FOLLOWING MARX

Historical Materialism Book Series

More than ten years after the collapse of the Berlin Wall and the disappearance of Marxism as a (supposed) state ideology, a need for a serious and long-term Marxist book publishing program has risen. Subjected to the whims of fashion, most contemporary publishers have abandoned any of the systematic production of Marxist theoretical work that they may have indulged in during the 1970s and early 1980s. The Historical Materialism book series addresses this great gap with original monographs, translated texts and reprints of "classics."

Editorial board: Paul Blackledge, Leeds; Sebastian Budgen, London; Jim Kincaid, Leeds; Stathis Kouvelakis, Paris; Marcel van der Linden, Amsterdam; China Miéville, London; Paul Reynolds, Lancashire.

Haymarket Books is proud to be working with Brill Academic Publishers (http://www.brill.nl) and the journal *Historical Materialism* to republish the Historical Materialism book series in paperback editions. Current series titles include:

Alasdair MacIntyre's Engagement with Marxism: Selected Writings 1953–1974
Edited by Paul Blackledge and Neil Davidson

Althusser: The Detour of Theory, Gregory Elliott

Between Equal Rights: A Marxist Theory of International Law, China Miéville

The Capitalist Cycle, Pavel V. Maksakovsky, Translated with introduction and commentary by Richard B. Day

The Clash of Globalisations: Neo-Liberalism, the Third Way, and Anti-globalisation, Ray Kiely

Critical Companion to Contemporary Marxism, Edited by Jacques Bidet and Stathis Kouvelakis

Criticism of Heaven: On Marxism and Theology, Roland Boer

Exploring Marx's Capital: Philosophical, Economic, and Political Dimensions, Jacques Bidet

Following Marx: Method, Critique, and Crisis, Michael Lebowitz

The German Revolution: 1917–1923, Pierre Broué

Globalisation: A Systematic Marxian Account, Tony Smith

Impersonal Power: History and Theory of the Bourgeois State,
Heide Gerstenberger, translated by David Fernbach

Lenin Rediscovered: What Is to Be Done? In Context, Lars T. Lih

Making History: Agency, Structure, and Change in Social Theory, Alex Callinicos

Marxism and Ecological Economics: Toward a Red and Green Political Economy, Paul Burkett

A Marxist Philosophy of Language, Jean-Jacques Lecercle and Gregory Elliott

The Theory of Revolution in the Young Marx, Michael Löwy

Utopia Ltd.: Ideologies of Social Dreaming in England 1870–1900, Matthew Beaumont

Western Marxism and the Soviet Union: A Survey of Critical Theories and Debates Since 1917
Marcel van der Linden

FOLLOWING MARX
METHOD, CRITIQUE, AND CRISIS

MICHAEL LEBOWITZ

Haymarket Books
Chicago, Illinois

First published in 2005 by Brill Academic Publishers, The Netherlands
© 2006 Koninklijke Brill NV, Leiden, The Netherlands

Published in paperback in 2009 by
Haymarket Books
P.O. Box 180165
Chicago, IL 60618
773-583-7884
www.haymarketbooks.org
ISBN: 978-1-608460-33-5

Trade distribution:
In the U.S., Consortium Book Sales, www.cbsd.com
In the UK, Turnaround Publisher Services, www.turnaround-psl.com
In Australia, Palgrave Macmillan, www.palgravemacmillan.com.au
In all other countries, Publishers Group Worldwide, www.pgw.com

Cover design by Ragina Johnson. Cover image by Vladimir Lebedev, 1918.

Printed in the United States on recycled paper containing 100 percent post-consumer
waste, in accordance with the guidelines of the Green Press Initiative,
www.greenpressinitiative.org.

This book was published with the generous support of the Wallace Global Fund.

10 9 8 7 6 5 4 3 2 1

Library of Congress Cataloging-in-Publication Data is available.

For a new generation of Marxist political economists who recognise that methodology and politics are not separate spheres isolated from one another.

Contents

Acknowledgements xi

Introduction   To Follow Marx xiii

PART ONE

CRITIQUES OF POLITICAL ECONOMY

Chapter One   The Fallacy of Everyday Notions 5

Chapter Two   Another Crisis of Economic Theory:
The Neo-Ricardian Critique 17

Chapter Three   The Neo-Ricardian Reduction 35

Chapter Four   Is 'Analytical Marxism' Marxism? 39
Appendix   Roemer's Self-Criticism 62

PART TWO

THE LOGIC OF *CAPITAL*

Chapter Five   Following Hegel: The Science of Marx 69

Chapter Six   Explorations in the Logic of *Capital* 87

PART THREE

ESSAYS IN THE THEORY OF CRISIS

Chapter Seven   Marx's Falling Rate of Profit: A Dialectical View   103
   Appendix   129

Chapter Eight   The General and the Specific in Marx's
   Theory of Crisis   131

Chapter Nine   Understanding Sweezy   157
   Appendix   Learning from Paul M. Sweezy   188

PART FOUR

ESSENCE AND APPEARANCE

Chapter Ten   Marx's Methodological Project as a Whole   195

Chapter Eleven   What Is Competition?   205

Chapter Twelve   Too Many Blindspots About the Media   217

Chapter Thirteen   The Theoretical Status of Monopoly-Capital   225

Chapter Fourteen   Analytical Marxism and the Marxian
   Theory of Crisis   247

Chapter Fifteen   In Brenner, Everything Is Reversed   273

PART FIVE

CONSIDERING THE OTHER SIDE OF *CAPITAL*

Chapter Sixteen   The Silences of *Capital* 303

Chapter Seventeen   Beyond the *Capital* of Uno-ism 319

Chapter Eighteen   Situating the Capitalist State 327

Chapter Nineteen   The Politics of Assumption,
    the Assumption of Politics 339

Bibliography 359

Index 367

Acknowledgements

Portions of this work have previously appeared in 'The Current Crisis of Economic Theory', *Science & Society*, Winter 1973–4, pp. 385–403; 'Is "Analytical Marxism" Marxism?', *Science & Society*, Summer 1988, pp. 191–213; 'The General and the Specific in Marx's Theory of Crisis', *Studies in Political Economy*, 7, Winter 1982, pp. 5–25; 'Too Many Blindspots About the Media', in *Studies in Political Economy*, 21, Autumn 1986; 'Learning from Paul Sweezy', *Studies in Political Economy*, 74, Fall 2004; 'The Silences of *Capital*', *Historical Materialism*, 1, September 1997, pp. 134–45; 'In Brenner, Everything is Reversed', *Historical Materialism*, 4, 2000, pp. 109–29; 'The Politics of Assumption, the Assumption of Politics', *Historical Materialism*, 14, 2, June 2006, pp. 29–47; 'Analytical Marxism and the Marxian Theory of Crisis', *Cambridge Journal of Economics*, 18, 1994, pp. 163–79; 'Review of Robert Paul Wolff, *Understanding Marx*', *Queen's Quarterly*, Spring 1987, pp. 239–41; 'Really Returning to Marx's *Capital*: A Reply to Robert Albritton', *History of Economic Ideas*, 12, 2, 2004, pp. 79–84; 'Marx's Falling Rate of Profit: A Dialectical View', *Canadian Journal of Economics*, 9, 2, May 1976, pp. 232–54; 'Situating the Capitalist State', in Antonio Callari et al (eds.), *Marxism in the Post-Modern Age: Confronting the New World Order* (New York: Guilford Publishers, 1995); 'The Theoretical Status of Monopoly Capital', in Stephen Resnick and Richard Wolff (eds.), *Rethinking Marxism: Essays for Harry Magdoff and Paul Sweezy*, New York: Autonomedia, 1985.

Permission to reprint is gratefully acknowledged.

Introduction

To Follow Marx

What does it mean to follow Marx?

To come *after*? That is to say, to come after in *time*?

To come after in *space* – i.e., to take the same path? Who follows in the same path? The disciple, certainly. But also the hunter, the detective, the tracker.

And, then, there is another meaning of follow: to understand, to grasp, to follow the *logical* path.

Which of these do I mean in the title of this book? All of them. Even that of the disciple, the student? Yes. But, not a disciple who would attempt to explain away 'the often paradoxical relationship of this theory to reality' and to demonstrate that, contrary to appearance, the master is nevertheless correct. As Marx understood, that is not at all a true follower but one who ensures the disintegration of the theory.[1]

Rather, my attempt to follow Marx is an attempt to rescue and retrieve that theory. Although Marx transformed the terrain before us through his work, many who came after him in time nevertheless lost their way. Not only those who consciously selected a fork in the road that Marx rejected, thinking that the smoother path would take them to the same destination (and ending up, perhaps to their own surprise, by going in the opposite direction). There are others as well: precisely because the path that Marx cleared has become overgrown through neglect, it has not been difficult to get lost when travelling in the dark.

This is a book about Marx's method. But, it is a book about method with a difference. Not simply because, following the lead of Lukács and Lenin about

---

[1] Lebowitz 2003, p. 21.

the centrality of the concept of the totality for Hegel and Marx, it offers a particular explanation of the relation of the inner structure of capital to its necessary forms of existence in competition. It is different also because it is not an abstract argument about Marx's method – at every step of the way, this book contains specific applications to concrete questions.

There is a reason for this unique combination of theoretical abstraction and concrete application. This book started out as a collection of essays on specific topics – e.g., neo-Ricardian theory, analytical Marxism, the falling rate of profit, crisis theory, monopoly capital, Paul Sweezy, advertising and the capitalist state. Essays on these topics dating back to the early 1970s had been published separately in journals such as the *Canadian Journal of Economics*, *Science & Society*, *Cambridge Journal of Economics* and *Historical Materialism* as well as in several volumes. Indeed, bringing together these essays from disparate sources into a single collection (which often I had been urged to do) was the original purpose of the volume.[2]

But, something happened along the way. In fact, these essays, though on apparently scattered topics, were in reality not so separate. Connecting them, first of all, was the influence of the *Grundrisse* and then Hegel which I read in the 1970s. More significant, however, was their relation to the understanding developed in a paper on Marx's methodological project that I presented in 1980 but never published. (I had left the paper to the gnawing criticism of the mice – although my basement study meant that the threat to the mss. was less from the praxis of the mice and more from a slime attack by banana slugs.) As I began to conceive of the volume, it occurred to me that – given the extent to which this unpublished manuscript demonstrated the underlying methodology in these essays and their unity – it was logical to retrieve the essay and to include it in the collection.

Yet, as I proceeded, I recognised that the published essays could be grouped in accordance with specific parts of the methodology paper. So, the next step was to divide up the latter into its relevant sections. Once divided, however, each segment took on a life of its own and started to grow. The result is that where there was one essay on methodology, there now are four (five,

---

[2] Although the editions of Marx cited in these essays vary, most readers of this literature are accustomed to citations from different editions and should have little difficulty.

if you count the exploration in the logic of capital, my exercise in coquetting with Hegel's *Logic*, which I retrieved from this period as well). They form, effectively, an extended essay of their own:

Chapter 1. The Fallacy of Everyday Notions
Chapter 5. Following Hegel: the Science of Marx
Chapter 6. Explorations in the Logic of *Capital*
Chapter 10. Marx's Methodological Project
Chapter 11. What is Competition?

These five chapters may be read in sequence as a single work – just as the individually published pieces can be read as discrete units. However, I believe that the special strength of this book comes from the particular combination of a developed conception of Marx's methodology and the theoretical practice which flows from this.[3] It makes for a book on Marx's method with a significant difference.

Perhaps one aspect of that difference will be apparent if I confess to the original working title of the volume: 'the tragedy of Marxist economists'. An important part of the tragedy I had in mind was the preoccupation (judging from journal submissions) of so many Marxist economists with two questions – the falling rate of profit and the 'transformation problem'. Marxist economists having absorbed their colleagues' identification of mathematics and science (a rather different conception of science from Marx's), the potential for deploying a modicum of mathematics elevated these as critical problems to be resolved by Marxist scientists. Accordingly, given my belief that much of the time and energy spent on these two questions could be allocated to rather better uses, it was my intention to demonstrate the waste of scarce resources here and on related matters.

---

[3] It should be noted that the way in which the contents of the book developed has some implications for its form. For one, it means both that different editions (e.g., of *Capital*) are used for reference in different chapters depending on when the work was originally written. Although this is not customary, it is quite trivial as a problem and does succeed in conveying the character of the book. Perhaps more significant, certain passages from Marx are repeated in the chapters developing the methodology and then in those applying it. In fact, I think this is a rather fortunate development because it reinforces and, indeed, colours passages which are important in tracing Marx's path.

There were already several essays for the volume involving the question of the falling (or not-falling) rate of profit, so it was simply a matter of developing an essay in relation to the transformation question. Happily, rationality was restored, and my self-imposed discipline never to spend time writing about the transformation of values into prices (when there were more important things to do) prevailed. (Readers, though, will detect a few slighting comments and a footnote on this matter.) Having changed the focus in this respect, I dropped 'tragedy' from the title.

And, yet, this book remains one about tragedy (although not solely that of Marxist economists). That economists can write about Marx without understanding the centrality of the sale of labour-power in his analysis of capitalism; that Hegel can be treated as non-essential for grasping Marx simply because those doing so have no understanding of Hegel (a mistake that Lenin acknowledged when reading the *Science of Logic*); that there can be discussions of Marx's crisis theory without exploring his assumptions; that Marx's many statements about the relation of competition to the inner laws of capital (including his repeated comments about how everything is reversed in competition) produce a cognitive dissonance that is resolved through their repression – these are but a few of the tragedies that help to explain why would-be followers of Marx lose their way.

Given the failure of theorists to understand Marx's methodology – in particular, his conception of the inner structure of capital – it is small wonder that my argument in *Beyond 'Capital'* that Marx did not complete the development of capitalism as a totality in *Capital* could be viewed as heresy by some – i.e., as hardly the work of a follower. The final section of this book, however, takes up some of the implications of my argument about the other side of capital and demonstrates, I hope, that a follower can continue a journey.

PART ONE

CRITIQUES OF POLITICAL ECONOMY

Part One
Critiques of Political Economy

While I have argued in *Beyond 'Capital'* that Marx should be understood as engaging not in a critique of *all* political economy but, rather, in a critique of the political economy of *capital*, there is a begged question. What precisely is that political economy of capital (as distinct from the political economy of the working class)?

Few Marxists would have difficulty in describing neoclassical economics (in general, as opposed to some of its tools) as the political economy of capital. The parallels to the vulgar economics Marx criticised are striking (as Chapter 1 argues). But, what about critiques of neoclassical economics and new, improved versions of Marxian economics? To what extent do they break with the political economy of capital and to what extent are they merely different forms?

The neo-Ricardian (or Sraffian) critique of neoclassical economics promised much: at the time of writing the essay which forms the basis of Chapter 2, it seemed to demolish technically the standard economics. But, was it ever a rejection of the logic of capital itself? Perhaps the ease with which it was ultimately swept aside reflects its limited challenge. Nevertheless, while its tendency to obscure Marx's critical distinction between labour and labour-power contributed to its confusion about the source of the surplus in capitalism, its target (the apologetics of neoclassical theory) was always clear.

In contrast, the appearance on the scene of the self-titled 'analytical Marxism' or 'no bullshit Marxism' group had a quite different object – the desire to make Marxism (and thus its authors) respectable to their neoclassical colleagues. In particular, methodological individualism became the banner behind which they marched against the bullshit (which, predictably, was ultimately revealed to be Marxism itself). Following Gramsci's advice that, in the battle of ideas, one should challenge the best of the opposition, Chapter 4 ('Is "Analytical Marxism" Marxism?') demonstrates the difference between Marxism and 'analytical Marxism' by unravelling John Roemer's model and revealing that its celebrated conclusions reflect its neoclassical assumptions.

Ironically, though, this Part opens with an insight derived from one of the above group, Jon Elster – Marx's emphasis upon the 'fallacy of composition'. Chapter 1 ('The Fallacy of Everyday Notions') explores this phenomenon in economic thought and concludes that its emergence is inherent in vulgar economics, theory which starts from the way things appear. This essay, written specifically for this collection, introduces the themes of appearance and essence which run throughout this volume. By stressing the importance of understanding the centrality of the sale of labour-power and the reproduction of the working class, it also focuses upon an essential element in the political economy of the working class.

Chapter One
The Fallacy of Everyday Notions

The fallacy of composition

Back when he presumably considered himself a Marxist, Jon Elster called attention to Marx's repeated focus upon a common logical error – the 'fallacy of composition'.[1] Elster defined this error as the position that 'what is possible for any single individual must be possible for them all simultaneously'.

It was a revelation to me. Of course, it was impossible to miss its presence in *Capital*. The classic case, cited by Elster, concerns the securing of profit or surplus-value by selling above value. Can surplus-value have its origin in a 'mark-up' over the value of the commodity? Marx's well-known response was: Yes, an individual capitalist can add a mark-up to his value and therefore secure a surplus-value; however, *all* capitalists cannot do so because they are also purchasers: 'the capitalist class of a given country, taken as a whole, cannot defraud itself'.[2]

Once Elster articulated the point, I saw it everywhere. (Not only in Marx: any individual country can drive down wages, environmental standards, etc and can be internationally competitive, but....) Can a worker become a capitalist? Of course. Any worker – with the proper combination of skill

---

[1] Elster 1978, p. 99.
[2] Marx 1977a, p. 266.

and fortune – may become an exploiter of other people's labour, a capitalist. But, the same can not be true for all workers at once: where there is no labour to be exploited, 'there would be no capitalist nor capitalist production'.[3] Can capitalists decide to lend their money-capital for interest rather than employ it in industry? Any individual or group of capitalists can, but all capitalists can not do so:

> Taken generally, i.e. when we apply it to the whole social capital, as is done by some vulgar economists and even given out as the basis of profit, of course, this is of course quite absurd.... But, as we have said above, for the individual capitalist this is in fact how it is.[4]

This is not only a question about the differing characteristics and conditions facing the whole and its parts; also relevant (as Marx notes in his discussion of the last example) is the way in which parts interact and affect the conditions of existence of each other. As the *Grundrisse* (that rich mine for the understanding of Marx's thought-processes) indicates, any single worker can engage in self-denial and save. Yet, if workers *generally* act this way, it would affect the total amount of spending and there would be damage to general consumption: 'the loss would be enormous...and hence also to production, thus also to the amount and volume of exchanges they could make with capital, hence to themselves as workers'. Indeed, the effect of all workers attempting to achieve what is possible for a single worker would be to nullify the efforts of each: 'If they all save, then a general reduction of wages will bring them back to earth again'.[5]

This early identification of what may be called a 'Keynesian' fallacy of composition argument is only one example of the effects of the interaction of individual actors. Every capitalist, Marx noted, 'would like the workers of *other* capitalists to be the greatest consumers possible of *his own* commodity'.[6] The mass of workers 'with the exception of his own workers, appear not as workers, but as consumers'.[7] Since each capitalist in his actions forgets that other capitalists are trying to restrict the consumption, i.e., the wage of their

---

[3] Marx 1977a, p. 1079.
[4] Marx 1981b, p. 501.
[5] Marx 1973, pp. 285–6.
[6] Marx 1973, p. 420.
[7] Marx 1973, p. 419.

own workers, however, Marx indicated that the effect of the competition of capitals, 'their indifference to and independence of each other', is a tendency to crisis (cf. discussion in Chapter 14, 'Analytical Marxism and the Marxian Theory of Crisis').[8]

Marx's stress upon the whole, appropriately, led him to criticise any theory which proceeds from particular cases to establish general principles for the whole. Commenting, for example, on the argument that capital accumulation leads to rising wages and therefore to an increase in the supply of labour, he proposed that economists were confusing the relation of all workers and the total social capital 'with the laws that distribute the working population over the different spheres of production'. What the economists see, he argued, is not the response of the total population but, rather, 'the local oscillations of the labour-market in a particular sphere of production'.[9] Yes, the working population will rise in one sector with relatively rising wages, but, here again, the experience in the individual case differs from what is true of the whole.

The point is really very simple – the subject is the whole. The working class taken as a whole, the capitalist class taken as a whole, capitalism as a whole. To know Marx is to know (1) that the whole is not the sum of the individual parts taken separately and (2) that the way things appear to the individual actors actually involved – even if the events in question occur over and over again – cannot be the basis for our understanding of the whole. There is, in short, a big difference between Appearance and Essence.

Everyday notions

Yet, Marx definitely was not arguing that the individual actors were deluded. On the contrary, the individual capitalist 'is right in believing' that his profit is not derived solely from the labour exploited by him:

> This is quite correct as far as his average profit is goes. How much this profit is mediated by the overall exploitation of labour by capital as a whole, i.e., by all his fellow-capitalists, this interconnection is a complete mystery to him.[10]

---

[8] Marx 1973, p. 420.
[9] Marx 1977a, pp. 791–2.
[10] Marx 1981b, p. 270.

Consider how things appear to the individual capitalist – indeed, how they truly are for him. What that capitalist wants is profits – the excess of the selling price of his commodity over its cost-price. The first thing he must do is obtain his necessary inputs and to do everything possible to lower the costs of those necessary inputs. Paying rent for land, interest for money-capital, wages for labour are preconditions of the process of production.[11] Thus, 'it is precisely wages, interest and rent that go into this production as limiting and governing amounts of price. These therefore appear to him as the elements determining the price of his commodities'.[12] Accordingly, in his calculations as to how to act within competition, the capitalist – who only moves among the forms on the surface – takes into account the relative prices of necessary inputs; if, in one country, wages and rent are relatively low whereas, in another, interest is relatively low, 'then a capitalist in the first country will use more land and labour and a capitalist on the other relatively more capital'.[13]

But, it is not simply obtaining inputs at the lowest possible price that determines whether the individual capitalist will achieve his goal – it is also a matter of using purchased inputs economically. Thus, anything that can be done to get more production from a given quantity of inputs will be pursued. There is a logic, then, to increasing the workday – prolonging it and intensifying it. Not only does the capitalist get more output from each worker but he also economises in this way on fixed capital.[14] By the same logic, too, the individual capitalist has an interest in increasing productivity in order to lower the cost-price of his commodities. 'He pockets the difference between their costs of production and the market-price of the other commodities, which are produced at higher production costs'.[15]

That difference is the difference between his production and that of his competitors. Every step of the way, that individual capitalist is conscious of one reality in particular – competition. His ability to meet his production costs and to secure profits, the basis for his reproduction as capitalist, all depend upon his ability to defeat his competitors. He is, indeed, driven by competition – both as an innovator and as a follower. For example, if he is

---

[11] Marx 1971, pp. 480, 508, 512.
[12] Marx 1981b, p. 1014.
[13] Ibid.
[14] Marx 1981b, p. 170.
[15] Marx 1981b, p. 373.

successful in increasing productivity, Marx commented, there is additional output to be sold. 'Other things being equal, the capitalist's commodities can only command a more extensive market if their prices are reduced'.[16] To increase his sales and his share of the market, the capitalist cheapens his commodities:

> he attains the object he wishes to attain, if he puts the price of his goods only a small percentage lower than that of his competitors. He drives them from the field, he wrests from them at least part of their sales, by *underselling them*.[17]

Faced with this initiative, the competitors must, in turn, act to reduce their cost-prices if they are to survive; they are compelled by competition to adopt the new method.[18] The price, accordingly, continues to fall and the advantage of the particular individual capitalist disappears as the new method becomes universal. The stage is set for the further driving down of prices in the search for profits.

No one could possibly criticise the individual capitalist for looking upon the costs of his inputs as the basis of commodity prices (rather than beginning from the concept of the value of commodities), and Marx certainly does not:

> Experience shows here in theory, and the self-interested calculation of the capitalist shows in practice, that commodity prices are determined by wages, interest and rent, by the prices of labour, capital and land, and that these price elements are in fact the governing elements of price formation.[19]

Similarly, it is not a surprise to Marx that an individual capitalist, when innovating to increase productivity, has no idea about the inner connection between the productivity of labour and the value of labour-power:

> When an individual capitalist cheapens shirts, for instance, by increasing the productivity of labour, he by no means necessarily aims to reduce the value of labour-power....

---

[16] Marx 1977a, p. 434.
[17] Marx 1977b, p. 223.
[18] Marx 1977a, p. 436.
[19] Marx 1981b, p. 1014.

His interest, as noted, is simply on reducing his costs relative to that of his competitors. Nevertheless, to the extent that he contributes in this way to the reduction of necessary labour, his actions make real 'the general and necessary tendencies of capital'.[20]

Why should the individual capitalist have any sense of any underlying inner relations? They are not his concern. All that matters to him is his own reproduction:

> The interconnection of the reproduction process is not understood, i.e. as this presents itself not from the standpoint of individual capital, but rather from that of the total capital.[21]

The problem, in short, is not with the individual actors. They perceive reality correctly – as it applies immediately to them. Marx's critique, rather, was with those people who analyse the system as a whole on the basis of the way things appear to the actual agents of capitalist production. The vulgar economist, Marx argued, 'does nothing more than to translate the peculiar notions of the competition-enslaved capitalist into an ostensibly more theoretical and generalized language, and attempt to demonstrate the validity of these notions'.[22] Vulgar economics is 'nothing more than a didactic and more or less doctrinaire translation of the everyday notions of the actual agents of production'.[23]

Since those everyday notions, though, are rooted in the real conditions facing individual capitals, the perceived relationships – like the apparent movement of the sun around the earth – *persist*. Precisely because capitalism is a totality, a system of reproduction, its forms of existence are themselves constantly reproduced:

> The secret reason why these products of the dissolution of commodity-value constantly appear as the premises of value formation itself is simply that the capitalist mode of production, like every other, constantly reproduces not only the material product but also the socio-economic relations, the formal

---

[20] Marx 1977a, p. 433.
[21] Marx 1981b, p. 983.
[22] Marx 1981b, p. 338.
[23] Marx 1981b, p. 969.

economic determinants of its formation. Its result thus constantly appears
as its premise, and its premises as its results.[24]

Capital, in short, constantly produces its forms of existence. Because it
does, it constantly produces everyday notions – 'the forms of appearance
are reproduced directly and spontaneously, as current and usual modes of
thought', Marx stressed.[25] And, theories based upon these forms obscure all
inner connections: 'capital yields the capitalist profit, year in year out; land
yields the landowner a ground rent; and labour-power...yields the worker
wages'.[26] On the surface of things, 'rent, profit and wages thus appear to grow
out of the roles that the earth, the produced means of production, and labour
play in the simple labour process'.[27] By elaborating the external connections in
its 'ostensibly more theoretical and generalized language', vulgar economy in
this way justifies the natural necessity of the existing distribution of income.
It turns 'into apologetics the notions of agents trapped within bourgeois
relations of production', presenting a dogma which 'corresponds to the self-
interest of the dominant classes'.[28]

We are describing, of course, neoclassical economic theory – which has
taken that ostensibly more theoretical and generalised language to new
heights. At every step of the way, it starts from the way that things appear to
the individual actors, from the results of capitalist production; and, remaining
at the surface, it takes those results (for example, individuals in different
classes with different endowments, tastes, etc) as its presuppositions and
proceeds from there into a consideration of production (fleetingly) and from
there to incomes. Starting, in short, from these individuals as presuppositions,
they 'close the circle' – i.e., construct an apparent totality proceeding from
appearance, general equilibrium as the highest form of vulgar economy.
And – what a surprise! – once again, incomes magically correspond to the
contributions made by their recipients, that soothing message offered by
vulgar economy.

Insofar as its surface totality fails to explain its initial presuppositions (for
example, individual wealth endowments and preference patterns), treating

---

[24] Marx 1981b, p. 1011.
[25] Marx 1977a, p. 682.
[26] Marx 1981b, p. 960.
[27] Marx 1981b, p. 964.
[28] Marx 1981b, pp. 956, 969.

them as exogenously given, that theory begins from foundations which are 'suspended in mid-air as principles and primary concepts'. Hegel's comment about such approaches to theory is as relevant as ever: 'Those fare best who without much thought, accept these principles as given, and thence forward use them as fundamental rules of their understanding.'

What neoclassical theory lacks in logical coherence, however, it makes up by its immediate correspondence to appearance which, normally reproduced, is accessible for its apparent verification. The reappearing movement of the sun around the earth may be predicted with a rather high degree of probability without any knowledge of the real movements.

Yet, as that old teacher noted, such 'sciences' are a kind of 'witches' circle' where the initial assumptions are mingled in with the deductions:

> The obstruction in the method becomes apparent when in its course it attempts to exhibit the derivative, which in fact contains the grounds of the primary assumptions.[29]

The conclusions of neoclassical economics are already present in the assumptions it draws from appearances. But, so also is the basis for its obstruction – as the vulnerability of neoclassical economics to the fallacy of composition reveals.

'All the mystifications of the capitalist mode of production'

Consider Marx's analysis of the wage. The wage is the payment for the sale of labour-power, what the worker receives for selling the property right to use his capacity to work for a limited period. Following from this sale of labour-power, we have the essence of the productive relations of capitalism: 'the worker works under the control of the capitalist to whom his labour belongs', and the capitalist has the property rights in the products of labour.[30]

This is the precondition for the generation of surplus-value – a coercive relation in which capital is able to compel the performance of surplus labour, where the labour the worker performs for the capitalist exceeds the labour necessary to reproduce the worker as wage-labourer. Understanding the

---

[29] Hegel 1929, Vol. II, pp. 87–8.
[30] Marx 1977a, pp. 291–2.

significance of this point – that the worker sells her labour-power rather than a certain amount of labour – is absolutely essential. Once we do, we can grasp the generation of surplus-value as the result of capital's victories in class struggle and can recognise all the subdivisions of surplus-value (e.g., profit, rent, interest) as premised upon exploitation within the process of capitalist production.

But, consider the *form* of the wage – what the wage necessarily looks like to the individual capitalist: 'On the surface of bourgeois society the worker's wage appears as the price of labour, as a certain quantity of money that is paid for a certain quantity of labour.'[31]

It looks like this on the surface – because a certain quantity of labour is exactly what the individual capitalist is purchasing in order to engage in production.

A theory which starts from the forms of appearances, therefore, *must* conclude that the capitalist pays for (all) the labour he receives, that surplus-value accordingly cannot come from exploitation of workers because workers get in accordance with what they contribute – in short, that rent, profit and wages grow out of the role played by the land, produced means of production, and labour in the production process. The 'Trinity Formula' flows logically from the form of the wage, and 'nothing is easier to understand than the necessity, the *raison d'être*, of this form of appearance'.[32]

That is why Marx stressed 'the decisive importance' of the form that the wage necessarily takes:

> All the notions of justice held by both the worker and the capitalist, all the mystifications of the capitalist mode of production, all capitalism's illusions about freedom, all the apologetic tricks of vulgar economics, have as their basis the form of appearance discussed above, which makes the actual relation invisible, and indeed presents to the eye the precise opposite of that relation.[33]

The problem with reasoning from the perspective of the individual purchaser of labour-power is *precisely* that the 'interconnection of the reproduction process is not understood, i.e. as this presents itself not from the standpoint

---

[31] Marx 1977a, p. 675.
[32] Marx 1977a, p. 681.
[33] Marx 1977a, p. 680.

of individual capital, but rather from that of the total capital'. If 'a certain quantity of money…is paid for a certain quantity of labour', what ensures the reproduction of the working class?

And there we have the question that Marx was so determined to stress (so much so that he concluded Volume I of *Capital* on this note) – the necessity for reproduction of this social relation, the necessity that workers be reproduced as dependent upon capital and thus compelled to sell their labour-power in order to survive. The reproduction of the working class *in general* is at the core of Marx's focus upon the value of labour-power; however, it is a concept inherently invisible on the surface because the sale of labour-power necessarily appears as the sale of labour.[34] Going beyond this form of appearance is critical. Without that distinction between labour-power and labour, it is impossible to understand why the 'maintenance and reproduction of the working class remains a necessary condition for the reproduction of capital'.[35]

So, it is not an accident that, after what would seem like a logical conclusion to Volume I of *Capital* (the expropriation of the expropriators), Marx added a further chapter – 'The Modern Theory of Colonization'. Something unusual happened in the New World ('the colonies'): the working class was *not* reproduced naturally. Wage-labourers *escaped*: 'the worker receives more than is required for the reproduction of his labour capacity and very soon becomes a peasant farming independently, etc, the original relation is not constantly reproduced'.[36] In this situation, 'the social dependence of the worker on the capitalist, which is indispensable' was not secured. And, the result, Marx commented, was that workers lost 'along with the relation of dependence, the feeling of dependence on the abstemious capitalist'.[37] What was invisible on the surface in the Old World could not be denied in the New – 'the secret' that the reproduction of the worker as wage-labourer is 'the absolutely necessary condition for capitalist production'.[38] Q.E.D.

Nevertheless, 'the great beauty of capitalist production', is that the unique circumstances which yielded this essential insight into the necessary condition

---

[34] Lebowitz, 2003, pp. 124–7.
[35] Marx 1977a, p. 718.
[36] Marx 1988, p. 116.
[37] Marx 1977a, pp. 935–6.
[38] Marx 1977a, pp. 716, 940.

of existence of capital are not normally present.[39] Characteristically, capitalist production 'makes the actual relation invisible, and, indeed, presents to the eye the precise opposite of that relation.' Accordingly, translating 'the everyday notions of the actual agents of production' into a more theoretical form cannot reveal that relation. Rather, 'the essential relation must first be discovered by science'.[40]

Just as no individual capitalist concerns himself with the reproduction of the working class, so also does this matter fall outside the scope of theories which build upon everyday notions. While the distinction between the reproduction of the individual capitalist and capital as a whole is not the source of *every* fallacy of composition characteristic of capitalism, it ensures that the fallacy of composition is inherent rather than contingent. Some capitalists can gain at the expense of others, some workers can get high enough income to save and escape wage-labour – since capital and wage-labour exist as many capitals and many wage-labourers, there are many possible variations.

But, which ones are consistent with reproduction of the working class and capital as a whole? The fallacy of composition points to the inherent flaw in neoclassical economics – that it is 'nothing more than a didactic and more or less doctrinaire translation of the everyday notions of the actual agents of production.' Only 'when viewed as a connected whole', when we view capitalist and worker not as individuals but 'in their totality, as the capitalist class and the working class confronting each other' – i.e., when we turn away from the way things necessarily appear to individual actors, can we understand the essential structural requirement for the existence of capitalism as a system – the necessity for the reproduction of wage-labourers.[41]

---

[39] Marx 1977a, p. 935.
[40] Marx 1977a, p. 682.
[41] Marx 1977a, pp. 711, 713, 717, 732–3.

Chapter Two

Another Crisis of Economic Theory: The Neo-Ricardian Critique

At the 1971 meeting of the American Economics Association, Joan Robinson told a large and receptive audience for her keynote address that economic theory again faced a crisis similar to that of the 1930s.[1] But, this time, instead of depression and the question of whether orthodox theory could deliver the goods, 'The Second Crisis of Economic Theory' related to *what* goods and for *whom*.[2]

Expressing concern over matters ranging from the destruction of the environment and the quality of life to continued poverty and inequities in income distribution, Robinson noted that the crisis centered both on the allocation of resources and on the distribution of income. And, here, she pointed to the 'evident bankruptcy of economic theory which for the second time has nothing to say on the questions that, to everyone except economists, appear to be most in need of an answer'.

The crisis, of course, relates to capitalism itself. And, it should be noted, it is a crisis more fundamental than that of the 1930s. To question what production is for and who should receive the fruits of that production

---

[1] The review-essay of Hunt and Schwartz (eds.) 1972 (now revised for incorporation in this volume) was originally published as 'The Current Crisis of Economic Theory', *Science & Society*. Winter 1973–4.

[2] Robinson 1972.

is to question production for surplus-value. It is to question the very core of capitalist society.

So foul a sky clears not without a storm. And a recent book, *A Critique of Economic Theory*, is directed to the economists (in service and in training) who will have to weather this second storm.[3] The core of the book deals with one central issue: the critique of the neoclassical theory of income distribution, that theory which has done yeoman ideological service by 'proving' that everyone gets the income he deserves. Drawing upon the 'Cambridge Criticism' or neo-Ricardian critique initiated by Piero Sraffa, the editors have assembled a splendid sequence of essays which make it possible for the reader who is prepared to follow the arguments to understand the nature of the critique which has shattered, from within, the hegemony of neoclassical economic theory.

Thus Dobb and Meek place the neoclassical theory historically; Robinson, Dobb and Nuti assess the significance of the Sraffa model; Robinson and Garegnani dispose of attempted defenses by Samuelson and other prominent neoclassical economists; and Dobb and Medio relate the critique to Marxian economics. In the course of the essays, a number of the critical tenets of the neoclassical faith fall by the wayside. Dobb and Meek, for example, point out that neoclassical economics is not fundamentally different from the vulgar economics which Marx criticised. Several articles (Robinson, Garegnani and Johansen) demonstrate that consideration of marginal utility and consumer demand adds little or nothing in the determination of equilibrium prices.[4]

In relation to the marginal product of capital, Dobb, Robinson and Garegnani show that attempts to relate the return to capital to its contribution are based on circular reasoning since it is impossible to conceive of a quantity of capital independent of the profit rate. And, finally, Garegnani disposes of the production function and the marginal productivity theory of distribution by demonstrating that there is no unique relationship between the degree of capital intensity and the distribution of income.

---

[3] Hunt and Schwartz (eds.) 1972.

[4] Sherman's essay, which tries to reconcile the labour theory of value with neoclassical theory, seems somewhat out of place in this volume. Sherman treats Marx's 'price theory' as special cases of neoclassical price theory rather than recognising the latter as a special and trivial case itself.

What does it all mean? It means simply that justification of the distribution of income by reference to technology and technique has lost its theoretical underpinning. The theoretical nexus between the return to the owner of capital and the contribution of means of production has been shattered; the result is to expose as pure ideology the dictum of J.B. Clark (anticipated much earlier in J.B. Say's catechisms) that 'what a social class gets is, under natural law, what it contributes to the general output of industry'. What then is there to replace technological determination of income distribution? As Nuti points out, as long as everyone gets his 'fair' share according to his individual contribution to the production process, there is no place for class struggle. In short, the critique of neoclassical theory makes possible the reintroduction of power and social relations into academic economics; it makes possible a return to political economy.

And the demonstration of the need for a return to political economy is precisely the intent of the editors of *A Critique of Economic Theory*. As Hunt and Schwartz indicate in a scathing introduction which deals with the training of new economists, the ideological nature of economic science, and its pretensions to objectivity, academic economics has been a realm where things are in the saddle and ride mankind, an economics of inhumanity. The editors end with a call for a new political economy which can demystify modern economics and help young people to discover a 'world of passionate possibilities'. It is pertinent, however, to ask what kind of political economy it shall be. Given the embrace of the 'Sraffa-Marx model' by one of the editors, it is necessary to explore the nature of that model and to consider its limitations as a basis for a new political economy.[5]

The Sraffa-Marx model?

By developing a model which, given technical conditions of production and the real wage, determines relative prices and the rate of profits, and also by demonstrating the possibility of 're-switching', Sraffa lays the groundwork

---

[5] Since the concern here is not with Sraffa's critique of neoclassical theory or his solution for the transformation problem, the focus and evaluation is somewhat different from that in earlier treatments in this journal. *Cf.* Meek 1961 and Hunt and Sherman 1972.

for much of the current critique of neo-classical theory.[6] Similarly, as Medio shows in one of the Hunt/Schwartz volume's finest essays, Sraffa provided the basis for a solution to the 'transformation problem' which has haunted many Marxists.[7] The praise of Marxists for the initiator of the demolition of the old vulgar economy has accordingly been well-taken. However, from a Marxist perspective, there are serious problems with the Sraffa model. Simply stated, it suppresses the sale of labour-power, obscures the source of surplus, and implicitly treats the value analysis of *Capital* as an 'unnecessary detour'.

With the exception of Medio's essay and some comments by Nuti, a critical view of the Sraffian (or neo-Ricardian) critique is absent from *A Critique of Economic Theory*. This lack would have been evident if due attention had been given to Marx's criticisms of classical political economy (and, particularly, Ricardo and the Ricardian school). For the treatment of capital as a thing rather than as a relation, the inability to explain clearly the source of profits, the tendency to find formal solutions which begin from surface forms as a premise, the conception of production relations as natural rather than historical – all these problems, and some others which Marx identified in Ricardian economics, reappear in the Sraffa model.

Consider, for example, Sraffa's central equation for his standard system:

$$r = R\,(1 - w),$$

where r is the rate of profit; R, the ratio of net product (surplus) to the means of production; and w, the wage per unit of labour (or alternatively, the wage share of national income). While it is possible to reduce the Sraffian equation to a more familiar Marxian equation, the view of the surplus and the wage in the Sraffian system is critical. Rather than the Marxian concept of surplus-value, the Sraffian surplus (or net product or national income) includes the share of both capitalists and workers. Similarly, the wage simply limits the portion of the surplus which can serve as profits.

---

[6] Sraffa 1960.
[7] Medio's essay, 'Profits and Surplus-Value: Appearance and Reality in Capitalist Production,' is an original essay which provides the framework for a number of comments in this section.

What are the implications of treating the wage as a share of a pre-existing surplus rather than as an input? As Sraffa noted, there are alternative ways of viewing the wage. One, which he employs in his earliest examples, would be to consider the wage as part of a necessary input – as a subsistence for workers. Another, which Sraffa prefers, would consider a portion of the wage as subsistence and a portion as a share of surplus. In choosing to treat the whole wage as a portion of the surplus, Sraffa avoids the problem of determining inputs into the production of wage-labourers where subsistence is socially rather than physiologically determined.

Despite, however, Dobb's comment that nothing in principle is involved in the way Sraffa deals with the wage, only one of Sraffa's three alternatives pertains to the real relations of capitalist production. Only by considering the *entire* wage as the cost of a necessary input can the fact be grasped that, in capitalist production, the purchase of labour-power is a necessary precondition of production; and this clearly is as true in the case of a social subsistence as in that of a physiological subsistence.

As Marx took pains to note, one can not be indifferent to the form of representing a relationship. To represent a relationship in the manner in which it appears on the surface and to 'conceal the very transaction that characterizes capital, namely the exchange of variable capital for living labour-power' is to perpetuate the mystification of real relations.[8] And this is what occurs in the Sraffa model, which substitutes for the sale of labour-power a division of a pre-existing surplus.

Thus, in the Sraffa model, capitalist and worker face each other and divide up the spoils *outside and after* the production process. As in the case of the money-capitalist, the worker stands outside the production process and claims a share of the surplus (presumably on the basis of having parted with a use-value prior to production). As the counterpart of fetish capital, we have fetish labour.

One characteristic of this system is that the necessaries of consumption are treated the same as luxuries in that they do not enter into the production of other commodities – because in the world of *Production of Commodities by Means of Commodities* labour-power is not a commodity. By abolishing the sale of labour-power and thus obscuring the nature of capital as a relation,

---

[8] Cf. Marx 1977a, Chapter 18.

Sraffa has developed a model which may be appropriate for another social system but which can not be considered consistent with the Marxian analysis of capitalism.[9]

Given the treatment of labour-power, there are obvious problems in divining the source of surplus in the Sraffa model. For Marx, explanation of the existence of surplus-value was the essential problem; and he found it in the 'non-equivalent exchange' where, because labour-power was sold as a commodity, the worker did not receive the use-value of labour (contribution to production).[10] But, for Sraffa, this question does not exist – because this particular exchange is not present.

The Sraffian surplus or net product emerges simply from a technical relationship: a given set of techniques of production produces a given R (or ratio of surplus to means of production). But where does the surplus or net product come from? Recalling Marx's comment about the self-evident nature of Lucretius's observation that 'out of nothing, nothing can be created', it is appropriate to ask whether the Sraffian surplus comes out of nothing.

The key to the Sraffian surplus is to be found in his interpretation of Ricardo in his introduction to that writer's collected works. In Ricardo's corn (wheat) industry, there is an excess of physical quantity of output over the physical quantity of input (expressed in the same commodity, corn). As Sraffa noted, this comparison of physical quantities made it possible to determine the rate of profit 'independently of value'.[11] The excess, determined by a technical relationship, sets R; and, with a given R, the rate of profits varies with the corn-wage.

This Ricardian model is generalised by Sraffa. In his first example, Sraffa produces a physical surplus in the wheat industry (rather than the

---

[9] One can easily envision the decision by associated workers to divide up a Sraffian surplus into wages, bonuses and 'profit' (for the purpose of accumulation). A workers' council, an Owenite co-operative or a socialist economy may, in fact, make as its basic decision its desired rate of accumulation, which will determine the necessary profit rate and, given R, the level of wages. To demonstrate the good fit of the Sraffa model to a distinct social system is to underscore its inappropriateness as a representation of capitalism.

[10] Edward Nell has recently described the fallacy of the neoclassical extension of the theory of exchange from product markets to factor markets and provided an extremely useful diagram to counter the 'circular flow' promulgated in elementary economics texts. Edward Nell, 'Economics: the Revival of Political Economy', in Blackburn (ed.) 1973.

[11] Sraffa 1960, p. 93.

'unproductive' iron industry) and allocates the surplus between the two industries through relative prices. The example is extended to several industries, all producing a net product or surplus, and then generalised. (Sraffa's 'standard' or composite basic commodity performs the same function as corn in Ricardo's model, permitting a direct comparison between inputs and outputs). Throughout, there is no explanation of how it is possible that a surplus can emerge. How can there be a commodity (or set of commodities) which reproduces more than is required for its own replacement? This question, for which Marx proposed an answer, is not posed by Sraffa (who excludes labour-power as such a commodity).

What the approach all boils down to is the assumption of a technical process by which some use-values are transformed into more use-values. (That the latter set may not involve a higher value than the former set is not considered; to do so would require investigation of the source of exchange-value and surplus-value.) It is reminiscent of Marx's comments about McCulloch (a follower of Ricardo), who turned use-values into exchange-values and 'transformed commodities into workers'.

Agriculture, of course, has, since the physiocrats, been the favorite example in this use-value approach because it permits comparability of inputs and outputs. Yet, in Marx's comments on Torrens's case of a corn surplus, he notes that 'even considered physiologically, as use-value', the surplus-product already exists in the form of manure, air, water, light and salts in the soil. In short, in the sphere of production of use-values, use-values which exist independent of human intervention must be considered as inputs; out of nothing, nothing can be created.[12]

In contrast to the use-value approach, Marx emphasised the socially-necessary input of human labour, an approach which focuses on the productivity of labour and its implications. In the case of agriculture, he viewed the action of nature as permitting an exceptional increase in the productivity of labour. The result of the 'gratuitous service' of nature was that commodities requiring a low expenditure of human productive energy were produced. And, to the extent that these commodities entered into the production of workers, a high productivity (or low value of necessaries of

---

[12] Marx's comments on McCulloch and Torrens appear in the section, 'Disintegration of the Ricardian School', in Marx 1971.

consumption) permitted the existence of a surplus over the requirements for replacement of labour-power.

There is a relatively simple extension of Marx's approach to sectors other than agriculture. In addition to the role of nature, Marx called attention to the importance of science and long-lived fixed capital in affecting the productivity of labour. In particular, he identified the growing gap between the fixed capital employed in production and the depreciating portion of that fixed capital as a powerful and ever-increasing influence on the productivity of labour (and thus also on the production of surplus-value).[13] The 'gratuitous service of past labour', like that of natural forces, was seen as a major factor in lowering the value of individual commodities, reducing the value of labour-power and increasing the rate of surplus-value.[14]

Nature, science, technology and the products of past labour – all viewed by Marx in terms of their effect on the productivity of labour and the production of surplus-value – are subsumed by Sraffa in the technical conditions of production. R, reflecting technique, determines the production of a surplus; and the distribution of that surplus is left to social institutions. This is John Stuart Mill with a vengeance. Production is consigned to the technical and natural sphere, while distribution is historical and social, a matter of human institutions. This complete severance of production relations and distribution relations is central to the Sraffa model; and for those who would invoke a 'Sraffa-Marx model', it is well to note Marx's comment about the 'insipidity of the economists who treat production as an eternal truth, and banish history to the domain of distribution'.[15]

In view of the above discussion, the observation that Sraffa downgrades the value analysis of Volumes I and II of *Capital* will be no surprise. However, in considering the effect of the Sraffa model and neo-Ricardian theory on the approaches economists are likely to be taking in the future, this question deserves special comment. A model which poses a direct relationship among wages, the rate of profit and relative prices can quite naturally be expected to treat the value analysis of Volume I and II of *Capital* as an 'unnecessary detour'.

---

[13] Note that when fixed capital is considered, Sraffa's R is significantly affected by the growth of long-lived fixed capital.

[14] Marx 1977a, Chapter 15, Section 2; Chapter 24, Section 4.

[15] McLellan 1972, p. 30. For some of Marx's comments on Mill, see p. 151, and also Marx 1981b, Chapter 51.

It is significant that, using an approach which he has identified as Sraffian or pre-Marxian, Samuelson concluded that Volume I's exploration of value and surplus-value was a 'digression' and that the Volume III 'transformation' of values into prices is simply an 'erase and replace' exercise performed between two mutually exclusive approaches.[16]

In order to understand the true sense in which relationships among wages, prices and profits are central to Marx's model, it is necessary to recall the nature of the methodology of *Capital*. The development from Volume I to Volume III is an illustration of what Marx described as the 'scientifically correct method', that of reasoning from abstract concepts to concrete forms as a way of grasping in our minds those concrete forms. The whole point of Marx's 'detour' was to understand the forms which economic categories assume on the surface of society – as well as to criticise the political economy which *directly* relates the surface forms without determining their underlying and essential links. It was not, on the other hand, meant as a demonstration that the abstract concepts *are* the reality, a position which Marx described as Hegel's error.[17]

From this perspective, once the inner connections of categories have been grasped, consideration of relationships among concrete forms does not require us to reproduce, each time, the process by which that understanding was reached. The appropriate test, then, of a model relating categories is whether it is informed by an understanding of the inner connections of those forms. By this test, the neo-Ricardian model fails because it obscures the essential character of capitalist production.[18]

A 'Sraffa-Marx model', thus, is an unlikely amalgam; and a new political economy based on the Sraffa model is unlikely to reveal a world of passionate possibilities. Those who do not take the 'detour' will not be aware of the path Marx sketched out to a world of 'passionate possibilities'. For it is in Volume I of *Capital* that Marx described in detail the drive of capital to press into service

---

[16] In his 'counterattack,' Samuelson has indicated he is prepared to come to terms with Sraffa – but not with Marx. Cf. Samuelson 1971 1973. Note that Medio also argues in this context that 'the neo-Ricardian theory, while providing the analytical tools for a correct solution of the "transformation problem", at the same time denies its relevance'.

[17] Marx, 'The Method of Political Economy', in McLellan (ed.) 1972, pp. 33–5.

[18] The Medio and Johansen models in the Hunt and Schwartz book, on the other hand, pass this test.

nature, science and the products of past labour in its search for surplus-value. And, in the resulting diminution of necessary labour-time and the value of labour-power, which produced an increase in relative surplus-value, Marx saw not only the cost to the individual labourer (in the form of degradation, self-estrangement and exploitation) but also the possibilities for the complete development of the potentialities that lie within human beings.

The increase in the productive powers of social labour, transmitted increasingly through the crystallised social labour with which living labour works, becomes the basis for the reduction of the portion of the workday which workers require to produce their means of subsistence. Under capitalist relations, the superfluous time takes the form of surplus-labour which brings with it, among other things, the superfluous employment of labour in the circulation sphere.[19] Yet, this superfluous or disposable time is potentially the basis for free human activity, that activity which is 'not dominated by the pressure of an extraneous purpose which must be fulfilled, and the fulfillment of which is regarded as a natural necessity or a social duty'.[20] It is this scope for free activity – true human wealth, which Marx saw as the foundation for real social labour and for the evolution of full human potential, intellectual and social – as an end in itself.[21] These are the passionate possibilities for humanity for which capitalist production paves the way but for which removal of capitalist relations are a necessary condition of realisation.

By focusing on labour-time and the productivity of social labour, value analysis permits recognition of fixed capital as both the result and condition of social labour; it allows us to understand our social relationships as such – rather than as the properties of things, as the properties of the material elements of production. At the same time, by placing time at the centre of its analysis, it points to the significance of both the length and division of the workday and also the squandering within capitalist relations of the

---

[19] The problems of unrealised surplus-value and the need for labour in the circulation sphere, while abstracted from here, are clearly germane to a discussion of the distribution of income. These questions will also be omitted by those who forsake the 'detour'. Cf. Lebowitz 1972.

[20] Marx 1971, p. 257. Other comments on disposable time and free activity appear especially in McLellan (ed.) 1972, pp. 138–49 and also in Marx 1977a, Chapter 17, Section 4.

[21] Marx 1971, p. 257. See also Marx 1965, pp. 84–5.

substance of wealth, labour-time.[22] Value analysis, accordingly, directs attention to the need to move beyond capitalist relations to a society in which the developing productivity of social labour serves as the basis for the free and full development of all people.

Consider, then, the nature of a theory such as that of Sraffa which, clinging to use-value, observes only a world of commodities (but not labour-power as a commodity); which incorporates past labour, science and nature within technique (and separates this from living labour); and which attributes production of a surplus not to social labour and the specific social relationship within which it is performed but to technique itself (to nature, science and technology). Such a theory is simply a theory of alienated economics. In addition to the general inability to pass beyond things to people, it reflects a world in which all applications of science, natural forces and products of labour on a large scale confront individual labourers only as something extraneous; where the worker 'looks at the social nature of his labour, at its combination with the labour of others for a common purpose, as he would at an alien power'.[23]

This separation of technique from living labour in the theory mirrors a stage in the development of capitalism – an intensified growth of fixed capital, where wealth as measured in use-value appears to be the result of fixed capital rather than of living labour. Neo-Ricardian economics describes a world in which the development of productive forces has separated scientific labour and the technological application of science from direct labour, a bewitched world in which science and technology are viewed as independent and alien powers. It is a theory which does not go beyond the way matters appear to the participants in capitalist production. It reinforces a situation in which the conditions of labour dominate labour itself, where things are in the saddle still riding mankind. It is, indeed, an alienated economics. But is it also more than that?

---

[22] 'In the final analysis, all forms of economics can be reduced to an economics of time.' Marx, quoted in McLellan (ed.) 1972, pp. 75–6.
[23] Marx 1981b, p. Chapter 5; Marx, n.d., pp. 378–9.

The social basis of the neo-Ricardian critique

As noted above, the main thrust of the neo-Ricardian critique of neoclassical economics has been to undermine the latter's theoretical justification of the distribution of income and, in particular, the return to the owners of capital. By demolishing the theoretical credibility (if not the ideological credibility) of the marginal productivity theory of distribution, neo-Ricardian theory has severed the link between the productive contribution of capital goods and the pecuniary return to the owners of capital. But it is important to consider both the perspective from which this attack has been made and its objective nature.

In its political form, this attack on the theoretical justification of the return to the owners of capital is specifically on the ownership of capital itself. Recalling Keynes's vision of the 'euthanasia of the rentier', Joan Robinson notes that 'the wealth generated by technical progress, capital accumulation, work and business acumen, thus drop into the laps of rentiers while they sit at home or occupy themselves with other tasks'.[24] Critically, this attack is on the ownership of capital rather than on the relation of capital itself. Thus Robinson earlier argued:

> If the capitalists fully lived up to Marx's description and really invested the whole surplus there would be no need for socialism. It is the rentier aspect of profit, as a source of private wealth, which Marshall emphasizes, that makes the strongest case for socialism.[25]

Accordingly, Robinson's prescriptions are arguments for ending the private ownership of capital rather than the capitalist relation.[26]

In arguing against the preconception that the ownership of capital is a productive function, the neo-Ricardian view does not challenge the function of capital itself.[27] Rather, it is an attack on the parasitical character of ownership of capital. Its perspective reminds one of Marx's description

---

[24] Robinson 1967, p. 58.

[25] Robinson 1955, p. 18.

[26] 'Rentier consumption, however, could be eliminated while savings out of profits are still needed to finance investment.' Robinson 1967, pp. 61, 80.

[27] It is interesting to note that Sraffa's R appears in Goodwin's essay in the Hunt and Schwartz book as 'capital productivity,' the inverse of the capital-output ratio. Since science and technology necessarily appear as someone else's property, as powers belonging to capital, this is not a surprising twist.

of the way functioning capitalists viewed their own activity 'as opposed to the inactivity, the non-participation of the money-capitalist in the production process'.[28] Robinson's view, then, of our 'highly peculiar economic system' is important to recognise:

> In the main, industry and trade are now dominated by *managerial* capitalism, that is by companies nominally owned by a shifting population of shareholders and actually run by salaried staff.[29]

It is from the perspective of that 'salaried staff' that the neo-Ricardian view is best understood.

Marx long ago described the effects of the development of capitalist production (and, in particular, the emergence of the joint-stock company) on the division between the money-capitalist and the functioning capitalist, the owner of capital and the functionary of capital, the juridical owner and the economic owner of capital. With the transformation of the actually functioning capitalist into a manager of other people's capital and of the owner of capital into a mere money-capitalist, the function of capital becomes less and less an attribute of the ownership of capital.[30] Like feudal lords whose functions within feudal society also were separated from them, owners of capital are increasingly perceived as superfluous.[31] That this perception would be clearest among those who face the owners of capital, the functioning capitalists (or their intellectual representatives), is not at all surprising.

Yet it is not only the opposition of functionaries of capital to owners of capital which underlies the neo-Ricardian position; there is also the opposition of science and technology to direct labour. In its tendency to attribute the surplus to technique, to separate science and technology from direct living labour and to obscure the nature of wage-labour (and capital), neo-Ricardian theory reflects the position of a special sphere within the social division of labour, that of scientific and technological labour.

---

[28] Marx 1981b, Chapter 23.
[29] Robinson 1967, pp. 56, 58.
[30] Marx 1981b, Chapters 23, 27. Marx 1971, p. 'Addenda on 'Revenue and its Sources. Vulgar Political Economy'.
[31] 'Their position is similar to that of the feudal lords whose exactions in the measure that their services became superfluous with the rise of bourgeois society, became mere outdated and inappropriate privileges and who therefore rushed headlong to destruction.' Marx 1971, p. 315.

The process of capitalist development which 'estranges from him (the labourer) the intellectual potentialities of the labour-process in the same proportion as science is incorporated in it as an independent power' is a two-sided process.[32] Just as mental (scientific and technological) labour appears to the manual labourer only in the form of fixed capital, as the property of another and as a means of exploitation, so also does manual labour appear to the mental labourer only as the object and mere appendage of fixed capital, the source of productiveness and wealth. The product of social labour, within existing social relations, intervenes to hide from both the social nature of their labour. As long as the conditions of labour dominate labour itself, this unity necessarily appears as an opposition, an opposition intensified with the shift from a simple labour process to a scientific labour process.

In contrast to the first opposition, the political form of the second opposition underlying neo-Ricardian theory is as yet latent. Nevertheless, it is possible to infer some of its characteristics from the nature of the theory. Given the complete severance of relations of distribution from relations of production, abstract considerations of social justice would lead to proposals for greater equality of income rather than for the abolition of wage-labour itself. Similarly, given the orientation to production of use-value and the lack of consideration for the alienating nature of production, this position would emphasise expansion of commodity production and, in particular, accumulation. And, with the emphasis on growth and accumulation and the attribution of surplus to technique, there would be a tendency to view wages as a necessary evil (which, however, tend to check the potential for accumulation) and, accordingly, an inclination to respond with incomes policies (especially after the removal of 'inequities') when wage demands 'get out of hand.' From this perspective, not only the claims of owners of capital but also those of trade unions are viewed with askance.

Once the objective nature of neo-Ricardian theory is recognised, the conflict between neoclassical and neo-Ricardian theory can be understood as more than just the result of the fortuitous resurrection of an earlier, better theory. It becomes possible to consider the social roots of that conflict and to situate neoclassical theory itself. We are brought directly back to Bukharin's characterisation of neoclassical theory in 1914 as the objective theory of the

---

[32] Marx 1977a, Chapter 25, Section 4; Chapter 14, Section 5.

rentier, as the 'ideology of the bourgeois who has already been eliminated from the process of production'.[33]

In this context, it is useful to recall Bukharin's advice:

> Marxism must give an exhaustive criticism of the latest theories, which must include not only a methodological criticism, but a sociological criticism, as well as a criticism of the entire system as pursued to its furthest ramifications....
>
> A criticism of the capitalist system is of the utmost importance for a proper understanding of the events of the present day. And, in so far as a criticism of the bourgeois theories may smooth the path for such an understanding, such criticism has an abstract theoretical value.[34]

The second crisis of economic theory: a postscript

The 'Second Crisis of Economic Theory' was not a crisis of Marxist economic theory. Nor was it meant to describe the state of neo-Ricardian theory. Rather, it was the assertion that neoclassical theory, the theory which dominates academic economics, once again had no answer to the crises of capitalist society.

The First Crisis of Economy Theory was also a crisis confined to neoclassical economic theory. And despite the existence of Marxist theory which went to the roots of the economic crisis, the solution to the first theoretical impasse (a crisis in the macroeconomic component of neoclassical theory) was Keynes. Would history repeat itself in the second crisis?

After all, neo-Ricardian theory is quite consistent with the work of Keynes and his successors. As Medio noted, 'a neo-Ricardian approach – in contrast to a Marxian one – to the problem of value and distribution may be associated with theories which attribute to profits some "objective" social role.'[35] He had in mind here the neo-Keynesian macroeconomic theory of income distribution, which determines the rate of profit via the rate of accumulation and the capitalists' propensity to save. Once the rate of profit is determined in this manner, the Sraffian system (which has one degree of freedom) is closed,

---

[33] Bukharin 1972, p. 31.
[34] Bukharin 1972, pp. 9–10.
[35] Hunt and Schwartz (eds.) 1972, p. 328. See also Nuti's comments: pp. 226–7.

and there is no place for alternative methods of closing the system such as a subsistence wage or the rate of surplus-value.[36]

In 1973, when this essay was originally written, it really looked like the neo-Ricardian critique had decisively undercut the legitimacy of neoclassical theory. Thus, I suggested that a likely result would be an end to the 'schizophrenic state of the arts' in which two incompatible and alien theories in micro-theory and macro-theory had co-existed uneasily since the absorption of Keynesian theory (with many of its central ideas cast off) in the 'neoclassical synthesis'.[37] With the emergence of neo-Ricardian theory, the suggested solution to a crisis in the microeconomic aspect of neoclassical theory, Keynesian theory now had its own microeconomic component and could detach itself from neoclassical theory. The completion of the Keynesian system in itself would be the result of Cambridge Criticism, Part Two.

Of course, it did not happen this way at all. Not only did the neo-Ricardian critique essentially disappear from the horizon (without its criticism ever being answered) but neoclassical theory proceeded to develop a macroeconomics once again rooted in its microeconomic theory. Why was neoclassical theory able to weather this particular theoretical challenge? Not because of the autonomous development of thought. The neo-Ricardian critique of the ownership of capital and Keynesian social democracy disintegrated as finance capital and neoliberal reconstruction advanced.[38] The ability of capitalism to weather its structural crisis gave strength to its traditional ideological prize-fighters.

But, as suggested above, the theoretical challenge posed by the neo-Ricardian critique never threatened the logic of capital itself. While questioning the link between income and contribution and the ability to derive the value of capital in means of production independent of the profit rate, the neo-Ricardian critique never identified capital as the result of the exploitation of workers. It was, in this respect, an internal dispute within capitalist economics. Yet, understanding its limits does not mean that it was appropriate to attack

---

[36] It is significant that Sraffa himself treats the rate of profit as the independent variable and suggests it may be 'determined from outside the system of production, in particular by the level of the money rates of interest'. Sraffa 1960, p. 33.

[37] Robinson describes the disposition of some of Keynes's ideas as follows, 'put to sleep', 'lost', 'smothered', 'wound up in a cocoon'. Robinson 1972.

[38] Lebowitz 2004.

it rather than to utilise its criticisms in the course of struggle. Bukharin understood this well:

> We have another reason also for devoting attentive study to bourgeois economics. The ideological struggle, like any other direct practical struggle, must make use of the rule: utilize all the oppositions within the ranks of the enemy, all their disagreements between themselves.... A criticism of bourgeois economics aids the development of the proletariat's own economic science.[39]

---

[39] Bukharin 1972, pp. 160–1. See also Sweezy's comments below in Chapter 9, Appendix.

Chapter Three
The Neo-Ricardian Reduction

Once a philosopher who considered Marx 'merely a philosopher of the human condition', Robert Paul Wolff has apparently become a neo-Ricardian economist who views Marx as 'a theoretical economist before all else'.[1] With this new perspective, which more than anything else took shape as the result of a set of lectures on value theory by John Eatwell, it is not surprising that Wolff considers neo-Ricardian linear reproduction models of an economy with a surplus as the key to the 'rehabilitation' of Marx as a powerful and relevant economist, or that he identifies distribution of the surplus as 'the central social and economic issue in any society'. What is surprising, however, is that his book's principal contribution to understanding Marx occurs only through consideration of its flaws and that he admits his failure to capture Marx's 'deepest and most powerful insights' in his models.

Wolff's problems begin with the three-sector (corn, iron, labour) model of an economy without a surplus (simple material reproduction) introduced in his opening chapter on the concept of reproduction. Whereas the inputs for the production of iron and corn include 'units of labor': the appropriate output in the third sector is 'workers'. With four variables

---

[1] Review of Wolff 1984 in *Queen's Quarterly*, Spring 1987, pp. 239–41.

(corn, iron, labour, and workers) but only three processes or equations, the critical question becomes the manner of closing the system. Marx's particular insight was to conceptualise a specific variable – the workday (the relation of units of labour to workers), determined exogenously to the technical requirements of the linear reproduction model; he thus directs us immediately to consider the character of the social relations of production which set a workday and to grasp that a model of material reproduction cannot be based exclusively upon technical relations.

In contrast, Wolff performs a 'Ricardian reduction' (allowing one variable to represent two relations) in order to close his system. He assumes that the technical inputs required to produce workers are those necessary to permit them to be able to work 'for one unit of time'. Thus, he sets up a fixed technical relation between the worker and the unit of labour. The workday disappears as a variable. But, so also (as Marx noted with regard to Ricardo's similar reduction) does the recognition of coercion in the capitalist workday. In short, Marx's central distinction between labour-power and labour (workers and units of labour) is obliterated by simple assumption in the formal model.

Although the resulting problems are already apparent in the inferences he draws from his model of simple reproduction, they become critical when Wolff introduces his model of an economy with a surplus: 'improvements in the techniques of corn and iron production allow larger outputs to be achieved with the same inputs'. His conclusion is that 'there now arises...a physical surplus'. And, with the emergence of such a surplus, three questions become central: Who gets the surplus? How do the surplus-getters get the surplus? and, What do they do with it? These are the fundamental questions, he proposes, that all classical political economy was trying to answer – which leads him to consider the answers of Smith, Ricardo and Marx.

Yet, there is a critical question which has been begged: Why should we assume there is a physical surplus? Once we recognise the existence of a variable for the length and intensity of the workday, it is appropriate to ask why, under conditions of increased productivity, workers do not reduce the workday? Put another way, why do the workers not capture the benefits of rising productivity through increased leisure (at home or on the job)?

This is precisely at the core of Marx's distinction between labour-power and labour. If we have failed to understand the centrality of the workday as a variable, we do not understand precisely why a surplus emerges. While recognising the uniqueness of Marx's interest in the 'deeper problem' (Why is there in general profit, and not nothing?) and understanding that the answer to 'the qualitative and quantitative riddle of the origin of profit' lies in the distinction between labour-power and labour (for no other product can we 'distinguish between the commodity itself and the commodity's employment, between labor-power and labor'), Wolff nevertheless makes no such distinction in his formal models and simply assumes the existence of a surplus.

Much of what follows in the book is predictable. After deploying his model of an economy with a surplus to demonstrate that it requires less than an hour of labour to 'replenish a worker's ability to labor for an hour' (the worker – or, more precisely, labour – is exploited), and total profits equal surplus-labour extracted, Wolff travels the familiar terrain of the transformation problem (with all its misunderstandings) to discover that 'Marx's solution to Ricardo's problem' fails except under very unique conditions. 'This is, really a rather devastating discovery!' Additional devastating discoveries follow in Wolff's concluding chapter, 'Envoi: Some Doubts about Marx's Theory of Value and Exploitation', where he proceeds to use corn rather than labour as a measure in his models and learns that it takes less than one unit of corn to produce a unit of corn – thus, the exploitation of corn. Yet 'the extraction of surplus corn value from the corn inputs does not require anything resembling a distinction between corn and "corn power"'. Accordingly, Wolff proposes that 'we have, it seems to me, raised questions about the foundations of Marx's critique of capitalism and classical political economy'.

The real question, however, concerns the adequacy of Wolff's understanding and formal modelling of Marx. Having assumed a surplus, it can be expressed in any basic input. But does this have anything to do with Marx? As Wolff himself belatedly recognises, 'little or nothing' of Marx's particular conception of labour 'found its way into the formal structure of our model of a capitalist economy'. He confesses 'There is in fact no place in the formal analysis at which the labor/labor-power distinction gets introduced'. Completely lost as to how the error made its way into the system and how it is to be resolved, Wolff concludes by expressing the hope that future models may make it 'possible to complete the analytical reconstruction of Marx's political economy in a way that preserves his deepest and most powerful insights. But that is, appropriately, the subject of a separate book'.

Having acknowledged that he failed to capture Marx's central insight in his models, the mystery here is why (once the owl of Minerva finally took wing) this book (with this title) was ever published.

Chapter Four
Is 'Analytical Marxism' Marxism?

Introduction

G.A. Cohen, Jon Elster, John Roemer – without
question, these are prolific writers with an impressive
series of articles and books, who have become a
significant presence in commentaries and discussions
of Marxism in recent years. My first inkling, though,
that more had emerged on the scene came from a
1983 article by John Gray (passed on by a sceptical
friend); for the 1983 article hailed the emergence
of 'a powerful new school of Analytical Marxism,
led by such outstanding figures as G.A. Cohen,
Jon Elster and John Roemer, with whose works the
future of Marxism, if it has any, must henceforth be
associated'.[1]

Is there indeed such a school? The evidence on
the existence of somesuch self-defined group is
overwhelming. In his *Making Sense of Marx*, Elster
notes that Cohen's *Karl Marx's Theory of History* came
as a 'revelation': 'Overnight it changed the standards
of rigour and clarity that were required to write on
Marx and Marxism.' Accordingly, he notes, a small
group of like-minded colleagues formed and began
a series of annual meetings in 1979. Their discussions
were decisive for the shaping of Elster's book – and,

---

[1] Gray 1983, p. 1461.

in particular, the contributions of Roemer (subsequently stated in his 'path-breaking' *A General Theory of Exploitation and Class*) were 'crucial'.[2]

In turn, Roemer begins the latter book by noting his particular indebtedness to Cohen and Elster, indicating among those who were helpful several others who also appear on Elster's list.[3] Mentioned on both lists, Erik Olin Wright corroborates the existence of the group, its annual meetings and its orientation toward 'analytical Marxism' in the preface to his recent book, *Classes*; in addition, he testifies that its 'new ideas and perspectives have had a considerable impact on my thinking and my work'.[4] Finally, definitively embracing the self-designation of 'analytical Marxism' is Roemer's new collection by that name – a collection which includes three essays each by Roemer, Elster and Cohen plus individual efforts by several others.[5]

So, what do the adherents themselves see as the constituent elements in analytical Marxism? For Wright, the central intellectual thread is the 'systematic interrogation and clarification of basic [Marxian] concepts and their reconstruction into a more coherent theoretical structure'.[6] Similarly, as noted, Elster identified 'rigour and clarity' as the underlying principle in the formation of the group. The most explicit self-description of analytical Marxism, however, comes from Roemer in his Introduction to his collection: 'analytically sophisticated Marxism' – pursued with 'contemporary tools of logic, mathematics, and model building' and committed to 'the necessity for abstraction', to the 'search for foundations' of Marxian judgements, and to 'a non-dogmatic approach to Marxism'.[7] An impressive set of elements, to be sure. Where do we apply for candidate status in this analytically correct fellowship?

More than rigour, however, sets analytical Marxism apart – as John Gray's praise for this 'powerful new school' makes clear. For, hailing the early

---

[2] Elster 1985, pp. xiv–xv. Elster especially thanks Cohen and Roemer for their comments. He does not identify other group members but, included among those thanked for pre-publication help are Pranab Bardham, Robert Brenner, Lief Johansen, Serge Kolm, Adam Przeworski, Ian Steedman, Robert van der Veen, Philippe van Parijs and Erik Wright.

[3] Roemer 1982. These include Lief Johansen, Serge Kolm and Erik Wright.

[4] Wright 1985, p. 2. Wright identifies among the members of the group Cohen, Roemer, Elster, van Parijs, van der Veen, Brenner, Przeworski and Hillel Steiner.

[5] Roemer 1986a. Included in this collection are essays by Bardham, Brenner, Przeworski, Wright and Allen Wood.

[6] Wright 1985, p. 2.

[7] Roemer 1986a, pp. 1–2.

Austrian criticisms of Marx by Böhm-Bawerk, von Mises and Hayek (and that of right-wing US economist Paul Craig Roberts) and genuflecting before 'the prodigious virtuosity of capitalism' and the marvels of the market, Gray was far from a sympathetic commentator on Marxism ('the first world view in human history that is genuinely self-defeating'); his praise for analytical Marxism occurs in the context of a lengthy anti-Marxist polemic ('The System of Ruins').

The practitioners of analytical Marxism can not, of course, bear the responsibility for what others (like Gray) write about them. They bear responsibility only for their own work. But, consider that work. Included by Elster as 'dead' in Marx (in his most recent book, *An Introduction to Karl Marx*) are the following: 'scientific socialism'; 'dialectical materialism'; Marxian economic theory – in particular, its two 'main pillars' – the labour theory of value ('intellectually bankrupt') and the theory of the falling rate of profit; and, 'perhaps the most important part of historical materialism' – the 'theory of productive forces and relations of production'.[8] Similarly, in a long march through Marxian economics, Roemer left intact only the Marxian theory of exploitation in his *Analytical Foundations of Marxian Economics*; he then proceeded in *A General Theory of Exploitation and Class* to find even this final survivor inadequate.[9] Exploitation, Roemer now informs us, is simply inequality. But what, then, is the difference between the analytical-Marxist position and that of non-Marxist philosophers such as Rawls? Roemer answers that 'it is not at all clear'; 'the lines drawn between contemporary analytical Marxism and contemporary left-liberal political philosophy are fuzzy'.[10]

One must wonder what really is left of Marxism in analytical Marxism. In what follows, we will examine some of this work (especially that of Elster and Roemer) in order to explore the extent to which it can be considered 'Marxist'. The conclusion is that analytical Marxism is not Marxism – and that, indeed, it is, in essence, *anti*-Marxist.[11]

---

[8] Elster 1986, pp. 188–94.
[9] Roemer 1981.
[10] Roemer 1986a, pp. 199–200.
[11] [When I made this point in the original essay, I thought I was being bold and provocative. Re-reading the essay now, it seems to me that any other evaluation was always ludicrous.]

'Neoclassical' or 'rational-choice' Marxism?

There are several alternative labels which have been attached to analytical Marxism and its practitioners; they include neoclassical Marxism, game-theoretic Marxism and rational-choice Marxism. Consideration of these labels themselves provides a good point of entry into an examination of analytical Marxism.

'Neo-classical Marxism', as Patrick Clawson described Phillipe van Parijs's article on the falling-rate-of-profit controversy, would appear on the face of things to be an oxymoron.[12] How could such a construct exist? After all, neoclassical economic theory begins from the atomistic individual – conceived as ontologically prior to the whole, the particular society. This is its 'Cartesian' heritage, so well analysed by Richard Levins and Richard Lewontin, which it shares with methodological approaches in other spheres:

> The parts are ontologically prior to the whole; that is, the parts exist in isolation and come together to make wholes. The parts have intrinsic properties, which they possess in isolation and which they lend to the whole.[13]

In neoclassical analysis, we have atomistic individuals who, with exogeneously given assets and techniques, enter into relations of exchange with each other in order to satisfy exogeneously given wants; and society is the sum-total of these arrangements of exchange.

Nothing could be further from Marx's perspective. To begin with the isolated individual for whom the various forms of social connectedness are a 'mere means toward his private purposes' was simply 'twaddle'.[14] 'Private interest,' Marx emphasised, 'is itself already a socially determined interest, which can be achieved only within the conditions laid down by society and with the means provided by society'. To be sure, it is the interest of individuals, of private persons; 'but its content, as well as the form and means of its realization, is given by social conditions independent of all'.[15]

Thus, in the dialectical (in contrast to the Cartesian) perspective, parts have no prior independent existence as parts. They 'acquire properties by virtue of

---

12 Clawson 1983, p. 108.
13 Levins and Lewontin 1985, p. 269.
14 Marx 1973, p. 84.
15 Marx 1973, p. 156.

being parts of a particular whole, properties they do not have in isolation or as parts of another whole'.[16] Marx's starting point, accordingly, is to develop an understanding of society as a 'connected whole', as an organic system; it is to trace the intrinsic connections and to reveal the 'obscure structure of the bourgeois economic system', the 'inner core, which is essential but concealed' on the surface of society.[17] Only then does Marx proceed to explore what is real *within this structure* for the individual agents of production and how things necessarily appear to them.

Having developed, for example, 'the general and necessary tendencies of capital' on the basis of the concept of capital (capital as a whole), it was then possible to demonstrate how 'the immanent laws of capitalist production' were manifested through the actions of individual capitalists in competition.[18] As Marx noted repeatedly in the *Grundrisse*, 'competition executes the inner laws of capital; makes them into compulsory laws towards the individual capital, but it does not invent them. It realizes them'.[19] To *begin* analysis, on the other hand, with those individual capitals (and with the connections as they appear in competition) produces a distortion of the inner structure because 'in competition everything always appears in inverted form, always standing on its head'.[20]

From this perspective, there is absolutely no compatibility between the atomistic approach of neoclassical economics and Marxism. 'Neo-classical Marxism' is either not neoclassical or it is not Marxism. Can we say the same, though, about 'Game-Theoretic' or 'Rational-Choice' Marxism? In a recent essay, Alan Carling has proposed 'Rational-Choice Marxism' as the label most characteristic of the work in question, describing its distinctive presupposition as the 'view that societies are composed of human individuals who, being endowed with resources of various kinds, attempt to choose rationally between various courses of action'.[21] But, is this just neoclassical economics by another name? Roemer's description of rational-choice models (in an essay entitled 'Rational Choice Marxism') as 'general equilibrium theory, game theory and

---

[16] Levins and Lewontin 1985, pp. 273, 3.
[17] Marx 1968, p. 165; Marx 1981b, p. 311.
[18] Marx 1977a, p. 433.
[19] Marx 1973, pp. 414, 552, 651, 751–2.
[20] Marx 1968, p. 165.
[21] Carling 1986, pp. 26–7.

the arsenal of modeling techniques developed by neo-classical economics' might seem to suggest as much.[22]

However, it is critical not to confuse particular techniques with their original emergence or the use which has been made of those techniques; to do that would be to repeat the unfortunate experience of Marxian economics with calculus – rejected as 'bourgeois' despite Marx's own significant explorations of this technique.[23] In short, if it is a question of the appropriation of these techniques within a Marxian framework, then analytical Marxism may have much to offer.

Consider game theory and game-theoretic approaches. Characteristic of both Elster and Roemer is a very strong emphasis on 'game-theoretic' modelling; indeed, Roemer's general definition of exploitation is explicitly game-theoretic. Does this approach have a place in Marxist theoretical work? If we insist that Marxist analysis must begin from a consideration of the 'whole', the establishment of the inner structure of society, before examination of how that whole must appear, it is not obvious that game theory as such is inappropriate here.

Game theory begins with the specification of the 'game'; that is, it explicitly sets out the set of relations within which the actors perform.[24] On the face of it, there is nothing inconsistent here with Marxism, which begins from the specification of a given set of relations of production and then proceeds to explore how the particular actors will behave rationally – and the dynamic properties (the laws of motion) inherent in the particular structure.

The key, of course, will be the specification of the game and the actors. A game, for example, in which the actors are identified as the competing sellers of a common commodity, exploring their rational strategies, inhabits the terrain of the competition of capitals which, for Marx, executes but explains nothing about the inner laws of capitalism. By contrast, a game in which the parties are a capitalist and 'his' wage-labourers (and which proceeds to explore the strategies and actions of each party) would appear to correspond closely to Marx's own approach. In this latter game, the relations between capitalist and wage-labourer are identical with those of the coalition of capitalists and the

---

[22] Roemer 1986a, p. 192.
[23] Gerdes 1985; Struik 1948.
[24] For an introduction to game theory, see Bradley and Meek 1986.

coalition of wage-labourers; that is, the relation of the capitalist to his own workers is the 'essential relation' of capital and wage-labour.[25]

Similarly, a game which explores the relation between the feudal lord and his peasant tenants (or, between the coalition of lords and that of peasants – the two approaches are seen here as identical so long as neither introduces matters appropriate to intra-coalition relations) would seem to permit an examination of the essential character of feudal relations of production. What does the lord want, what are the strategies available to him, what are the potential gains (and risks) from each? What does the peasant (peasant community) want, what are the potential strategies and returns? What (in a continuing game) is the 'appropriate' solution or outcome to the particular game – and, significantly, what aspects of the behaviour of the parties in this particular interaction tend to undermine (rather than preserve) the existing solution/outcome and, indeed, the particular game itself?

Stated in this way, there appears to be nothing at all inconsistent between game theory as such and a Marxist approach; indeed, not only may we speculate that Marx would have been quick to explore its techniques but we can go further and suggest that Marx's analysis was inherently a 'game-theoretic' analysis.[26]

Yet, the above description of the feudal 'game' has a certain specificity; for, it is a game which may best be designated as a 'collective game'. Its actors are classes (or class representatives, *Träger*, the bearers of a relation). There is no place here for the autonomous, atomistic individual; nor have we introduced (yet) intra-class interactions. It is simply assumed that the coalition of lords acts in the same way as the Abstract Lord – that our examination of the latter in its specific interaction with the Abstract Peasant yields the essential insights into the coalition or class of lords in its interactions with the class of peasants.

In short, in the collective game, classes act. *The* feudal lord and *the* peasant interact – but individual feudal lords and individual peasants do not interact with each other. Similarly, in the collective game for capitalism, capital (the capitalist) and wage-labour (the worker) interact – but factors emanating from the posited existence of competing capitalists and wage-labourers are seen as

---

[25] Marx 1973, p. 420.
[26] See, for example, Maarek's elaboration of Marx's theory of surplus-value using game theory, Maarek 1979, pp. 124–34.

secondary to the establishment of the essential capital/wage-labour relation. As Maarek indicates, in his discussion of Marx's theory of surplus-value, 'it is just as if there were a single centre of decision in each class, a "collective" capitalist and a "collective" worker, with the two classes confronting each other like two autonomous blocks'.[27]

The collective (or class) game, thus, puts to the side any consideration of the ability of the particular coalitions to engage successfully in collective actions (i.e., the issues posed by Mancur Olson in his *The Logic of Collective Action*) in order to explore first in detail the character of the relation between classes as defined by relations of production.[28] All questions of whether individual agents will find it in their individual interest to engage in collective action (to achieve class goals), all matters relating to 'free-rider' problems, etc. are not the principal matter of enquiry of the collective game. *Epistemological priority is assigned to the determination of the structure within which individuals act.*

Yet, intra-coalition matters are not outside the purview of a Marxian analysis (anymore than the consideration of how a class-in-itself becomes a class-for-itself). The manner in which capital attempts to divide workers and to encourage competition among them in order to secure its own goals is an important part of Marx's exploration of a rational strategy for capital in the strategic game of capital and wage-labour. Further, Marx makes a critical statement about intra-coalition issues on the side of workers when he concludes that when workers act in their individual self-interest, the result is the *worst* strategy for workers as a whole.[29] As important as Marx's insights on these intra-coalition matters are, it is essential to recognise that they can occur only *after* the prior specification of the collective game.

In contrast to the collective game, on the other hand, what we may designate as the 'individual game' has a different starting point. Beginning from the position that there are no supra-individual entities which act in the real world ('capital' does nothing, etc.), it asserts the necessity to consider the behaviour of the individual unit at a *pre-coalition* level in the war of all against all. Thus, no longer at the core of enquiry is the character of the class relation. Substituted is a different problematic, the neoclassical problematic – the outcomes which

---

[27] Maarek 1979, p. 132.
[28] Olson 1965.
[29] Lebowitz 1988.

emerge from the interactions of atomistic individuals. At its best, the over-riding question in the individual game becomes one of why coalitions emerge, why (and in what sense) there are classes-for-themselves.

Thus, a game-theoretic approach in itself can not be said to be inconsistent with a Marxist analysis. Rigour is *not* the dividing line between Marxism and 'analytical Marxism'. Rather, the central issue is the nature of the problematic within which such techniques are employed. It is precisely in this context that 'analytical Marxism' should be considered.

Methodological individualism and microfoundations

At the core of analytical Marxism is the categorical imperative – *there shalt be no explanation at a level above that of the individual unit.* Thus, Elster opens his *Making Sense of Marx* by announcing that he will begin 'by stating and justifying the principle of methodological individualism'. The doctrine is quite uncompromising: 'all social phenomena – their structure and their change – are in principle explicable in ways that only involve individuals – their properties, their goals, their beliefs and their actions'.[30]

To explain, Elster proposes, it is necessary 'to provide a *mechanism*, to open up the black box and show the nuts and bolts, the cogs and wheels, the desires and beliefs that generate the aggregate outcomes'.[31] Accordingly, methodological individualism abandons the macro-level for the micro and rejects an explanation which does not proceed from individuals; it stands in opposition to methodological collectivism, which 'assumes that there are supra-individual entities that are prior to individuals in the explanatory order'.[32]

As Elster is well aware, however, Marx's discussions about 'humanity', 'capital', and especially 'capital in general' as collective subjects are inconsistent with this doctrine of methodological individualism. Citing one of Marx's statements on competition in the *Grundrisse*, Elster indeed comments, 'One could not wish for a more explicit denial of methodological individualism'.[33] He immediately, however, evokes an alternative authority – John Roemer.

---

[30] Elster 1985, p. 4.
[31] Elster 1985, p. 5.
[32] Elster 1985, pp. 5–6.
[33] Elster 1985, p. 7.

In this respect, it is important to recognise that Elster has read Marx closely, and that not the lack of familiarity of relevant passages (although his interpretations are rather questionable at times) but, rather, the *rejection* of these as grievous errors and as 'near-nonsense' underlies his argument. What is to be rescued is the Marx who makes 'sense', the Marx who sounds like a methodological individualist. Elster's project, simply, is to get rid of the bad Marx and preserve the good – the separation of the 'misguided framework' from what he sees as valuable in Marx.

The very same themes can be found in Roemer's essay on method in *Analytical Marxism*. Roemer asserts 'Marxian analysis requires micro-foundations'.[34] How, he asks, can we say that the entity, capital, does anything (e.g. divides and conquers workers) 'when in a competitive economy there is no agent who looks after the needs of capital'? When Marxists argue in such a manner, he proposes, they are guilty of 'a lazy kind of teleological reasoning'.[35] Again, the identified project is the necessity to find micro-mechanisms: 'What Marxists must provide are explanations of *mechanisms*, at the micro level, for the phenomena they claim come about for teleological reasons'.[36]

The logic behind this analytical-Marxist position can be seen most clearly in Phillipe Van Parijs's response to Clawson's description of his position as one of 'Neoclassical Marxism'. Noting the contrast between *'rational-man* (or individualistic) and *structural* (or systematic) explanations', Van Parijs indicates that structural explanations which refer to a structural imperative (e.g., a requirement flowing 'from the system itself') are 'unambiguously rejected by 'Neoclassical Marxism'.[37] Why? Because 'no explanation of B by A is acceptable unless one specifies the *mechanism* through which A generates B.'

Yet 'mechanism' has a rather specific meaning for Van Parijs here. For example, the propositions that can be derived from the structured collective game of capital and wage-labour (like capital's tendency to intensify the workday or develop productive forces) would fail his test for acceptability. This is clear from his subsequent proposition: 'Or, equivalently, no explanatory theory is acceptable unless it is provided with *microfoundations*'.

---

[34] Roemer 1986a, p. 192.
[35] Roemer 1986a, p. 191.
[36] Roemer 1986a, p. 192.
[37] Van Parijs 1983, p. 119.

How Proposition II is *equivalent* to Proposition I is something that Van Parijs considers so self-evident that it need not be mentioned!

Clearly missing from his discussion is the critical proposition which states that 'the *only* mechanism by which one can explain is one with microfoundations'. This, of course, is the only mechanism by which one *can* get from I to II, and it is the core of the matter. For, if we do accept that missing proposition, it of course follows that 'Marxism needs microfoundations'.[38]

But, *why* should we accept the proposition that microfoundations are the only mechanism by which one can explain? All we have are assertions. But where is the proof? Where is the demonstration that 'methodological collectivism' cannot provide a valid (and, indeed, better) explanation? Where is the basis for describing such 'structural' explanations as misguided, near-nonsense, disastrous scientific practice?[39] Are we to assume the point, drawing its force from neoclassical conventionism, is self-evident?

Elster notes that a methodological-collectivist explanation 'frequently takes the form of functional explanation'.[40] However, even if the analytical Marxists were able to find examples of functionalist or teleological arguments conducted at the supra-individual level, it would not prove that methodological collectivism *necessarily* leads to functionalist or teleological argument. Indeed, Przeworski, Brenner and Elster themselves all explore collective games in essays in *Analytical Marxism*.

Further, an acceptable methodological-individualist (or micro-) argument *would not constitute a sufficient refutation* of an explanation of social phenomena based upon the concept of supra-individual entities. Marx's argument that the competition of capitalists executes the inner laws of capital is a rejection of methodological individualism and micro*foundations* – but not of the real existence of individual capitals and micro-phenomena. The conclusion that only microfoundations can explain aggregate outcomes requires far than the assertions of analytical Marxism.

Ultimately, the proof of the pudding is in the eating. So, rather than criticise the Cartesian reductionism of analytical Marxism abstractly, let us look at the best that analytical Marxism has to offer, its success story. Consider specifically

---

[38] Van Parijs 1983, p. 120.
[39] Elster 1985, p. 4.
[40] He admits, though, that there is no necessary logical connection. Elster 1985, p. 6.

Elster's answer to Marx's explicit denial of methodological individualism – Roemer's 'pathbreaking' work on exploitation. Elster describes this centrepiece of analytical Marxism as an approach

> generating class relations and the capital relationship from exchanges between differently endowed individuals in a competitive setting....The overwhelmingly strong argument for this procedure is that it allows one to demonstrate as theorems what would otherwise be unsubstantiated postulates.[41]

What, however, is *wrong* with the so-called 'unsubstantiated postulates'? Recall that Marx's procedure was to begin his examination of capitalism from the postulate of capitalist and wage-labourer in which the relation is specified as one in which the worker has sold the property right over labour-power – with the necessary result both that the worker works under the direction of the capitalist and that the worker has no property rights in the product of labour. Marx, in short, begins from the specification of a particular set of relations of production.

Now, we may ask – where did those unsubstantiated postulates come from? And, the answer is obvious – from history, from real life, the real concrete. The sale of labour-power, work under the direction of the capitalist and the absence of workers' property rights in the product of labour are the historical premises of the discussion; and, they are brought to the theoretical discussion as the exogenous point of entry. So, there is indeed a theoretically unsubstantiated postulate – the capital/wage-labour relation. What is critical, however, is what Marx proceeds to *do* on the basis of this premise. He explores the nature of the interaction between capitalist and workers in the collective game and generates the dynamic properties inherent in that structured relationship.

Now, consider what Elster has said about Roemer's approach: Roemer will generate the class relationship from individuals; he will demonstrate the capital/wage-labour relation as a 'theorem'. An immediate response might be – but, this is a *different* theoretical object; what Marx takes as his starting point, Roemer sees as his object. Yet, it is important to remember that, in Marx's dialectical analysis, a central requirement will be to demonstrate that what was a mere premise and presupposition (an unsubstantiated postulate)

---

[41] Elster 1985, p. 7.

of the theory is itself reproduced within the system – i.e., is a result. In this respect, both Marx and Roemer have the *same* object – to demonstrate the production of the class relation. But, their starting points are different: Marx beginning from the observation of the concrete relationships and Roemer from... Roemer from *where*?

We will put that question aside for the moment. Let us ask first – what are we to conclude if both Roemer and Marx, having started out from different places, arrive at the same destination? Are we to conclude that Roemer's successful arrival (the derivation of the class relation from atomistic individuals) proves that you cannot get there from Marx's starting point? Obviously not. To conclude this would be to confuse explanation and necessitation. At best, Roemer's arrival will have demonstrated Marx's argument that competition executes the inner laws of capital – i.e., that many capitals, the necessary form of existence of capital, manifest through competition the inner nature of capital. On the other hand, if we have Roemer's derivation, do we *need* Marx's.

But, there is a begged question in all this: does Roemer *really* arrive at that same point, the point which for Marx is both premise and result – the historically given capitalist relations of production? Now we will consider Roemer's starting point. Elster has already told us – 'differently endowed individuals'. But, let Roemer explain more fully. His model 'has "explained" some phenomena, in deriving them from logically prior data. In *A General Theory of Exploitation and Class* [GTEC], the data are: differential ownership of the means of production, preferences and technology. Everything is driven by these data; class and exploitation are explained to be a consequence of initial property relations'.[42]

We see, not surprisingly, that Roemer *also* starts from 'logically prior data' which are not the subject of his analysis (i.e., an unsubstantiated postulate). It *happens* to be the same logically prior data with which neoclassical economics (in particular, neoclassical general-equilibrium theory) begins. And, Roemer proposes that, on the basis of those same neoclassical premises, he has succeeded in demonstrating the existence of exploitation and class – a classic case of hoisting neoclassical economics by its own petard.

---

[42] Roemer 1986b.

Let us think, though, about those logically prior data. (This particular success may be a poison draught for Marxism.) Where do they come from? Roemer answers – history. 'The historical process which gives rise to the initial endowments where my model begins is not a subject of my analysis. That is a topic for an historian.'[43] History thus has yielded a set of individuals who, with given preferences and technology, have differential property endowments. *Is that it?* Has history presented us with a group of atomistic individuals who have no prior connections, no prior interactions – individuals who are ontologically prior to the society?

Obviously not. What we have, rather, is that an analyst has decided to model the individuals *as if* they were initially outside society and then entered into society to exchange. The starting point, then, is not history – but history mediated by an ideological assumption, one identified by Marx as early as 1843.[44] It is easy to understand such an operation when conducted by a neoclassical economist – but a *Marxist*?

Roemer's instrumentalist response, however, would be that if the model succeeds in explaining the desired phenomena, then clearly the 'model has made the right abstractions: it has ignored things which are not crucial to its topic and has focused our attention correctly'.[45] Methodologically, this is not objectionable practice – since Marx similarly engages in abstraction and puts aside questions pertaining to the members of the set or coalition; however, many Marxists will find the idea that 'society' is an appropriate victim of Occam's Razor rather troublesome. Nevertheless, rather than debating this issue, it is more pertinent to consider whether the model has indeed succeeded in its object – whether, in short, Roemer's model makes 'the right abstraction'.

Roemerian exploitation

In discussing Roemer's success in generating as theorems both classes and exploitation within capitalism, we must limit ourselves to selected aspects of his theory as developed in his book and subsequent articles.[46] We will not

---

[43] Roemer 1986b.
[44] Marx 1975.
[45] Roemer 1986b.
[46] Some other issues are raised in my review of Roemer's book in Lebowitz 1984.

concern ourselves, for example, with the exploitation that Roemer discovers in his linear production model of an economy of simple-commodity producers with differential asset ownership since the inequality that Roemer finds here is manifestly 'rent', and its designation as 'exploitation in the Marxian sense' would necessitate holiday pay for his words; nor, for similar reasons, will we consider Roemer's 'socialist exploitation'.

The core argument in *GTEC* occurs when Roemer introduces a labour market into his model of individuals with differential endowments of productive assets. He demonstrates that, as a consequence of optimising behaviour, those individuals with low endowments will end up selling labour-power and will be exploited, whereas those who have high endowments will hire labour-power and will be exploiters. The argument, generating the classical-Marxist proposition, appears quite powerful.

Roemer proceeds, however, to introduce a credit market (rather than a labour market) and proceeds to demonstrate a functionally equivalent result: those with low endowments hire capital and are exploited while those with high endowments rent capital and are exploiters. Accordingly, Roemer offers his 'isomorphism theorem' that 'truly it does not matter whether labour hires capital or capital hires labour: the poor are exploited and the rich exploit in either case'.[47]

Now, this theorem (whose clauses successively skewer Marxian and neoclassical economists) is central to all that follows. Roemer himself draws the robust inference that 'the fundamental feature of capitalist exploitation is not what happens in the labour process, but the differential ownership of productive assets'.[48] *Yet, precisely the wrong conclusion has been drawn from the isomorphism theorem: rather than revealing the power of Roemer's analysis, it exposes its weakness.*

Consider what has occurred. Logical priority has shifted from specific relations of production to property relations; their connection has been inverted. Rather than seeing capitalist property relations (KP) as the product of capitalist relations of production (KRP), Roemer argues that differential ownership of productive assets necessarily yields capitalist relations of production, exploitation and class. Since, further, this can be demonstrated

---

[47] Roemer 1982, p. 93.
[48] Roemer 1982, pp. 94–5.

to occur with *either* a labour or credit market, it follows that unequal property endowment plus a factor market are sufficient to generate 'class relations and the capital relationship' (as theorems).

Let us, however, stress what Marx saw as critical elements in capitalism. These are: (1) the sale of the property right over labour-power by the person who owns no means of production; and, (2) the purchase of this property right by an owner of means of production whose goal is valorisation (M-C-M'). The two elements here clearly *presuppose* capitalist property relations (KP) – the specific inequality in property ownership. However, KP is not sufficient to yield these two elements – since (as Roemer demonstrates) it is obvious that KP can *also* support: (1a) the hiring of means of production by someone who owns only labour-power and (2a) the renting of the same by the owner of means of production. *KP is a necessary but not sufficient condition for capitalism (KRP).*

In short, two quite distinct régimes can be generated on the basis of Roemer's logically prior data, the initial property relations. A simple question reveals that difference: *who owns the product of labour?* In 1/2, property rights in the product of labour belong to the owner of means of production (who also purchased the property rights over the disposition of labour-power); in 1a/2a, on the other hand, it is the owner of labour-power who possesses the property right over the product. It is not difficult to establish that Marx's analysis of capitalism refers to 1/2 – but *not* to 1a/2a.

For Marx, the situation in which the purchase of labour-power did not occur was explicitly *precapitalist*. Where there is formal subsumption of labour by capital (the initial form of the capital relation), he noted that 'the relations of capital are essentially concerned with controlling production and . . . therefore the worker constantly appears in the market as a seller and the capitalist as a buyer . . .'.[49] In contrast to formal subsumption, on the other hand, was the case where capital is to be found but 'where it has not emerged as the direct purchaser of labour and as the immediate owner of the process of production' (as with, e.g., usury and merchant-capital). 'Here we have *not yet* reached the stage of the formal subsumption of labour under capital.'[50]

---

[49] Marx 1977a, p. 1011.
[50] Marx 1977a, p. 1023.

Characteristic of precapitalist relations was precisely the credit-market case that Roemer presents. Thus, in the *Grundrisse*, Marx commented that the relation in which the producer, still independent, faces means of production which are independent 'forming the property of a particular class of usurers...necessarily develops in all modes of production resting more or less on exchange'.[51] Here, the worker 'is not yet subsumed into the process of capital. The mode of production therefore does not yet undergo essential change'. There is, *of course*, exploitation – indeed, the 'most odious exploitation of labour'. In the mode of production itself, capital is still

> materially subsumed under the individual workers or the family of workers....What takes place is exploitation by capital without the mode of production of capital....This form of usury, in which capital does not seize possession of production, hence is capital only formally, presupposes the predominance of pre-bourgeois forms of production.[52]

Marx similarly observed that 'capital arises only where trade has seized possession of production itself, and where the merchant becomes producer, or the producer mere merchant'.[53]

In short, specifically capitalist relations of production (KRP) as examined by Marx require more than unequal distribution of property in means of production (KP); *they also require that capital has 'seized possession of production'* (true for 1/2 but not 1a/2a), that capital directs the process of production, that production is subordinated to the goals of capital. *Only* with this second element do we necessarily have two essential characteristics of the capitalist labour process – that 'the worker works under the control of the capitalist to whom his labour belongs' and 'the product is the property of the capitalist and not that of the worker, its immediate producer'.[54] Only here is it characteristic that, rather than the worker employing means of production, means of production employ the worker (a metaphor that captures Marx's conception).

Thus, Roemer's 'logically prior data' cannot select between capitalism and precapitalism. Does it matter? Consider what follows from 1/2 which does

---

51 Marx 1973, p. 853.
52 Ibid.
53 Marx 1973, p. 859.
54 Marx 1977a, pp. 291–2.

not follow from 1a/2a. The performance of surplus-labour will be compelled (given by M-C-M' and the sale of the property right over labour-power) – i.e., there will be exploitation specific to capitalist relations. The capitalist – but not the worker – will gain by increasing the intensity, etc. of labour; the capitalist – but not the worker – will be the direct recipient of gains resulting from increased productivity and thus has an incentive to alter the production process. Capitalist exploitation will be the basis of capital accumulation; KRP will be a sufficient condition for the reproduction of KP, for capitalist distribution relations.

By contrast, under 1a/2a (the credit-market case), it is the *producer* who gains from increased labour and productivity and who decides over the process of expanded reproduction. (Consider how this collective game would differ from the capitalist game.) Potentially, this producer *may* succeed in securing means of production for self as the result of intensive efforts. Unlike the case of 1/2, the credit-market case is, in fact, a 'transitional' relationship. The dynamic properties, the laws of motion, inherent in the two structures clearly differ.

What 'phenomena', then, have been derived from Roemer's logically prior data, unequally endowed atomistic individuals? What theorems have been successfully demonstrated by means of this prime example of methodological individualism? We find that there is no distinction between a capitalist and a precapitalist relation, no distinction between specifically capitalist exploitation based on capitalist relations of production and precapitalist exploitation based merely on unequal property endowments. Roemer, of course, is entitled to call anything he wants capitalism (as is Milton Friedman) – *but it should not be confused for a moment with Marx's (and a Marxist) concept of capitalism.*

Thus, Roemer does *not* arrive at the same destination as Marx. Rather than strengthening the case that we can proceed from individuals with differing property endowments to generate capitalist relations of production and capitalist exploitation, the very indeterminacy apparent in his model (the isomorphism theorem) undermines his argument. Still, it might be responded that all this simply proves that Marx was *wrong* to distinguish between capitalist exploitation (where 1/2 holds) and precapitalist exploitation based upon unequal property endowments (1a/2a) – since exploitation is the same in both cases. To answer this argument, we must briefly consider Roemer's model.

One of the critical problems in Roemer's model is his assumption of a common production function for all régimes. Precluded *by definition* is any effect of particular relations of production on the production function. By assuming, for example, in his linear-production models that a unit of labour-power exudes a certain quantity of labour (i.e., the quality and intensity of labour are presumably given technically), he not only effectively assumes away the content of the Marxian distinction between labour-power and labour but also leaves us with production considered merely as a technical process transforming inert inputs into final products. Thus, the distinction Roemer *once* acknowledged between the neoclassical and Marxist approach – that the Marxist asks 'how hard are the workers labouring?' fades away.[55]

What is the implication? Consider the difference between the credit-market model and the labour-market model. In the former, the producers secure the fruits of their own labour (i.e., own the product). They choose whether or not to select leisure on the job. Presumably, there are no inherent problems of shirking, no necessary costs of surveillance and monitoring, etc. – which would be reflected in the production function. To assume the same production coefficients in the case of the labour-market model, however, is to presuppose that workers who have no property rights in the products of their labour will behave the same as those who do. (Nor should we ignore the likelihood, in the labour-market case, that the choice of technique and the division of labour will be determined not solely by technical efficiency but also by the need to monitor easily and to reduce the ability of producers to engage in coalitions.)

Although Roemer concludes that capitalist exploitation does not require domination at the point of production because 'the class and exploitation relations of a capitalist economy using labour markets can be precisely replicated with a capitalist economy using credit markets', his models generate these results *only because of his hidden assumptions*.[56] In a model in which producers wish to maximise leisure (which includes leisure in the 'pores' of the workday), the assumption of unchanged technical coefficients in the two cases amounts to assuming the existence of an efficient (and costless) capitalist monitoring process – without acknowledging it! One can only abstract from the requirement of capitalist domination by assuming (as Roemer does explicitly!) that the delivery of labour for the wage is 'as simple and enforceable a transaction as the delivery of an apple for a dime'.[57]

---

[55] Roemer 1981, pp. 143–5.
[56] Roemer 1986a, p. 268.
[57] Roemer 1986a, p. 269.

In short, Roemer's discovery that the labour-market case and the credit-market case yield equivalent solutions and that, accordingly, capitalist domination is not necessary reflects merely the ideological assumption he has imposed upon his model. Having *assumed* that productive relations do not matter, Roemer finds little difficulty in then 'proving' that they do not matter; he is, of course, not the first to believe that he has proven what is merely embedded in his assumptions.

'Just' exploitation

For others in the analytical-Marxist camp, Roemer's discovery that capitalist exploitation requires neither labour-power as a commodity nor domination in production has been most persuasive. Wright, for example, initially resisted the argument that capitalist domination was unnecessary for exploitation but then yielded – maintaining, however, the importance of a link between domination in production and class relations.[58] Subsequently, he succumbed on this latter point as well (accepting Roemer's theory as the framework for his own empirical analysis) and announced, 'I now think that Roemer is correct on this point'.[59] Elster, too, is unequivocal; after presenting Roemer's conclusion, Elster characteristically declares, 'I believe that Roemer's argument is an irrefutable objection to the "fundamentalist" view that exploitation *must* be mediated by domination in the labour process'.[60]

Once the specific characteristics of capitalism and capitalist exploitation have been obliterated (leaving only unequal endowments), however, can meditations on 'just' exploitation be far behind? Posing the question 'Should Marxists be Interested in Exploitation?', Roemer responds with his 'verdict... that exploitation theory is a domicile that we need no longer maintain: it has provided a home for raising a vigorous family who now must move on'.[61] Having emptied the house of all its contents, Roemer's up-market move is to 'the modern concept' of exploitation as 'an injustice in the distribution of income resulting from a distribution of endowments which

---

[58] Wright 1982, p. 331.
[59] Wright 1985, p. 72.
[60] Elster 1985, p. 181.
[61] Roemer 1986a, p. 262.

is unjust'.[62] Exploitation, in short, is simply inequality – 'the distributional consequences of an unjust inequality in the distribution of productive assets and resources'.[63]

The obvious implication is that exploitation/inequality is not unjust if the original inequality in property endowments *itself* was not unjust. While this point is indeed explored by Roemer, it is Elster who most clearly draws out the logic of the analytical-Marxist argument. We judge exploitation unjust, he proposes, because 'exploitation in history has almost always had a thoroughly unclean causal origin, in violence, coercion, or unequal opportunities'.[64] But, what if there were a 'clean path' of original accumulation? What if people differ in their time preferences? What if some people choose to save and invest rather than consume (thereby building up a capital stock)? 'Could anyone object if they induce others to work for them by offering them a wage above what they could earn elsewhere?'.[65] Here, Elster notes, is a 'powerful objection, that must be taken seriously by anyone who sets out to defend Marx's theory of exploitation'.[66]

Thus, as counterexamples to the view that exploitation is inherently unjust, Elster and Roemer each present a two-person case where, as the result of the patterns of capital asset ownership and leisure preferences, the asset-poor person 'exploits the rich person'.[67] Elster's conclusion from this example is that 'It demonstrates, I think conclusively, that exploitation is not inherently wrong'.[68] In a second example ('more relevant for real-life problems'), Elster posits two people with the same skills and capital but a different orientation toward present consumption. One postpones consumption and thus accumulates capital – enough ultimately to pay the other to work for him – at a wage that exceeds what he could gain by himself. 'True, he will be exploited – but who cares?' From this, Elster concludes that 'the example suggests that exploitation is legitimate when the unequal capital endowments have a "clean" causal history'.[69]

---

[62] Roemer 1986a, p. 199.
[63] Roemer 1986a, p. 281.
[64] Elster 1986, p. 99.
[65] Elster 1985, p. 226.
[66] Elster 1985, p. 227.
[67] Roemer 1986a, pp. 274–7; Elster 1986, p. 98.
[68] Elster 1986, p. 98.
[69] Elster 1986, p. 99.

All that is left to exploitation, thus, is the contingent character of original accumulation. Since exploitation has been severed from any connection to the capitalist process of production and rests solely upon the pre-existence of unequal endowments, all that remains is the question as to whether property rights were violated in the formation of those differential endowments. Having begun by inverting the connection between property relations and relations of production in an organic system, Elster and Roemer find from their contingent stories of original accumulation that 'exploitation is not a fundamental moral concept'.[70] Sadly, Marx's own argument that, even if capital was originally acquired by a person's own labour (the cleanest possible path to accumulation), 'it sooner or later becomes value appropriated without an equivalent' is just one more element that disappears in the course of making 'sense' of Marx.[71]

Conclusion

Despite all of the above, it would be quite wrong to conclude that analytical Marxism has little to offer Marxists. In fact, these writers pose important questions and challenges. They reject, in particular, teleological reasoning in Marx; it *should* be rejected. Similarly, functional explanations are viewed as suspect. They *are* – and, where they appear, they should be scrutinised. Analytical Marxism, in this respect, can keep us on our toes.

Further, there are aspects of the work of these writers which can be incorporated easily into Marxist analysis. Roemer's examination of exploitation as an implicit counterfactual proposition points to a way around the neoclassical objection that the very sale of labour-power proves that the wage-labourer benefits (compared to the existing alternative of non-sale). As we have seen in Chapter 1, Elster's early discussion of the 'fallacy of composition' (what is possible for one member of a set is not necessarily true for all members simultaneously) strikes directly at attempts to reason from the position of the isolated individual (and all such Robinsonades of neoclassical economics). And, as we will see in Chapter 14, Cohen's 'locked-room' parable dramatically poses the contrast between the individual worker's ability to

---

[70] Ibid.
[71] Marx 1977a, p. 715.

escape the status of wage-labourer and the structural inability of the class as a whole to do so.[72]

These last two examples, in particular, provide powerful arguments against neoclassical conventions. I regularly introduced them in the first week of my class in Marxian economics – as an introduction to the question as to why Marx saw the necessity to begin from the consideration of an organic whole (which is, of course, precisely *contrary* to the methodological imperative of analytical Marxism).

Nevertheless, not only is there not much of Marx left in 'analytical Marxism' but its essential thrust (as traced above) is *anti*-Marxist. So why do these writers wish to retain their connection to *any* kind of Marxism? The answer, it appears, is that they consider themselves socialists and that the Marxist 'label does convey at least that certain fundamental insights are viewed as coming from Marx'.[73] And, as Elster puts it, 'if, by a Marxist, you mean someone who can trace the ancestry of his most important beliefs back to Marx, then I am indeed a Marxist'.[74]

Yet, if selected beliefs and insights detached from a Marxian framework were sufficient for designation as Marxism, then the term would lose all integral meaning. For, situated in an alternative framework, those selected beliefs acquire quite different properties. The transformation, within the neoclassical framework, of Marx's theory of exploitation (one of Elster's 'most important beliefs') into a conception of distributive justice which accepts the possibility of 'just exploitation' illustrates this fundamental dialectical principle quite well. What makes 'analytical Marxism' anti-Marxist is that the beliefs and insights once absorbed from Marx have been incorporated within an anti-Marxist framework, and the parts have acquired properties from that whole.

---

[72] Cohen 1986. It also, I suggest in Chapter 14, significantly undermines the methodological-individualist credo.

[73] Roemer 1986a, p. 2.

[74] Elster 1986, p. 4.

Appendix

Roemer's Self-Criticism

While viewing the Marxian research agenda as worth pursuing, in his *General Theory* John Roemer expanded his list of the mistakes of Marxian economics.[75] Subsequently, in *A Future for Socialism*, he turned his attention to socialism, arguing that, while 'socialism is an ideal worth pursuing', 'socialists have made a fetish of public ownership'.[76] Not surprisingly, given his own trajectory, socialism has become for him primarily a matter of equality of ownership; and, having made such a taxonomic determination, it is not a major leap for him to declare that 'the link between public ownership and socialism is tenuous'.[77]

Although the adequacy and logic of Roemer's models of market socialism deserve separate attention, this later work is of particular interest on this occasion because it can be read as an unacknowledged self-critique of the most celebrated product of his 'analytical-Marxist' period. Given that neoclassical general-equilibrium (or Walrasian equilibrium) theory is at the core of all his central conclusions in his *General Theory*, one would anticipate a similar place for it in Roemer's models of socialism. Nevertheless, while *A Future for Socialism* ventures on a few occasions into this familiar territory, the substance of Roemer's argument is a rejection of the adequacy of such a body of theory.

No one familiar with the history and current interpretation of the classic debate over market socialism will be surprised. After all, Walrasian analysis was the basis of Oskar Lange's argument in the 1930s that a market-socialist economy could satisfy the static efficiency criteria of neoclassical economics as well as (or, indeed, better than) a capitalist economy.[78] Yet, it is widely recognised now that, in stressing problems of information, incentives and innovation, the Austrian school (in the person particularly of Friedrich Hayek)

---

[75] Roemer 1982.
[76] Roemer 1994, pp. 1, 20.
[77] Roemer 1994, p. 20.
[78] Lange 1964 [1938].

had the better of the argument with Lange. Roemer, indeed, acknowledges this, noting that the criticisms of market socialism by Hayek (and updated by Janos Kornai) are 'for the most part on the mark' – so much so that Roemer identifies his purpose as the reformulation of the concept of market socialism 'in response to the Hayekian critique of its intellectual ancestor'.[79]

Specifically, for Roemer, the challenge becomes one of designing institutions for market socialism that can solve principal-agent problems and, in particular, can ensure that technical innovation will take place.[80] In order that socialism can emulate the dynamic efficiency of capitalism, there is necessarily a focus upon monitoring – (a) monitoring workers to ensure that they work hard, (b) monitoring managers to ensure that they operate firms efficiently and innovate and (c) monitoring the monitors. Given that Roemer accepts the mechanisms present in capitalism for monitoring workers, he turns his attention to designing socialist counterparts to capitalism's institutional solutions to the latter two agency problems and generates in this process his proposals for a coupon economy and socialist *keiretsu*.

Consider, though, the paradigm shift that this focus represents. 'A principal-agent problem arises when one actor (a principal) must engage another (the agent) to perform a task', where the actors have differing interests and differing information; under these circumstances, monitoring and supervision is necessary to ensure that the agent does what the principal wants.[81] Yet Roemer's understanding of the pervasiveness of such problems is precisely what is absent in his earlier 'isomorphism theorem': not only are the principals (and thus the goals) different on his 'Credit Market Island' and 'Labor Market Island', but it is assumed that there are no such principal-agent problems in either – that, as pointed out in Chapter 4 above, there are no inherent problems of shirking and no costs of surveillance and monitoring. Thus, in insisting now upon the importance of such matters, Roemer has demolished the entire basis for his conclusion in *A General Theory* that capitalist exploitation does not require domination at the point of production (and that unequal property endowments are a sufficient condition).

---

[79] Roemer 1994, pp. 1–2, 30–2.
[80] Roemer 1994, Chapters 5, 9.
[81] Roemer 1994, p. 37.

Given *A General Theory*'s place in the laurels of analytical Marxism, its unintended repudiation (as Roemer has moved on to questions about the future of socialism) should close an interesting chapter in Marxist intellectual history. One hopes that Marxists can go on from here to a no less productive or rigorous (but definitely less anti-Marxist and self-congratulatory) chapter.

PART TWO

THE LOGIC OF *CAPITAL*

Part Two
The Logic of *Capital*

One of the questions which emerged in the preparation of this book was determination of the point when the heavy questions of dialectics, method, and Hegel would be introduced. Should this precede Part I's critiques of political economists? Should it follow Part III's essays on the theory on the theory of crisis?

In the end, I decided that it was important to introduce in Part I the ideas of holism and of an underlying essence before exploring how one develops an understanding of that whole. Further, since the opening essay of Part III is explicitly a dialectical view of *Capital* and the matter of the falling rate of profit, it seemed appropriate to let the more abstract discussion of dialectics and dialectical derivation in Part II precede and serve as an introduction to the application to capital as a whole and crisis theory.

However, it will not come as a great shock to me that some readers would prefer to put off entering into the swamp of dialectics a bit longer. For that reason, I am happy to inform those of you in this situation that it is possible to proceed directly from Part I to Part III without floundering seriously. Although the essays in Part III were written under the influence of Marx's *Grundrisse* and Hegel's *Logic* (which play a clear role in this Part), they were published and presumably read without any such prelude of the chapters in Part II, which appear in print for the first time.

Chapter 5 ('Following Hegel: the Science of Marx') returns to a question introduced in Chapter 1. If we recognise the problems of understanding based upon daily observation (i.e., the fallacy of everyday notions), how can we develop an understanding which goes beyond appearances? The essay develops Marx's conception of 'science' and shows its relation to Hegel's *Logic* and Marx's early critique of political economy. The process of dialectical reasoning which rises from the abstract to the concrete is then illustrated in Chapter 6 ('Explorations in the Logic of *Capital*').

Chapter Five
Following Hegel: The Science of Marx

Defining science

> The vulgar economist thinks he has made a
> great discovery when, as against the revelation
> of the inner connection, he proudly claims that
> in appearance things look different. In fact, he
> boasts that he holds fast to appearance and
> takes it as ultimate. Why then have any science
> at all?[1]

The inner connection vs. appearance – over and
over again, Marx stressed that the point of science
in political economy is to reveal the inner connection
in contrast to outer appearances. Classical political
economy (by which he generally meant Ricardo), he
proposed:

> seeks to reduce the various fixed and mutually
> alien forms of wealth to their inner unity by
> means of analysis and to strip away the form
> in which they exist independently alongside one
> another. It seeks to grasp the inner connection in
> contrast to the multiplicity of outward forms.[2]

---

[1] Marx and Engels 1965, pp. 209–10.
[2] Marx 1971, p. 500.

For Marx, this was what science was all about. Because Ricardo sought to discover the hidden, inner relation of a multiplicity of apparently independent phenomena, Marx was drawn to his work in political economy:

> Ricardo's theory of values is the scientific interpretation of actual economic life.... Ricardo established the truth of his formula by deriving it from all economic relations, and by explaining in this way all phenomena, even those like rent, accumulation of capital and the relation of wages to profit, which at first sight seem to contradict it; it is precisely that which makes his doctrine a scientific system.[3]

Here was a theme to which Marx returned fifteen years later. By beginning with the determination of value by labour-time, the starting point for the understanding of the 'internal coherence' and physiology of capitalism, Marx noted, Ricardo 'forces science to get out of the rut,...in general, to examine how matters stand with the contradiction between the apparent and the actual movement of the system. This then is Ricardo's great historical significance for science'.[4]

And that is the perspective that pervades *Capital*: the necessity of science begins from the understanding that there is an enormous gap between appearance and essence. If we do not acknowledge this, we cannot understand *Capital*. 'All science,' Marx proclaimed, 'would be superfluous if the form of appearance of things directly coincided with their essence.'[5] Precisely because we cannot rely upon the way things appear, we need scientific explanations – explanations which often appear paradoxical and contrary to everyday observation. It is 'paradox that the earth moves round the sun and that water consists of two highly inflammable gases. Scientific truth is always paradox, if judged by everyday experience, which catches only the delusive appearance of things'.[6]

Indeed, Marx's paradigm for science was often the explanation of the movement of the planets – a case where perception and everyday experience offer an inverted explanation. Discussing relative surplus-value in *Capital*, he commented that 'the apparent motions of the heavenly bodies are intelligible

---

[3] Marx 1976b, p. 124.
[4] Marx 1968, p. 166.
[5] Marx 1981b, p. 956.
[6] Marx 1985b, p. 127.

only to someone who is acquainted with their real motions, which are not perceptible to the senses.'[7] This gap between everyday appearances and scientific explanation was invoked again in *Value, Price and Profit* with respect to the appearance of the wage; there, Marx indicated that 'having once made sure of the real movement of the celestial bodies, we shall be able to explain their apparent or merely phenomenal movements'.[8] And he returned in his discussion of the wage-form in *Capital* to the problem of inverted appearances: 'that in their appearance things are often presented in an inverted way is something fairly familiar in every science, apart from political economy'.[9]

Yet, as we noted in Chapter 1 ('The Fallacy of Everyday Notions'), a gap between appearance and essence in matters relating to political economy is not at all an accident. Insofar as the necessary conditions for the reproduction of the whole differ from those relevant to the individual actors taken separately, we cannot rely upon the way things must appear to the individual actors (their 'everyday notions'). Political economy which does not go beyond those appearances, Marx stressed, is not science.

Beyond appearance

But, what made Marx so sensitive to a gap between essence and appearance? There is no way that we can ignore the importance of Hegel here. Knowledge, Hegel proposed, seeks to go beyond immediate appearances to essence. To understand the truth of Being, it 'penetrates further, assuming that behind this Being there is something other than Being itself, and that this background constitutes the truth of Being'.[10] And this was what Marx believed: the search for essence, the attempt to understand the whole, the hidden inner connection of the parts, the 'obscure structure', is science. It is 'one of the tasks of science to reduce the visible and merely apparent movement to the actual inner movement'.[11]

Understanding this link between Marx's conception of the 'work of science' and Hegel's idea of the search for an Essence which lies beyond immediate

---

[7] Marx 1977a, p. 433.
[8] Marx 1985b, p. 128.
[9] Marx 1977a, p. 677.
[10] Hegel 1929, II, p. 15.
[11] Marx 1981b, p. 428.

Appearance (which Lenin described in his marginal notes as the 'theory of knowledge') is absolutely critical.[12] Without grasping the connection, we fail to understand Marx's methodological project.

The idea that scientific truth ('always paradox, if judged by everyday experience') is not attainable through induction and empiricism was shared by Marx and Hegel. On the surface, we immediately see a multiplicity of outer forms – chaos and noise; all variables appear to be 'absolute, free, and indifferent towards each other'.[13] And, so, we attempt to look for patterns, to identify the regularities in events, to posit principles, theories, laws about the relation between variables. To discover the universal in given particulars is definitely an advance in understanding.

Yet Hegel understood that there are inherent limits in the 'laws' we develop:

> Appearance and Law have one and the same content.... Consequently, Law
> is not beyond Appearance but is immediately *present* in it; the realm of Laws
> is the quiescent counterfeit of the existing or appearing world.[14]

The problem, as Lenin immediately grasped in his reading of the *Science of Logic*, is that our laws simply do not tell us enough: 'Law is the enduring (the persisting) in appearances'. The concept of law is one of the stages of cognition, but every law is 'narrow, incomplete, approximate'.[15]

The problem with the laws that we develop upon the basis of observation is that even repeated observations do not go beyond appearances: I see the sun rise every day in the East and move to the West where it sets, and I can even predict successfully the sun's route around the Earth in the future without knowing anything about the real processes involved. The ability to predict (under controlled conditions) and true knowledge, however, are quite different things.

Consider Hegel's comments on the law of gravity, which posits a relation between two variables – space and time. What do we know from the fact that stones fall when dropped? The assertion of our law 'means most likely that this experiment must have been tried at least with a good many, and from that we

[12] Lenin 1963, p. 129.
[13] Hegel 1929, II, p. 31.
[14] Hegel 1929, II, pp. 134–5.
[15] Lenin 1963, pp. 150–1.

can by analogy draw an inference about the rest with the greatest probability or with perfect right'. Yet probability is not truth: 'be the probability as great as it may it is nothing as against truth'.[16] Missing is any understanding of *necessity*: 'a proof is still required, that is, a mediation for cognition, that the law not only operates but is *necessary*. The law as such does not contain this proof and its objective necessity.'[17]

Necessity. Insofar as laws and theories are developed on the basis of empiricism (in accordance with the best fit, the highest regression coefficient), the inherent necessity for those regularities discovered is hidden. Insofar as we have not reduced those appearances to their inner unity by means of analysis, we thus do not understand those laws. The economists, the young Marx commented, do not understand their own laws because they do not grasp the inner relations:

> Political economy starts with the fact of private property; it does not explain it to us. It expresses in general, abstract formulas the *material* process through which private property actually passes, and these formulas it then takes for *laws*. It does not *comprehend* these laws, i.e., it does not demonstrate how they arise from the very nature of private property.

And, the result? Political economy does not understand *necessity*. It explains simply by reference to greed and competition:

> As to how far these external and apparently accidental circumstances are but the expression of a necessary course of development, political economy teaches us nothing.

Science involves going beyond those external appearances. 'Now, therefore, we have to grasp the intrinsic connection', Marx announced in 1844.[18] But, how to proceed? For the scientist in political economy, there are no chemical reagents or microscopes to help. In their place, abstract thought, the 'power of abstraction' is the instrument we must use.[19]

---

[16] Hegel 1967, p. 290.
[17] Hegel 1929, II, p. 134.
[18] Marx 1975d, pp. 270–1.
[19] Marx 1977a, p. 90.

Abstract thought – the scientist's instrument

The 'scientifically correct method', Marx declared in the *Grundrisse*, begins with the 'simplest determinations' and concepts from which we can logically deduce a conception of the whole not as chaos but as 'a rich totality of many determinations and relations'. This is the way, Marx proposed, that 'the thinking head…appropriates the world':

> the method of rising from the abstract to the concrete is the only way in which thought appropriates the concrete, reproduces it as the concrete in the mind.[20]

Any Hegelian would recognise this reasoning. Although Marx completely rejected Hegel's premise that the movement from abstract to concrete, from simple to complex in the process of thought parallels the *real* process of development, 'the process by which the concrete itself comes into being',[21] he accepted Hegel's principle that the simple, abstract, universal term must be the starting point for cognition, the way to understand:

> It is easier for Cognition to seize the abstract simple thought-determination than the concrete, which is a manifold concatenation of such thought-determinations and their relations: and this is the manner in which the concrete is to be apprehended.[22]

Marx's reference, indeed, to the approach to the 'rich totality of many determinations and relations' echoes Hegel's argument that 'the abstract must everywhere constitute the beginning and the element in which the particularities and rich shapes of the concrete spread out'.[23]

Of course, this simple abstraction, the starting point for the scientifically correct method, does not itself drop from the sky for Marx. As he noted, the first step in scientific inquiry is to begin with concrete study. The real society is 'the point of departure for observation and conception', and we need to 'appropriate the material in detail, to analyse its different forms of development and to track down their inner connection'. The latter is critical because, by itself, empirical observation can only produce a 'chaotic

---

[20] Marx 1973, pp. 100–1.
[21] Marx 1973, pp. 101–3, 107–8.
[22] Hegel 1929, II, p. 443.
[23] Hegel 1929, II, p. 444.

conception of the whole' – a conception which has no grasp of the underlying interconnections.[24]

Thus, Marx described the way in which the early economists had proceeded to discover through analysis a small number of abstract general relations which would become the starting point for the process of abstract thought. But this, too, was Hegel's point; the formation of the simple abstract begins from immediate existence – it is the result of the cognitive process of Definition, which reduces 'this wealth of the manifold determinations of intuited experience to the simplest moments'.[25] The precondition of the 'scientifically correct method' was the consideration of immediate concrete experience, but, for both Marx and Hegel, it was abstract thought (and *only* abstract thought) which allows one to go beyond the inherent limitations of appearance:

> Abstracting thought must not be considered as a mere setting-aside of the sensuous material, whose reality is said not to be lowered thereby; but it is its transcendence, and the reduction of it (as from mere appearance) to the essential.[26]

Reading Hegel's criticism here of Kant and others for whom 'the abstract is counted of less worth than the concrete', Lenin commented that '*Essentially*, thought proceeding from the concrete to the abstract – provided it is *correct* ... – does not get away *from* the truth but comes closer to it.' And, he noted further:

> the abstraction of *value*, etc., in short *all* scientific (correct, serious, not absurd) abstractions reflect nature more deeply, truly and *completely*. From living perception to abstract thought, *and from this to practice*, – such is the dialectical path of the cognition of *truth*, of the cognition of objective reality.[27]

Lenin returned to this very point in his comments upon Hegel's *Lectures on the History of Philosophy*: 'The movement of cognition *to* the object can always only proceed dialectically: to retreat in order to hit more surely – to fall back, the better to leap (to know?).'[28]

---

[24] Marx 1977a, p. 102; 1973, p. 100–1.
[25] Hegel 1929, II, pp. 437, 439.
[26] Hegel 1929, II, p. 222.
[27] Lenin 1963, p. 171.
[28] Lenin 1963, pp. 279–80.

Moving 'from living perception to abstract thought' – followed by the process of 'rising from the abstract to the concrete' – is exactly what Marx proposed in his *Grundrisse* discussion of the method of political economy. But this was not the first time he approached political economy.

The young Marx's critique of political economy

When people turn to Marx's 1844 manuscripts, it is generally the discussion of alienation which is their focus – the alienation from one's product, from the act of labour, from one's own nature, from nature and other human beings. It is all very important, and the link to his later work is essential.

But, think about Marx's *method* in 1844. Having proposed that the economists do not understand their own laws, Marx argued that that 'we have to grasp the intrinsic connection'. But, *how*? 'We proceed from an *actual* economic fact,' Marx declared.[29] That 'fact', drawn from his reading of the political economists, was that 'the worker becomes all the poorer the more wealth he produces'. Marx took this simple point, explored various sides of the relationship that would generate such a result, and developed a new concept:

> We took our departure from a fact of political economy – the estrangement
> of the worker and his product. We have formulated this fact in conceptual
> terms as *estranged, alienated* labour. We have analysed this concept – hence
> analysing merely a fact of political economy.[30]

From living perception to abstract thought – the development of a *new* concept. Not estranged labour, not alienated labour – but a concept which is enriched by the idea of labour as both sold and foreign, a combination greater than the sum of its parts. And, now? 'Let us see, further, how the concept of estranged, alienated labour must express and present itself in real life.' From the concrete observed to the abstract to the concrete *understood* – the path illustrated in the following Figure 5–1:

---

[29] Marx 1975d, p. 271.
[30] Marx 1975d, p. 278.

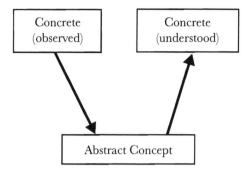

Figure 5–1. The Method of Political Economy

By way of thought, rising from the abstract toward an understanding of the concrete, Marx proceeded to argue that, although it *appears* that private property produces alienated labour, we see the reverse – that private property (specifically, private property in the results of other people's labour) is a *result*. The worker produces the capitalist:

> Through *estranged, alienated labour*, then, the worker produces the relationship to this labour of a man alien to labour and standing outside it. The relationship of the worker to labour creates the relation to it of the capitalist (or whatever one chooses to call the master of labour). *Private property* is thus the product, the result, the necessary consequence, of *alienated labour*, of the external relation of the worker to nature and to himself.[31]

Now, this is not something apparent on the surface. It is only 'by analysis', by analysis of the concept, that we understand that the private property Marx is discussing is a result. Logically, through the power of abstraction, a result has been produced which is the opposite of what is apparent to the senses: through analysis of this concept of alienated, estranged labour, it is shown 'that though private property appears to be the reason, the cause of alienated labour, it is rather its consequence'.[32] The entire starting point of political economy, in short, is wrong – inverted. The (unacknowledged) presupposition of the political economists is, in fact, a result. They do not understand their own theories.

---

[31] Marx 1975d, p. 279.
[32] Ibid.

But, Marx's process of deduction does not stop there. There is also the logical exploration of the capitalist and *'capital*, that is, of private property in the products of other men's labour'.[33] We have looked at one side; we now must consider, Marx proposes, the *other* side of the relation of private property, the side of the non-worker – 'the relation of the *non-worker to the worker and to the product of his labour'*.[34] But the manuscript breaks off.

A true loss for anyone trying to trace Marx's argument. Yet, where Marx's logical examination of the side of capital took him in the missing pages is clear from the remaining manuscript fragments: capital and labour are shown to be identical (as each concept passes over into the other), as antitheses, as dependent upon each other for their existence, and 'they reciprocally develop and promote each other as *positive* conditions'.[35] A unity of opposites in which these opposites are identical, are necessary to each other, and produce each other – where we can not abolish one without the other – Marx's concept of estranged, alienated labour expresses and presents itself in real life as a particular whole, capitalism as a whole.

And, it is this conception of these two opposites forming a single whole that Marx brought forward to *The Holy Family*[36] and, most explicitly, to *Wage-Labour and Capital*:

> *Thus capital presupposes wage-labour; wage-labour presupposes capital. They reciprocally condition the existence of each other; they reciprocally bring forth each other.*
>
> *To say that the interests of capital and those of labour are one and the same is only to say that capital and wage-labour are two sides of one and the same relation. The one conditions the other, just as usurer and squanderer condition each other.*[37]

Well before writing *Capital*, in short, Marx looked upon capitalism as 'a total, connected process' which 'produces and reproduces the capital-relation itself; on the one hand the capitalist, on the other the wage-labourer'. It is no accident that, in *Capital*, Marx quoted *Wage-Labour and Capital* on the unity of these two sides of capitalism; the conception of this whole was clearly

---

[33] Marx 1975d, p. 246.
[34] Marx 1975d, p. 281.
[35] Marx 1975d, pp. 283–5, 289.
[36] Marx and Engels 1975, pp. 35–6.
[37] Marx 1977, pp. 214–15.

present in that earlier work (and, as we have seen, was the product of his theoretical activity in 1844).[38]

Yet, it is essential to remember not only this unity of capital and wage-labour but also their opposition. Wages and profits 'stand in inverse ratio to each other'; and, within this relation, the interests of capital and wage-labour are diametrically opposed.[39] Class struggle between these two inseparable opposites, the 'two sides of a single whole', is the contradiction that drives capitalism forward, is the source of its motion.[40]

There is 'nothing simpler for a Hegelian', Marx announced in 1857, 'than to posit production and consumption as identical'. This comment followed Marx's own *tour de force* lesson in Hegelian dialectics – where he had revealed that the concepts of production and consumption (although apparently opposites) are immediately identical, presuppose and are means for each other, and reciprocally bring forth each other.[41]

One might *also* say, though, that there was nothing simpler than for a Hegelian to posit the unity of those opposites, capital and wage-labour. Hegel's logical exploration of Being and Nothing in his *Science of Logic* is the prototype for such exercises; and his comment that 'nowhere in heaven or on earth is there anything which does not contain within itself both being and nothing' resonates in Marx's response to that political economy which does not understand its own laws – 'how they arise from the very nature of private property':

> Just as we have derived the concept of *private property* from the concept of *estranged, alienated labour* by *analysis*, so we can develop every *category* of political economy with the help of these two factors; and we shall find again in each category, e.g., trade, competition, capital, money, only a *particular* and *developed* expression of these first elements.[42]

There is, in short, so much that can be found in the young Marx which helps us to understand *Capital*. However, if Marx had proceeded no further

[38] Marx 1977a, pp. 724, 724n.
[39] Marx 1977b, pp. 219–20.
[40] Marx 1975d, pp. 289, 294; 1975, p. 35.
[41] Marx 1973, pp. 90–3.
[42] Hegel 1929, I, p. 138; Marx 1975d, pp. 271, 281.

than this, we would have had the Marx of the *Manifesto* but not the Marx of *Capital*.

The scientifically correct method

What Marx developed in his manuscripts for the *Grundrisse* went far beyond his early critique of political economy. In 1844, Marx moved from his *'actual economic fact'* to abstract thought and then proceeded upon what he would later call the 'scientifically correct method' of logically developing a growing understanding of the concrete as 'a rich totality of many determinations and relations'.[43] Yet, we must admit that, in 1844, Marx *did not* begin from an actual fact – i.e., from the real concrete. Rather, he began from the theories of political economists – he read closely a number of writers (for example, Smith, James Mill, Ricardo, Sismondi, Say, etc) and subjected their work to a logical critique which goes beyond the surface to identify inner connections in the categories they had developed.

In 1857, however, Marx proceeded from quite a different empirical base. By then, Marx had absorbed himself in studying not only the work of economists but also the real economic movements about which he wrote regularly in the press of this period. (At the very same time as he was writing the notebooks for his *Grundrisse*, he also was recording the progress of the business cycle of the time.) Thus, we can truly say now (unlike before) that Marx had begun from the real society as 'the point of departure for observation and conception', that he had appropriated 'the material in detail' and prepared himself 'to analyse its different forms of development and to track down their inner connection'.

Yet, Marx had prepared himself in another way, too. As it happened, he had recently had the opportunity to re-read Hegel's *Science of Logic*, finding it 'of great use to me as regards *method* of treatment'.[44] While he was referring particularly at the time to his examination of the rate of profit, in fact, the deepening of the influence of Hegel's dialectical method is evident throughout the *Grundrisse*.

Whereas his 1844 starting point was the concept of estranged/alienated labour, the mature Marx's logical journey to the understanding of capitalism

---

[43] Marx 1973, pp. 100–1.
[44] Marx and Engels 1983, p. 249.

began with the commodity. In the course of analysing the characteristics of money in his *Grundrisse* notebooks, it had become clear to him that the contradictions he was uncovering were already latent within the commodity; and, as he proceeded into an exploration of capital and the relation of capital and wage-labour, he identified the commodity as the logical starting point for the study of capitalism.[45]

In retrospect, the commodity seems like an obvious choice. Given his growing recognition that the purchase of labour-power as a commodity is a unique characteristic of capitalism – one which ensures that the product of workers is estranged, alienated and a power over them as the result of a free transaction, it made much sense to begin by understanding exactly what a commodity is and what its sale entails. But this transparency is all in retrospect – it reflects Marx's success in tracking down the inner connections.[46]

Of course, identifying the appropriate starting point is one thing; there remains the question as to how 'the thinking head' can proceed from there to appropriate the world. What is the method of deduction by which one ascends from the simple abstract to the rich totality of many determinations and relations? To understand the concrete totality, that 'universal, all-sided, *vital* connection of everything with everything', Lenin commented, it is necessary to develop concepts that 'likewise must be hewn, treated, flexible, mobile, relative, mutually connected, united in opposites, in order to embrace the world'.[47] And, this is what Marx did. As Hegel had before him, Marx developed and showed the connection between categories through a process of dialectical derivation.

By means of his dialectic of negativity, Hegel proceeded in his *Science of Logic* from concept to concept in a seamless web. The essential question he asked was – what does this concept imply, what is outside this concept but intimately connected to it? For Hegel, as Lenin indicated, both the 'necessity of connection' and 'the immanent emergence of distinctions' were central.[48]

To the extent that a concept can be shown to imply a further concept, it can be said to contain within it a distinction, a negation, which demonstrates that it is not adequate in itself. The 'dialectic moment' with respect to the first

---

[45] Marx 1973, pp. 320, 881.
[46] Marx 1977a, p. 102.
[47] Lenin 1963, p. 146.
[48] Lenin 1963, p. 97; Hegel 1929, I, p. 66.

term, then, is the grasping of 'the *distinction* that it implicitly contains', the Other which is latent within it.[49] This is the second term, and when we *initially* encounter it, we understand it merely as the opposite of the first, as that which stands outside the first term.

However, that second term is clearly *richer* than that which preceded it – it contains more. It is

> a new concept, but a higher richer concept than that which preceded; for it has been enriched by the negation or opposite of the preceding concept, and thus contains it, but contains also more than it, and is the unity of it and its opposite.[50]

Our interrogation of the second term leads us to understand *the relation* of the two terms, their unity: 'The second term on the other hand is itself the determinate entity, distinction or relation; hence with it the dialectic moment consists in the positing of the *unity* which is contained in it.'[51]

In short, having developed the concept of its opposite from the first or immediate term, Hegel proceeded to demonstrate that the second term (although encompassing the content of the first term) was also deficient in itself; further progress in understanding occurs only by grasping fully the relation of the two terms, by understanding the unity of these specific opposites. The third term (the negation of the negation) contains and preserves within it the content of the first two terms while, at the same time, transcending the one-sidedness of each. In this respect, the third term is clearly a richer, fuller concept.

Yet, this third term is itself a new first term, a new immediacy; that is, it is not a stopping point. Since this new understanding, in its turn, can be shown to contain within it a distinction, Hegel explained that 'cognition rolls forward from content to content. This progress determines itself, first, in this manner, that it begins from simple determinatenesses and that each subsequent one

---

[49] Hegel 1929, II, p. 477.

[50] Hegel 1929, I, p. 65.

[51] Hegel 1929, II, p. 477. Henri Lefebvre (1968, p. 31) defined the 'dialectical moment' as 'that expedient of the mind which finds itself obliged to move from a position it had hoped was definitive and to take account of something further...'. Similarly, in his account of the 'systematic dialectic' of Hegel and Marx, Chris Arthur (1998, p. 450) comments that 'the basis of the advance is generally that each category is *deficient* in determinacy with respect to the next and the impulse for the transition is precisely the requirement that such deficiency must be overcome...'.

is richer and more concrete.' In this way, every step of the process is one of 'dialectical progress [that] not only loses nothing and leaves nothing behind, but carries with it all that it has acquired, enriching and concentrating itself upon itself'.[52] Not only do we, in this way, move from the simple category to the 'rich totality of many determinations and relations' but all subsequent categories contain within them the beginning.[53]

When you look for it, it is not difficult to find dialectical reasoning in *Capital*. Starting from his concrete observations and proceeding from there to abstract thought, Marx's progress through categories involves a process of constant enrichment by which he develops a concept of the concrete totality. He discovers money as latent within the commodity, identifies capital in circulation as a specific unity of commodity and money, discovers capital in production as a distinction within capital in circulation, and he presents capital as a whole as the unity of capital in production and capital in circulation.[54] As illustrated in the exercise in the following chapter, 'Explorations in the Logic of *Capital*', it is possible indeed to present Marx's dialectical derivation (in this case, journeying from the commodity to money) in a blatantly Hegelian manner – namely, one that does far more than 'coquette' with Hegel's 'mode of expression.'[55]

Marx's methodological project, however, differed in many ways from Hegel's.[56] In particular, Marx's reasoning rested upon his appropriation of the empirical and theoretical material in detail with the result that the real subject, society, was always before him. Thus, whereas Hegel's discussion is propelled forward by the discovery of logical deficiencies, for Marx, it is the defect in the theory *relative to the concrete totality* which is critical. As Lenin noted with respect to *Capital*, 'Testing by facts or by practice respectively, is to be found here in *each* step of the analysis.'[57]

Marx as well clearly rejected Hegel's association of the logical order of categories with the historical order, the sequence in which the economic categories were 'historically decisive' – a rejection which Lukács called Marx's

---

[52] Hegel 1929, II, pp. 482–3.
[53] Marx 1973, p. 100.
[54] The steps in the derivation of this whole are set out in Lebowitz 2003, pp. 59–63.
[55] Marx 1977a, p. 103.
[56] Lebowitz, 2003, pp. 52–9.
[57] Lenin 1963, p. 320.

'methodologically decisive criticism of Hegel'.[58] Nevertheless, the intellectual discipline that Marx absorbed from Hegel guided him: he understood the importance of not introducing any category before its premises had been developed and, accordingly, of not omitting the intermediate terms (a failing of Ricardo and classical political economy). Categories do not drop from the sky. Thus, step by step, Marx could demonstrate the logical connection of the whole, a whole composed of various aspects which 'stand to one another in a necessary connection arising out of the nature of the organism'.[59]

The foundations of a wholly new science

'The basic idea is one of genius', Lenin declared about Hegel's conclusions. Recognition of the 'universal, all-sided, *vital* connection of everything with everything' and the development of the concepts which permit us 'to embrace the world' is at the core of Hegel's work:

> A river and the *drops* in this river. The position of *every* drop, its relation to the others; its connection with the others; the direction of its movement; its speed; the line of the movement – straight, curved, circular, etc. – upwards, downwards. The sum of the movement.... There you have *à peu près* [approximately] the picture of the world according to Hegel's *Logic*, – of course minus God and the Absolute.[60]

How is such a conception of the vital connection of everything with everything developed? For Hegel and Marx, it was through the process of dialectical reasoning. But, that particular labour process of abstract reasoning was, for Marx, merely the purposeful activity 'by which thought appropriates the concrete, reproduces the concrete in the mind'.[61] His goal was to grasp capitalism as an organic system, a 'structure of society, in which all relations coexist simultaneously and support one another'.[62] The prize that is won through Marx's 'power of abstraction' is the understanding of that concrete totality.

---

[58] Marx 1973, pp. 106–7; Lukács 1978, pp. 108–10.
[59] Marx 1975a, p. 11.
[60] Lenin 1963, pp. 146–7.
[61] Marx 1973, p. 101.
[62] Marx 1976b, p. 167.

We need, in short, to distinguish between the concrete totality and the method by which the thinking head appropriates that world. It is important not to 'fetishise' moments within the reasoning process. Precisely because, in the very process of dialectical thought, terms, concepts and moments are altered in their meaning and significance – precisely because this dialectical method involves the constant enrichment of concepts – it is inherent that the meaning and definition of moments within the totality will *differ* from that which they possess when they are first encountered in the process of abstract thought.

The commodity, for example, looks different after development of the concepts of money, capitalist circulation and capitalist production and capital as a whole – and the same is true of money and, indeed, capital itself. They must. In dialectical reasoning, terms and moments are introduced in a one-sided manner, developing their all-sidedness only in the course of the construction of the totality. It is only, however, when we have successfully developed that 'totality of thoughts' that we can understand fully its elements.

Understanding the elements of capitalism not as 'independent, autonomous neighbours' extrinsically or accidentally related, but as 'the members of a totality, distinctions within a unity', which act upon each other is essential if we are to explain 'apparent or merely phenomenal movements'.[63] Proceeding from the point of view of the totality, we recognise that the surface of society does not permit us to see the 'obscure structure of the bourgeois economic system' – that is, the 'inner core, which is essential but concealed'.[64] Thus, rather than accepting outward appearances, we search for what lies behind these, what produces the regularities that form the basis of those 'laws' which in themselves do not demonstrate how these patterns 'are but the expression of a necessary course of development'.[65]

By understanding the inner connections, we can 'reduce the visible and merely apparent movement to the actual inner movement'. For Marx, the development of the concept of the totality as the vantage point from which to view all phenomena is the task of science.[66] As he could say about Ricardo, he 'forces science to get out of the rut, ... in general, to examine how matters

---

[63] Marx 1973, pp. 90, 99.
[64] Marx 1968, p. 165; 1981, p. 311.
[65] Marx 1975d, p. 271.
[66] Marx 1981b, p. 428.

stand with the contradiction between the apparent and the actual movement of the system'. Here, it can be said, is Marx's 'great historical significance for science'.[67] As Lukács commented:

> The category of totality, the all-pervasive supremacy of the whole over the parts is the essence of the method which Marx took over from Hegel and brilliantly transformed into the foundations of a wholly new science.[68]

---

[67] Marx 1968, p. 166.
[68] Lukács 1972, p. 27.

Chapter Six

Explorations in the Logic of *Capital*

Consider this chapter an artefact dating back to around 1979 – a document which was developed for distribution to students in my 'Introduction to Marxian Economics'. Accordingly, I am reproducing in the form in which they would have received it. As can be seen, the full development proceeds from commodity to money and comes to a pause at the point where capital is introduced; however, the opening outline and the logic itself should allow one to continue the exploration.

*   *   *

The following pages are part of an initial attempt to set out the development in *Capital* in an unequivocal dialectical form. To avoid any possible misunderstanding of what I am doing, I have 'coquetted' with Hegel's manner of presentation in the *Science of Logic* by summarising in advance the moments of the argument at each point.

The discussion follows the treatment in *Capital* (using the *Grundrisse*) and quotations are from the Penguin/Vintage edition. Since only what is required for logical transitions is included – thus excluding 'testing' and all commentary on appearances – the pages may be useful as a short (though heavy) guide through these sections. However, in some cases, the order of presentation and position of elements varies slightly from that of Marx, and one can conclude from that what one wants.

The logic of *Capital*

I. The commodity in its immediacy is the elementary form of the wealth of capitalist society. Upon investigation, it is found to contain a distinction – Money.

II. The relations of commodity and money are money as mediator for commodity and commodity as mediator for money (money as an end).

III. Capital as self-expanding value, as value for itself, is the unity of commodity and money; it lies beyond them but takes their forms in the sphere of circulation. Upon investigation, capital in circulation is shown to contain a distinction – capital in the sphere of production.

IV. The relations of capital in circulation and in production are production as a mediator for circulation and circulation as a mediator for production (reproduction).

V. Capital in reproduction, as unity of production and circulation of capital, is capital as a whole, capital as a totality.

1. *The commodity*

A. The commodity immediately appears as the elementary form of the wealth of society. In itself, it is an object which satisfies human needs and which is a product of labour. But, it is also a bearer of exchange-value. The dual character is determined as use-value and value and, further, as product of useful, concrete labour and product of abstract human labour.

B. As a value, the commodity exists as a relation between commodities in which the contradiction within a commodity is posited as an external relation.

C. In *exchange*, the opposites of use-value and value are united, and the commodity is shown to be in-and-for-itself only through an Other. The becoming of a commodity is also the becoming of a specific commodity which is the universal expression of value, or *money*.

A.

To begin, a commodity is an object which satisfies human needs and which is a product of labour. But it is more than that also – because 'a thing can be useful, and a product of labour, without being a commodity'.[1] A commodity

---

[1] Marx 1977a, p. 131.

is also a bearer of exchange-value. Thus, in addition to its aspect as a thing of use, its qualitative side, a commodity also has a quantitative side – a side which presents itself as a quantitative relationship between differing use-values, or as exchange-value. The commodity thus appears as a use-value and an exchange-value.

But, for differing use-values, differing qualities, to be compared quantitatively, to exist in a quantitative relationship, they must first be qualitatively the same in some aspect; they must have some property which permits comparison, a quality other than their particular qualities as use-values. This common property which unites them and permits their quantitative comparison is their quality as products of labour. Yet, it is not as products of specific, concrete labour that commodities are equal; rather, it is as products of abstract, homogeneous, universal labour. Specific, concrete labour is labour which forms the specific, material quality of commodities, forms them as use-values. Abstract human labour, on the other hand, is the quality of labour which forms commodities as values – permitting their quantitative comparison.

The labour contained in commodities is both concrete and abstract, both specific and universal, both separate and part of the total labour of society. Thus, the dual nature of labour in commodities underlies the determination of the commodity as a use-value and a value.

B.

The labour contained in a commodity, however, manifests itself in different ways in accordance with its quality as concrete or abstract labour. As concrete labour, it is manifested in a specific and distinct material form – as a use-value; and, as a use-value, the commodity appears separate and distinct – as a thing-in-itself. But, as abstract labour, the labour contained in the commodity is not manifested in a manner which permits the commodity to appear as a thing-in-itself. The value of a commodity has no form – is not expressed – in the body of the given commodity. As the crystallisation of abstract labour, value is intrinsically social; and, thus, its form of expression must be social. The value of a commodity, accordingly, can only be expressed through another commodity. As a value, a commodity necessarily is a thing which exists in relation to another commodity.

Thus, insofar as there exists another separate and distinct commodity, the value of a commodity can be expressed in the body of the second commodity which has the position of equivalent. The value of the first commodity is expressed – and only expressed – in the use-value of the second commodity. A particular use-value, thus, is the manifestation of the quantity of value contained in the first commodity. (The expression of value in money, the money-form of value, which develops with the emergence of a particular commodity as a universal equivalent, is already latent here.)

Within this relation between the two commodities, the two necessarily stand in opposition. They exclude each other: only one can be the equivalent, only one the commodity whose value is expressed; only one can be the material embodiment of value, only one can display its social character as value. Yet, each presupposes the existence of the other and is necessary for the other. Thus, the two opposites are 'inseparable moments, which belong to and mutually condition each other' in this relation which is the form of value.[2]

However, each side of this relation is one-sided. If the second commodity as equivalent manifests the value of the first, then the first commodity can only exist as use-value in relation to the second as value. 'The internal opposition between use-value and value, hidden within the commodity, is therefore represented on the surface by an external opposition...'.[3] In the form of value, which reveals the internal distinctions within the commodity, use-value – the product of specific, concrete, separate labour – stands opposite value – the product of abstract, homogeneous, directly social labour – as two separate commodities. This one-sidedness is cancelled, i.e., the commodity is revealed as a thing-in-and-for-itself, only as the commodity passes into its opposite, only in the process of *exchange*.

C.

Exchange is that process in which the commodity which is the relative form of value passes over into its opposite, in which it takes the position of the equivalent. Thus, the relative no longer merely *expresses* its value in the equivalent, an ideal process occurring in the form of value, but *realises* its value in exchange. Exchange is that process in which the opposites contained within the commodity are united – in which use-value and value, concrete and abstract labour, separate and directly social labour, qualitative and

---

[2] Marx 1977a, p. 140.
[3] Marx 1977a, p. 153.

quantitative side, are one in the commodity. Thus, exchange is the 'truth' of the commodity, the 'truth' of use-value and value, etc. It is the Becoming of the commodity as a thing-in-and-for-itself, as that which becomes by passing through its opposite (the equivalent) which is itself, its own form.

Thus, a commodity is a commodity only insofar as it exists in exchange, in movement. The commodity is not a thing at rest; it is motion and its activity is the process of exchange. Exchange is the affirmation of the commodity; and it is only in the act of exchange that a use-value is proved to be value, that particular labour is proved to be useful for others, that concrete labour is abstract labour, that private and separate labour is social labour – that a commodity is a commodity.[4] *Before* exchange, in the form of value, a commodity is not as yet a commodity.[5] Thus, an unsold commodity is a negation of a commodity – and, similarly, a commodity which has already passed through exchange (unless its end is to return to exchange) is a negation of a commodity. In the former case, it is not a commodity because it is not a use-value; in the latter, because it is *only* a use-value.

Considered further, exchange may be seen itself as having a two-fold determination, as containing two moments. In one of those, the relative form of value is immediate: use-value becomes value (or sale); in the other, the equivalent form is immediate: value becomes use-value (or purchase). Each of these moments of exchange presupposes the existence of the other. Every sale, viewed from the opposite side, is a purchase; and, similarly, every purchase has as its counterpart a sale. Thus, there cannot be a sale without a purchase.

These two processes, sale and purchase, are, on the other hand, polar opposites. Sale is the positing of the commodity as the expression of homogeneous, abstract universal labour – entirely indifferent to a particular form. Purchase, on the other hand, is the positing of the commodity as the expression of particular, concrete and useful labour – as a material form useful to the purchaser. Further, these processes exclude each other (in the same manner as the relative and equivalent forms of value exclude each other): only one process, sale, can be the passage into abstract labour; only one process, purchase, the passage into concrete labour, Thus, exchange of *commodities* posits a seller on one side and a buyer on the other. In the

---

[4] Marx 1977a, p. 180.
[5] Marx 1977a, p. 181.

exchange of commodities, the same person can not act as seller and buyer at the same time.

The exchange of commodities must be understood, accordingly, as the unity of two separate and distinct acts – sale and purchase – which are carried out by separate individuals at opposite poles. This exchange which is the becoming of the commodity has a particular *quality* – which sets it apart from exchange of products.

Thus, simple or direct exchange of two products (i.e., barter) is not adequate to the concept of the commodity because here each seller is simultaneously a buyer – and is a seller only insofar as he is a buyer. (There is a direct identity between the exchange of one's own product and the acquisition of another's product.) Here, each seller looks at the commodity opposite her not as the expression of homogeneous abstract labour (i.e., is not indifferent to its content) – but as the expression of a particular useful concrete labour. This exchange, thus, is an exchange of use-values rather than one of use-value and value. The polar opposition of use-value and value disappears because value has no independent existence.

Even though *expanded* exchange – characterised by a growth in the number and variety of direct exchanges, demonstrates that a product may pass into many particular equivalents (and thus is indifferent to form, revealing a universal within particulars), the defect that each particular exchange remains an exchange of use-values, that seller and buyer are not distinct, is not remedied. Thus, it is only where value has an independent existence, separate from any particular use-value – which presumes the existence of general exchange, itself a social product – that the exchange of *commodities* occurs.

Yet, this independent existence for value is that of a commodity as universal equivalent, as indifferent to any particular use-value, – or *money*. Thus, the process of exchange of commodities, which is the becoming of the commodity, is *simultaneously* the process of the formation of money. In the exchange of commodities, we find the apparent development of the commodity for itself; but, on further investigation, we find that the commodity can only be for itself by passing into money, the independent expression of value. The commodity must posit itself doubly, must have a double existence – in commodity and money. All this follows from the initial determination of the commodity as a unity of use-value and value. For the commodity as such to exist, value must take an independent form and this is 'achieved by the differentiation of commodities into commodities and money'.[6] And, the process of exchange of commodities – the unity of the opposite acts of sale and purchase – is the process in which this intrinsic nature of the commodity becomes manifest; it 'produces a differentiation of the commodity into two elements, commodity and money, an external opposition which expresses the opposition between use-value and value which is inherent in it'.[7]

Thus, an adequate concept of the commodity requires grasping not merely that the commodity exists only in motion – but that it exists only in motion with money.

2. *Money*

A. In its immediacy, money is the distinction contained within commodity – the independent form of value. As equivalent, it expresses the value of commodities; as distinct object, it is the means of realising their value. But, equally, money is in the form exchangeable with all commodities and is the means of purchase. Money thus is the mediator between commodities.

B. Money is mediator for commodities both in the representation of value, where it serves as measure of value, and also in the exchange of commodities, where it serves as medium of circulation. Money appears here as wholly dependent on commodities, but it can be seen to be independent in its quality as the embodiment of wealth, which points beyond money as a mere mediator of commodities.

C. Money as an end-in-itself, as wealth, exists both as a representation of wealth, outside of circulation, and as a means of realising wealth, within circulation. The commodity here appears as mediator for money in the accumulation of wealth. But, this is shown to point to another quality – self-expanding value, value-as-end, or *capital* – for which both commodity and money are mediators.

A.

Money, as we see from the analysis of the commodity, is itself a commodity, one which has been differentiated from other commodities to stand as the

---

[6] Marx 1977a, p. 181.
[7] Marx 1977a, p. 199.

independent form of value. Thus, money is the equivalent in the form of value; it is the commodity whose body, whose use-value, expresses the value of commodities which are in the relative form of value. Accordingly, it must have definite properties (durability, divisibility, etc.), a certain quality, which permits it to serve as the form of value; the value of each commodity must be capable of expression as a certain number of units (e.g., ounces) of the money-commodity. In this sense, money is the standard of price, which is the representation of value in money.

Money, though, is more than the form in which value is represented. It is also a distinct object which stands opposite commodities and which is a means by which their value may be *realised*. Thus, in relation to money as value, each commodity exists as use-value and its value is only in an ideal form – as its price. Actual exchange with money, or sale, is the means by which the commodity's price is realised. Thus, as the independent form of value, money provides both the material for the expression of value of commodities and also the basis for the realisation of that value in sale.

Yet money is more than value. Just as the commodity exists really as use-value and ideally as value (in price), so also does money exist really as value and ideally as use-value. The use-value of money as such (i.e., apart from its particular use-value) is a social use-value, a use-value arising out of its social function – that it exists in a form immediately exchangeable for all commodities. Money stands as the universal commodity (the representation of abstract, social labour) in relation to which all commodities are particular equivalents; its use-value is that it represents the particular use-values of all commodities. And, just as in the case of the ideal existence of value in the commodity, the use-value of money is realised in actual exchange, in purchase. In addition to representing use-values, money is also an actual means of purchase, a means of acquisition.

Thus, like the commodity, money is both value and use-value; it has a double existence given by its social function. Unlike the commodity, on the other hand, money can represent the value of another commodity and be the means of realising it, can represent the use-values of all commodities directly and be the means of acquiring them. Money, accordingly, is the mediator between commodities – it is for commodities what they cannot be themselves, and it must be by its very nature.

B.

In its position as mediator for commodities, money functions both with respect to the representation of value and also in relation to exchange. Through money, one commodity is revealed as the equivalent of another commodity; it expresses its value in money, which, in turn, is the representation of the use-value of another commodity. These commodities are, first of all, equivalents as possessing prices, which reveal the relative quantities of value contained within them. Thus, money here is the measure of value; it shows commodities to each other as exchange-values.

Money, accordingly, is the *real* third to which commodities must be equal before they can be compared directly with each other. Just as abstract human labour is the *immanent* measure of value which permits the comparison of the value of commodities, so also is money (the external representation of abstract labour) the external measure of value. Money plays this central role within the world of commodities of mediating the relation of commodities. Yet, within the position of mediator, the quality of money is fleeting; one commodity can be directly compared with another in accordance with price (which appears immanent) – the mediation of money thus apparently disappears. What remains is the ideal transformation of one commodity into another, the ideal metamorphosis of the commodity.

Money also is a real mediator for commodities. By functioning as a means for realising the value of a commodity (through the process of sale, C–M) and also as a means of acquiring the use-value of another commodity (through the process of purchase, M–C), money permits the real transformation of one commodity into another. Money here is medium of circulation, where circulation is understood as the double positing of exchange, as sale and purchase as two separate and complementary acts. Sale (C–M) and purchase (M–C), processes which are separate and distinct in time and space, thus are a unity within the process of circulation (C–M–C); they are opposite phases within one process, the real metamorphosis of the commodity.

In the circulation of commodities (C–M–C), money appears as a fleeting moment, a fleeting aspect of the exchange of product against product, of use-value for use-value; money is wholly subsumed within the metamorphosis of the commodity as such. Yet, money does not therefore disappear. Each sale is a purchase and each purchase, a sale. Thus, the first phase of a given metamorphosis (C–M) is the second phase of another (M–C); and, the second phase of the given metamorphosis (M–C) is the first (C–M) of yet another. Money is thus constantly in circulation, constantly functions as a mediator for commodities, existing as a residue within circulation. We have here the circulation of money or money as coin. Money here is wholly dependent upon commodities; as coin, its circulation depends on that of commodities.

However, money in this form is not adequate to the concept of money. It exists here solely as value and not as use-value; it exists in a form in which any time spent *as money* is pure loss, is negation of its function within the metamorphosis of the commodity. But, money is more than the mere medium of circulation – and this is revealed in the very circulation of commodities, in selling in order to buy (C–M–C). Precisely because money is the independent form of value, because it has the use-value of immediate exchangeability with all commodities, sale is not necessarily followed by an immediate purchase. Because money is independent value, is independent of commodities, it may remain at rest, may be negated as coin following a sale; the separation and separability of purchase and sale for this reason contains the possibility of crisis.

Similarly, it is because money is value become independent that purchase can precede sale. Here, money exists ideally in purchase as measure (M–C) and really in sale (C–M); selling is selling to *pay* rather than selling to buy. Money here exists as means of payment – which presupposes the independence of money. Buyer and seller are transformed into debtor and creditor through the extension of credit. (Still another side is where money is *borrowed* to purchase in advance of sale; here, again, sale becomes selling to pay rather than to buy.)

The independence of value as money is most clear in the case of money as world-money. Here, money in its commodity-form is shown as universal commodity, as universal means of payment, as universal means of purchase – as, indeed, 'the absolute social materialisation of wealth as such (universal wealth)'.[8] Its mode of existence (as precious metal and specie) here becomes adequate to its concept as the form of abstract human labour.[9]

Thus, money is more than mere medium, mere conduit between use-values; it is also use-value itself because it is the embodiment of social wealth. Yet, this is as yet latent within its position as mediator. Money at rest (as negation

---

[8] Marx 1977a, p. 242.
[9] Marx 1977a, p. 241.

of coin), money as means of payment, money as world-money – all exist within money as mediator of commodities, as measure of value and medium of circulation. They point, on the other hand, to another quality inherent in money, one whose emergence is the result of social processes – money as wealth, money as end-in-itself.

C.

Money becomes an end-in-itself, is in-and-for-itself, because it is the universal commodity for which all commodities are particular equivalents. That is, all commodities appear as particular monies, particular embodiments of money, the independent form of value. Money here is wealth, the universal embodiment of abstract labour – but wealth as One, in contrast to wealth diffused and fragmented in its commodity-forms. Thus, money is the general 'compendium' of wealth. The wealth of society appears as money, the material representation of abstract human labour.

In money-as-end, the commodity appears as a mere means, as an imperfect embodiment of money. Money, as a distinct object, is the object of desire rather than a particular use-value. But, since money as a distinct object has a uniform quality, it is as quantity that it is an end, as quantity of wealth. Thus, money as wealth is its own measure, and the commodity appears as a means for a greater quantity of money. Sale (C–M) here appears as its own end, selling not to buy or to pay, but selling to acquire money.

Accumulation of wealth, then, appears as the accumulation of money, the accumulation of a greater quantity of units of the money-commodity. In money as hoard, in the process of hoarding, money becomes independent of circulation, is removed from circulation to stand as representation of wealth. However, money as hoard is only an ideal representation of wealth; it is only latently wealth. To be realised as wealth, it must return to circulation, to interaction with the form of *wealth as many* – commodities.

Money as real wealth thus is money which exchanges with commodities with the goal of more money. It is money which passes into a commodity-form to return to money; it is buying (M–C) to sell (C–M). The commodity here is real mediator for money in the circulation of money as wealth (M–C–M); it is the means of acquisition of more wealth through circulation (M–C–M').

Thus, the circulation of commodities *here* is dependent on the circulation money as wealth. Money is here independent; the commodity is dependent.

The commodity appears as a fleeting moment, a fleeting aspect of the expansion of money as wealth, Thus, any time spent in the commodity-form of wealth appears as pure loss, a negation of the function of the commodity within the circuit of wealth. This dependence of the commodity is itself personified in the dependence of commodity-owners upon the owner of money, Mr. Money-bags, when money develops its inherent quality as end-in-itself.

Money, thus, develops its full quality as the independent form of value when it exists as use-value in relation to the commodity as value, when it goes beyond its position of mere mediator and becomes end. Yet, money is itself merely value. In the movement of money as wealth, value is common and present in all forms; thus 'both the money and the commodity function only as different modes of existence of value itself'.[10] It is *value* which moves successively and endlessly through the forms of money and commodity in this process of expansion; it is value and not either money or commodity which is the subject of this process. Neither is independent; both are dependent. What is independent is self-expanding value, self-valorising value – capital, for which commodity and money are mere forms.

Capital, self-expanding value, in the form of money passes into the form of commodity and returns to a money-form as more capital, as surplus-value in addition to original value (M–C–M′); this is the process of circulation of capital, in which money and commodity are a unity as capital.

Money, thus, is in-and-for-itself only by passing into capital, self-expanding value. It differentiates itself into money which is spent and money which is advanced, into money as money and capital.

---

[10] Marx 1977a, p. 255.

PART THREE

ESSAYS IN THE THEORY OF CRISIS

Part Three

Essays in the Theory of Crisis

Chapter 7, on Marx's falling rate of profit, was one of my first essays after reading the *Grundrisse* and grasping the dialectics that had been hidden (at least from me) in *Capital*. That reading, too, led me immediately to Hegel (and that is responsible in particular for the understanding here of the concept of capital's 'barrier'). After all, if dialectics are important, we should make the attempt to understand where Marx learned this. How, indeed, can we understand the three volumes of *Capital* except dialectically? As the book's essays (and opening quote in the chapter) stress, we cannot.

Linking all the essays in this Part is the rejection of what Paul Sweezy (cited in Chapter 8) called the 'fetishisation' of the tendency of the rate of profit to fall (FROP). Chapter 8 ('The General and the Specific in Marx's Theory of Crisis') reinforces the argument in the previous chapter on the significance for FROP of a particular assumption about the bias of productivity increase and further proposes that the FROP emphasis has obscured what is specific and unique about capitalism. In a significant addition to this essay (drawing upon Marx's *1861–3 Economic Manuscripts* which were not earlier available), I have strengthened the demonstration that Marx recognised his own assumption about productivity changes. Why, then, the importance assigned by so many to FROP? One may suggest that anything that looks like it can be handled with a little bit of mathematics and made to look inevitable has great appeal to mathematical determinists.

Perhaps it was especially his rejection of FROP and his stress upon the importance of realisation problems (a true sign of 'Keynesianism' and 'reformism') that produced a tendency for self-proclaimed Marxist economists to sneer at Paul Sweezy's work. Chapter 9 on Paul Sweezy was written originally for an edited collection on political economy in the twentieth century (accompanying essays on Maurice Dobb, Joseph Schumpeter and

Joseph Steindl, among others). The long-distance call that I received from him in Vancouver shortly after I sent it to him, saying that I got it 'right', remains one of my proudest memories. The Appendix, written after his death in 2004, draws upon some early letters from him and shows him to be more of a revolutionary than his Lilliputian critics.

Chapter Seven
Marx's Falling Rate of Profit: A Dialectical View

It is impossible completely to understand Marx's
Capital, and especially its first chapter, without having
thoroughly studied and understood the whole of
Hegel's *Logic*. Consequently, half a century later none
of the Marxists understood Marx!![1]

Introduction

The 'Poet of Commodities', as Edmund Wilson
described Karl Marx, has suffered the familiar fate
of poets translated from their native language by
indifferent translators; he has been judged mediocre,
a minor post-romantic. But, to appreciate this
particular poet, it is necessary to know something
about his language, the significance of his terms, his
method – which is to say, the dialectical method.[2]

And, nowhere is this necessity to locate Marx
within the context of dialectics more pressing than in
relation to the 'tendency of the rate of profit to fall',
a tendency that, some might assure us, is really a
tendency to rise, or to be indeterminate, or to fall only
ultimately (perhaps in some lonely 'last instance').
For, when working on his 1857–8 notebooks, which
have become known as the *Grundrisse*, Marx informed
Engels:

---

[1] Lenin 1963, p. 180.
[2] Wilson 1953, p. 289 ff.

By the way, things are developing nicely. For instance, I have thrown overboard the whole doctrine of profit as it has existed up to now. In the method of treatment the fact that by mere accident I again glanced through Hegel's *Logic* has been of great service to me.[3]

To be sure, it is precisely in the *Grundrisse* that Marx threw overboard the classical argument on the falling rate of profit and initially developed an alternative. But there is more there. The *Grundrisse* (only recently translated into English) provides an invaluable guide to the reading of *Capital* and to the understanding of the dialectical nature of Marx's argument, an argument for which Hegel's *Logic* was indeed of great service.

To understand the significance which the falling rate of profit had for Marx, it is necessary to consider the dialectical nature of *Capital* (and this is particularly true, given the fragmentary nature of the material, for Volume III of *Capital*). Such a reading reveals the significant differences between the falling rate of profit as understood by classical political economy and by Marx and shows what Marx offered as a counterpart to the classical position.

Capital: a dialectical view

The structure of capital

One of the clearest characteristics of the *Grundrisse* is the extent to which Marx developed the concept of capital as a unity containing two elements: production and circulation. 'The total production process of capital,' he stressed, 'includes both the circulation process proper and the actual production process. These form the two great sections of its movement, which appears as the totality of these two processes'.[4] Over and over again, throughout this work, there is both the explicit description of capital as a unity of production and circulation and also the *development* of capital as a dialectical unity.

But, if capital, the concept, is a unity, then what might we expect to find in *Capital*, the work? Here, it is enough to note the method of dialectical

---

[3] Marx and Engels 1965, p. 100.
[4] Marx 1973, p. 620.

exposition that permeates *Capital* and is most explicit in the discussion of the form of value in its opening chapter. That method is the full examination and consideration of one side of a relationship (such as the relative form of value), followed by examination and consideration or development of the other side of the relation (such as the equivalent form of value), and, finally, the consideration of the relationship 'as a whole'.

This general approach, in which consideration of the 'whole' is a starting point for examining the defects or inadequacy of this whole itself and thus for passing beyond it, is also employed by varying one part of a relationship while holding the other explicitly constant, then reversing this procedure, and, finally, considering all factors variable and noting their interaction. The latter is the method used in looking at relative and absolute surplus-value (i.e. by considering the division of the workday and then expanding the surplus portion of that day, holding the necessary portion constant, followed by reducing the necessary portion, and, finally, considering both changes) and in examining the rate of profit.

If capital *itself* is a unity, then the logical method of exposition is quite clear. It is to consider, first, the production process of capital fully, then the development of the circulation process of capital, and, thirdly, capital as a whole (and then to move beyond). It is crucial to recognise that this is precisely what Marx did in setting out the structure of *Capital*. Volume I is entitled 'The Process of Capitalist Production'; Volume II, 'The Process of Circulation of Capital'; and Volume III, 'The Process of Capitalist Production as a Whole'.

Thus it is essential for an understanding of *Capital* to see the care with which it is presented as a dialectical unity. And should anyone have missed this dialectical structure, the opening lines of Volume III are there as a signpost for the confused traveller. In Volume II, Marx notes, 'it developed that the capitalist process of production taken as a whole represents a synthesis of the processes of production and circulation'. However, he pointed out that Volume III could not 'confine itself to general reflection relative to this synthesis'. It had to go beyond to consider the various forms which capital assumed 'on the surface of society'.[5]

This structure tells us that we can not hope to understand *Capital* by reading (or publishing) only the first volume on the production of capital. To do so

---

[5] Marx 1959, p. 25.

is explicitly to take a one-sided (and therefore flawed) view of capital. And, certainly, it tells us (as we shall see) that 'Marxian models' which draw solely on elements related to the production of capital are similarly one-sided. But the structure says more. It tells us that the critical opposition within capital is between production and circulation, between, in other words, the matters examined in Volume I and those of Volume II. We must do more than simply note this point, which follows logically from the very structure of *Capital*; to understand *Capital*, it is necessary to grasp 'the contradiction between production and realisation – of which capital, by its concept, is the unity'.[6]

Production and circulation: the unity of opposites

For Marx, it was self-evident that the production of capital required the act of exchange to be made real. Since surplus-value was contained in the value of commodities, it was necessary that commodities be truly commodities (i.e. that they be exchanged) in order that surplus-value be realised. Without exchange, he argued, 'the production of capital as such would not exist, since *realization* as such cannot exist without exchange'.[7] The sphere of circulation, the sphere of commodities and money, thus was the sphere in which the 'real self-positing' of capital occurred, the sphere of 'its self-realization as exchange-value'.[8]

Accordingly, production of capital without the act of circulation was inconceivable to Marx. To ignore this and to treat 'production as directly identical with the self-realization of capital', which Marx suggested was a failing of classical political economy, was to ignore the specific characteristics of capitalist production, which required circulation of commodities for the realisation of value and surplus-value.[9] At the same time, however, circulation required production because 'it cannot ignite itself anew through its own resources. . . . Commodities constantly have to be thrown into it anew from the outside, like fuel into a fire'.[10] The production of capital and the circulation of capital thus exist in an inseparable relationship to each other.

---

[6] Marx 1973, p. 415.
[7] Marx 1973, p. 447.
[8] Marx 1973, p. 260.
[9] Marx 1973, p. 410; Marx 1957, p. 92.
[10] Marx 1973, pp. 254–5.

Within this relationship, however, circulation was the negation of production. Every moment capital existed in the sphere of circulation was 'pure loss', time outside the sphere of production of capital. 'As long as capital remains frozen in the form of the finished product, it can not be active as capital, it is *negated* capital'.[11] In this sense, circulation, although necessary to the production of capital, is a barrier to the production of capital.

Any reduction, accordingly, of the time which capital spends in circulation is an increase in the time in which it can be productive. The abolition of circulation-time – its negation – would thus be the equivalent of the highest possible production of capital.[12] To the extent, then, that capital has a tendency toward self-expansion, toward growth, this tendency must involve the attempt to reduce circulation-time to a minimum; and this is to say that capital attempts to transcend itself, its own nature, 'since it is capital itself alone which posits circulation time' as a necessary part of the production of capital.[13] The growth of capital thus means the necessity to go beyond a barrier which is inherent in capital itself.

Growth and barrier in capital

It has often been noted that Marx had few rivals (even among the worst apologists) in his laudatory account of the 'positive' aspect of capital. It is inherent in the nature of capital, he argued, that it constantly drives to go beyond its quantitative barrier: 'The goal-determining activity of capital can only be that of growing wealthier, i.e. of magnification, of increasing itself'.[14] And, in 'capital's ceaseless striving' to expand itself was its 'historic mission', that it develops the productive power of labour, that it 'strives towards the universal development of the forces of production'.[15]

In its drive to expand, capital, this self-expanding value, treats what were the inherent limits of earlier modes of production as mere barriers to be dissolved:

---

[11] Marx 1973, pp. 535, 546.
[12] Marx 1973, pp. 545, 630.
[13] Marx 1973, p. 629.
[14] Marx 1973, p. 270.
[15] Marx 1973, pp. 325, 540.

capital drives beyond natural barriers and prejudices as much as beyond nature worship, as well as all traditional, confined, complacent, encrusted satisfactions of personal needs, and reproductions of old ways of life. It is destructive towards all of this and constantly revolutionizes it, tearing down all the barriers which hem in the development of the productive forces, the expansion of needs, the all-sided development of production, and the exploitation and exchange of natural and mental forces.[16]

This 'universalizing tendency of capital, which distinguishes it from all previous stages of production', thus tends toward the absolute development of productive forces and to the destruction of all previous limits to the productivity of labour.[17]

Yet, as we have seen in the discussion of circulation, the other side of capital, capital contains its own barriers. Capital cannot remain in the sphere of production; it must pass through the sphere of circulation to realise itself, and the time it spends there is a barrier to the productive force of capital.[18] In the sphere of circulation, capital encounters a barrier 'in the available magnitude of *consumption* – of consumption capacity'.[19] This means that, if capital is to grow, so also must the consumption capacity: 'a precondition of production based on capital is therefore the production of a *constantly widening sphere of circulation*'.[20]

To the extent, however, that capital grows by striving to restrict workers' consumption to a minimum, by striving 'to reduce the relation of necessary labour to surplus-labour to the minimum,' it simultaneously creates a barrier to exchange.

> The boundless enlargement of its value – boundless creation of value – therefore absolutely identical here with the positing of barriers to the sphere of exchange, i.e. the possibility of realization – the realization of the value posited in the production process.[21]

It is the contradiction of capital that its barriers, just as its tendency to grow, are inherent in its very nature:

---

16 Marx 1973, pp. 649–50, 410.
17 Marx 1973, p. 540.
18 Marx 1973, pp. 539, 545.
19 Marx 1973, p. 405.
20 Marx 1973, p. 407.
21 Marx 1973, p. 422.

> Contradiction in the capitalist mode of production: the labourers as buyers
> of commodities are important for the market. But as sellers of their own
> commodity – labour-power – capitalist society tends to keep them down
> to the minimum price.[22]

For Marx, then, it was necessary to recognise both tendencies in capital, the
tendency to grow and the tendency to create barriers to growth. Accordingly,
he considered inadequate the position of economists who emphasised
only one side. Thus he criticised 'economists who, like Ricardo, conceived
production as directly identical with the self-realization of capital – and hence
were heedless of the barriers to consumption'. On the other hand, he similarly
considered limited the view of 'those, who like Sismondi, emphasized the
barriers of consumption'. The former, he argued, had better 'grasped the
positive essence of capital'; the latter had 'better grasped the limited nature
of production based on capital, its negative one-sidedness'. 'The former more
its universal tendency, the latter its particular restrictedness'.[23]

The structure of *Capital* thus reveals the attempt to consider both aspects
of capital. Volume I, with its emphasis upon the growth, the accumulation,
the positive aspect of capital, stands as a reproof to the underconsumptionist
position; Volume II, on the other hand, with its emphasis on the necessary
circuit through which capital must move and the conditions for realisation
of capital, is a criticism of the position that considers 'supply without regard
to demand,' that treats the realisation of capital posited in the production
process as 'its *real* realization'.[24]

The two sides are united in Chapter 15 of Volume III, on 'internal
contradictions of the law'. Here, it is explained that the production of surplus-
value, which is limited only by the productive power of society, 'completes
but the first act of the capitalist process of production – the direct production
process'. The 'second act of the process,' on the other hand, the act in which
commodities must be sold, is limited by the 'consumer power of society', a
power which has been restricted by the relations of production.[25]

It is here, in the bringing together of 'Acts One and Two', that the contradiction
of the capitalist mode of production is revealed: 'the more productiveness

---

[22] Marx 1957, p. 316n.
[23] Marx 1973, p. 410.
[24] Marx 1973, pp. 410–11.
[25] Marx 1959, p. 239.

develops, the more it finds itself at variance with the narrow basis on which the conditions of consumption rest'.[26] Thus, there is continued 'rift' between the tendency toward absolute development of the productive forces and the 'limited dimensions of consumption under capitalism', between the historic task of capital, 'the unconditional development of the social productivity of labour', and 'its own corresponding relations of social production'.[27]

Capital thus contains within itself both the tendency to grow and its own barrier to that growth: 'The *real barrier* of capitalist production is *capital itself*'.[28]

Capital as finite

To identify a contradiction in the Hegelian/Marxian sense, however, is not to speak of a logical impossibility, an impasse; it is to indicate a source of movement, change, and development. And to identify a barrier is *not* to speak of an absolute limit. A barrier is a limit which can be negated, which can be surpassed: 'by the very fact that something has been determined as barrier, it has already been surpassed'.[29] Indeed, the surpassing of barriers is the way in which a thing develops: 'the plant passes over the barrier of existing as a seed, and over the barrier of existing as blossom, fruit or leaf'.[30]

Certainly, this tendency to surpass its own barriers exists also in capital: 'Capital is the endless and limitless drive to go beyond its limiting barrier. Every boundary is and has to be a barrier for it'.[31] Thus, faced with limits in the existing sphere of circulation, capital drives to widen that sphere. 'The tendency to create the *world market* is directly given in the concept of capital itself. Every limit appears as a barrier to be overcome'.[32] And, as it strives 'to tear down every spatial barrier' to exchange and to 'conquer the whole earth for its market', capital also strives 'to annihilate this space with time, i.e. to reduce to a minimum the time spent in motion from one place to another'.[33]

---

[26] Marx 1959, p. 240.
[27] Marx 1959, pp. 245, 251.
[28] Marx 1959, p. 245.
[29] Hegel 1929, I, p. 146.
[30] Hegel 1929, I, p. 147.
[31] Marx 1973, p. 334.
[32] Marx 1973, p. 408.
[33] Marx 1973, p. 539.

Similarly, in its attempt to expand the 'consuming circle within circulation', capital also turns to the 'production of *new* needs and discovery and creation of new use values':

> Hence exploration of all of nature in order to discover new, useful qualities in things; universal exchange of the products of all alien climates and lands; new (artificial) preparation of natural objects, by which they are given new use values. The exploration of the earth in all directions, to discover new things of use as well as new useful qualities of the old; such as new qualities of them as raw materials etc.; the development, hence, of the natural sciences to their highest point; likewise the discovery, creation and satisfaction of new needs arising from society itself.[34]

Thus, in its tendency to drive beyond every barrier to production, capital posits Growth as the third term in the sequence: Growth–Barrier–Growth. Though its barriers are constantly overcome, however, they are just as constantly posited, 'and in as much as it [capital] both posits a barrier *specific* to itself, and on the other side equally drives over and beyond *every* barrier, it is the living contradiction'.[35]

This sequence of Growth–Barrier–Growth, which we have identified, is so fundamental to Marx's view of capital that it is a prime candidate as Marx's paradigm for the capitalist mode of production. In contrast to static paradigms, such as optimisation or market equilibrium, Marx poses a dynamic paradigm, the law of motion. Though it is not very familiar as a paradigm in economics, there is a certain similarity to theories of the growth of the firm. Alfred Chandler's descriptive sequence of Growth–Rationalisation–Growth in his *Strategy and Structure* is one with which Marx would have been quite at home.[36]

Yet, this process of creating barriers, transcending them, and creating them anew is endless. Indeed, it was in the course of exploring the relationship between Ought and Barrier that Hegel demonstrated the manner in which the concept of Finitude passed into Infinity:

---

[34] Marx 1973, pp. 408–9.
[35] Marx 1973, pp. 410, 421.
[36] Chandler 1969, pp. 383–96.

> The Finite (containing both Ought and Barrier) thus is self-contradictory;
> it cancels itself and passes away....[But] the finite in perishing has not
> perished; so far it has only become another finite, which, however, in turn
> perishes in the sense of passing over into another finite, and so on, perhaps
> ad infinitum.[37]

Is capital, then, infinite? Does its ability to drive beyond all barriers mean
that the capitalist mode of production, though changing and developing, is
an absolute form for the development of the productive powers of labour?
For it to be other than infinite, i.e. for it to be finite, it must be incapable of
surpassing a particular barrier. One barrier must, in fact, be its Limit. And,
if capital has a Limit, then it is finite and must perish:

> its perishing is not merely contingent, so that it could be without perishing.
> It is rather the very being of finite things, that they contain the seeds of
> perishing as their own Being-in-Self and the hour of their birth is the hour
> of their death.[38]

Marx's argument is precisely this: capital is a relative and historical form for
the development of the productive forces, rather than an absolute or infinite
form, because it comes up against an inherent barrier which is, in fact, its
limit. Accordingly, the capitalist mode of production is finite.

The tendency of the rate of profit to fall

'The Day of Judgement'

It is hardly surprising that Marx should be fascinated by the place occupied
by the 'Stationary State' in the theories of classical political economy. Quoting
extensively from Ricardo's account of how the decline in the rate of profits
would lead to an end to all accumulation, Marx commented, 'This, as Ricardo
sees it, is the bourgeois "Twilight of the Gods" – the Day of Judgement'.[39]

For, what was the 'Stationary State' but an account of the end to capital, the
end to self-expanding value, the end to the 'historic mission' of developing

---

[37] Hegel 1929, I, p. 149.
[38] Hegel 1929, I, p. 142.
[39] Marx 1968, p. 544.

the social productivity of labour? And what was the declining profit rate, the negation of capital itself, but the identification of a limit to the capitalist mode of production? Could one wonder at 'the terror which the law of the declining rate of profits inspires in the economists'?[40] Thus Marx commented about Ricardo (who, as noted, emphasised the 'positive essence' of capital) that

> What worries Ricardo is the fact that the rate of profit, the stimulating
> principle of capitalist production, the fundamental premise and driving force
> of accumulation, should be endangered by the development of production
> itself.[41]

Of course, the falling rate of profit and the 'Stationary State' were not identified by the classical school as signalling the end of a particular mode of production. Given their tendency to 'eternalise' capitalist production, all growth of production and development of social productivity were seen as coming to a halt. Nevertheless, Marx suggested that there was a vague awareness, an intuition, in Ricardo that something deeper was involved, that capitalist production itself was 'not an absolute, but only a historical mode of production corresponding to a definite limited epoch in the development of the material requirements of production'.[42]

An immanent limit in production?

Marx rejected the entire basis of the classical argument, an argument resting upon the assumption of declining productivity in agriculture. This external natural barrier could be surpassed by capital through changes in social relations in agriculture and, in particular, by putting science (especially the chemical sciences) to work for capital. Indeed, he projected the possibility that, at some point, productivity gains in agriculture would exceed those in industry.[43] Thus Marx considered it 'strange that Ricardo, Malthus, etc. constructed general and eternal laws about physiological chemistry at a time when the latter hardly existed'. And he commented that, in assuming

---

[40] Marx 1971, p. 447. Note also Marx's comment about McCulloch giving 'vent to a veritable jeremiad about the fall in the rate of profit' (p. 186).
[41] Marx 1959, p. 254.
[42] Ibid.
[43] Marx 1968, p. 110.

declining productivity of labour in agriculture, Ricardo 'flees from economics to seek refuge in organic chemistry'.[44]

The central criticism of Ricardo's falling-rate-of-profit argument, however, was that it confused the rate of profit with the rate of surplus-value.[45] Accordingly, the only way for the rate of profit to fall was with a decline in the ratio of profits to wages. Nor were Ricardo and the classical school alone in this respect: although Carey rejected the linking of the declining profit rate to declining productivity, he nevertheless connected the decline with an increase in the relative share of labour. Similarly, Bastiat concluded that the falling rate of profit was associated with the fact that 'the worker's share has grown larger'.[46] In short, the conventional wisdom held that the falling rate of profit was a product of a decline in the rate of exploitation, and also, for the classical economists, declining productivity.

It is not very surprising, therefore, that Marx chose to demonstrate that even if the rate of surplus-value was constant (i.e. did not fall) there was nevertheless a tendency for the rate of profit to fall, and that, furthermore, this tendency was a concomitant of *rising* productivity. It is, on the other hand, quite surprising, in the light of the *whole* of Volume I of *Capital* and numerous comments in Volume III and elsewhere, that anyone could assume that Marx *believed* that the rate of surplus-value was constant (i.e. did not rise). Thus he noted (in contrast with the conventional wisdom):

> The tendency of the rate of profit to fall is bound up with a tendency of the rate of surplus-value to rise, hence with a tendency for the rate of labour exploitation to rise.... The rate of profit does not fall because labour becomes less productive, but because it becomes more productive.[47]

But did Marx *really* believe that there was a tendency for the rate of profit to fall? There were, after all, the 'countertendencies,' and the analytical basis for concluding that, ultimately, the tendency would prevail over the countertendencies was never entirely clear. Most significantly, we should consider Marx's last work on the rate of profit, the 1875 notebook, 'The Relation of the Rate of Surplus-Value to the Rate of Profits' (written ten

---

[44] Marx 1973, pp. 752, 754.
[45] Discussed most fully in Marx 1968, p. 373 ff.
[46] Marx 1973, pp. 558, 754–5, 385.
[47] Marx 1959, p. 234.

years after the bulk of the material incorporated in Volume III of *Capital* by Engels). This long notebook remains untranslated, but a summary of it is the basis for Chapter 3 of Volume III of *Capital*.[48]

In this particular chapter, Marx proceeds by considering the effect on the rate of profit of changes in the organic composition of capital while holding (or attempting to hold) the rate of surplus-value constant; he then reverses this procedure, and, finally, allows both to vary. The basic conclusion derived is that changes in the rate of profit will be determined by the relative rates of change of the organic composition of capital and the rate of surplus-value. He offers no reason here to assume that the rate of increase of the organic composition of capital will exceed that of the rate of surplus-value, and there is no mention of a falling rate of profit.

Thus, one could argue that there is no necessary tendency for a declining rate of profit in Marx – that 'it all depends'. That it all depends on the relative strengths of tendency and countertendencies, on the relative rates of change of the organic composition of capital and the rate of surplus-value. But, besides neglecting the importance Marx attached to the tendency of the rate of profit to fall in relation to the intensity of competition and the tendency toward centralisation of capital, however, an argument for 'a tendency of the rate of profit to be indeterminate' offers a syncretic rather than a dialectical solution to the problem of the rate of profit.

It is necessary, then, to return to the problem of the falling rate of profit and its relation to the 'Stationary State', the check to expansion of capital, the concept of Limit. Consider the manner in which Marx originally developed his position, in which he threw 'overboard the whole doctrine of profit as it has existed up to now'. Capital, Marx argued, as self-expanding value, sought to expand without limits: 'The quantitative boundary of the surplus-value appears to it as a mere natural barrier, as a necessity which it constantly tries to violate and beyond which it constantly seeks to go'.[49] In short, it acts as if it faces only barriers to be transcended.

Yet, the central point that Marx made in the *Grundrisse* is that surplus-value contains a limit given by its very nature – that surplus-value is surplus-labour. 'The identity of surplus gain with surplus labour – absolute and relative – sets

---

48 Marx 1957, Preface, pp. 2–5; Marx 1959, Preface, pp. 3–5.
49 Marx 1973, pp. 334–5.

a qualitative limit on the accumulation of capital'.[50] That limit is established by the length of the workday, the number of workers, and the degree of productivity (which determines the extent of necessary labour). In other words, Marx argued that there was a limit to the production of surplus-value, a point central to the proposition on the rate of profit which he advanced.

The critical elements in Marx's argument on the falling rate of profit as he developed it in the *Grundrisse* are as follows:

1. There is a limit to the amount of surplus-labour per worker, and this limit is given by the length of the workday.
2. Relative increases in surplus-labour per worker are always smaller than relative increases in productivity (or productive force) – since 'the multiplier of the productive force' is the 'divisor' of necessary labour per worker. Thus, 'surplus labour (from the worker's standpoint), or surplus value (from capital's standpoint) does not grow in the same numerical proportion as the productive force'.[51]
3. As the limit to surplus-labour per worker is approached, i.e. as the portion of surplus-labour in the workday rises, increases in surplus-labour per worker resulting from given increases in productivity tend to decline.

    > Surplus value rises but in an ever smaller relation to the development of the productive force. Thus the more developed capital already is, the more surplus labour it has created, the more terribly must it develop the productive force in order to realize itself in only smaller proportion.[52]

4. Increases in productive forces are the equivalent of increases in capital relative to the number of workers: 'an increase in the productive force means that a smaller quantity of labour sets a larger quantity of capital in motion'.[53]

It followed from these propositions that increases in surplus-labour per worker must be relatively smaller than increases in capital per worker, namely that increases in the amount of surplus-labour per worker cannot

---

[50] Marx 1973, p. 375.
[51] Marx 1973, pp. 335–6.
[52] Marx 1973, p. 340.
[53] Marx 1973, pp. 389, 380, and this section in general.

compensate for decreases in the number of workers relative to capital. (See the appendix for a demonstration of points raised in this section.) The rate of profit, the ratio of total surplus-value to capital, must decline. 'The profit rate is therefore inversely related to the growth of relative surplus value or of relative surplus labour, to the development of the powers of production, and to the magnitude of the capital employed as (constant) capital within production'.[54]

The above argument is fundamentally the same as that subsequently introduced with minor changes in form. Thus, the later version focuses on the rate of surplus-value (surplus-labour per worker relative to necessary labour per worker) and the organic composition of capital (total necessary labour relative to total capital); and the basic argument becomes the inability for the rate of surplus-value to rise as rapidly as the organic composition of capital.

The argument as developed in the *Grundrisse* is also the essential version. When Marx wanted to explain why he felt there were limits to the increase in the rate of surplus-value, he reverted to the form of explanation appropriate to the *Grundrisse* version:

> Now, however much the use of machinery may increase the surplus labour at the expense of the necessary labour by heightening the productiveness of labour, it is clear that it attains this result, only by diminishing the number of workmen employed by a given amount of capital.... It is impossible, for instance, to squeeze as much surplus value out of 2 as out of 24 labourers. If each of these 24 men gives only one hour of surplus labour in 12, the 24 men give together 24 hours of surplus labour, while 24 hours is the total labour of the two men.[55]

Thus, the falling-rate-of-profit argument is based on the limit to the workday (inherent in the identity of surplus-value and surplus-labour) and on the 'contradiction which is immanent in it' (the production of surplus-value), that 'of the two factors of the surplus value created by a given amount of capital, one, the rate of surplus value cannot be increased, except by diminishing the other, the number of workmen'.[56]

---

[54] Marx 1973, p. 763.
[55] Marx 1906, pp. 444–5.
[56] Marx 1906, p. 445.

This is essentially an argument about the necessary decline in the *maximum* rate of profit! Even if we were to assume that surplus-labour per worker were equal to the entire workday (due to enormous increases in productivity), even if we were to assume that the workday were equal to the calendar day (24 hours), there would still be a tendency for the rate of profit to fall given by the limit to surplus-labour (24 hours) and by the reduction in the number of workers relative to capital.[57] Thus, the falling rate of profit is an absolute, ultimate barrier which cannot be surpassed by increases in productivity (relative surplus-value) or extensions in the workday (absolute surplus-value). The declining rate of (maximum) profit is a limit to the production of surplus-value, a limit immanent in production.

However, there are definite problems in the above argument. One is that it may be demonstrated that the rate of profit determined here initially *rises* as capital per worker increases. More fundamental is the question of the 'given amount of capital,' i.e. the *value* of the capital. There are two issues relating to the fourth point in the account of the elements in Marx's argument: first, are productivity increases the result of increases in *capital* relative to the number of workers? And, second, does capital relative to the number of workers increase?

First, we may note that, for Marx, it is the *technical* basis or technical composition – the 'definite quantity of means of production, machinery, raw materials, etc.' in relation to a 'definite number of labourers' – which determines the level of productivity rather than the aggregate values of those components, the value-composition of capital or the organic composition of capital.[58] Changes in the organic composition of capital which are the result of changes simply of values do not affect the level of productivity:

> As soon, therefore, as this proportion is altered by means other than a mere change in the value of the material elements of the constant capital, or a change in wages, the productivity of labour must likewise undergo a corresponding change.[59]

---

[57] 'To produce the same rate of profit after the constant capital set in motion by one labourer increases ten-fold, the surplus labour-time would have to increase ten-fold, and soon the total labour-time, and finally the entire 24 hours of a day, would not suffice, even if wholly appropriated by capital' (Marx 1959, p. 390).

[58] Marx 1959, p. 143.

[59] Marx 1959, p. 51.

Accordingly, it is possible for there to be increases in means of production per worker (leading to increased productivity) at the same time as there are 'mere' changes in the value of those means of production – such that there is no increase in capital per worker.

What, then, does happen to the value of means of production, in the context of increases in productivity? If we were to assume that productivity increases occurred evenly throughout the economy, or, at least, that relative rates of productivity gain in the departments producing articles of consumption and means of production were the same, then the relationship of the average value of means of production to the value of labour-power would remain constant. At a result, the organic composition of capital would 'mirror' the technical composition. This would appear to be the most appropriate 'general assumption'.

Under this 'neutral' technological-change assumption, however, it can be demonstrated that capital per worker *falls* with an increase in the technical composition of capital. In short, the tendency is for the rate of profit to rise! Therefore, unless we assume that the average value of means of production rises relative to the value of labour-power (that is, the value composition of capital rises relative to the technical composition), the rate of profit will tend to rise. Such a 'labour-saving' technical bias is not necessarily an inappropriate assumption, since Marx recognised the possibility of differing sectoral rates of productivity change, as in the case of industry and agriculture.

However, the 'falling rate of profit' would then rest on restrictive conditions which could be removed by one of the 'countertendencies' – economies in the use of constant capital. And the search for such economies would be heightened itself by a fall in the rate of profit.[60] As in the case of the classical argument based on the assumption of declining productivity, the falling rate of profit as developed by Marx is shown to be a mere barrier which can be surpassed rather than a limit immanent in production. There is no Limit within the production of capital, in Act One.

---

[60] Marx 1959, Chapter 5, *passim*.

The Second Act

But all this talk about laws of rising rates of profit, while full of sound and fury, actually signifies nothing, because there is no profit rate in the act of production. A profit rate presupposes profits, and profits only emerge through exchange, namely in the act of circulation.

The failure to recognise that capital is only made real through the exchange of commodities can produce strange 'Marxian models', in which the rate of profit is high because the rate of surplus-value is high which, in turn, is due to high unemployment. If one assumes that production is 'directly identical with the self-realization of capital', then it is no difficult task to 'prove' that the rate of profit is highest when unemployment is at its highest possible level and wages at their lowest possible level. Marx, however, saw that it was necessary to be able to *sell* the commodities before there was (and one could talk about) a rate of profit.

The rate of profit was introduced in Volume III of *Capital*, that is, after Volume II. Logically, it belongs in the 'synthesis of the processes of production and circulation'. Yet the whole discussion on the falling rate of profit has tended to proceed as if there were no Volume II. All of the elements deployed in the argument (e.g. the rate of surplus-value, the organic composition of capital, etc.), are of Volume I vintage. It is as if Volume II were never written, as if economists are able to do what capital cannot do – ignore the process of circulation. This is, of course, in the classical tradition, which is one reason why Marx considered the physiocratic model superior to that of classical political economy.[61]

What must be ascertained is the significance of *position* in the argument. Does the meaning and significance of an element change with a change in its position in a dialectical argument? For there can be no doubt that, while Marx's concept of the falling rate of profit was developed in the context of the act of production (as in the case of the classical argument), it is introduced only in the 'Second Act'.

One of the fundamentals of the dialectical method is the process of enrichment of concepts in the course of development. The new concepts that

---

[61] Marx 1957, pp. 92, 99.

emerge out of consideration of opposites contain more than those which preceded. What results is

> a new concept, but a higher, richer concept than that which preceded; for
> it has been enriched by the negation or opposite of that preceding concept,
> and thus contains it, but contains also more than it, and is the unity of it
> and its opposite.[62]

Thus, by 'dialectical progress', the concept 'not only loses nothing and leaves nothing behind, but carries with it all that it has acquired, enriching and concentrating itself upon itself'.[63]

Enrichment of concepts is precisely what occurs in Volume II of *Capital*. Thus, the rate of surplus-value which emerges by the end of Volume II is no longer the same as that which emerged from Volume I; it is now the *annual* rate of surplus-value, a concept which draws upon the turnover period (production-time and circulation-time) of capital and thus the number of turnovers which capital can make in a year.[64] Similarly, the total capital advanced is no longer simply capital expended on elements of production – means of production and labour-power. Added to this are sales expenses (including the cost of salesmen, which now 'appears as an additional investment of capital'), office expenses, and costs of storage.[65] Significantly, the concept of capital tied up in inventories ('lying-fallow') during the time of circulation is introduced.[66]

Although the arguments developed in the various manuscripts assembled by Engels for Volume II were written years after the fragments available for Volume III of *Capital*, many of the questions had been worked upon earlier (as in the case of turnover-time and capital tied up in circulation, considered at length in the *Grundrisse*).[67] And, it is clear that these new definitions were to play an important role in Volume III:

> In the process of circulation the time of circulation comes to exert its influence
> alongside the working-time, thereby limiting the amount of surplus value
> realizable in a given time span. Still other elements derived from circulation

---

[62] Hegel 1929, I, p. 65.
[63] Hegel 1929, II, p. 483.
[64] Marx 1957, Chapter 16.
[65] Marx 1957, p. 133 and Chapter 6.
[66] Marx 1957, Chapter 15; Marx 1973, pp. 547–8.
[67] Marx 1957, Preface, pp. 1–5.

intrude decisively into the actual production process. The actual process of production and the process of circulation intertwine and intermingle continually, and thereby adulterate their typical distinctive features. The production of surplus value, and of value in general, receives new definition in the process of circulation, as previously shown. Capital passes through the circuit of its metamorphoses.[68]

The rate of profit had to take into consideration the points developed in Volume II (as Marx advised Engels); and this included not only issues in relation to the annual rate of surplus-value but also those relating to the additional outlays of capital. The latter necessarily lowered the rate of profit, 'an effect arising from every new investment of additional capital whenever such capital is required to set in motion the same mass of variable capital'. They reduced the rate of profit 'because the advanced capital increases, but not the surplus value'.[69]

The time of circulation, the barrier to capital, necessarily has a critical effect on the rate of profit. Time of circulation affects both the number of turnovers in a year and also the amount of capital tied up in inventories ('frozen in the form of the finished product'). The former is derived from the relation of the sum of production-and-circulation time to a year; and the latter stands in relation to capital in production in accordance with the ratio of time of circulation to time of production.[70] Thus, an increase in the time of circulation, the negation of production-time, both reduces the annual surplus-value (and annual rate of surplus-value) and increases the capital tied up in inventories: 'the capital outlay is greater, the surplus value smaller and its proportion to the capital advanced is also smaller'.[71] An increase in the time of circulation accordingly reduces the rate of profit, negates capital.

But why should time of circulation increase? For the very reasons noted earlier in this chapter. While the time of circulation is affected by such factors as the distance to markets, ultimately it is based upon 'consumption capacity', upon the 'consumer power of society'. And the drive of capital to expand the production of surplus-value by reducing necessary labour relative to

---

[68] Marx 1959, p. 43.
[69] Marx 1959, pp. 286, 293; Marx and Engels 1965, p. 205.
[70] Marx 1959, Chapter 15; Marx 1973, pp. 653–7, 666.
[71] Marx 1971, p. 392.

surplus-labour and the number of workers relative to means of production creates barriers to the realisation of capital. A gap opens, a gap between the productive power of society and the consuming power.

Rising circulation-time reflects this growing gap; it reflects the difficulty of selling. (Within the extended reproduction model, this can be expressed by relating the time of circulation in Department II directly to the rate of surplus-value and the organic composition of capital.) And, increasing circulation-time produces involuntary inventory investment and reduced cash flows, i.e. increased capital tied up in circulation and reduced turnover of surplus-value, both characteristics of the falling rate of profit.[72] What follows are pressures on the money market and, ultimately, restriction of production; it is the crisis of 'overproduction', the forcible assertion of 'the unity of the two phases that have become independent of each other'.[73] It is the increase in circulation-time which leads to the crisis; 'the crisis occurs not only because the commodity is unsaleable, but because it is not saleable within a *particular period of time'*.[74]

The rate of profit thus can only emerge in the interaction between production and circulation of capital, which means that it depends on the relationship between variable capital and total capital (including capital in circulation) and also the annual rate of surplus-value – the 'enriched' concepts. And the decline in the rate of profit is the way in which the contradiction between production and circulation of capital expresses itself, via the emergence of unsold commodities and the increase in circulation-time. It is no more possible to eliminate from Marx's argument the tendency for the rate of profit to fall than it is to eliminate the sphere of circulation of capital.

However, this tendency for the rate of profit to fall resulting from the increase in the time of circulation is explicitly a cyclical rather than a secular tendency. 'Permanent crises do not exist'.[75] They contain within themselves the means of their solution – the restriction of production, destruction of capital. Thus this declining rate of profit is a barrier rather than a limit; it does not produce an ultimate limit to the expansion of capital in the manner of the classical argument.

---

[72] Marx 1957, pp. 148, 287–91.
[73] Marx 1957, pp. 103, 283, 291; Marx 1968, p. 500.
[74] Marx 1968, p. 514.
[75] Marx 1968, p. 497n.

Is there, then, no secular tendency for the rate of profit to decline? We should consider whether, in its efforts to surpass the barrier of the falling rate of profit, capital creates conditions which lead to a secular decline in the rate of profit, which transform the barrier into a limit.

As Marx often noted, one of the principal responses to the falling rate of profit was

> an exertion of capital in order that the individual capitalists, through improved methods, etc., may depress the value of their individual commodity below the social average value and thereby realize an extra profit at the prevailing market-price.[76]

The falling rate of profit was an inducement to innovation in production: 'Improvement, inventions, greater economy in the means of production, etc., are introduced...when profit falls below its normal rate'.[77] Thus, all the tendencies described in Volume I of *Capital* are means of surpassing the barrier of the falling rate of profit – centralisation, rising organic composition of capital, rising rate of surplus-value, etc. (It is the Growth–Barrier–Growth sequence.) Of course, the very means used to surpass the barrier necessarily posit it anew.

But there is also the attempt to widen the sphere of circulation – the sales effort. Individual capitals will find it advantageous to hire circulation agents, to expand capital in circulation, as a way to reduce the time of circulation of their own capital, as a way to expand their share of the market.[78] The falling rate of profit induces innovations in circulation. To the extent that competitors, faced with increasing circulation-time as the result of the initial innovation, follow suit, the advantage of the innovator declines and what remains is an expansion of selling expenditures. A growing amount of capital is diverted from the development of the productivity of labour; the 'historic mission' of capital is thwarted by the conditions within which capital moves.[79] But this, of course, means that more capital is required to set in motion the same variable capital; the rate of profit falls. The attempt to go beyond the barrier produces

---

[76] Marx 1959, p. 253.
[77] Marx 1968, p. 26.
[78] Marx 1959, pp. 275, 291.
[79] Lebowitz 1972, pp. 334–8.

a falling rate of profit; and this follows logically from a dialectical view of *Capital*.

Yet can we stop here? The sales effort also involves the attempt to create new needs, and this means to create new needs for workers. 'To each capitalist, the total mass of all workers, with the exception of his own workers, appear not as workers but as consumers'.[80] But what is the effect of creating new needs for workers? *Capital*, which posits the value of labour-power as dependent on historically developed social needs, has nothing to say about the growth of needs. And, the reason is made clear in the *Grundrisse*: *Capital* was originally intended as only the first of six books, and in order to avoid 'confounding everything' the standard of necessary labour (or needs) was assumed constant in *Capital*. Changes in needs were to be considered in the book on 'Wage-Labour', the third book in Marx's work on political economy (which, of course, remained unwritten).[81]

The effect of the creation of new needs where workers are organised in trade unions is to lead to demands for higher wages. Thus the contradiction of the capitalist mode of production emerges in a different form. On the one hand, each capital attempts to restrict wages to a minimum, and this restricts the ability of workers as buyers of commodities. On the other hand, each capital attempts to generate new needs in workers, and this leads to increased wage demands. The result of the effort to widen the sphere of circulation is therefore a tendency to reduce the rate of surplus-value. Accordingly, the result of efforts to surpass the barrier of the falling rate of profit produces the tendency for a falling rate of profit: 'Capitalist production seeks continually to overcome these immanent barriers, but overcomes them only by means which again place these barriers in its way and on a more formidable scale'.[82]

The final act

Dialectics is the study of things from all sides:

> the endless process of the discovery of new sides, relations, etc.... the endless
> process of the deepening of man's knowledge of the thing, of phenomena,

---

[80] Marx 1973, p. 419.
[81] Marx 1973, p. 817; Lebowitz 2003 and see Chapter 16 below.
[82] Marx 1959, p. 245.

processes, etc., from appearance to essence and from less profound to more profound essence.[83]

And the dialectical consideration of the falling rate of profit constantly produces new aspects also, as in the case of circulation costs and the effect of the creation of new needs on the rate of surplus-value.

But are *these* limits? In fact, there is no reason to suggest that these can be the basis of the falling rate of profit as Limit, as opposed, simply, to the repositing of the barrier, at a higher level. There is nothing to suggest that these, too, cannot be surpassed by greater exertions of capital.

So, finally, we must be explicit, must give a name to the place which the falling rate of profit occupies in Marx's view of capital. Examination of *Capital* demonstrates very clearly that Marx did not view – indeed rejected by his method – the falling rate of profit as a limit. Marx's falling rate of profit is far more fundamental than the falling rate of profit as immanent limit in production, which, once revealed as a theory of the falling maximum rate of profit, can be seen to have very little to do with the relations of production of capital.

Rather, the falling rate of profit, which emerges out of production and circulation of capital, out of the forces and relations of production of capital, is the ever-present, the inseparable barrier of capital. The falling rate of profit is the negation of capital, and, as dialectics tells us, its existence ensures the growth, movement and development of capital: 'Contradiction is the root of all movement and life, and it is only insofar as it contains a Contradiction that anything moves and has impulse and activity'.[84] Without contradiction, no movement; without the falling rate of profit, no innovation, no rising productivity of labour, no rising organic composition of capital, etc., in other words, no movement.

Thus, the drive of capital to go beyond its barrier, expressed as the negation of capital, is the law of motion of capital. It is the means by which capital perfects, universalises itself. Yet, if the falling rate of profit is a barrier which can be surpassed and not a limit, then is the capitalist mode of production infinite?

---

[83] Lenin 1963, p. 222.
[84] Hegel 1929, II, p. 67.

Marx's answer to this question necessarily takes us beyond the issue of the falling rate of profit, just as it took Marx beyond the standpoint of an economist. Although Marx clearly viewed the creation of ever-more-formidable barriers as part of the development of capital, a breakdown [*Zusammenbruch*] is not part of Marx's economic model. It is necessary to be explicit about why Marx viewed the capitalist mode of production as a relative rather than an absolute form for the development of the productivity of labour, and about Marx's counterpart to the classical 'Stationary State' ushered in by the falling rate of profit.

What, in Marx's view, made capital finite is that people become *increasingly conscious* that these barriers to capital as a form for the absolute development of human productive powers are inherent in capital, that they are inherent results of the relations of production within which capital moves. Thus, 'the limitations of the capitalist mode of production come to the surface'. They include a falling rate of profit which 'must be overcome constantly with crises' and the determination of production by a 'definite rate of profit, rather than the relation of production to social requirements, i.e. to the requirements of socially developed human beings'.[85] They include the waste of capital in circulation, the diversion of capital from its 'historic mission' of increasing productivity, the immiseration resulting from the creation of needs more rapidly than they can be fulfilled, and alienation, the fact that

> the working-out of the productive forces, of general wealth, etc., knowledge, etc., appears in such a way that the working individual *alienates* himself; relates to the conditions brought out of him by his labour as those not of his *own* but of an *alien wealth* and of his own poverty.[86]

Thus, it is conscious human beings who recognise that capital is its own barrier, who are the limit to capital. The universality towards which capital irresistibly strives encounters barriers in its own nature, which 'at a certain stage in its development, allow it to be recognized as being itself the greatest barrier to this tendency, and hence will drive towards it own suspension (abolition, transcendence)'.[87] That limit is the proletariat, created, united, and expanded by capital in the course of its development. What capital produces,

---

[85] Marx 1959, p. 253.
[86] Marx 1973, p. 541; Lebowitz 1975.
[87] Marx 1973, p. 410.

'above all, is its own grave-diggers. Its fall and the victory of the proletariat are equally inevitable'.[88] This occurs as the proletariat becomes conscious of the nature of capital, conscious that the relations of production of capital are the barrier to the absolute development of social productivity.

Thus, the writing of *Capital*, the 'popularisation' of Marx's ideas, was a profoundly political act. It was the attempt to bring consciousness of the inherent barriers in capital to the proletariat, the carrying out of Marx's early project – the uniting of philosophy and the proletariat. To the end, Marx remained the philosopher of *praxis*, of human action.

Capital thus comes to an end, not with the decline of the productivity of the soil, but with the emergence of the conscious individual who grasps 'his own history as a *process* and the recognition of nature (equally present as practical power over nature) as his real body'.[89] And it is followed not by some 'Stationary State', but by the removal of the 'limits to growth', by the absolute 'development of human productive forces, in other words the *development of the richness of human nature as an end in itself*'.[90]

---

[88] Marx and Engels 1962, p. 45.
[89] Marx 1973, p. 542.
[90] Marx 1968, pp. 117–18.

Appendix

Marx's *Grundrisse* model on the falling rate of profit may be described simply in the following set of equations:

$$s = d-w, \qquad (1)$$

where s, w, and d are, respectively, surplus-labour per worker, necessary labour per worker (or the value of labour-power expressed in labour hours), and the length of the workday (assumed constant);

$$w = U/q, \qquad (2)$$

where U and q are, respectively, use-values entering into a worker's consumption (assumed constant), and the productivity of labour;

$$q = \sigma k, \qquad (3)$$

where σ and k are, respectively, a constant representing 'efficiency' of capital, and capital per worker (in labour hours); and

$$P' = s/k \qquad (4)$$

where P', surplus-labour per worker relative to capital per worker, is defined as the rate of profit.

It follows, then, from (1) and (2) that surplus-labour per worker rises at a decreasing rate with increases in productivity and has its limit in the length of the workday. Further, it can be demonstrated that, with increases in capital per worker, the rate of profit initially rises but approaches zero at its limit.

As noted in the text, however, the above argument is incorrect both because k, defined in labour hours, must be affected itself by increases in productivity and also because the productivity of labour is more appropriately related to the technical composition of capital. In relation to the latter point, we must introduce a new equation in place of (3):

$$q = \gamma t, \qquad (3')$$

where t and γ, respectively, are the technical composition of capital (means of production per worker), and a constant representing the efficiency of means of production.

In order, then, to establish what happens to capital per worker as productivity increases, it is necessary to determine the relationship between k and t:

$k = (C+V)/N; t = K/N,$

where C, V, K, and N are, respectively, constant capital (in labour hours), variable capital (in labour hours), means of production, and the number of workers.

Now, let p represent the average value of means of production (in labour hours) such that:

$C = Kp$

Given that $w = V/N$, we can define β as the relationship between the average value of means of production and the value of labour-power:

$\beta = p/w.$

Now, let us assume β constant, the assumption of no bias in technological change. Then

$C/V = (K/N) (p/w) = t\beta.$

Accordingly, under this assumption, changes in the organic composition of capital (C/V) will 'mirror' changes in the technical composition t.

Substituting, we can solve for k as follows:

$k = (C + V)/N = (C/N) + (V/N) = (Kp/N + V/N = tp + w = t\beta w + w = w(t\beta + 1) = (U(t\beta+1))/q.$ (5)

Differentiating (5) with respect to q, we find that capital per worker falls as productivity increases.

Accordingly, as discussed in the text, we may conclude that, assuming d, U, γ and β constant, within the sphere of production the tendency is for the rate of profit to rise.

Chapter Eight

The General and the Specific in Marx's Theory of Crisis

Introduction[1]

Economic cycles tend to generate complementary theoretical movements, and so it is not surprising that, at the present time, we are experiencing a boom in the crisis-theory sector. We 'see' crisis all about us – in falling rates of profit, capital-strikes, capital flight, unemployment, raw material shortages and falling real wages. And, thus, there is the attempt, in some, to demonstrate that it all proves that Marx was right (or, in some extreme cases, to prove that they themselves were right).

Yet, the question must be posed as to whether we have an adequate theoretical basis to analyse the individual concrete crisis of the present. Can we indeed speak of a crisis of capitalism as such at this point? Or, is it simply a crisis of capitalism in Canada, or in North America, or in developed capitalist countries, or in specific capitalist sectors? Or, is it a crisis which is independent of capital as such – that is, a natural or ecological crisis, an approach to an entropy state which affects *all* forms of production?

[1] This paper was originally presented to the Society for Socialist Studies at the annual meeting of Canadian Learned Societies in Halifax in May 1981. I am grateful for the encouragement and comments of editors and reviewers for *Studies in Political Economy*. In addition, I have also benefited particularly from comments of Paresh Chattopadhyay, Harry Magdoff, Max Nemni, James O'Connor and Paul Sweezy.

The question is – how will we know a crisis of capital as such when we see it?

Certainly we must be wary of any discussions framed in terms of growing capitalist competition, of Japanese and German capital vs. US capital, of capital in the newly industrialising countries (NIC), such as South Korea, Taiwan, Singapore, Hong Kong, etc. vs. developed capitalist countries, and so forth. That poses simply the question of *particular* crises. But, there are always particular crises in capitalism; any increase in productivity implies a crisis for the particular capital or capitals which are *not* so advancing, but this does not mean a crisis for capital as a whole. On the contrary, it is the very continued life-process of capitalism, the process of capital acting upon itself to execute its inner laws. As Marx noted, to try to explain these intrinsic tendencies simply as results of competition therefore means to concede that one does not understand them.[2] Thus, the starting point for analysis must be capitalism as a whole, world capitalism; as severe and protracted as a particular crisis may be, it can only be understood by situating it within the whole.

But, can we speak legitimately of 'crisis'? For Marx, a crisis was a 'violent eruption', a 'momentary and forcible solution of the existing contradictions'; it was not long-term or permanent.[3] What was significant about a crisis is that it revealed the existence of a barrier to capital. Given the essential nature of capital as self-expanding value, a crisis was a manifestation of an inherent check on its growth, a moment in which capital has come up against barriers which thwart its impulse, which negate its essence. It is, of course, the existence of barriers – rather than their momentary and forcible solutions – which is the subject of Marxian crisis theories.

Thus, while the particular form of an individual crisis (for example, a crisis in money-capital, a crisis in commodity-capital, etc.) may be a matter of chance and contingency, the concept of the barrier itself is meant to establish *necessity*. Does capital have inherent barriers, which come to the surface in crises – and, if so, what are they?

Whatever its nature, a barrier to capital is necessarily manifested in a decline in the rate of self-expansion of capital, that is, in the rate of profit. To say, then, that capital tends to face barriers to its growth is to say that capital tends

---

[2] Marx 1973, pp. 651, 751–2.
[3] Marx 1959, p. 244.

to face a falling rate of profit. (Capital's tendency to transcend all barriers – which does not abolish the barriers as such – produces, on the other hand, a tendency for the rate of profit to rise.) It takes a giant leap of the imagination, however, to move from *a* tendency of the rate of profit to fall – which is inherent in the concept of a barrier to capital – to *the* historically specific argument for the tendency of a falling rate of profit (hereafter designated as FROP). Unfortunately, the very existence of the FROP argument has been a barrier to the understanding of barriers to capital and, thus, a barrier to analysis of individual concrete crises.

The tendency of the rate of profit to fall: a critique

Certainly, there has been much written about Marx's argument with respect to the falling rate of profit (FROP). It has been buried (complete with prominent obituaries) and resurrected (amidst exultations that it 'lives') with a frequency that suggests that we are dealing with a religious phenomenon rather than with an analytical proposition. For this very reason, one must be apologetic for entering once again into this ideal world of rising organic compositions of capital and constant or bounded rates of surplus-value. The only justification which can be offered is that investigation of FROP may yet reveal something which has been hidden behind it, something which has gone on behind the backs of the various FROP-disputants.

Let us recall what FROP is all about: 'This law, and it is the most important law of political economy, is that the *rate of profit has a tendency to fall with the progress of capitalist production*'.[4] That 'law' clearly is about the long term, and this is why FROP 'has caused a great deal of anxiety to bourgeois political economy':

> The whole of the Ricardian and Malthusian school is a cry of woe over the day of judgement this process would inevitably bring about, since capitalist production is the production of profit, hence loses its stimulus, the soul which animates it, with the fall in this profit.[5]

---

[4] Marx 1994, p. 104.
[5] Marx 1994, pp. 104–5.

Not surprisingly, this very same 'law' that has been a source of anxiety to the supporters of capitalism has become a source of faith for some of the opponents of capitalism that the day of judgement will soon arrive. Indeed, we often are treated to the spectacle of attempts to demonstrate that concrete declines in the rate of profit are proof of FROP at work, even where the former are produced by declining rates of exploitation, which are no part of Marx's FROP story. Such a performance is characteristic of the disciple, who as Marx noted with respect to the disciples of Ricardo, tries to solve 'a series of inconsistencies, unresolved contradictions and fatuities...with phrases in a scholastic way':

> Crass empiricism turns into false metaphysics, scholasticism, which toils painfully to deduce undeniable empirical phenomena by simple formal abstraction directly from the general law, or to show by cunning argument that they are in accordance with that law.[6]

'So where does this tendency for the general rate of profit to fall come from'?[7] The familiar-FROP scenario proposes, it is known, that increases in the value-composition of capital (C/V), reflecting the growth in means of production per worker, ultimately tend to exceed increases in the rate of surplus-value (S/V). Aside from some confusion over assumptions about the rate of surplus-value (constancy, 'limits', etc), it is now generally recognised that the whole matter revolves around the course of the ratio of dead to living labour $(C/(V + S))$; if the growth of $C/(V + S)$ can be demonstrated as necessary, then the rate of profit must indeed ultimately fall.[8]

Now, on the face of it, a growth in dead to living labour $(C/(V +S))$ appears to be a necessary tendency – given capital's tendency to substitute machinery for living labour and to increase productivity. Yet all that this tells us is that the mass of machinery and raw materials per living labour rises, that is, that the technical composition of capital tends to rise. The condition for $C/(V + S)$ to rise is that productivity in the production of means of production must not grow as rapidly as the technical composition itself. If, however, the rate of growth of productivity in the production of means of production is equal

---

[6] Marx, n.d., p. 87.
[7] Marx 1994, p. 104.
[8] See the discussion, for example, in the preceding chapter and, for example, in Van Parijs 1980.

to the rate of increase in means of production per living labour, *then there is no increase in the ratio of dead to living labour*. Further, the preceding chapter indicates that in this case the value-composition of capital will rise (following from the decline in variable capital as the result of productivity increases) but that it will increase less than the rate of surplus-value – and, thus, the result will be a *rising* rate of profit rather than a falling rate of profit.

In short, the whole familiar FROP picture may be seen to rest on the assumption of an uneven growth in productivity, on a lag in the growth of productivity of labour in the sector producing means of production (Department I). But, how can this special assumption be an explanation for a *necessary* tendency for the rate of profit to decline? If we think of capital-as-a-whole, surely its intrinsic laws should result from a general rather than a specific assumption about productivity? Capital's tendency to develop productive forces and to reduce the quantity of labour necessary to produce particular use-values obviously applies to the production of means of production as well as to articles of consumption. For this reason, 'economies in constant capital' as such are not a *counter*-tendency to capital's general tendency. Nevertheless, Marx explicitly treated the reduction in the value of elements of constant capital (as the result of productivity growth) as merely a 'counter-acting' tendency; only in 'isolated cases' did he suggest that the value of constant capital might remain the same (or fall) as its mass increased.[9] But why *only* in 'isolated cases'?

It is important to understand that the problem in the FROP-scenario is not at all that Marx failed to recognise the importance of an assumption about productivity in the production of means of production. Indeed, he was far more aware of this critical point than many subsequent disciples. Writing in the *Grundrisse* (where the basic elements of his FROP argument were first developed), Marx argued that the composition of capital would remain the same if 'productivity increases at the same time not only in the given branch of production, but also in its conditions'. On the other hand, a rise in the constant component of capital emerges 'if the objective conditions of production...remain unchanged in value'.[10] In short, Marx's very argument

---

[9] Marx 1959, p. 231.
[10] Marx 1973, pp. 773, 771.

for the growth in the composition of capital explicitly rested upon the uneven development of productivity:

> If the force of production increased simultaneously in the production of the different conditions of production, raw material, means of production and means of subsistence, and in the [of production] determined [them], then their growth would bring about no change in the relation between the different component parts of the capital.[11]

He returned to this same question several years later in his *Economic Manuscripts of 1861–3*. There, he did extended calculations for the rate of profit, demonstrating the effect of increases in productivity in the sector producing means of production. Productivity increases in cotton weaving involve increases in raw materials per worker; assuming productivity in the production of yarn constant, there is an increase in the value composition of capital (C/V), and if the rate of surplus-value remains unchanged, the effect is that the rate of profit falls:

> In I b), where the productivity of weaving increases threefold and wages remain the same, but the yarn, etc., retains its old price, we have a fall in the rate of profit. In this case the rate of profit falls from 50% to 25%.[12]

Further, Marx indicated that, where the rate of surplus-value rose as the result of productivity increases, the rate of profit also fell (but in this case only to 36%):

> We have equally a fall in the *rate of profit* under III, where wages fall in the same proportion as the productivity of labour [rises]. But raw materials, etc., remain the same here as before the threefold increase in the productivity of labour, as under I a).

In contrast, in the two cases where Marx considered equal productivity increases in the production of the input (yarn) to those occurring in weaving, there was *no* fall in the profit rate. Where the rate of surplus-value was constant, the rate of profit remained the same, whereas, in the case where necessary labour falls 'in the same proportion as the productivity of labour

---

[11] Marx 1973, p. 770.
[12] Marx 1994, p. 29.

grows', the rate of profit rises to 80%.[13] In short, the *only* case that corresponds to the FROP story introduced in Chapter 13 of Volume III of *Capital* is where productivity in the sector producing material inputs is assumed constant. Marx concluded in his 1861–3 manuscript that it would appear 'that the rate of profit cannot *fall* unless' (1) the value of labour-power rises ('Ricardo's assertion') or (2)

> there is a rise in the *value of constant capital in relation to variable*. And the latter would appear to be restricted to cases where the productive power of labour does not rise *equally* and *simultaneously* in all the branches of production which contribute to produce the commodity.[14]

Again, the same point about uniform productivity changes is made in the very exposition of FROP in Chapter 13 of *Capital*, Volume III. Marx clearly indicated there that the rate of profit would tend to fall despite a higher rate of surplus-value 'outside of a few cases (for instance, *if the productiveness of labour uniformly cheapens all elements of the constant, and the variable, capital)*'.[15] Of course, the probability of achieving equal and simultaneous increases in productivity for all sectors approaches zero, and, among the many contingencies we can imagine (which Marx did not explore above), is a threefold increase in productivity in the sector producing means of production but none in the using sectors. But Marx's specification of this condition in which the rate of profit would not fall was deliberate: not only did he repeatedly acknowledge the importance for FROP of lagging productivity in Department I but he also offered an unequivocal explanation as to why a uniform increase in productivity would be limited to 'isolated cases'.

Discussions of the rise in the technical composition of capital, the increase in the quantity of means of production per living labour, often focus solely upon fixed capital, the instruments of labour which are a 'condition' of the growth of the productivity of labour without thinking about the *other* part of the increase, the 'consequence' of this rising productivity of labour – i.e., the relatively growing mass of raw materials which workers transform.[16] Marx, though, stressed the latter; whereas the size and value of machines

---

[13] Marx 1994, pp. 26–9.
[14] Marx 1994, pp. 33–4.
[15] Marx 1959, p. 222. Emphasis added.
[16] Marx 1977a, p. 773.

employed tended to rise less than the productivity growth which follows from their use, the 'growing productivity of labour is expressed precisely in the proportion in which a larger quantity of raw material absorbs a definite quantity of labour'.[17] With growing productivity, there was a tendency for the value of raw materials to form 'an ever-growing component of the value of the commodity-product':

> If the productivity in wool spinning is trebled, then, provided the conditions of production of the wool remained the same, three times as much time as previously would have to be spent, three times as much capital would have to be expended in wool production.[18]

For this reason, it was critical for the value of constant capital (and the rate of profit) that the increased requirements for objects of labour, raw materials, be 'counterbalanced by a proportionate decrease in the value of the raw material arising from the growing productivity of the labour employed in its own production'.[19]

What was the likelihood of this? It is certainly possible that productivity gains in the production of instruments of labour (machines, etc.) – once this sector is characterised by the specifically capitalist mode of production – counterbalance the growing use of those instruments. One, indeed, could as easily argue for a *higher* than average rate of growth of productivity as a lower one here – in other words, it would take an artificial assumption to posit lagging productivity gains for instruments of labour. But, for Marx, the situation is precisely the opposite in the case of the objects of labour. *Over and over again, he argued that it was likely that productivity in the production of raw materials would tend not to increase as rapidly as productivity in general (and, accordingly, the growing requirements for raw materials).* Thus, he noted quite early in Volume III of *Capital* that it was 'quite comprehensible' that productivity in agriculture and the extractive industries might decline and thereby produce an increase in constant capital.[20] And, the reason for this uneven development of productivity was that, here, *more than social conditions* were determinate:

---

[17] Marx 1959, p. 107; 1994, pp. 133, 289.
[18] Marx 1959, p. 107; 1968, p. 128.
[19] Marx 1959, pp. 105 107.
[20] Marx 1959, pp. 56–7.

The development of the productivity in different lines of industry proceeds at substantially different rates and frequently even in opposite directions....Productivity of labour is also bound up with natural conditions, which frequently become less productive as productivity grows – inasmuch as the latter depends on social conditions....Consider the mere influence of the seasons, for instance, on which the bulk of raw material depends for its mass, the exhaustion of forest lands, coal and iron mines, etc.[21]

Again, he noted the 'peculiar nature of agriculture', where even increases in the technical composition of capital might not generate an increase in productivity:

In agriculture (as in mining) it is not only a matter of the social, but also of the natural, productivity of labour which depends on the natural conditions of labour. It is possible for the increase of social productivity in agriculture to barely compensate, or not even compensate, for the decrease in natural power.[22]

This distinction between production processes which were immediately dependent upon nature and those that were not was one Marx had made earlier in his manuscripts. Considering the growth in the technical composition of capital, Marx asked if ten times as much cotton can be worked on by a spinner as the result of technical change, why should not the cotton itself *also* be produced ten times as productively, 'that is, why should the *value* ratio not remain the same?' Marx's answer was unequivocal:

To this it is quite easy to answer that some kinds of raw materials, such as wool, silk, leather, are produced by animal organic processes, while cotton, linen, etc are produced by vegetable organic processes and capitalist production has not yet succeeded, and never will succeed in mastering these processes in the same way as it has mastered purely mechanical or inorganic chemical processes....As far as coal and metal (wood) are concerned, they will become much cheaper with the advance of production; this will however become more difficult as mines are exhausted, etc.[23]

---

[21] Marx 1959, p. 255.
[22] Marx 1959, p. 748.
[23] Marx 1971, p. 368.

These organic processes, too, affected not only the *long-term* prospects for development of productivity in the production of raw materials, but also the tendency for this production to lag behind in boom periods. Thus, Marx called attention to a tendency for 'relative underproduction' of raw materials:

> It is in the nature of things that vegetable and animal substances whose growth and production are subject to certain organic laws and bound up with definite natural time periods, cannot suddenly be augmented in the same degree as, for instance, machines and other fixed capital, or coal, ore, etc whose reproduction can, provided the natural conditions do not change, be rapidly accomplished in an industrially developed country.[24]

We have here, then, a clear explanation for the growth in $C/(V + S)$, that is, for the value of raw materials to increase: there is a necessary lag in productivity because productivity depends, in part, on natural conditions. Precisely because the productivity of labour in the production of raw materials 'is bound up with *natural conditions*', it is only in 'isolated cases' that the value of constant capital remains the same or falls while its mass increases.[25] FROP, accordingly, is a necessary tendency.

Was Marx, then, in this respect a 'minor post-Ricardian', fleeing 'from economics to seek refuge in organic chemistry' to generate the basis for a tendency of the rate of profit to fall?[26] There are some similarities – for both Ricardo and Marx, the rate of profit tends to fall as the result of the accumulation of capital. Further, we can see that, like Ricardo, Marx recognised the link between falling profit rates and natural barriers. Marx's discussion is bound up with his description of crises in the nineteenth century; he notes that a growth in the number of cotton mills, an increase in the number of spindles per worker tended to outrun the production of raw materials, and generated a shift to raw materials produced under less favourable conditions. The issue is that in capital's thrust to expand, it tends to expand the production of instruments of production more rapidly than that of objects of labour. There is the tendency toward the 'relative over-production of machinery and other fixed capital' and the relative under-production of raw materials.[27] 'Although

---

[24] Marx 1959, pp. 116–17.
[25] Marx 1968, pp. 516–17; 1959, p. 231.
[26] Marx 1973, pp. 754, 752; 1968, p. 18.
[27] Marx 1959, pp. 117–27.

the raw material would have been sufficient for the *old level of production*, it will be insufficient for the *new.... It is a case of *overproduction of fixed capital...*'.[28] The fall in the rate of profit here is the direct result of capital's thrust to expand.

But, there are major differences between Ricardo and Marx. In particular, Marx rejected the idea that the fall in the rate of profit is the product of diminishing productivity leading to a fall in the rate of surplus-value. On the contrary, it is the result of *rising* productivity; *that* is what generates the necessary increase in raw materials per worker (which is the expression of the growth of social productivity). The very same development of productive forces (for example, the improvement of machinery) which tends to increase social productivity and to increase the rate of surplus-value also tends to increase the constant portion of capital:

> The rate of profit does not fall because labour becomes less productive, but because it becomes more productive. Both the rise in the rate of surplus value and the fall in the rate of profit are but specific forms through which growing productivity of labour is expressed under capitalism.[29]

Further, in contrast to Ricardo's stress upon declining productivity in agriculture, for Marx the natural barrier that generates a falling rate of profit does not require *diminishing productivity* but only a *relative* decline:

> Even in this case a fall in profit would prove not that the yield of cotton cultivation had declined, but only that it had not become more productive in the same ratio as cotton manufacturing. Therefore only a relative reduction in its productivity, despite the absolute increase in it. Ricardo, however, thinks that agriculture must become more unproductive absolutely. It would only demonstrate that industry and agriculture do not develop to the same degree in bourgeois production. If they do not do this, that alone is sufficient to explain the decline in the rate of profit.[30]

What we are describing here is the tendency for capital to come up against barriers in the sphere of production in its attempt to expand. The rate of profit tends to fall if productive forces cannot expand sufficiently in the sectors which produce the 'conditions of production', where 'the growing

---

[28] Marx 1968, pp. 516–17.
[29] Marx 1959, p. 234.
[30] Marx 1994, p. 34.

productivity of labour would lead capital to encounter a barrier in the not-growing mass of raw material and machinery'.[31] Yet capital was successful in surmounting a barrier in the production of instruments of labour. It did so by developing the production of machines by machines – through the spread of the 'specifically capitalist mode of production'. It was precisely the transformation of the mode of production in this sphere, the production of its own presupposition of instruments of labour, which gave capital 'an adequate technical foundation' and allowed it to 'stand on its own feet'; it is that which gave capital the power to expand production 'by leaps and bounds', and it is why there is no reason to assume that productivity will tend to lag in production of instruments of labour.[32]

Why, then, is there the suggestion that the same ability to transcend a barrier to its growth is not present for capital with respect to a barrier of raw materials? Cannot capital here also transform the mode of production, produce its own presuppositions on a new technical foundation and give itself the power to expand by leaps and bounds? While Marx did not deny the possibility of increasing production here with the development of productive forces, he remained conscious of the natural, organic side of production:

> Agriculture forms a mode of production *sui generis*, because the organic process is involved, in addition to the mechanical and chemical process, and the natural reproduction process is merely controlled and guided; extractive industry (mining is the most important) is likewise an industry *sui generis*, because no reproduction process whatever takes place in it, at least not one under our control or known to us.[33]

As he noted with respect to the products of extractive industry, they are products of labour (and thus accessible to productivity increase) insofar as they are brought to light and given form – but they are not themselves produced by labour: 'But they are not reproduced, since we do not yet know how to create metals'.[34]

The problem here is that, unlike the case of instruments of labour, capital cannot *wholly* transform the production of raw materials. *Nature itself stands*

[31] Marx 1973, p. 775.
[32] Marx 1977a, pp. 504–6.
[33] Marx 1973, p. 726.
[34] Marx 1973, p. 716n.

outside the reproduction of capital; it is a point of departure but not a point of return.
Thus, nature is always present as a barrier to the growth of capital. When
capital produces its own presuppositions, preconditions, premises – they do
not include nature. For this reason, the very growth of capital necessarily
generates a tendency for the rate of profit to fall.[35]

It is obvious, however, that this barrier of raw materials is not specific to
capital and capitalist relations of production. Nature does not stand only
outside the reproduction of *capital*. In short, investigation of FROP reveals
the existence of a barrier which is not specific to capital but which is a *general*
barrier; it allows us to develop a concept which has been hidden behind FROP
and to thereby distinguish between barriers which are general to all social
formations and those which are specific to capital. There are, indeed, barriers
to the growth and expansion of capital, and they need to be distinguished.
Discussing the development of machinery, Marx commented:

> As soon as the general conditions of production appropriate to large-
> scale industry have been established, this mode of production acquires
> an elasticity, a capacity for sudden extension by leaps and bounds, which
> comes up against no barriers but those presented by the availability of raw
> materials and the extent of sales outlets.[36]

The two barriers identified here point to the existence of a general barrier and
also a specific barrier to capital; the concepts of general and specific barriers
will be considered separately and then in their interrelation.

General barriers

Just as it is a 'rational abstraction' to identify the common and general
elements in every epoch of production, and to distinguish these from those
elements which are specific to a particular form of production, so also is
it a rational abstraction to distinguish those barriers to the development

---

[35] Marx 1973, p. 716n. But, this does not 'rescue' FROP as such. On the contrary. I
agree with Paul Sweezy's characterization of the tendency toward 'the fetishization of
the falling tendency of the rate of profit'. I have only attempted here to reveal what
lies hidden behind FROP which is not apparent in the discussions. I am grateful to
Harry Magdoff and Paul Sweezy for forcing me to be more explicit on this point.
Cf. Sweezy 1974.

[36] Marx 1977a, p. 579.

of productive forces which are general from those which are specific to a particular form of production.[37] In the labour process, that 'appropriation of what exists in nature for the requirements of man (which) is common to all forms of society in which human beings live', there are *two* general barriers to the development of productive forces – human beings and nature.[38] The *form* which these barriers take within capitalist production, however, is specific – as is the means of transcending these general barriers.

Consider the barrier of human beings. It is not unique to capitalist production that growth of productive forces may, at some point, come up against a barrier in the form of available supplies of labour-power. Under given conditions of production, rapidly growing production will entail increased labour requirements which, sooner or later, may exhaust the existing supply of labour. Where the conditions of production remain unchanged, the effect will be to check the rate of growth of production (and thus also the growth of labour requirements) until such time as increases in the supply of labour permit more rapid increases in production. The pattern, thus, will be one of waves and cycles imposed by the barrier of human beings. This barrier, on the other hand, can be transcended by the alteration in the technical conditions of production, by using the products of past labour to increase the productivity of present labour, that is, by the development of social productivity. Thus, we can see in Eastern-European countries (which may be characterised as 'actually existing socialism') precisely the effect of this general barrier: rapid development occurred to a substantial extent on the basis of an 'extensive model' of development, drawing upon available supplies of labour for industry. Reduced increments in the supply of labour, however, have checked that rate of growth of production – and point to the necessity to surmount that barrier through a significant shift to 'intensive' growth, a rise in social productivity.[39]

The *capitalist* form of this general barrier of human beings, of course, was described at length by Marx in Chapter 25 of Volume I of *Capital*, 'The General Law of Capitalist Accumulation'.[40] In its drive to expand, capital reaches a point 'at which the requirements of accumulation begin to outgrow the customary

---

[37] Marx 1973, p. 85.
[38] Marx 1977a, p. 290.
[39] Cf. Lebowitz 1985.
[40] Marx 1977a, p. 763.

supply of labour, and a rise of wages therefore takes place.' The result is a reduction in surplus-value, a fall in the rate of profit and, finally, a lessening of the rate of accumulation – which removes the 'disproportion between capital and exploitable labour-power'.[41] As Marx, however, emphasised, capital drives beyond this barrier (given by the rate of natural increase in the working population) by increasing the technical composition of capital. (The very increase in the wage, in paid labour, increases the scope for capital to introduce machinery.) Thus, capital turns any potential limits to its self-expansion given by the supply of labour into a mere barrier by the production of a relative surplus population; it produces a 'relatively redundant working population'.

> Independently of the limits of the actual increase of population, it creates
> a mass of human material always ready for exploitation by capital in the
> interests of capital's own changing valorization requirements.[42]

Thus, we see that capital faces and transcends the general barrier of human beings in its own specific way – the development of social productivity occurs in opposition to and at the expense of living labour. Yet, it is critical to recognise that it is a *general* barrier and not one *specific* to capital; it is capitalist relations of production which give this general barrier its specific antagonistic and inverted character – as described by Marx in 'The General Law of Capitalist Accumulation'.[43]

As we have already seen from our investigation of FROP, nature also is a barrier to capital, but not one which is specific to capital. The tendency for instruments of production to be able to be 'augmented' faster than the products of nature, the tendency for raw materials to emerge as a bottleneck sector, that is, the tendency for nature to emerge as a barrier to the development of productive forces – all this follows from the pattern which Marx described and which he noted was not simply the result of 'the peculiarity of the bourgeois mode of production'.[44] Indeed, the existence of a pattern of growth of productive forces leading to shortages of raw materials and, thus, generating a slowdown in growth, i.e., waves and cycles emanating

---

[41] Marx 1977a, p. 770.
[42] Marx 1977a, pp. 782, 784.
[43] Marx 1977a, pp. 798–9.
[44] Marx 1959, p. 255.

from the 'raw-materials barrier', has long been identified in Eastern-European countries. Where such a barrier is operative, the only means of transcending it is through the development of science, the increase of productivity in these bottleneck sectors, the development of substitutes, etc; and, where such efforts are successful, they may generate long periods in which productive forces can develop rapidly without the immediate pressure of the raw materials barrier, offering the prospect of 'long waves'.

Again, the capitalist form of this general barrier has the form of movements in value and value-categories: the relative value of raw materials rises, the value-composition of capital increases and the rate of profit falls. (Note that it is the *maximum* rate of profit, a ratio independent of capitalist relations of production, which falls in this case.) Similarly, the very concept of capital as self-expanding value indicates the manner in which this barrier is transcended. Increased values of raw materials indicate the spheres in which capital can expand most rapidly. Or, in other words, the potential of high profit rates (and rents) directs capital into those very sectors which are bottlenecks. The increased technical composition of capital in these spheres, the attempt to increase productivity in raw materials production, the marshalling of science to develop substitutes – all these are part of the process by which capital attempts to transcend the barrier in order to posit its growth once more:

> Hence exploration of all of nature in order to discover new, useful qualities in things;...new (artificial) preparation of natural objects, by which they are given new use values. The exploration of the earth in all directions, to discover new things of use as well as new useful qualities of the old; such as new qualities of them as raw materials etc; the development of the natural sciences, hence, to their highest point...is likewise a condition of production founded on capital.[45]

Where capital is successful in negating this barrier, its success again takes the form of a period of relatively declining raw-material values, a declining value-composition of capital and a rising rate of profit. In short, the very existence of the general barrier of nature and capital's tendency to drive beyond all barriers will tend to generate long waves and swings of a 'Kondratieff-type'

---

[45] Marx 1973, p. 409.

(although there is no reason to assume a mechanical regularity for such waves)*.

Here again, then, there can be little question that it is a general barrier that capital faces and transcends in its own specific way. Given capital's over-riding thrust for surplus-value, this barrier also takes on a specific antagonistic and inverted character:

> Moreover, all progress in capitalist agriculture is a progress in the art, not only of robbing the worker, but of robbing the soil; all progress in increasing the fertility of the soil for a given time is a progress towards ruining the more long-lasting sources of this fertility. . . . Capitalist production, therefore, only develops the technique and the degree of combination of the social process of production by simultaneously undermining the original sources of all wealth – the soil and the worker.[46]

It is precisely these original sources of wealth, nature and human beings, which exist as general barriers to capital. They stand outside capital: they are premises and presuppositions of capital, but they are not results of capital; they are not part of the reproduction of capital – although the reproduction of capital is dependent upon them. Unfortunately, standard Marxian accounts of capitalist development have by and large failed to recognise these as general barriers – barriers to which other forms of production are also subject. Accordingly, they have also failed to distinguish adequately capital's *specific* barrier – which does *not* characterise other forms of production.

The specific barrier of capital

In his examination of crises in the *Theories of Surplus Value*, Marx charged Ricardo with an 'inability to grasp the specific form of bourgeois production'. Treating capitalism as 'a mode of production without any definite specific characteristics', Ricardo could not therefore admit that:

> the bourgeois mode of production contains within itself a barrier to the free development of the productive forces, a barrier which comes to the surface

---

[46] Marx 1977a, p. 638.

in crises and, in particular, in *over-production* – the basic phenomenon in crises.[47]

But, what was this specific barrier contained within capital itself? The concept emerges in the *Grundrisse*: following an extensive discussion of capital's tendency to drive beyond all barriers to its growth, its tendency to develop productive forces, needs, science and social productivity, Marx then noted that the 'universality towards which it irresistibly strives encounters barriers in its own nature'.[48] Accordingly, he set out to demonstrate logically 'that capital contains a *particular* restriction – which contradicts its general tendency to drive beyond every barrier to production'.[49]

Inherent in capital, Marx argued, coinciding 'with the nature of capital, with the essential character of its very concept', there were limits – limits given by the fact that capital produced its products as commodities, that its over-riding purpose of production was surplus-value, that it could only realise that goal through the sale of commodities and that capital *itself* narrowed the sphere of circulation. It was this, a restriction of production particular to capital, which was 'the foundation of *overproduction*, the fundamental contradiction of developed capital'.[50]

The particular restriction of production, simply stated, was that the very nature of capital, the capitalist relation of production, was such as to posit production only insofar as it was production of surplus-value *and* only insofar as that surplus-value was realisable: 'it posits necessary labour only *to the extent and in so far as* it is surplus labour and the latter is *realizable* as *surplus value*'.[51] Yet, at the same time, the very nature of capital is that it attempts 'to restrict the worker's consumption to the amount necessary to reproduce his labour capacity,' and strives 'to reduce the relation of this necessary labour to surplus labour to the minimum'.[52] In short, every capitalist tries to restrict the consumption of his own worker, 'his ability to exchange, his wage, as much as possible'; and 'the relation of *every* capitalist to *his own* workers is the *relation as*

---

[47] Marx 1968, pp. 527–9.
[48] Marx 1973, p. 410.
[49] Marx 1973, p. 415.
[50] Marx 1973, pp. 415–16.
[51] Marx 1973, p. 421.
[52] Marx 1973, p. 422.

such of *capital and labour*, the essential relation'.[53] The very positing of growth within the sphere of production is thus at the same time, 'absolutely identical here with the positing of barriers to the sphere of exchange, i.e. the possibility of realization'.[54] What capital does in the sphere of production comes back to haunt it in the sphere of circulation because it is *not* an abstract, externally juxtaposed sphere of circulation but, rather, one characterised by capitalist relations of production.

Thus, capital, by its nature, posits a barrier to labour, to productive activity, to value creation, to the development of productive forces – in spite of its tendency to expand these boundlessly, in spite of its tendency toward 'universality': 'And in as much as it both posits a barrier *specific* to itself, and on the other side equally drives over and beyond every barrier, it is the living contradiction'.[55] Capital, in short, has the tendency to come up against its own 'specific barrier'; it has the tendency to expand production without regard for the limits posed by itself, without regard for the limits of a sphere of circulation marked by capitalist relations of production. Thus, its specific barrier 'comes to the surface in crises' and is 'the foundation of overproduction, the fundamental contradiction of developed capital'. *That specific barrier is constituted by the capitalist relations of production.*

Although Marx's position as developed in the *Grundrisse* has recently been characterised by Makoto Itoh as 'an excess commodity theory of the underconsumptionist type', it is entirely wrong-headed to describe this as an underconsumptionist or, for that matter, an overproductionist position.[56] That obscures the critical point that Marx was making about the specific difference of capitalist production. Marx's position was a capitalist-relations-of-production position; it was that capitalist relations of production were capital's unique fetter on the development of productive forces, a particular restriction not characteristic of other forms of production.

On this identification of the specific barrier of capital, Marx remained consistent. Writing subsequently on the question of crises, he emphasised

---

[53] Marx 1973, p. 420.
[54] Marx 1973, p. 422.
[55] Marx 1973, p. 421.
[56] Itoh 1978, p. 132.

the need to isolate 'the special aspects of capital which are *peculiar* to it as capital'.[57] And, he found that:

> Over-production is specifically conditioned by the general law of the production of capital: to produce to the limit set by the productive forces, that is to say, to exploit the maximum amount of labour with the given amount of capital, without any consideration for the actual limits of the market or the needs backed by the ability to pay;...while on the other hand, the mass of producers remain tied to the average level of needs, and must remain tied to it according to the nature of capitalist production.[58]

Similarly, in Volume II of *Capital*, he returned to the question of capital itself as the contradiction, as the barrier:

> Contradiction in the capitalist mode of production: the labourers as buyers of commodities are important for the market. But as sellers of their own commodity – labour-power – capitalist society tends to keep them down to the minimum price.[59]

Finally, the whole argument was brought together in Chapter 15 of Volume III of *Capital*, 'Exposition of the Internal Contradictions of the Law'. Here, Marx indicates that the realisation of surplus-value is limited by a 'consumer power based on antagonistic conditions of distribution', that the growth of productivity 'finds itself at variance with the narrow basis on which the conditions of consumption rest', and that a continual rift ensues 'between the limited dimensions of consumption under capitalism and a production which forever tends to exceed this immanent barrier'.[60] To those who would deny that overproduction is *necessary*, he replies that they are ignoring 'barriers of this specific, capitalist mode of production':

> The contradiction of the capitalist mode of production, however, lies precisely in its tendency towards an absolute development of the productive forces, which continually come into conflict with the specific *conditions* in which capital moves, and alone can move.[61]

---

[57] Marx 1968, pp. 512–13.
[58] Marx 1968, pp. 534–5, 512–13.
[59] Marx 1957, p. 316n.
[60] Marx 1959, pp. 239–40, 251.
[61] Marx 1959, p. 252.

Thus, again and again, there is emphasis on this specific barrier of capital, the barrier to the development of productive forces which is its own relations of production. We see that surplus-value cannot be realised 'under the conditions of distribution and consumption peculiar to capitalist production', that production 'comes to a standstill at a point fixed by the production and realization of profit, and not the satisfaction of requirements'. It is all summed up in the phrase: 'The *real barrier* of capitalist production is *capital itself*'.[62]

Not only in crises, however, is the specific barrier of capital – capital and wage-labour, 'the essential relation' – manifested. That barrier 'comes to the surface' in these moments, but its specific fetter on the development of productive forces may be discerned in other ways. Capital will introduce labour-saving machinery not at the point where it involves a net saving of labour (i.e., increased social productivity), but only at the point where it involves a net saving of *paid* labour. Does this not reveal that it is not the development of social productivity (lower labour requirements) but surplus-value which is the over-riding goal of capital?[63] Similarly, the very necessity to divert capital to the sphere of circulation in order to foster the realisation of surplus-value is testimony to the manner in which the development of productive forces comes into 'conflict with the specific conditions in which capital moves, and alone can move'.[64]

Yet, we must also note the manifestations of the specific barrier from the side of wage-labour. The resistance of workers to the 'domination of capital' – the fact that capital is 'constantly compelled to wrestle with the insubordination of the workers'; the constant struggle by workers to secure the realisation of needs which capital itself generates – the struggle as the worker 'measures his demands against the capitalists' profit and demands a certain share of the surplus value created by him'; the struggle to reduce the length and intensity of the workday, to 'set limits to the tyrannical usurpations of capital'; the struggle against fixed capital and machinery which appear only as the attributes of capital; all this coincides with the very nature of the capitalist system. Here, 'all means for the development of production undergo a dialectical inversion so that they become means of domination and

---

[62] Marx 1959, pp. 253, 245.
[63] Marx 1977a, p. 515.
[64] Cf. the preceding chapter and Lebowitz 1972.

exploitation of the producers', and 'the working-out of the productive forces, of general wealth, knowledge, etc appears to the worker not as his own but as an *'alien wealth'*.[65] All this coincides with the specific barrier of capital – the capitalist relations of production.

Finally, the fact that the development of productive forces is accompanied by the displacement and redundancy of workers and that its development *to the extent* that 'it would put the bulk of the population out of the running... would cause a revolution', is another aspect of the unique capitalist barrier to the development of productive forces:

> This is another manifestation of the specific barrier of capitalist production, showing also that capitalist production is by no means an absolute form for the development of the productive forces and for the creation of wealth, but rather that at a certain point it comes into collision with this development.[66]

How impoverished, then, is the perspective of those theorists who de-emphasise this specific barrier of capital (for fear of 'underconsumptionism') in favour of explications of FROP, that particular manifestation of a general barrier. What is obscured is precisely the *differentia specifica* of capital. The point is not, however, that capital has a specific barrier rather than the general barriers; the point is – it has *both*.

The general and the specific

Despite the distinction which has been drawn between the two categories of barrier to which capital is subject, it is important to note some common elements. The existence of both barriers – those specific to capital and those which are not specific to capital – is not a chance or contingent characteristic. It is *necessary* – given either by what is common to all production or by what is specific to capital. Further, the form of a general barrier in capitalism is always its specific capitalist form, is always refracted through the prism of capitalist relations. (A general barrier *as such* exists in no particular society but

---

[65] See Lebowitz 2003.
[66] Marx 1959, p. 258. See Chapter 14 for a further discussion of the specific barrier.

is always 'within and through a specific form of society'.) Thus, the potential for confusion between the specific barrier of capital and the specific capitalist form of a general barrier is obvious.

Indeed, Marx did not distinguish adequately between general barriers and specific barriers, between specific capitalist forms of general barriers and the specific capitalist barrier; his disciples have followed him in this respect. Marx's own failings can be understood by the times in which he wrote. Struggling against theorists who either argued that there were no necessary barriers but only chance or contingent events or, on the other hand, that there were only general barriers as such, Marx's thrust was to demonstrate that there were indeed *capitalist* barriers, but the distinction between capitalist forms of general barriers and specific capitalist barriers was not clearly drawn. Nor is that surprising: there were at the time no other real forms of production before him that were clearly oriented to the development of productive forces. Thus the task of distinguishing between general and specific barriers to the development of productive forces was not one which history had placed before him. Of course, the same can not be said for his modern disciples, who continue to confound the specific and the general at a time when history (i.e., class struggle) has produced *another form of production* which is subject to general barriers to the development of productive forces, subject indeed to its own special barrier, but *not* subject to capital's specific barrier (at least as is manifested in overproduction of commodities).[67]

The failure to distinguish between specific and general barriers has meant that both have tended to disappear from theoretical view into an indeterminate void. It has meant, for example, that the very concept of a general barrier emanating from nature or human beings has appeared as something which is *not* a barrier for capital and as distinctly 'non-'Marxian'; and, thus the very concept of a natural or ecological crisis becomes the province of Malthus, the Club of Rome, petty-bourgeois despair and capitalist conspiracy. On the other side, the specific capitalist forms of general barriers have displaced the specific capitalist barrier – inexorably rising organic compositions of capital, vanishing reserve armies of labour and FROP take the foreground in place of class struggle; and the charge of 'neo-Ricardianism' with respect to struggles

---

[67] For a consideration of the specific barrier of 'actually existing socialism' and its relation to economic crises, see Lebowitz 1985; 1986; 2000.

within distribution is made by those who have *unwittingly* retreated to organic chemistry.

The failure to distinguish between the specific and the general has also meant that their interaction and interpenetration could not be explored. The manner in which each necessarily passes over into the other is hidden. The drive of capital to expand, on the one hand, and the drive of workers in capitalism to realise the needs which capital itself generates, on the other, produces the tendency for capital to introduce machinery which increases productivity and brings with it growing raw-material requirements. The specific here passes into the general – there is *both* the tendency for production to expand more rapidly than the market and also for the values of raw materials to rise, the value-composition of capital to grow and the rate of profit to fall. Describing the crises of the 1840s, Marx noted that 'the rising demand for raw materials naturally went hand in hand with a market flooded with manufactures'.[68] Capital, in short, grows by leaps and bounds and 'comes up against no barriers but those presented by the availability of raw materials and the extent of sales outlets'.

Thus, the emergence of the general barriers within capitalism has its roots in capitalist relations of production; and, precisely because the specific *necessarily* passes over into the general, it is impossible to accept a radical-ecology position that does not begin with the need to dispose of capitalist relations of production. Of course, within actually existing socialism, there too the general emerges out of *that* specific (as, indeed, it must in every case – since there is no *production in general*); yet, as noted earlier, the general does not everywhere have the particular inverted and antagonistic character which marks its capitalist form.

Similarly, the general necessarily passes over into the specific. The decline of unemployment and the relative underproduction of raw materials tend toward a fall in the rate of profit. This is the specific form of general barriers. But the response of capital is not *merely* to the form of the general barrier itself, but is a response within its own relations of production; there is the attempt to drive down real wages and to increase the length and intensity of the work-day (for the working class as a whole) in order to increase the rate of surplus value and thereby posit capital's growth again. Thus, the potential result of

---

[68] Marx 1959, p. 122.

the general barrier is the intensification of class struggle (as the general returns to the specific); the long down-swing of a Kondratieff-type wave may provide a conjuncture particularly favourable to revolutionary activity.

Of course, it is *possible* that either the specific or the general barrier may, in fact, be the basis of a limit to capital, that is, that capital as such may not be able to transcend it. However, we can not establish the *necessity* that any such barrier will be a limit, given our understanding of capital's tendency to drive beyond all barriers. The only limit that Marx identified to capital was the proletariat; and a necessary (though not sufficient) condition was that the proletariat recognise the barriers in capital's own nature, recognise that the real barrier is capital itself, namely, the specific barrier of capital. For this reason, emphasis on the specific barrier of capital, capital's unique tendency to hold back the development of productive forces and the realisation of needs, strikes directly at the heart of capital.

How, then, do we situate the *general* barrier – especially the general barrier of nature? Despite the potential noted in the passage of the general to the specific, it must be recognised that the very character of the general barrier permits an ensuing crisis to be viewed as a crisis of the 'economy' rather than of capital, as a crisis requiring 'sacrifice' by all; in short, there is nothing inherent in the general barrier which challenges the hegemony of capital.

Realisation of the potential present in the passage of the general to the specific requires that the roots of the general in the specific (that is, in capitalist relations of production) be revealed and, further, that the general barrier as such be distinguished from the specific antagonistic and inverted capitalist form in which it presents itself. It calls for the demonstration that the problem is not 'production as such' but its capitalist form; that capitalism develops only 'by simultaneously undermining the original sources of all wealth – the soil and the worker;' and, here, the general barrier may indeed prove to be part of the basis for a limit to capital.[69]

---

[69] James O'Connor commented in a letter that substantially different political perspectives may emerge from one's view as to whether capitalist relations of production 'hold back' development of productive forces – or whether they 'destroy' them.

In any event, the separate existence of the general barrier cannot be denied; nor can it continue to be presented in FROP-form as the specific barrier. Rather, it is necessary to be precise in distinguishing those aspects of the current crisis which immediately manifest the specific barrier of capital and those which are the capitalist manifestations of general barriers. For, it is clear, the current crisis is a unity of the specific and the general.

Chapter Nine
Understanding Sweezy

Biographical note

Described by the *Wall Street Journal* as 'the "Dean" of radical economics', Paul Sweezy has more than any other single person kept Marxist economics alive in North America.[1] One work would be sufficient to have achieved this – *The Theory of Capitalist Development* (first published in 1942). During the period of the 1950s and 60s, this was the book to which one turned to learn about Marxist economics. As Meghnad Desai testified years later (in the Introduction to his own text in Marxian economics):

> There was in those days one book that students could read if they wanted to acquaint themselves with Marx's thought. *The Theory of Capitalist Development*, when all is said and done, still remains a classic introduction to Marxian economics.... It was a definitive statement of a certain period about how Marx and his system were a key to the understanding of capitalism. While the book comes in for much casual criticism today, Paul Sweezy can be credited for having kept the eventual prospect of a revival of Marxian economics alive.[2]

---

[1] Lifshultz 1974, p. 54.
[2] Desai 1979, pp. 1–2.

Similarly, two German writers, Gerd Hardach and Dieter Karras, commented in 1974 that 'as an analytical and exhaustive resumé of the history of Marxist theory up to the 1930s, Sweezy's book is still without any rivals today'. Lending support to Desai's point, they noted that, on the eve of the rebirth of West-German Marxism, the 1959 German edition of the book 'made available to the German reader a theoretical tradition which had been very largely produced in German-speaking areas and then subsequently effectively suppressed by fascism and the post-war restoration'.[3]

Yet, *The Theory of Capitalist Development* was not only an introduction to Marxian economics and a transmission of a theoretical tradition. Sweezy also initially formulated there his general theory of capitalist stagnation. It is a theory which has been offered to explain not only the Depression conditions of its origin but also the postwar boom (the 'Golden Age') and the subsequent crisis of the 1970s and 80s.

More than the author of a single text, however, Paul Sweezy has probed for answers about society and social change in many directions. His questions in relation to Maurice Dobb's *Studies in the Development of Capitalism* in 1950 triggered a major debate on the transition from feudalism to capitalism whose echoes reverberate today – just as a later exchange with Charles Bettelheim would pose critical questions about the transition to socialism. From his book on the Cuban Revolution (with associate Leo Huberman) to his emphasis on capitalism as a world system to his essays on postrevolutionary societies, Sweezy has addressed the important questions of our time; and no one could say (as he has about neoclassical economists) that he has concerned himself with 'smaller and decreasingly significant questions' with the result that there is 'a truly stupifying gap between the questions posed and the techniques employed to answer them'.[4]

For many, though, it is for his joint work with Paul Baran, *Monopoly Capital*, that he will be remembered. Begun in the mid-50s, a time of 'full-fledged McCarthyism' when 'it was practically impossible for Marxist dialogue to exist with the U.S. academy', the book became upon its publication in 1966 the introduction to radical economic analysis for an entire generation of

---

[3] Hardach, Karras and Fine 1978, p. 60.
[4] Paul M. Sweezy, 'Toward a Critique of Economics,' *Monthly Review* (January 1970) reprinted in Sweezy 1972, p. 58.

university students and an important influence on the New Left of the period.[5] But Sweezy has never rested on his laurels. In *Monthly Review* (the magazine founded in 1949 by Sweezy and Huberman), he and his co-editor Harry Magdoff continued to analyse current economic developments and to explore their theoretical significance. After over a half-century of Marxist scholarship, the Dean of radical economics continued to guide (and to receive graciously) younger colleagues and students.

None of this is the trajectory which could have been predicted at the time of Sweezy's birth in New York City on 10 April 1910. Sweezy's father was a banker, one of five vice presidents of the First National Bank (a predecessor of the Citibank), and Paul had the background appropriate to the scion of a wealthy family. He attended Phillips Exeter Academy and then went on to Harvard (as had his brother Alan before him). During his time there from 1928 to 1932, he edited the *Harvard Crimson* and was trained in the standard neoclassical economics.[6]

There was no sign here of his future path. And, there certainly was no indication that this banker's son would become the object of a McCarthyite witch hunt by a New Hampshire subversive activities committee. Questioned in 1953, he was found guilty of contempt of court and sentenced to jail. While out on bail, he appealed against the charge which was ultimately overturned in 1957 by the US Supreme Court in one of the landmark decisions on McCarthyism.[7]

The year of his graduation, 1932, was, of course, a time of troubles. The period was one of stock market crash, bank failures, the onset of the Depression of the 1930s, the rise of Hitler and the First Soviet Five-Year Plan. And, as for so many others, these events represented a challenge to the education Sweezy had received. What, after all, did this have to do with the neoclassical economics that he had studied at Harvard?

Sweezy recalls arriving in London in 1932 for a graduate year at the London School of Economics with a feeling of 'confusion edged with resentment at the irrelevance of what I had spent the last four years trying to learn'. There, however, he found graduate students actively debating the issues of the day,

---

[5] Sweezy 1987, p. 15.
[6] Michael Hillard, 'Harry Magdoff and Paul Sweezy: Biographical Notes', in Resnick and Wolff (eds.) 1985, p. 400.
[7] Lifshultz 1974, p. 55; Sweezy 1987, p. 8.

a 'continuous state of intellectual and political ferment;' and, it was there that he first came into contact with Marxism. He returned to Harvard after that year 'a convinced but very ignorant Marxist'.[8]

Changes had begun at Harvard as well. Graduate students and younger faculty were beginning to take an interest in Marxism. (Among those with whom Sweezy was to have many discussions about Marxism was Shigeto Tsuru, who later contributed an Appendix to *The Theory of Capitalist Development* comparing the reproduction schemes of Quesnay, Marx and Keynes.)[9] Perhaps the most significant development for Sweezy, however, was that he met and became a student of Joseph Schumpeter who had joined the Harvard faculty in 1932. The atmosphere around Schumpeter was one certain to stimulate a young economist: he organised informal seminars and discussion groups and attracted economists from around the world. What Sweezy received there, along with others in the 'Schumpeter circle', was encouragement and an atmosphere of intellectual clash and excitement. He was to describe this period subsequently as the most stimulating of his life.[10]

As it happens, Sweezy took only one formal course from Schumpeter, a small graduate seminar of four or five people which included Oscar Lange and which Wassily Leontief also attended. Yet, he went on to become Schumpeter's assistant in an introductory graduate course in economic theory and a very close friend.[11] With Schumpeter on his thesis committee, he completed his doctoral dissertation in 1937 on the coal cartel during the English Industrial Revolution (for which he was awarded the David A. Wells Prize for best essay in economics by the Harvard Economics Department).

During this time, Sweezy worked at becoming 'a self-educated Marxist'. In this, too, Schumpeter was central. For, despite his own diametrically opposite political perspective, Schumpeter was 'a unique figure. He understood the importance of Marxism'. A contemporary of Hilferding and Austro-Marxists such as Otto Bauer, he had constructed his own theory of capitalism as a deliberate alternative to Marxism. Thus, 'he paid Marxism the compliment

---

[8] Hillard, in Resnick and Wolff (eds.) 1985, p. 400; Sweezy 1981, pp. 12–13.
[9] Sweezy 1956, p. vi.
[10] Sweezy 1951, pp. xxii–xxv.
[11] Sweezy 1987, p. 5.

of understanding and recognizing that it was the most important intellectual trend of the time'.[12]

In 1938, Sweezy became an instructor at Harvard, teaching a course on the economics of socialism (in which he had previously assisted). Attempting to increase the level of treatment of Marxism in the course, he proceeded to teach himself and to absorb the European (especially German) traditions in Marxist thought. *The Theory of Capitalist Development* was written over these years – 'started more or less as an effort in self-clarification'. Completed soon after the United States entered World War II, the book was published shortly before he went into the US Army in 1942.[13]

The early work

Yet, *The Theory of Capitalist Development* was not Sweezy's first book or contribution. In a study undertaken in 1937 for the National Resources Committee (a New Deal agency), he demonstrated that, contrary to the Berle and Means classification of a substantial number of leading US corporations as 'management-controlled', it was possible to identify eight clearly definable 'interest groups', industrial and financial alliances among the large corporations.[14] To understand the control of corporations, Sweezy stressed the importance of a 'knowledge of the general policies of the companies and individuals involved'.[15] Citing the policies of the investment banking firm of J.P. Morgan & Co. and its alliance with the First National Bank of New York (his father's bank) in the first and most important of the interest groups, he proposed that not only stock ownership but also banking and underwriting relations were critical in tracing industrial and financial alliances.[16]

Within a few years, however, Sweezy proceeded to explain that the dominant role that had been played by the investment banker in the consolidation of the large firms had now declined. In part the result of the sharp decline in economic expansion during the Depression, an important

---

[12] Ibid.
[13] Sweezy 1987, p. 2; Hillard, in Resnick and Wolff (eds.) 1985, p. 401.
[14] 'Interest Groups in the American Economy', in National Resources Committee, *The Structure of the American Economy*, Part 1, Appendix 13 (Washington 1939) reprinted in Sweezy 1953.
[15] Sweezy 1953, p. 162.
[16] Sweezy 1953, pp. 163, 168.

explanation was 'the vast internal financial resources' at the disposal of existing large corporations which significantly reduced their necessity to resort to the capital market. Thus, the dominance of financial over industrial capital could be seen as a 'temporary stage' of capitalist development.[17] It was a point subsequently underlined in his criticism of Hilferding in *The Theory of Capitalist Development*, where Sweezy stressed the growing importance of internal corporate financing and his preference for Lenin's concept of 'monopoly capital' over that of Hilferding's 'finance capital'.[18]

Monopoly was the theme as well in Sweezy's thesis, published in 1938 as *Monopoly and Competition in the English Coal Trade, 1550–1850*. Using the records of the coal owners, Sweezy drew upon current theoretical developments in the theory of imperfect competition and applied the microeconomist's tools (in a manner to be discovered many years later by the 'New Economic History') to explain the behaviour of the owners and, in particular, the reasons for the emergence of excess capacity in the industry in the nineteenth century. A demand curve facing producers which was relatively elastic above the existing price and relatively inelastic below that price tended to generate, he argued, high profits and a relatively stable price. Under the existing cartel arrangements, his model also predicted 'growing individual plants with a *tendency* towards more growth than is warranted by the increase in demand'.[19]

What was particular to the early nineteenth-century English coal combination, however, now had become general as the result of the growth of large-scale production which generated a tendency for 'productive capacity to outrun the market'. The threat of cutthroat competition (and its implications for profits) engendered combination – but the fostering of monopoly would itself 'serve further to contract markets and outlets for investment'.[20]

The 'kinked demand curve' described (and presented complete with the discontinuity in the marginal revenue curve) in this study was subsequently to become well-known and influential as the result of Sweezy's article,

---

[17] Paul M. Sweezy, 'The Decline of the Investment Banker', *Antioch Review* (Spring 1941) in Sweezy 1953, pp. 192, 195.
[18] Sweezy 1956, pp. 166–9.
[19] Sweezy 1938, p. 119.
[20] Sweezy 1938, pp. 148–9.

'Demand Under Conditions of Oligopoly', published in the following year.[21] Yet, the extension to current policy implications had occurred first in Sweezy's comments upon a paper by A.P. Lerner, 'The Relation of Wage Policies and Price Policies', at the December 1938 meetings of the American Economics Association. There, he stressed the point subsequently made in his article that under conditions of the kinked demand curve the only effect of an increase in wages may be reduced profits (rather than a change in the short-run equilibrium of price and output).[22]

The *Theory of Capitalist Development*

When Sweezy published his *Theory of Capitalist Development*, he had already established a reputation as an important young scholar as the result of his essay on the oligopolistic demand curve. With this book, however, he added significantly to that reputation. For the book introduced many to a tradition of Marxist scholarship hitherto inaccessible to Anglophones. To this day, it is often remembered for opening up the discussion of the problem of the 'transformation' from Marxian values to prices and for its consideration of the work of Ladislaus von Bortkiewicz on this question. Yet, on the Marxian questions of value theory, the falling tendency of the rate of profit and crisis theory, Sweezy's contribution was easily as important.

Sweezy is credited with having introduced into the discussion of Marx's theory of value the distinction between the 'quantitative-value problem' and the 'qualitative-value problem'. Despite the break with the English Marxist tradition of Maurice Dobb which stressed the basic continuity between the labour-cost approach of Smith, Ricardo and Marx (and, later, Sraffa), however, there has been a tendency to lump Sweezy together with Dobb as part of a single 'Anglo-American' tradition which effectively treats the Marxian and Ricardian theories as identical.[23]

That is, simply, incorrect. Indeed, the failure to understand Sweezy's early attempt to distance Marx's value theory from that of classical political economy left subsequent commentators unprepared for Sweezy's 1974

---

[21] Sweezy 1939.
[22] Sweezy 1939, p. 406. Information on the 1938 American Economics Association meetings comes from the Proceedings and Paul M. Sweezy.
[23] De Vroey 1981, p. 173; see also Elson 1979, pp. 116–22ff.

critique of Dobb's *Theories of Value and Distribution since Adam Smith: Ideology and Economic Theory*.[24] Criticising Dobb for making 'Marx seem much more like his predecessors and successors than he really was', Sweezy argued that the scope and depth of Marx's originality and his break with the classical tradition were lost in Dobb's account of the Ricardo-Marx-Sraffa tradition. In short, 'to speak of a Ricardo-Marx tradition can only be misleading for both bourgeois and Marxist economists'.[25]

The point, though, was not at all new: Sweezy had begun his discussion of value thirty-two years earlier by stressing 'the sharp break which divides his [Marx's] analysis from that of the classical school'.[26] And, central was the distinction between the 'qualitative-value problem' and the 'quantitative-value problem'. 'No longer can the economist afford to confine his attention to the quantitative relations arising from commodity production; he must also direct his attention to the character of social relations which underlie the commodity form'.[27]

Marx's distinction between 'abstract' labour and 'concrete' labour was at the core of the 'qualitative-value problem'. Abstract labour (or labour in general) was the labour represented in the value of the commodity; yet the critics of Marx's value theory had said 'hardly a word about abstract labor'.[28] The very concept of abstract labour, however, went beyond the forms of value on the surface, individual commodity prices, to consider the relations among human beings which were necessarily hidden by the commodity-form; at the centre of the qualitative-value problem was the 'fetish character of commodities'.

It was a clear *although unacknowledged* break with the position of Dobb. In elevating the qualitative-value problem, Sweezy cited as support 'the excellent note on value theory by Alfred Lowe, 'Mr. Dobb and Marx's Theory of Value''.[29] But 'Alfred Lowe' was Shigeto Tsuru – to whom Sweezy acknowledged his 'greatest debt' for many discussions.[30]

And Tsuru *had* openly criticised Dobb. He had argued that Dobb's very conception of value theory in his *Political Economy and Capitalism* [1937]

---

[24] See, for example, McFarlane 1982, p. 139.
[25] Sweezy 1974, pp. 482–3.
[26] Sweezy 1956, p. 23.
[27] Sweezy 1956, p. 24.
[28] Sweezy 1956, p. 34.
[29] Sweezy 1956, p. 25n.
[30] Sweezy 1956, p. vi.

'presupposes already a method quite opposite to that of Marx'.[31] Citing Hilferding's argument in the response to Böhm-Bawerk (which Sweezy later was to make widely available), Tsuru proposed that the essence of Marx's value analysis was 'the *qualitative* statement specifying the social relation of the capitalist mode of production'.[32] Why, after all, had Marx underlined 'the importance of distinguishing the two-fold character of labour in the commodity production, as contrasted with Mr. Dobb's vague definition of labour as "the expenditure of a given quantum of human energy"'?

Rejecting Dobb's argument that a theory of value must be quantitative in form and capable of expression in terms of 'quantitative entities in the real world', Tsuru argued that this was

> an insuperable task. For such an attempt has to involve factors both apparent and essential embracing the economic system as a whole. Society is the only accountant of socially necessary labor time.[33]

For Tsuru (whose honours thesis at Harvard College had explored Marx's methodology and commodity fetishism), Marx's 'insistence on the necessity of distinguishing between value and value-form' were critical; Dobb's focus on quantitative issues and distribution, on the other hand, was little different from that of classical political economy and, indeed, in some respects approached the 'pre-Marxian complacency' of Ricardo and John Stuart Mill.[34]

Sweezy's adoption of this distinction between qualitative and quantitative thus foreshadowed the subsequent debates over value which emerged among neo-Ricardians and Marxists in the wake of Sraffa's work. Indeed, Sweezy's discussion of the 'quantitative-value problem' also diverged significantly from the classical value tradition of embodied concrete labour in his stress upon the importance of 'demand'. Different traditions of value theory, then, were transmitted by Dobb and Sweezy, and this may help to explain why Sraffa's work subsequently had so much less of an impact among North-American Marxists.

The significance attributed to 'the falling rate of profit' (FROP) was another such distinction between Sweezy and Dobb (and the classical tradition).

---

[31] Tsuru, 'Mr. Dobb and Marx's Theory of Value', in Tsuru 1976, p. 99.
[32] Tsuru 1976, pp. 100–2.
[33] Tsuru 1976, p. 103.
[34] Tsuru 1976, pp. 101–4.

Identifying Dobb as an author who had 'concluded that Marx meant the law of the falling tendency of the rate of profit to be the primary explanatory principle so far as crises are concerned', Sweezy rejected this conclusion on two important grounds.[35] Firstly, emphasising Marx's consideration of 'counteracting tendencies', he questioned the theoretical foundations of the FROP tendency with respect to the assumption that the organic composition of capital *necessarily* increased more than the rate of surplus-value; the formulation, he proposed, was 'not very convincing'.[36]

Just as critical, however, was that Sweezy argued that Marx's view of crises and business cycles differed significantly from those of mainstream economists who assumed that 'the crisis is not the result but rather the cause of a shortage of effective demand'.[37] Implicit in the theory of value, he argued, was a theory of crisis which emanated from the inability of capitalists to sell commodities at their value.[38] And, at the root of such crises was the contradiction between the production of use-values and the goal of producing surplus-value, the fundamental contradiction of capitalism.[39]

This alternative explanation Sweezy labelled an 'underconsumption' theory of capitalist crises, and he proceeded to show its undeniable presence in Marx's texts. Yet, there was a critical gap – the theory had never been fully developed by Marx, and subsequent Marxists (like Rosa Luxemburg) who had turned their attention to the question had not succeeded in constructing a logical and detailed theory. The result was that 'the outstanding present-day English Marxist economist, Maurice Dobb, assigns a role to underconsumption which is distinctly secondary to that of the falling tendency of the rate of profit'.[40]

Completed, however, the underconsumption theory 'would have been of primary importance in the overall picture of the capitalist economy'.[41] To supplement Marx's work by carefully formulating the Marxian underconsumption theory, then, was the project Sweezy undertook.

---

[35] Sweezy 1956, pp. 147–8.
[36] Sweezy 1956, pp. 102–4.
[37] Sweezy 1956, p. 155.
[38] Sweezy 1956, p. 146.
[39] Sweezy 1956, p. 172.
[40] Sweezy 1956, p. 179.
[41] Sweezy 1956, p. 178.

The general theory of capitalist stagnation

'The real task of an underconsumption theory,' Sweezy proposed, 'is to demonstrate that capitalism has an inherent *tendency* to expand the capacity to produce consumption goods more rapidly than the demand for consumption goods.' Such a tendency may be manifested in two forms. Where an increase in capacity leads to overproduction and then curtailment of production, 'the tendency in question manifests itself in a crisis'. In a second case, however, capacity is *not* expanded 'because it is realized that the additional capacity would be redundant relative to the demand for the commodities it could produce. In this case, the tendency does not manifest itself in a crisis, but rather in stagnation of production'.[42]

As Sweezy noted, in *either* case, the existence of such a tendency significantly alters the fundamental questions economists must pose. Marx's comments in *Capital* imply, Sweezy argued, that

> stagnation of production, in the sense of less-than-capacity utilization of productive resources, is to be regarded as the normal state of affairs under capitalist conditions. If this view is adopted, the whole crisis problem appears in a new light. Emphasis shifts from the question: 'What brings on crisis and depression?' to its opposite: 'What brings on expansion?'.[43]

Here was the core of Sweezy's argument. And, it is one to which he has returned in various forms over the years. As he commented in 1980,

> If a monopoly capitalist economy tends toward stagnation – in the same sense that it always used to be assumed that a competitive capitalist economy tends toward full employment – then the problem to be explained is periods of sustained expansion and buoyancy.[44]

Much, indeed, of his work can seen as a variation around this theme, which was to become a *Leitmotiv*.

Actually, it is more accurate to describe Sweezy's argument in *The Theory of Capitalist Development* as an overaccumulation theory of crisis than as one of underconsumption. In the model presented, crisis is not triggered by an

---

[42] Sweezy 1956, p. 180.
[43] Sweezy 1956, p. 177.
[44] Sweezy 1980, p. 3.

increase in the rate of exploitation (rate of surplus-value) or by inadequate effective demand. Rather, it is the result of excessive additions to capacity: a relative expansion of fixed capital occurs (in his Appendix, see this version of his argument) because of an increase in the propensity of capitalists to invest and a tendency to substitute machinery for direct labour.

Assuming a constant relation between additions to means of production and potential additions to output, the expansion of capacity tends to exceed that which would be warranted: the actual increase in the demand for consumption goods is insufficient to justify those previous investment decisions. In this argument (as in early writings of Kalecki), the essential recognition is that investment is not only a component of aggregate demand; it also, importantly, increases productive capacity.

The central problem in the argument, however, is that, if the sector producing means of production expands sufficiently, there *will* be adequate income generated in that sector to warrant capacity increases in the consumption-goods sector – a point not recognised explicitly in the model. Sweezy's crisis theory then amounted to the argument that this condition would not *normally* be satisfied; thus, the general tendency would be one toward underconsumption/overaccumulation.

To understand why equilibrating growth in Department I (the sector producing means of production) was seen as a *special* case, we have to go back to Sweezy's comments on the argument of Tugan-Baranowsky. As Sweezy noted, Tugan demonstrated that the balance could easily be achieved if 'social production were organized in accordance with a plan'. In short, 'if the proportional division of output is precisely that which is prescribed by the equilibrium condition for expanded reproduction, then supply and demand must be in exact balance'.[45] Yet, such a condition as the *normal* case was contrary to the specific characteristic of capitalism – that it is a system in which the very purpose of production is not the harmonisation of production but the expansion of capital.

This did not mean that the prescribed equilibrium condition could not be achieved; it *could* – under special circumstances. (Indeed, in Sweezy's Appendix model, the general tendency would not exist at all if national income were growing at an increasing rate, which he suggested might be characteristic of

---

[45] Sweezy 1956, p. 166.

a 'young' capitalist country.) As Marx had done in presenting his discussion of the tendency of the rate of profit to fall, Sweezy followed his discussion of the general tendency toward underconsumption/overaccumulation with a consideration of 'counteracting forces'. Precisely because there *were* such counteracting causes, Sweezy proposed 'that for long periods the latter (tendency to underconsumption) may remain latent and inoperative'.[46]

The establishment of new industries was one such important counteracting force. Reminiscent of Schumpeter's business-cycle theory, insofar as the period of initial investments did not add correspondingly to output of consumption goods, the tendency was suspended; only when this process was completed and new consumption goods could come on stream was the general relation between additions to means of production and additions to consumption demand re-established. In this case (as well as that of faulty investment and state expenditures), the counteracting tendency exists to the extent that there is an increase in aggregate demand but not a corresponding increase in capacity.

Yet, Sweezy proposed that the strength of new industries as a counteracting force was dependent upon the relative share of total investment absorbed; although new industries would always continue to appear, their relative importance would decline as a country industrialised. 'One of the most powerful forces counteracting the ever-present tendency to underconsumption', thus, was disappearing.[47] It was not, however, the only such sea change.

A declining rate of population growth meant the dramatic eclipse of yet another of developed capitalism's critical counteracting forces. In stressing the relation between declining population growth and stagnation (a relation epitomised as 'the law of inverse relation between population growth and the tendency to underconsumption'), Sweezy was, of course, by no means alone.[48] Alvin Hansen's 1938 Presidential Address to the American Economics Association, 'Economic Progress and Declining Population Growth', had put this issue high on the list of explanations of the continuing sluggishness of the 1930s.[49]

---

[46] Sweezy 1956, p. 180.
[47] Sweezy 1956, p. 220.
[48] Sweezy 1956, p. 224.
[49] Hansen 1939.

Yet, rather than emphasising the benefical effects upon *demand* as Hansen had, Sweezy identified rapid population growth as extremely favourable to the expansion of capitalism because it ensured available reserves of labour. With the pressure to substitute machinery for labour thereby reduced, it followed from Sweezy's specific model that the danger of underconsumption was not present.

In the weakening, then, of these counteracting forces, Sweezy found an explanation for the progressive strengthening of the tendency to underconsumption. The prospect for mature and developed capitalist countries, thus, was increasingly one of chronic stagnation.[50] 'So far as capitalism is concerned,' he commented, 'we are undoubtedly justified in calling underconsumption a disease of old age'.[51]

But, what about the role of monopoly? Given Sweezy's earlier work, it appears as a strange failure that the growth of monopoly plays no role in this conclusion. After all, from the rigid prices and absence of price competition under conditions of oligopoly to the 'vast internal financial resources' of the large firms to the significance (noted in his thesis) of large-scale industry and combination in fostering excess capacity and the contraction of investment outlets, there was an explanation both for a growing tendency to underconsumption/overaccumulation and for this to be increasingly manifested in stagnation rather than crisis.

The *Theory of Capitalist Development* was not silent on the question of monopoly. In a later section, Sweezy described the tendency for higher prices and profits in the concentrated sectors, the disinclination to expand output in these sectors (because of the potential effect upon the profit rate), an increased bias toward labour-saving innovation, and the possibility that the growth of monopoly would lead to an increased rate of surplus-value thereby strengthening the tendency to underconsumption.[52] The effect of monopoly, in this respect, was clearly to *intensify* the inherent tendency of capitalism. On the other hand, Sweezy identified the growth of selling costs as the result of the non-price competition characteristic of concentrated industries as a counteracting force; this was the only one of the monopoly-

---

[50] Sweezy 1956, p. 226.
[51] Sweezy 1956, p. 189.
[52] Sweezy 1956, pp. 274–7.

related characteristics considered explicitly in the explanation of the general tendency to stagnation.[53]

Why was the discussion of monopoly not at the *centre* of Sweezy's theory of underconsumption? Because *something else* was there – Keynes and the secular-stagnation argument of his foremost North-American champion, Alvin Hansen (who joined the Harvard faculty in 1937). For, without question, Sweezy was profoundly influenced by Keynes and Hansen. As he noted in 1946, 'the sense of liberation and the intellectual stimulation that *The General Theory* immediately produced' may only be appreciated fully by those trained as economists in the period before 1936.[54] Similarly, reviewing Hansen's *Full Employment or Stagnation?* in 1938, he described the latter's analysis as 'brilliant and profound'; and, several years later, he hailed Hansen's contribution to a 'rebirth of scientific economics'.'[55] Certainly, the influence, in particular, of Hansen can be seen – not only in *The Theory of Capitalist Development* but also in a volume published in 1938 in which Sweezy collaborated, *An Economic Program for American Democracy*.[56]

Was Sweezy at the time, then, simply a left-wing Keynesian? Although there were elements in *The Theory of Capitalist Development* clearly drawing upon Keynes and Hansen, that is not sufficient to yield the conclusion that Sweezy can be considered a Keynesian – any more than Marx can be considered a Ricardian for similar reasons.[57] At issue is the framework within which those elements were incorporated. While Sweezy followed Hansen, for example, in stressing the importance of declining population growth, he offered an entirely different explanation – just as Marx had with the classical theories such as the falling rate of profit. More than anything else, Sweezy's work appears as a *critique* of the Keynesians from a Marxian perspective.

Rather than focussing upon the Keynesian elements in Sweezy, the real question is how Keynes, working within the neoclassical framework, came up with an argument so easily absorbed within a Marxian framework. As Marx had argued that the political economists did not understand the underlying

---

[53] Sweezy 1956, p. 283.
[54] Sweezy, 'John Maynard Keynes', *Science & Society* (Fall 1946) in Sweezy 1953, p. 257n.
[55] Sweezy, 'Hansen and the Crisis of Capitalism' in Sweezy 1953, pp. 268–70.
[56] Gilbert 1938. See the discussion in Lekachman 1966, pp. 154–6.
[57] Sweezy himself suggested this analogy in Sweezy 1981, p. 34.

basis of their own laws (theories), so also did Sweezy consistently stress that the Keynesians knew *what* was occurring in the Depression but did not understand *why*. ('Hansen understands very well *what* is wrong with our present-day economy, and that is all to the good. But ask the question of this book: *why* have matters turned out as they have? You will not find much by way of answer.')[58] The adequacy of proposed Keynesian solutions was, of course, the central problem.

The Keynesians, Sweezy indicated, did not see that the troubles were 'manifestations of the real nature of the capitalist system itself'.[59] Thus, while Keynes 'was able to demonstrate that his fellow economists, by their unthinking acceptance of Say's Law, were in effect asserting the impossibility of what was actually happening', Sweezy argued that Keynes was unable to proceed to a critique of existing society. Why? Because Keynes attributed the problems to 'a failure of intelligence and not to the breakdown of a social system'.[60] 'In general,' Sweezy commented, 'one can say that to the Keynesians the crisis of capitalism appears as a crisis of intelligence'.[61]

Nevertheless, Sweezy emphasised that, when it came to a clarification of the 'functioning of the capitalist mechanism', Marxists had much 'to learn from the work of Keynes and his followers'.[62] Indeed, some of Marx's work, he argued, 'takes on a new meaning and fits into its proper place when read in the light of the Keynesian contributions'.[63] And, he continued to stress that Marxists should not be afraid to learn from Keynes since 'most of the valuable Keynesian insights can be added' to the basic structure of Marxism.[64]

Yet, it was not many years before Sweezy would identify problems in *The Theory of Capitalist Development* as related to the general Keynesian intellectual environment in which he had been working. Initially, as he indicated in a 1950 response to Evsey Domar and several Japanese critics of his book, Sweezy declared his exposition of underconsumption crises in terms of net aggregates to be 'one of the weakest parts of the book' and argued that his

---

[58] Sweezy 1953, p. 272.
[59] Sweezy 1953, p. 273.
[60] Sweezy 1953, p. 258.
[61] Sweezy, 'Marxian and Orthodox Economics,' *Science & Society* (Summer 1947), reprinted in Sweezy 1953, p. 313.
[62] Sweezy 1953, p. 315.
[63] Sweezy 1953, p. 261.
[64] Sweezy 1987, p. 18.

aggregative analysis (attributable to Keynesian influence) was not suitable for exploring the question of underconsumption.[65] In subsequent years, however, he became increasingly critical of Keynesian theory's failure precisely because it was 'wholly on the macro level'.[66] The missing micro-element was that of monopoly.

The general theory in the Golden Age[67]

Upon Sweezy's return to Harvard after the War, it became clear that there were no prospects of being rehired with tenure after the completion of his existing contract. Although supported by Schumpeter for a tenure-track position, 'there was never any chance that they would take a Marxist'. Accordingly, financially secure enough that he did not have to rely upon an academic salary, Sweezy resigned his position and proceeded to work with Leo Huberman to establish *Monthly Review*.[68]

In its opening issue in May 1949, Sweezy noted recent government evidence confirming

> a phenomenon of great and growing importance, the extent to which the huge corporate giants now finance their expansion internally...and have consequently become independent of the capital markets generally and of banker control in particular.[69]

Moreover, he repeated his argument that the normal tendency of American capitalism was one of chronic depression and mass unemployment.

In the context of the postwar boom, however, Sweezy now had to explain why things looked different. It was not difficult – the massive military expenditures for World War II and the armaments build-up of the postwar period. Depression or stagnation, rather than a full employment equilibrium,

---

[65] Sweezy, 'A Reply to Critics', *The Economic Review* (April 1950), reprinted in Sweezy 1953, pp. 353–4, 360.

[66] Sweezy 1980, p. 3.

[67] An excellent collection of essays by (among others) Sweezy, Kalecki and Steindl relevant to the discussion in this section may be found in Foster and Szlajfer (eds.) 1984.

[68] Sweezy 1987, p. 4; Hillard, in Resnick and Wolff (eds.) 1985, p. 402.

[69] Sweezy, 'Recent Developments in American Capitalism', *Monthly Review* (May 1949), in Sweezy 1953, p. 118.

he argued in a 1952 restatement of his theory, must be regarded as the normal condition of developed capitalism; yet, new industries were a central factor capable of 'taking up the slack'. If these new industries are 'sufficiently numerous and important they may keep the system going at or near full capacity'.[70] In the development of the military-industrial complex, Sweezy had found a new and important counteracting force making the tendency to underconsumption 'latent and inoperative' in the postwar period.[71]

In the course of the Golden Age, however, Sweezy's theory was to undergo a quite significant shift. For a new element was to enter. Describing his theory in 1980, he indicated that it

> draws upon or combines a line of thought which originated with Michal Kalecki and attained its most complete expression in the work of Josef Steindl, published in the early 1950s, *Maturity and Stagnation in American Capitalism*.

Despite the 'strange failure of Keynesian theory' to make the connection between monopoly (at the micro-level) and stagnation (at the macro-level), Kalecki *had* integrated the two. 'And of course it was Kalecki's lead that Steindl followed up.'[72]

This acknowledgement of theoretical influence had appeared earlier in Paul Baran's and his book *Monopoly Capital* (which Sweezy described as a 'simpler version' of the Kalecki/Steindl argument). There, Baran and Sweezy praised Kalecki and Steindl for their integration of monopoly at the micro-level into their macro-models. And, they noted, 'anyone familiar with the work of Kalecki and Steindl will readily recognize that the authors of the present work owe a great deal to them'.[73]

Without question, the catalyst was Steindl's book, which Sweezy described in his 1971 Marshall Lecture as 'one of the most important and most neglected works of political economy of the last half century'.[74] That appreciation is recorded as well in his 1954 review of Steindl's book, where Sweezy proposed that, 'in successfully linking up the theory of investment with the theory

---

[70] Sweezy, 'A Crucial Difference Between Capitalism and Socialism', in Sweezy 1953, p. 347.
[71] See also Sweezy 1953, p. 364.
[72] Sweezy 1980, pp. 2–3.
[73] Baran and Sweezy 1966, p. 56.
[74] Sweezy, 'On the Theory of Monopoly Capitalism', in Sweezy 1972, p. 41.

of imperfect competition he has, I believe, made a contribution of the first importance'.

It is interesting what appeared at the time central to Sweezy. He summarised Steindl's theory as stressing that 'the driving force behind capital accumulation is internal corporate saving'. In a competitive industry, those savings were responsive to demand: with a shortage of productive capacity, the resulting high profit margins would increase internal savings and thus accumulation; similarly, excess productive capacity would generate competition which drives down profit margins and thus internal savings.

In oligopolistic industries, however, excess capacity was *not* remedied in this way because price competition was avoided, and 'for this reason there is a *permanent* bias in favor of high profit margins and excess capacity'. Further, excess capacity discourages additional investment whereas a variety of factors inhibit a flow of investment to competitive sectors. Thus, in Steindl's theory, there was an explanation of a long-term stagnation in capital accumulation linked to a secular decline in competition.[75]

As we have seen, however, *all these elements were already present in Sweezy's own work!* On the other hand, providing an organising principle for those elements could be seen as a central contribution. The place to examine the new combination is in *Monopoly Capital*, upon which Baran and Sweezy began work in the Spring of 1956 while Baran was in the process of completing his *Political Economy of Growth*.[76]

As they noted in their introduction, it was a work generated by, among other things, a dissatisfaction with the adequacy of existing Marxist analyses (including their own) of monopoly capitalism. Marxist theory could explain well the Depression of the 1930s, but fell short in dealing with a postwar period in which severe depression had not re-occurred. 'Nor have Marxists contributed significantly,' they commented,

> to our understanding of some of the major characteristics of the 'affluent society' – particularly its colossal capacity to generate private and public

---

[75] Sweezy 1954, pp. 531–3.
[76] Sweezy, 'Paul Alexander Baran: A Personal Memoir', in Sweezy and Huberman 1965, p. 29.

waste and the profound economic, political, and cultural consequences which flow from this feature of the system.[77]

At the core of the 'stagnation of Marxian social science' was the failure to place monopoly at the very centre of analysis. The project, an attempt to 'remedy this situation in an explicit and indeed radical fashion', was organised around 'one central theme: the generation and absorption of the surplus under conditions of monopoly capitalism'.[78]

Aside from the apparent terminological shift from surplus-value to the concept of the 'surplus', what stands out immediately here is the concept of the *absorption* of the surplus. Both aspects had been considered explicitly by Baran in his book (which had drawn upon Kalecki and Steindl as well as upon Sweezy). Indeed, writing to Sweezy in 1956 upon reading the galleys of *The Political Economy of Growth*, he had expressed the hope that the discussion of monopoly capitalism would help to push

> Marxist thought on Mono. Cap. off its dead center and into a deepened
> consideration of what we both agree is the crux of the matter: the generation
> and absorption of the economic surplus.[79]

As a concept, generation of the surplus did not present any particular difficulties at first sight. The opening discussion explored the ability of the large corporations to maintain high prices (and to avoid price competition) while at the same time cutting production costs. The lion's share of rising productivity thus captured, the projection was one of 'continuously widening profit margins'; unlike Sweezy's earlier argument, at the core was a growing rate of exploitation in the sphere of production.[80]

Implied, then, was a growth in the profit share of national product and, indeed, 'a law of monopoly capitalism that the surplus tends to rise both absolutely and relatively as the system develops'.[81] Yet, as Baran and Sweezy stressed in response to an argument by Nicholas Kaldor, this relative growth of the surplus would not necessarily be *apparent* in the national statistical

---

[77] Baran and Sweezy 1966, p. 3.
[78] Baran and Sweezy, pp. 3–8.
[79] Sweezy, 'Paul Alexander Baran: A Personal Memoir', in Sweezy and Huberman 1965, p. 53.
[80] Baran and Sweezy 1966, p. 71.
[81] Baran and Sweezy 1966, p. 72.

accounts. The issue was one of 'the problem of realizing surplus value', a problem more chronic than in Marx's time. For, only profits which are *realised* are recorded: 'potential profits...leave their traces in the statistical record in the paradoxical form of unemployment and excess capacity'.[82]

The geneaology of this argument is clear. It originated with Kalecki:

> Imagine, for instance, that as a result of the increase in the degree of monopoly the relative share of profits in the gross income rises. Profits will remain unchanged because they continue to be determined by investment which depends on past investment decisions, but the real wages and salaries and the gross income or product will fall. The level of income or product will decline to the point at which the higher relative share of profits yields the same absolute level of profits.[83]

Although Kalecki had considered the possibility of 'retarded growth' and the potential for growth of unutilised capacity, the immediate influence on *Monopoly Capital* came from Steindl. The reason, he had argued, why we do not observe a decrease in the wage share of income (or an increase in the profit share of income) as the gross profit margin rises is because the rise in the profit share exists only *potentially*; that is, it exists only as a tendency. Thus, the rise of oligopoly increases the production of surplus value, but the latter

> can be realized only to the extent to which there is a corresponding amount of investment and capitalists' consumption. If this amount does not increase, then the rise in the rate of surplus value *produced* will not lead to any increase in surplus value *realized*, but only to excess capacity.

For Steindl, then, the effect of a growing rate of exploitation in the sphere of production would not be reflected in an actual increase in the surplus secured but, rather, by a reduced degree of capacity utilisation 'so that there is a not a shift of actual income from wages to profits, but a shift of potential income of workers to wastage in excess capacity'.[84] It is the same point that Baran made in the Foreword to the 1962 edition of *The Political Economy of Growth*. Responding to Kaldor's criticism, he argued that a rising surplus

---

[82] Baran and Sweezy 1966, p. 76.
[83] Kalecki 1968, p. 61. See the discussion in Chapter 14 of the Kaleckian cross, pp. 263–4.
[84] Steindl 1976, p. 245.

is entirely compatible with a constant (and even rising) share of wages in national income 'simply because the increment of surplus assumes the form of an increment of *waste*'.[85]

The same point – and yet not quite the same. For, what had occurred was a *generalisation* of the category of 'waste'. As *Monopoly Capital* would indicate subsequently, the rising surplus can be absorbed or utilised in several ways: '(1) it can be consumed, (2) it can be invested, and (3) it can be wasted'.[86] Given the normal inability (always present in Sweezy's theory) of capitalist consumption and investment to absorb the surplus that monopoly capitalism was capable of producing, 'waste' (in the form of 'the sales effort', government expenditures and imperialism) now edged its way onto centre stage in the analysis.

Thus, what prevented the growth of excess capacity (one form of waste) which the Kalecki/Steindl theory would predict as the rate of exploitation rose was the growing reliance upon *other* forms of waste. Growing relative to capitalist consumption and investment, 'they increasingly dominate the composition of social output, the rate of economic growth, and the quality of society itself'.[87]

These were the days, remember, not of the Depression but of Galbraith's *Affluent Society*, Vance Packard's *The Waste Makers* and the Edsel. What was to be explained, in the context of a general theory of capitalist stagnation, was the relation between the 'colossal capacity to generate private and public waste' and the absence of depression. Here, the treatment of the sales effort was representative.

Although Marx had treated the expenses associated with selling commodities as a deduction from the total surplus-value, Baran and Sweezy proposed that the sales effort had 'come to play a role, both quantitatively and qualitatively, beyond anything Marx ever dreamed of'.[88] And, essentially, that new role was that advertising and other selling expenditures had become an important 'mode of utilization of the economic surplus'.[89] It was a waste of resources,

---

[85] Baran 1962, p. xxi.
[86] Baran and Sweezy 1966, p. 79.
[87] Baran and Sweezy 1966, p. 114.
[88] Baran and Sweezy 1966, p. 114.
[89] Baran and Sweezy 1966, p. 125.

but in the presence of unemployment and idle capacity, these resources would have otherwise remained unutilized: advertising calls into being a net addition to investment and income.[90]

This was a shift in position. Sweezy had earlier argued that growing sales expenses act as a counteracting force to the general tendency of capitalism toward underconsumption/overaccumulation insofar as they diverted expanding productive forces 'into socially unnecessary and hence wasteful channels'.[91] In *Monopoly Capital*, however, this waste of resources not only increased output but also 'the sales effort absorbs, directly and indirectly, a large amount of surplus which otherwise would not have been produced'.[92]

Clearly, more than the emphasis on the absorption of the surplus was new here. There also was a quite different operative concept – a surplus which would not be produced in the absence of waste such as advertising (but also government expenditures and imperialism). While that concept was consistent with the Kalecki/Steindl framework, here *Monopoly Capital* drew some of its distinctive characteristics from Baran. What had occurred was a shift from the concept of 'actual surplus' to that of 'potential surplus' – i.e., to the surplus which would be both produced and realised at the full employment level. As Baran had noted, the concept differed explicitly from Marx's surplus-value by including 'the output lost in view of underemployment or misemployment of productive resources'.[93]

In the context of Baran's own work on underdeveloped countries, the emphasis on the 'utilization of available unutilized or underutilized resources' and the need to mobilise the potential economic surplus for the development of productive forces echoed the concerns of classical economists (and his own early teacher, Evgenii Preobrazhensky).[94] Extension of the concept of potential surplus to monopoly capitalism, though, involved an important shift of focus. As Harry Magdoff had noted in relation to Baran's development of the concept, the potential surplus 'is an active, operative concept: it leads to

---

[90] Baran and Sweezy 1966, p. 127.
[91] Sweezy 1956, p. 286. See also the discussion in Steindl 1976, pp. 55–66.
[92] Baran and Sweezy 1966, p. 142.
[93] Baran 1957, p. 23n.
[94] Baran 1952, pp. 81, 83; Isaac Deutscher in Sweezy and Huberman (eds.) 1965, p. 94.

an understanding of the waste, inefficiency, and unfulfilled possibilities of monopoly capitalism'.[95]

The system, for Baran, thus required waste to absorb 'the overflowing economic surplus' or to provide 'an adequate stimulus to additional investment by expanding aggregate demand'; and, in this respect, *Monopoly Capital* followed his argument.[96] Not only drawing upon Kalecki and Steindl for the connection between monopoly and the tendency to stagnation, the book also extended Kalecki's treatment of a budget deficit and export surplus to the category of waste in incorporating the concept of the potential economic surplus.[97] The latter, however, was not an unproblematic element – especially with respect to the attempt to determine the potential surplus by adding to profits (and other property income) the various components of waste.[98] Yet, in combination with the Kalecki/Steindl framework, it enabled *Monopoly Capital* to offer an answer to its two questions: why a severe depression had not reoccurred and why monopoly capitalism was a wasteland.

For those who had not lived through the experience of the Depression, it was the *second* question (rather than the first) which was central. In the 1930s, Sweezy had asked the timely question, why does capitalism have a tendency for chronic unemployment and stagnation? In capitalism's Golden Age, *Monopoly Capital* now asked a question equally as timely. And, its answers found a receptive audience in the generation, emerging from the desert of the Cold War, whose only experience had been that of the postwar boom.

There was another important question, though. As Baran and Sweezy noted, there is in *Monopoly Capital* 'almost total neglect of a subject which

---

[95] Magdoff, 'The Achievement of Paul Baran', in Sweezy and Huberman (eds.) 1965, p. 77.
[96] Baran 1957, pp. 88–92.
[97] Kalecki 1968, p. 51.
[98] See, for example, Lebowitz 1966. Within this framework, selling expenses and taxes – *to the extent to which they are a charge against surplus-value* – reduce the realisable rate of exploitation and thus the slope of the profit share line (i.e., increase output but not profits). It is logical to add these in order to reconstruct the surplus generated within production. Estimating the surplus, however, by adding undifferentiated government expenditures and advertising (according to the theory that these 'absorb' a portion of the surplus) to profits means that profits made possible by the former are counted twice. *Cf.* Phillips, 'Appendix: Estimating the Economic Surplus', in Baran and Sweezy (eds.) 1965, pp. 369–91. For a more sympathetic view of the concept of the surplus, see the comprehensive discussion in Foster 1986, Chapter 2. See also the essays by Henryk Szlajfer in Foster and Szlajfer (eds.) 1984.

occupies a central place in Marx's study of capitalism: the labor process'. Questions such as the nature of work, the psychology of workers, the forms of working-class organisation, and so forth – 'all obviously important subjects', they acknowledged, 'which would have to be dealt with in any comprehensive study of monopoly capitalism' – were missing.[99] Although Sweezy subsequently proposed that the gap was present because he and Baran lacked 'the necessary qualifications' – the 'crucially important direct experience' of the capitalist labour process, the basis for the silence goes somewhat deeper.[100]

In ignoring the labour process, Baran and Sweezy insisted that they had not forgotten class struggle:

> The revolutionary initiative against capitalism, which in Marx's day belonged to the proletariat in the advanced countries, has passed into the hands of the impoverished masses in the underdeveloped countries who are struggling to free themselves from imperialist domination and exploitation.[101]

There was a reason for this. Several years earlier, Sweezy and Huberman had argued that rising wages of steel workers came at the expense of steel consumers; and, this was not unique to the particular industry:

> sharing increased monopoly profits between big corporations and strong unions has not been confined to steel but rather has been quite general in the monopolistically organized sectors of the economy.

The capitalist labour process and workers, thus, disappeared as subjects in *Monopoly Capital* because workers in monopoly capitalism were not themselves seen to be acting as subjects.[102] Organised labour had consigned itself 'to playing the role of junior partner in a Big Business-dominated society.'[103] In a country lacking not only a revolutionary movement but also a labour party,

---

[99] Baran and Sweezy 1965, pp. 8–9.
[100] Braverman 1974, p. x.
[101] Baran and Sweezy 1965, p. 9.
[102] The same silence was present in *The Theory of Capitalist Development* (Sweezy 1956). Sweezy's principal concern at that time, though, was to show that mature capitalism had an inherent tendency to stagnation; its failure to provide jobs, in short, was systemic rather than accidental or the result of a failure of intelligence. Those *without* jobs, thus, were the issue.
[103] Huberman and Sweezy 1960, pp. 357–61.

such a judgement was not surprising.[104] Sweezy expanded upon this point in 1967 noting that production workers had been able to capture a portion of the substantial increases in productivity but also citing Lenin's argument that imperialist 'booty' permits capitalists to 'bribe and win over to their side an aristocracy of labor'.[105]

Monopoly Capital, thus, answered another question: what happened to the working class? A less, rather than more, revolutionary proletariat in the developed countries was an inherent characteristic of the era of monopoly capital. Yet, capitalism had to be understood as a 'global system embracing both the (relatively few) industrializing countries and their (relatively numerous) satellites and dependencies'; and, in that global system, the revolutionary subjects had become 'the masses in these exploited dependencies'.[106]

It had become increasingly clear in the postwar period, Sweezy concluded in 1971, that 'the principal contradiction in the system, at least in the present historical period, is not *within* the developed part but *between* the developed and underdeveloped parts'.[107] That answer, too, found a receptive audience in a generation struggling against US imperial involvement in Vietnam and elsewhere around the world.

The general theory in a new age of crisis

In the retardation in economic growth which became apparent in the early 1970s, Sweezy found confirmation that, sooner or later, the inherent tendency of monopoly capitalism toward stagnation exerts itself. The period of the 1970s and 1980s was thus an opportunity to restate his theory in a context in which the effect of the tendency rather than that of the counteracting forces was manifest. Since this period was also one marked by his collaboration with Harry Magdoff (who, before the onset of McCarthyism had, among

---

[104] Sweezy and Magdoff subsequently suggested that the theoretical silence in *Monopoly Capital* was in part the reflection of this political silence: 'Marxism leads us to expect an intimate relation between revolutionary theory and revolutionary practise: where either is missing the other will be at the very least severely handicapped'. Sweezy and Magdoff 1974, pp. 7–8.

[105] Sweezy, 'Marx and the Proletariat', *Monthly Review* (December 1967) reprinted in Sweezy 1972, p. 163.

[106] Sweezy 1972, pp. 163, 165.

[107] Sweezy, 'Modern Capitalism', *Monthly Review* (June 1971) reprinted in Sweezy 1972, p. 13.

other things, served as the head of the current business analysis section of the US Department of Commerce), it meant that there was a strong empirical element in Sweezy's work in this period.[108]

More than a restatement of the theory, however, occurred. Significantly, in his explanations as to why the tendency to stagnation was latent and inoperative for so long a period, the centrality of waste as a category faded from the analysis – as did any consideration of the concept of potential surplus.

Waste, despite its thematic prominence, was never the *sole* 'counteracting force' identified in *Monopoly Capital*; new industries and wars (and their aftermath) remained part of the analysis. Thus, a wave of 'automobilization' in the context of postwar consumer liquidity as well as the enormous increase in arms spending were identified by Baran and Sweezy as important explanations of the postwar boom.[109] Similarly, in *Monthly Review* at the time, Sweezy and Huberman emphasised the importance of the postwar reconstruction boom of Western Europe and the stimulus of growing trade within the Common Market; within a year of the publication of *Monopoly Capital*, their list of factors explaining the boom included military spending, deficit finance, tax subsidies and the growth of consumer debt (but not 'waste' as such).[110]

To this list was added the civilian spinoff from military technology and, especially, US postwar economic hegemony (with its particular implications for the growth of world trade and capital). The specific combination of these factors, Sweezy argues, was sufficient to produce a unique stimulus to investment; it meant a major investment boom in key industries and rapid growth of capacity in all the leading capitalist economies (as well as some Third-World countries).

The war, indeed, 'altered the givens of the world economic situation'; a unique set of events had provided powerful counteracting forces. Yet, 'every one of the forces which powered the long postwar expansion was, and was bound to be, self-limiting'.[111] And so, with the exhaustion of the special

---

[108] Hillard, in Resnick and Wolff (eds.) 1985, p. 397.
[109] Baran and Sweezy 1965, pp. 244–5 and Chapter 8, 'On the History of Monopoly Capitalism' in general.
[110] Sweezy and Huberman 1962, p. 391; 1967, p. 4.
[111] Sweezy and Magdoff, 'Why Stagnation?', *Monthly Review* (June 1982), reprinted in Magdoff and Sweezy 1987a, pp. 35–6.

conditions, there followed increased levels of unemployment, excess capacity (on a world scale) and lagging investment – stagnation both realised and operative.[112]

The displacement of waste was not the only change to Sweezy's general theory of stagnation in the 1970s and 1980s. *Monopoly Capital* had focused upon characteristics reflecting the unique postwar position of US corporations relatively secure from capitalist competitors of other countries; and, as US international economic hegemony declined, so too did monopoly slip from the centre of the analysis.

In Sweezy's *Four Lectures on Marxism* (1981), the focus was upon the inherent tendency of capitalism toward overaccumulation, that tendency for productive power to grow 'more rapidly than is warranted by society's consuming power'. In this context, the significance attributed to monopoly was that it 'intensified' the contradictions of the accumulation process – both by enhancing the ability to accumulate and by choking off outlets for investment. More stress, similarly, was placed upon the significance of 'maturity' in the explanation as to why counteracting forces (such as, in particular, the effect of new industries) tend to become weaker.[113] *In a very real sense, thus, Sweezy returned in this period to earlier formulations of his theory.*

The Kalecki/Steindl link between monopoly at the micro-level and stagnation at the macro-level, however, has remained integral to his argument: 'the more monopolistic the economy, the stronger the tendency to stagnation'.[114] Stagnation, Sweezy argued, is a 'consequence of the specific form of overaccumulation of capital which characterizes capitalism in its monopoly phase'. Any attempt at analysis of developed capitalism, accordingly, must recognise the importance of monopolistic elements. Precisely because of its failure to incorporate this micro-element, Sweezy has argued that Keynesian theory could not explain the emergence of 'stagflation' in the 1970s.[115]

In the course of interpreting and analysing current developments from the perspective of his general theory, Sweezy (in conjunction with Magdoff) made *Monthly Review* during this period a unique medium in which to trace the

---

[112] For a discussion of world excess capacity in the steel industry as 'a harbinger of events to come', see Sweezy and Magdoff 1977.
[113] Sweezy 1981a, pp. 39, 42–3.
[114] Sweezy 1980, p. 3.
[115] Sweezy 1981b, pp. 4, 8.

changing fortunes of US capitalism. Two such developments are of particular interest. In the 'embryo of an adequate theory of inflation under conditions of monopoly capitalism', Sweezy and Magdoff argued in 1974 that the power of giant corporations to control prices and wages intensified the tendency toward stagnation; at the same time, however, it meant that attempts to stimulate the economy generated inflation.[116] Having ignored 'the monopolistic structure of the economy', however, (bastard) Keynesian technicians accordingly were confounded in their efforts to stimulate a stagnating economy because 'much of the increase in monetary demand was dissipated in inflationary price increases rather than in expanded output'.[117]

In addition to stagflation, the theoretical issue which Sweezy explored most in recent years was the growth of financial speculation. After years of noting the growth of debt (both private and public), he increasingly called attention to the coexistence of a stagnant production sector and a prosperous and expanding financial sector. In 1983, Sweezy and Magdoff emphasised that a growing part of money-capital was not directly transformed into productive capital, but, instead, was used to purchase financial instruments. There was no necessity, however, that this money would find its way, directly or indirectly, into real capital formation.

> It may just as well remain in the form of money capital circulating around in the financial sector, fueling the growth of financial markets which increasingly take on a life of their own.[118]

Following two years in which financial transactions proliferated and new financial instruments (options on futures, etc) multiplied, Magdoff and Sweezy suggested that 'the financial sphere has the potential to become an autonomous subsystem of the economy as a whole, with an enormous capacity for self-expansion'. In that growing divergence between a stagnant economy and a financial explosion, however, they noted in 1985 that one

---

[116] Sweezy and Magdoff, 'Keynesian Chickens Come Home to Roost', *Monthly Review* (April 1974) reprinted in Magdoff and Sweezy 1977, pp. 21–2.

[117] Sweezy 1980, p. 6; see also Sweezy 1979, p. 9.

[118] Magdoff and Sweezy, 'Production and Finance', *Monthly Review* (May 1983) reprinted Magdoff and Sweezy 1987a, pp. 96–7.

definite possibility was 'a bust of classic dimensions'. Indeed, the most remarkable thing was that it had not yet occurred.[119]

But, why has this been happening? Sweezy and Magdoff argued that behind the financial explosion was a growing concentration of wealth and income. There was

> a swelling of the pool of fresh savings seeking profitable investment outlets. However, since the demands on this pool for investment in the production of real goods and services have been declining, more and more of it has been flowing into purely financial channels, giving rise to a vast expansion of the financial superstructure of the economy and an unparalleled explosion of speculative activity of all kinds.[120]

The explanation is entirely consistent with Sweezy's general theory of stagnation. (Moreover, it can be related to the discussions by Kalecki and Steindl of 'rentiers' and 'outside' savings, respectively.)[121] In this respect, it may confirm Sweezy's oft-repeated view that understanding stagnation as the 'normal' state of a developed capitalist economy is a far more fruitful assumption than the full-employment assumption which underlies neoclassical economics.

Whether it was sufficient for Sweezy, on the other hand, is another matter; he became increasingly dissatisfied with the adequacy of our understanding of the relation between the spheres of finance and production:

> In economics, we need a theory which integrates finance and production, the circuits of capital of a financial and a real productive character much more effectively than our traditional theories do.[122]

Paul Sweezy continued until his death to analyse the characteristics of a mature capitalist economy – a work begun more than a half century ago. The Dean of radical economics remained an eager student of history, tracing the new forms of the stagnationist tendencies of monopoly capitalism. In all this, he retained the enthusiasm of his youth. Even his earlier pessimism about

---

[119] Magdoff and Sweezy, 'The Financial Explosion', *Monthly Review* (December 1985) reprinted in Magdoff and Sweezy 1987a, pp. 147, 149–150.

[120] Magdoff and Sweezy 1987b, pp. 13–14.

[121] *Cf.* Kalecki 1968, p. 159; Steindl 1976, pp. 113–21.

[122] Sweezy 1987, p. 19.

workers in developed capitalist economies was tempered with the passage of the Golden Age: if

> the global system has now entered a crisis phase that gives every sign of being irreversible, it is hard to avoid the conclusion that we are entering a new chapter in the history of the metropolitan working classes.[123]

No one would have been happier than Paul Sweezy himself. He ended, indeed, his Foreword to Harry Braverman's *Labor and Monopoly Capital* with these words:

> The sad, horrible heart-breaking way the vast majority of my fellow countrymen and women, as well as their counterparts in most of the rest of the world, are obliged to spend their working lives is seared into my consciousness in an excruciating and unforgettable manner.[124]

To help put an end to such a situation remained the goal of Paul Sweezy throughout. That, indeed, is the lesson that he drew from his general theory of stagnation: it

> teaches us that what we need is not the reform of monopoly capitalism but its replacement by a system that organizes economic activity not for the greater glory of capital but to meet the needs of people to live decent, secure, and to the extent possible, creative lives.[125]

---

[123] Sweezy 1981a, p. 86n.
[124] Braverman 1974, p. xii.
[125] Sweezy, 'Introduction', in Magdoff and Sweezy 1987a, p. 25.

Appendix

Learning from Paul M. Sweezy[126]

We all stand on other people's shoulders, and so many of us are indebted to Paul Sweezy for our own development. His death in February of this year reminded me how much I had learned from him. Ironically, though, my first publication in Marxian economics was a critique of Baran and Sweezy's *Monopoly Capital* in *Studies on the Left*.[127] I had read all three volumes of *Capital* – at least once – and felt that was sufficient to criticise my elders for their errors in deviating from Marx.

Subsequently, I came to know Paul Sweezy well. I visited him at the *Monthly Review* offices when I came to New York, and I often saw him (and Harry Magdoff) at the annual Socialism in the World conferences in Cavtat, Yugoslavia. We also corresponded over the years, and his death led me to look over letters I had saved and which I want to share.

Although I remembered how encouraging and supportive he was (as in our direct meetings), I was surprised to see how critical he was of what I was doing. (I clearly blocked all that out). I also was surprised to be reminded of his emphasis on the importance of engaging in debate. On 17 August 1982, after commenting favourably on an article I had published in *SPE*, he wrote:

> Finally, if an old man may presume to give advice to a young one, let me recommend (1) that you stop quoting Marx every second sentence, (2) that you develop your own style and formulations more freely, and (3) that you engage your contemporaries in more vigorous critical polemics. They badly need it.

The need to challenge bad Marxism and to be more effective was a theme which runs through our correspondence – whatever the particular issue that we were discussing. In the course of some correspondence, he asked on 12 June 1977 why I was spending so much time on this question of the falling rate of profit (FROP):

---

[126] These comments draw upon a presentation made at the tribute to Paul M. Sweezy at the conference, 'Karl Marx and the Challenges of the 21st Century', in Havana, 4–8 May 2004.

[127] Lebowitz 1966.

Not only is it, taken by itself, an egregious case of mechanistic theorizing; even worse, it fosters that kind of thinking everywhere else. You are right of course that the class struggle has to be restored to its rightful central position, but one has to guard against the notion that when one has said 'class struggle' one has also solved, rather than posed, the important questions.

Once again, what was needed was theoretical struggle:

> I'd like to see you get more into the business of attacking the traditional FROPists, ridiculing the 'forces of production' theories, laying low the sectarians, forcing all and sundry false Marxists to come out and do battle. You're on the right track, but are you being as effective as you ought to be?'

It was never a matter, though, of polemics for themselves. The point was always linked to Paul's commitment to revolutionary change:

> Most theory nowadays should be highly polemical, attacking and destroying false Marxism and restoring Marxism to its proper role, not as a body of formal theories, but as the only way to interpret history and *hence* as the only reliable guide to revolutionary action.

Nor was it a proposal that we simply go off and attack anyone who deviates in any way. One of our earliest subjects of discussion revolved around my criticism of the neo-Ricardians (or Sraffians). Paul worried that I was too harsh with them. We have to decide how to relate to them, he commented on 17 July 1974. 'Are they friends or enemies (actual or potential), and does our way of perceiving them and dealing with them have any bearing on the problem?' While he clearly saw this school of thought (and Maurice Dobb) as wrong, Paul knew who the real enemy was. On 30 December 1973, he wrote about the neo-Ricardians:

> The trouble with them is – and the point of view from which we should (sympathetically) criticize them – that in this day and age it makes no sense to dream of an effective critique of capitalism which is not Marxist. Those, like Dobb for example, who imagine that Sraffism is really a sort of variant of Marxism are on the wrong track. Our job is (1) to try to steer them onto the right track, and (2) to keep the young from following them on to the wrong one. In other words effectively to establish Marxism as what it is,

the definitive (although of course not in the sense of being incapable of indefinite further development) critique of capitalism with its necessary link to a revolutionary political position.

I cannot say that I followed Paul's advice enough (I still quote Marx a lot). But, I definitely learned much from him. In looking back over our correspondence, I was reminded of the story of the young man who decided his father knew nothing and then ten years later was shocked to discover how much his father had learned in the intervening years. Looking over those letters reminds me in particular that what moved Paul was his desire for revolutionary change.

PART FOUR

ESSENCE AND APPEARANCE

Part Four
Essence and Appearance

If we know the inner structure of capitalism, what is its relation to the way things appear? This is the central question addressed in the essays in this Part. The first two chapters (prepared for this volume) continue the discussion of method begun in Chapters 1, 5 and 6. Chapter 10 begins with a look at Marx's methodological project as a whole, placing the competition of capitals in the context of Marx's schema. Chapter 11 focuses upon competition, on the world of many capitals, and examines what competition is and what it does (offering an explanation of why everything is reversed in competition).

The previously published essays which follow all take up questions about the relationship between competition and capital as a whole in different ways. Thus, Chapter 12 provides an illustration of the inversion characteristic of competition and the confusion it creates (in this particular case, in the analysis of advertising and the media). Chapter 13's discussion of monopoly-capital then poses the question: if arguments at the level of competition cannot demonstrate necessity, what is the *inner* argument for the tendency for centralisation of capital? Chapter 14 returns to the question of crisis and the attack on Marxism by the 'analytical Marxists' by exploring the relation between the inner structural requirements of capital and the existence of economic agents indifferent to that structure.

Finally, Chapter 15 is a case study of where the methodological individualism celebrated by analytical Marxism leads. It looks at Brenner's explanation of the postwar crisis of capitalism and finds that his adherence to this school produces the displacement of class struggle by the competition of capitals, thus driving him to a conclusion which belies his own political perspective. The chapter's answer to the *New Left Review*'s anointment of Brenner as successor to Marx is revealed by its title: 'In Brenner, Everything is Reversed'.

Chapter Ten
Marx's Methodological Project as a Whole

If we understand the essence of capitalism, do we need to worry about the multiplicity of its outward forms? As we have seen in Chapters 1 and 5, appearances cannot be the basis for understanding the concrete totality that is capitalism. Rather, we need to proceed from observation of the concrete to the sphere of abstract thought – to move, as Lenin described the process, 'from living perception to abstract thought'.[1]

The 'scientifically correct method' that Marx described employs the scientist's instrument, 'the power of abstraction', and reasons from simple concepts to deduce an understanding of the whole as 'a rich totality of many determinations and relations'.[2] Through the process of dialectical reasoning, 'thought appropriates the concrete, reproduces the concrete in the mind'.[3] In this way, we grasp the concrete totality, understand the interconnections within the whole that are hidden from mere observation.

But, what is the relation between the initial observations, the multiplicity of appearances which are our point of departure, and the 'obscure structure', that 'inner core, which is essential but

---

[1] Lenin 1963, p. 171.
[2] Marx 1973, pp. 100–1; 1977a, p. 90.
[3] Marx 1973, p. 101.

concealed'?[4] Are those appearances *false*? We have already indicated in Chapter 1 that those appearances are not false for individual capitalists. But, should they be ignored because they are false *in general*?

Not if Marx was following Hegel with respect to the relationship between Essence and Appearance. 'Essence must appear', Hegel declared. Essence shows itself, is reflected on the surface.[5] Appearances, thus, are *forms* of essence. Accordingly, there are not two disconnected worlds – a world of appearances and an essential world, two worlds entirely independent of each other. Rather, there is an essential relation between essence and appearance, an essential relation between inner and outer.

We need to understand, Hegel proposed, reality or actuality as the unity of the inner core and its forms of existence. A particular inner produces a particular outer; a particular outer manifests a particular inner. Thus, essence and appearance are inseparably united as two sides of reality – the inner connections and the multiplicity of outward forms.[6] We cannot understand that reality if we understand it one-sidedly: if we stop the process of reasoning at the point where essence has been logically developed, we stop it prematurely because we do not understand essence if we do not understand why it appears as it does.

The appearance of capital as a whole

Capital as a whole, we saw earlier in Chapter 7, is a specific unity of production and circulation – a 'unity-in-process of production and circulation' whose moments are identified in the subtitles of the three volumes of *Capital*.[7] If we view that whole as the essence of capital, then its completion calls upon us to proceed at this point to consider the necessary forms of existence of capital, i.e., the appearance of capital as a whole.

Although we will never know precisely what Volume III of *Capital* would have looked like had Marx gone beyond the notes that he left behind for the volume, it certainly appears as if his plan was to focus upon capital's surface forms. Noting that the reproduction models (with which Volume II concludes)

---

[4] Marx 1968, p. 65; 1981b, p. 311.
[5] Hegel 1929, II, p. 107.
[6] Hegel 1929, II, p. 159.
[7] Marx 1973, p. 620.

demonstrated that 'the capitalist production process, taken as a whole, is a unity of the production and circulation processes', Marx indicated it was necessary to go beyond 'general reflections on this unity'. Rather, Volume III had to 'discover and present the concrete forms which grow out of the *process of capital's movement considered as a whole'.*

Having developed the concept of capital as a whole, the forms of capital on the surface and their link to the everyday notions of the actors, thus, now became Marx's special concern:

> The configurations of capital, as developed in this volume, thus approach step by step the form in which they appear on the surface of society, in the actions of different capitals on one another, i.e. in competition, and in the everyday consciousness of the agents of production themselves.[8]

But, what precisely is the relation between capital as a whole and the forms in which capitals 'appear on the surface of society'? We must remember that we are talking about a relationship between an inner core and an outer form; that is, we are considering elements of two different logical worlds. However connected those worlds may be, these elements pertain to different logical planes.

Marx was quite clear about this relation between the categories of the inner structure and those of the surface of society. Surplus-value, for example, is a category of the inner analysis; it does not exist at the level of the surface. In contrast, profit belongs in the category of outer forms; on the surface of society, surplus-value takes the form of profit:

> Surplus-value and the rate of surplus-value are... the invisible essence to be investigated, whereas the rate of profit and hence the form of surplus-value as profit are visible surface phenomena.[9]

Surplus-value, in short, is invisible. It is essence. It is a category discovered with the scientist's instrument, the power of abstraction. Profit, in contrast, is 'the form of appearance of surplus-value, and the latter can be sifted out from the former only by analysis'.[10] Only by the process of proceeding from the concrete to the abstract can we develop an understanding of surplus-value

---

[8] Marx 1981b, p. 117.
[9] Marx 1981b, p. 134.
[10] Marx 1981b, p. 139.

(and thus its surface form). Profit, Marx noted, is 'a transformed form of surplus-value, a form in which its origin and the secret of its existence are veiled and obliterated'.

At the level of the inner, exploitation as the basis for surplus-value can be demonstrated: 'in surplus-value, the relationship between capital and labour is laid bare'. In contrast, when we see surplus-value only in its form on the surface, we lose all understanding of its source. 'In the relation between capital and profit, i.e. between capital and surplus-value as it appears', capital appears to create a new value somehow through production and circulation. 'But how this happens is now mystified, and appears to derive from hidden qualities that are inherent in capital itself.'[11]

We move, in short, from the surface phenomenon (profit) by analysis; and, through the process of reasoning, we develop the concept invisible on the surface (surplus-value) which allows us to understand the concrete. That same distinction between inner and outer applies to value and price. We observe prices on the surface but their nature is entirely mystified. By developing the concept of value, an inner category, we can grasp the link to labour and from the concept of abstract labour to the nature of money. Indeed, without value, how could possibly we understand the nature of money and thus capital?[12]

All the inner connections revealed through the concept of value, however, are obliterated when considering market prices and prices of production (the 'law' or average around which market prices gravitate); these, too, are mere *forms* of value:

> The price of production is already a completely externalized and *prima facie* irrational form of commodity value, a form that appears in competition and is therefore present in the consciousness of the vulgar capitalist and consequently also in that of the vulgar economist.[13]

In the chapter that follows ('What Is Competition?'), we will explore the world of many capitals competing in the market, this world of surface forms that produces 'the everyday consciousness of the agents of production themselves'. However, here, where we are considering Marx's methodological project, an immediate question presents itself: *if value, surplus-value and the*

---

[11] Ibid.
[12] Marx 1981b, p. 295.
[13] Marx 1981b, p. 300.

rate of surplus-value do not exist on the surface whereas price, profit and the rate of profit are their respective forms and only exist on that plane, in what sense is it possible to talk about the 'transformation' of value into price?

If value, surplus-value and the rate of surplus-value are 'invisible essences', then the much-discussed question of 'transformation' must be understood not to be a *real* process but, rather, a *logical* process between two levels of abstract thought. We can see that price and profit are the *premise*, i.e., are categories of the real society which are the point of departure. When it comes, however, to attempting to understand, the categories of value and surplus-value precede price and profit but do not themselves exist alongside their forms.

Despite discussions of 'transformation', then, as a process involving 'unequal exchange' and redistribution of surplus-value, Himmelweit and Mohun made the point admirably many years ago: 'Redistribution is only meaningful if one can specify a state from which redistribution occurs and a state after such a redistribution'.[14] How could there possibly be a redistribution between an invisible essence and its surface form? Rather than a *real* redistribution of value and surplus-value, the 'transformation' of value into price is a logical test of the consistency of essence and appearance.

The moments of Marx's method

We are now at the point when we can be much more explicit in trying to reconstruct Marx's methodological project, a project which may be seen as incorporating a set of specific moments.

Moment I of Marx's method begins by observation of the concrete, capitalist society, appropriating the material in detail. From this point, as we have seen, Marx proceeds to Moment II, which has the task of moving from simple abstract concepts to complex, richer concepts to establish thereby the totality of thoughts. Here, we have the logical construction of essence, the interconnected whole in which:

> Every economic relation presupposes every other in its bourgeois economic form, and everything posited is thus also a presupposition, this is the case with every organic system.[15]

---

[14] Himmelweit and Mohun 1978, p. 98.
[15] Marx 1973, p. 278.

Understanding capitalism as a system, as an organic whole, is precisely the concern here. What are the conditions for the reproduction of the system? For the generation of surplus-value? For the realisation of surplus-value generated? Focus on the totality, this 'structure of society, in which all relations coexist simultaneously and support one another' allows us to identify the tendencies which are inherent and necessary rather than contingent.[16] The basic premise of Moment II is that we understand nothing about capitalism unless we grasp its inner connections, understand it as a totality.

Moment III in Marx's method continues the logical process; yet it has a qualitatively different nature. The purpose here is not to establish the inner connections because that has been achieved with the construction of the totality. Rather, the purpose in Moment III is to demonstrate the manner in which this totality must appear; we must explain appearance, explain the multiplicity of outward forms in which essence is manifested. Here we enter into a familiar world – a world of market prices, cost of production, long-run equilibrium prices, profits, profit rates, capital flows, interest rates, rent, etc – a world not of capital as a whole but of *many* capitals all acting upon each other. And the task is to demonstrate not only why capital appears as it does but also how the interaction of these parts generates the same tendencies revealed through the inner analysis, the analysis at the level of the whole.

When we understand not only the essence of capital but its forms, not only the inner tendencies but also the way in which those tendencies are manifested through the real actions of the many capitals in competition, then we understand capital in reality – the unity of its obscure structure and 'the concrete forms which grow out of the *process of capital's movement considered as a whole*'.

Yet Moment III is also not a stopping point because Moment III still is within the head, is 'merely theoretical'. The concept of the real, that unity of essence and appearance, remains a concept. 'The real subject retains its autonomous existence outside the head just as before.'[17]

Accordingly, it is necessary to relate the concepts which have been generated to the real concrete, the real world, which is the subject and the

---

[16] Marx 1976b, p. 167.
[17] Marx 1973, pp. 101–2.

presupposition. Thus, Moment IV involves *testing*...the stage of validation of the concepts. As Hegel noted:

> Equally untrue are...a notion [concept] which does not correspond with reality, and a reality which does not correspond with the notion [concept].[18]

Accordingly, the concept of the real (the unity of essence and its necessary form of appearance), 'the concrete in the mind', must be reconciled with the real concrete, the objective concrete. Moment IV thus returns to the starting point, to the point of departure, the real concrete; it is the return from abstract thought to the subject, the real world. As Lenin described the 'dialectical path of the cognition of *truth*, of the cognition of objective reality', it is the movement 'from living perception to abstract thought, *and from this to practice*'.

Asking whether the concept of value...a concept which plays a central role in Moment II had to be proven, Marx commented:

> All that palaver about the necessity of proving the concept of value comes from complete ignorance both of the subject dealt with and scientific method.

But there was, nevertheless, a proof:

> Even if there were no chapter on 'value' in my book, the analysis of the real relations which I give would contain the proof and demonstration of the real value relation.[19]

Thus, the 'correctness' of the analysis of real relations constitutes a proof; the ability to present the 'real movement' is the test of success in the 'cognition of objective reality':

> If this is done successfully, if the life of the subject-matter is now reflected back in the ideas, then it may appear as if we have before us an *a priori* construction.[20]

---

[18] Hegel 1929, II, p. 227.
[19] Marx and Engels 1965, pp. 209–10.
[20] Marx 1977a, p. 102.

As the return from abstract thought to the real world, Moment IV underlines the necessary unity of thought and its object, reveals the cognition of objective reality as a *process* – 'the eternal, endless approximation of thought to the object'.[21] For it points to the 'conditional' quality of cognition and a constant process of movement to transcend contradictions between the products of thought, the concrete in the mind, and the real concrete.[22] Testing the correctness of the products of abstract thought, as emphasised by Lenin, is a necessary part of this process of cognition:

> By checking and applying the correctness of these reflections in his practice and technique, Man arrives at objective truth.[23]

Yet, it is important to recognise that Moment IV does not come only at the end, only after the completion of Moments II and III. Describing *Capital*, Lenin noted that 'Testing by facts or by practice respectively, is to be found here in *each* step of the analysis'.[24] Indeed, as I have argued, 'it is the defect in the theory *relative to the concrete totality* which propels the discussion forward' and which demonstrates that 'the specific subject, society, is always present as the premise of this theoretical process'.[25] Just like that real subject, the process of testing is always present.

As Lenin discovered in his reading of Hegel, practice served for Hegel as the link in the analysis of the process of cognition and 'indeed as the transition to objective ("absolute", according to Hegel) truth'. And, as clearly indicated in his *Theses on Feuerbach*, Marx sided 'with Hegel in introducing the criterion of practice into the theory of knowledge'.[26] 'The question whether objective truth can be attributed to human thinking,' Marx noted, 'is not a question of theory but is a *practical* question. Man must prove the truth, i.e., the reality and power, the this-worldliness of this thinking in practice'.[27]

Moment IV, the *real* test of the results of the power of abstraction, of the science of Marx, thus is absolutely critical. And it was something that Marx clearly understood. As he wrote to Engels in 1867:

---

[21] Lenin 1963, p. 195.
[22] Lenin 1963, pp. 191–5.
[23] Lenin 1963, p. 201.
[24] Lenin 1963, p. 320.
[25] Lebowitz 2003, pp. 57–8.
[26] Lenin 1963, p. 212.
[27] Marx 1976a, p. 3.

As regards CHAPTER IV, it was a hard job finding *things themselves,* i.e., their *interconnection.* But with that once behind me, along came one BLUE BOOK after another just as I was composing the final *version,* and I was delighted to find my theoretical conclusions fully confirmed by the FACTS.[28]

Figure 10.1 depicts the four moments of Marx's methodological project as a whole. Considering that project as a whole, it can be seen as the concept of a process – the process of cognition, the process of the endless approximation of thought to the object, the real world.

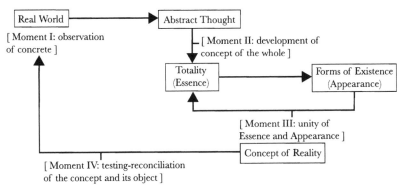

Figure 10.1. Marx's Methodological Project as a Whole

---

[28] Marx and Engels 1987, pp. 407–8.

Chapter Eleven
What Is Competition?

Competition is the world of markets, prices, profits, profit rates, interest, and rent. Competition is the world of many capitals, real capitals, capitals as they *really* exist. Capital, indeed, 'exists and can only exist as many capitals'.[1]

Thus, we leave behind the abstraction, capital as a whole. Here, we are no longer in the essential world where capital is a whole, a totality; rather, we are in the world of existence, the way essence must appear:

> The essence of capital, which, as will be developed more closely in connection with competition, *is* something which repels itself, *is* many capitals mutually quite indifferent to one another.[2]

As shown in Chapter 1, this world of competition is the source of everyday notions, the everyday consciousness of the agents of production themselves. And, rightly so. What capitalists are paying for their inputs – their materials and the wages, rent, interest they pay – are the real facts always before them; and, if they are not attentive to how these compare to what their competitors are paying, sooner or later reality imposes itself.

---

[1] Marx 1973, p. 414.
[2] Marx 1973, p. 421n.

This is the real world. There is no place here for invisible essences, for obscure, hidden structures. Assuming a real capitalist could see what is invisible (e.g., value, surplus-value), it would only confuse him in the battle of capitals. *And, yet, if we want to understand capitalism, this world is itself the source of great confusion.*

Inner truth

The essence of capital is that it is the sum of accumulated surplus-value, the fruits of exploitation of workers. Capital grows as the result of new exploitation. And its growth increases as the result of increases in length and intensity of the workday, the driving down of real wages, increases in productivity, and increases in the numbers of workers it exploits. *There is no other way for capital to grow.*

When we understand capital and its drive to grow, we understand why capital constantly attempts to lengthen and intensify the workday, drive down the real wage, and increase productivity to the best of its ability. Capital, we see, must increase the exploitation of workers in the sphere of production if more surplus-value is to be produced. However, since that surplus-value can only be made real in the sphere of circulation, capital must contrive to sell the commodities containing surplus-value and to do so as quickly as possible. Thus, as we saw in Chapter 7, capital drives to reduce the time of circulation to a minimum, to negate its negation, so it can return more rapidly to the sphere of production to generate surplus-value.

Here, we see the incredible power of Marx's development of the concept of capital as a whole. He demonstrates in the *Grundrisse* that latent within the very concept of capital are its necessary tendencies:

> The simple concept of capital has to contain its civilizing tendencies etc.
> *in themselves*; they must not, as in the economics books until now, appear
> merely as external circumstances. Likewise the contradictions which are
> later released, demonstrated as already latent within it.[3]

Thus, we see capital constantly coming up against barriers to its growth and seeking ways to drive beyond those barriers. Its attempt to speed up the

---

[3] Marx 1973, p. 414.

process of circulation, to generate new needs, to create a world market ('The tendency to create the *world market* is directly given in the concept of capital itself'), etc. – all these developments can be seen as coming from this 'germ' of the concept of capital in general.[4] Understanding the essence of capital means that we understand its inherent tendencies.

Marx's whole argument was an attempt to demonstrate this point. It is why his theoretical argument in the *Grundrisse* is developed on the basis of capital in general (an approach he then follows in *Capital*). Value/value of labour-power/ necessary labour/surplus-labour/absolute surplus-value/relative surplus-value/accumulation of capital – here is the sequence in which Marx reveals the nature of capital as the workers' own product turned against themselves; and it is by proceeding along this path that we understand capital's tendencies.

But, this understanding requires a commitment to science, the discipline to resist the siren call of appearances. All around us is not the essence of capital but its forms, and it is easy to yield to temptation and to incorporate elements of the concrete forms of capital into the explanation of capital's inner tendencies. Marx explicitly rejected this course. In his discussion of relative surplus-value in the *Grundrisse*, he pointed out that 'it is easy to develop the introduction of machinery out of competition and out of the law of the reduction of production costs which is triggered by competition'. (Indeed, it is *very* easy – Marx himself had done this very thing in *Wage Labour and Capital* before developing his method consistently in the *Grundrisse*.) But, he continued, 'we are concerned here with developing it [the introduction of machinery] out of the relation of capital to living labour, without reference to other capitals'.[5]

Why *without reference to other capitals*? Very simply because, as he noted in his discussion of relative surplus-value in Volume I, Chapter 12: 'the general and necessary tendencies of capital must be distinguished from their forms of appearance'.[6] Precisely because necessity can be grasped only through the inner argument, Marx added that 'it is not our intention here to consider

---

[4] Marx 1973, pp. 310, 408.
[5] Marx 1973, pp. 776–7.
[6] Marx 1977a, p. 433.

the way in which the immanent laws of capitalist production manifest themselves'.

So, if we grasp the necessary tendencies of capital only by considering capital as totality, where does competition come in? Does competition add anything to our understanding of those tendencies? If it does not, why not apply Occam's Razor and just ignore it?

Necessary appearance

There is no mystery, though, about exactly where competition comes in. Over and over again in the *Grundrisse*, Marx stressed that the competition of individual capitals is precisely the way that the inner tendencies of capital are made real. 'The seemingly independent influences of the individuals, and their chaotic collisions, are precisely the positing of their general law.'[7] This is Moment III of Marx's methodological project (see Chapter 10) – the place where we must understand the forms that capital takes on the surface:

> Competition merely *expresses* as real, posits as an external necessity, that which lies within the nature of capital; competition is nothing more than the way in which many capitals force the inherent determinants of capital upon one another and upon themselves.[8]
>
> Conceptually, *competition* is nothing other than the inner *nature of capital*, its essential character, appearing in and realized as the reciprocal interaction of many capitals with one another, the inner tendency as external necessity.[9]

For Marx, we see, competition is 'the real process of capital', the way the inner laws, the immanent tendencies, of capital as a whole are unveiled:

> Only in competition – the action of capital upon capital – are the inherent laws of capital, its tendencies realized.[10]
>
> Competition executes the inner laws of capital; makes them into compulsory laws towards the individual capital, but it does not invent them. It realizes them.[11]

---

[7] Marx 1973, p. 657.
[8] Marx 1973, p. 651.
[9] Marx 1973, p. 414.
[10] Marx 1973, pp. 651, 751.
[11] Marx 1973, p. 752.

Competition generally, this essential locomotive force of the bourgeois economy, does not establish its laws, but is rather their executor....Competition therefore does not *explain* these laws; rather, it lets them be *seen*, but does not produce them.[12]

Obviously, the *Grundrisse* is rich in explicit statements about competition of capitals as the outer form by which the inner tendencies of capital are realised. However, Marx says the same thing in his discussion of relative surplus-value in Chapter 12 of Volume I of *Capital*. There, again, the central point:

the immanent laws of capitalist production manifest themselves in the external movement of the individual capitals, assert themselves as the coercive laws of competition.[13]

What does all this mean? Very simply that this inner drive of capital, discovered through abstract thought *without reference to separate capitals*, necessarily appears in the real world as propelled *not* by class struggle but by competing capitalists. Competition is not the source of these tendencies, 'does not produce them'; however, capitalists necessarily view themselves as *driven*, as forced, by the actions of other capitalists (and they *are*). Rather than the inner impulse in which the struggle to increase exploitation is what drives capital forward, the inner tendency here appears as external necessity, as the external compulsion produced by competition.

Insofar as an individual capitalist's actions in driving down real wages and increasing productivity help to lower necessary labour, he contributes to the execution of the 'general and necessary tendencies of capital' – in this case, the inner tendency to drive up the rate of surplus-value.[14] But, competition also executes the inner laws of capital where individual capitalists succeed in finding ways to reduce their costs of circulation and the diversion of their capital from the sphere of production, where competition compels individual capitalists to increase accumulation at the expense of their consumption in order not to fall behind their competitors, and where individual capitals are driven to innovate in the creation of new use-values and the discovery of new markets for old use-values.

---

[12] Marx 1973, p. 552.
[13] Marx 1977a, p. 433.
[14] Ibid.

Where the inner tendencies of capital are realised through the reciprocal interaction of many capitals with one another, we can see the link between essence and appearance in Marx, between capital in general and its necessary form of existence as many capitals. However, we are able to identify the way in which competition realises capital's inner laws *only* because we have first discovered the latter.

Competition and contingency

All that appears is not necessary. Much of what happens in that real process of capitalist competition does not necessarily have its counterpart in the inner analysis. Rather than necessary, it may merely be contingent – a possibility 'whose Other or opposite equally is' possible.[15] Reality or actuality contains both necessity and contingency, and it is essential to distinguish between these.

For example, if observable trends in the rate of profit are the result of periods of uneven progress in the development of productivity, how can we view the resulting patterns as inherent and necessary rather than contingent and temporary? (See the discussion in Chapters 7 and 8.) Similarly, if subdivisions of capital (e.g., merchant-capital or finance-capital), categories or activities (e.g., advertising, fictitious capital, speculation) take on a growing role relative to industrial capital as such, is this a contingent development or an immanent tendency? In what sense, too, can it be said that the growth of monopoly capital is inherent in capitalist development?

Certainly, the particular quantitative determinations of the subdivision of surplus-value may develop a 'law-like' regularity as the result of the balance of forces (leading vulgar economists to propose separate laws to explain the level of each). Yet, as discussed in Chapter 5, persisting appearances are not sufficient to reveal necessity. Marx was very explicit in his recognition that those 'laws' may be purely external and not rooted in the essential characteristics of the system; thus, one could not be guided by surface phenomena.

In some cases, the apparent regularities may help 'those caught up in the practice of competition' to 'arrive at some idea, even if still a superficial one, of the inner connection of economic relations that presents itself within

---

[15] Hegel 1929, II, p. 177.

competition'. But, not all appearances suggest the general and necessary. Discussing the question of a natural rate of interest, Marx declared:

> Where, as here, it is competition as such that decides, the determination is inherently accidental, purely empirical, and only pedantry or fantasy can seek to present this accident as something necessary.[16]

How, then, can we distinguish between cases where outer phenomena have no inner basis (i.e., cases of contingency where the pattern is 'inherently accidental') and those where the outer is the manifestation of general and necessary tendencies? If we are to understand the phenomena before us, there is no alternative but to search for their inner basis. 'A scientific analysis of competition is possible,' Marx stressed, 'only if we can grasp the inner nature of capital'.[17]

If science means anything, it means that you cannot accept appearance as the basis of knowledge. As Marx commented in relation to Adam Smith's discussion of the rate of profit:

> Competition executes the inner laws of capital..., but it does not invent them. It realizes them. *To try to explain them simply as the results of competition therefore means to concede that one does not understand them.*[18]

In competition, everything is reversed

If we do not grasp the inner tendencies of capital, what do we understand from competition? Recall how often Marx's discussion of science comes back to the problem of the inverted appearance of the movement of the planets – how we need to grasp 'their real motions, which are not perceptible to the senses' before we can understand the apparent movement of the sun around the earth. He speaks of the 'paradox' presented by appearances, of how it is 'paradox that the earth moves around the sun.' (See Chapter 5.) Demonstrating that these references to the inversion of the world of appearance were not casual, Marx commented at another point:

---

[16] Marx 1981b, p. 485.
[17] Marx 1977a, p. 433.
[18] Marx 1973, p. 752. Emphasis added.

that in their appearance things are often presented in an inverted way is something fairly familiar in every science, apart from political economy.[19]

Competition inverts the inner connections. And, we have already seen why it does for the individual capitalist; making advances for the costs of his inputs is the precondition for his activity –

it is precisely wages, interest and rent that go into this production as limiting and governing amounts of price. These therefore appear to him as the elements determining the price of his commodities.[20]

But, it is *not* only for the individual capitalist that everything is reversed, that 'all the determinants appear in a position which is the *inverse* of their position in capital in general. There price determined by labour, here labour determined by price etc. etc.'[21] There is an inherent basis for this reversal.

Value and surplus-value are the logical premises for developing the internal connections and coming to an understanding of the conceptual totality of capitalism. They are, further, the logical premises for understanding the subdivisions of value and surplus-value. Yet, as Marx stressed, value and surplus-value are 'invisible essences' – in contrast to the visible surface phenomena of price and profit, respectively. These inner premises for understanding the interconnections do not and cannot appear as such; they do not exist on the surface.

However, the *forms* of these logical premises do appear. And they appear not as premises but as *results, indeed as sums*! Thus, the abstract social labour of society appears as the sum of concrete labours; value appears as price – the sum of cost-price plus profit; and, surplus-value appears as profit, as rent, as interest (as their sum, if anyone bothers to add them up) – which all appear to be derived from independent sources. How different from the inner analysis! There it is clear that value pre-exists its subdivision: the length of a line

is not determined by the lengths of the segments into which it is divided. It is rather the relative lengths of the latter that are limited in advance by the limits of the line of which they are parts.[22]

---

[19] Marx 1977a, p. 677.
[20] Marx 1981b, p. 1014.
[21] Marx 1973, p. 657.
[22] Marx 1981a, p. 462.

On the surface, the whole must appear as the sum of pre-existing parts. Given that the subdivisions of surplus-value in competition are elements of the cost of production for the individual capitalist, for example, they 'appear upside-down, as formative elements of surplus-value'; added to wages, these subdivisions appear as formative elements of price.[23] If we do not delve beneath the surface, the result is inevitable:

> In competition, therefore, everything appears upside down. The finished configuration of economic relations, as they are visible on the surface, in their actual existence, and therefore also in the notions with which the bearers and agents of these relations seek to gain an understanding of them, is very different from the configuration of their inner core, which is essential but concealed, and the concept corresponding to it. It is in fact the very reverse and antithesis of this.[24]

It is not easy to focus consistently on that essential but concealed inner core and to distance oneself from the visible pattern of economic relations. For Marx, the problem of mixing up inner and outer was dramatically illustrated by Adam Smith's confusion. Smith first demonstrated that value is resolved into profit, rent and wages,

> and then he proceeds the other way round, regards the prices of wages, profit and rent as antecedent factors and seeks to determine them independently, in order to compose the *price of the commodity* out of them. The meaning of this change of approach is that first he grasps the problem in its *inner relationships*, and then in the *reverse form, as it appears in competition.*[25]

Thus, we find in Smith both the inner and the outer – both 'the intrinsic connection existing between economic categories or the obscure structure of the bourgeois economic system' and also 'the connection as it appears in the phenomena of competition and thus as it presents itself to the unscientific observer'. Having initially grasped that inner connection, Smith became

---

[23] Marx 1981b, p. 1011.
[24] Marx 1981b, p. 311.
[25] Marx 1968, p. 106.

obsessed ... with the *connection, as it appears in competition*, and in competition everything always appears in inverted form, always standing on its head.[26]

The problem with competition

Does it *matter* that in competition everything is reversed? Does it matter if we think the sun revolves around the earth? In neither case does it matter if you are going to go about your daily life. But it matters if we truly want to understand the basis of appearances. If 'the interconnection of the reproduction process is not understood, i.e., as this presents itself not from the standpoint of the individual capital, but rather from that of the total capital', then we will never grasp that what the worker sells is labour-power rather than a specific quantity of labour.[27]

The problem is not simply that competition's reversal of the inner connections inherently masks the nature of exploitation. Insofar as we live in the world of competing capitals which drive each other forward 'with a constant *march, march!*', as commented, there is a natural tendency to attribute the inner drive of capital to competition.[28] Thus, Ernest Mandel, in his 'Introduction' to Volume I of *Capital*, for example, described 'the basic drive' of capitalism as 'the drive to accumulate capital' and declared that this drive 'is essentially explained by competition, that is by the phenomenon of "various capitals"'.[29]

---

[26] Marx 1968, pp. 165, 217. But, Smith should not be overly condemned for the ease with which he glided from an inner analysis ('the inner connection, the physiology') to the surface ('the external phenomena of life, as they seem and appear'). After all, how many readers of *Capital* have been sensitive to the inverted order when Marx (1977a, p. 770) states, 'To put it mathematically the rate of accumulation is the independent, not the dependent variable; the rate of wages is the dependent, not the independent variable.' Yet, what is the rate of accumulation? It depends upon the surplus-value generated (and realised), and this in turn depends upon the value of labour-power. Indeed, the *inner* logic as developed through Volume I proceeds from value to the value of labour-power to surplus-value to accumulation. If there is an *inner* dependent variable, it is the rate of accumulation. The level at which Marx's Volume I, Chapter 25 discussion takes places needs to be looked at carefully.

[27] Marx 1981b, p. 983. See the discussion in Chapter 1 above.

[28] Marx 1973, p. 413.

[29] Marx 1977a, p. 60. Mandel explains the 'basic drive' by competition of capitals despite his understanding (Marx 1977a, p. 62) that Marx viewed capital accumulation 'at two different and successive levels of approximation' and that the Volume I discussion, considering 'capital in general', looked at accumulation 'essentially in

Unfortunately, using competition to explain the basic drives of capitalism prevents you logically from stressing class struggle over any other struggle generated by competition (or, for that matter, from stressing production over circulation). *In the world of competing capitals, nothing privileges exploitation or class struggle*: all inputs are viewed simply as costs; and, all reductions in costs (whether in production or circulation and whether these involve reductions in, for example, what is paid for labour, use of land or money-capital) are of equal importance. Thus, increasing exploitation (although not, of course, in these terms) and economising upon rental payments both are simply responses to the external compulsion exerted by alien capitals.

If capital *really* existed as One – i.e., if the phenomenal form of capital corresponded to its essence – then it would be clear on the surface that the only way that capital grows is through the exploitation of workers and that it is the class struggle between capital and wage-labour that drives the system forward. Insofar as capital exists in the form of many capitals, however, science is necessary. That science must do what all other sciences do:

> seek to uncover the essence which lies hidden behind commonplace appearances, and which mostly contradicts the form of commonplace appearances (as for example in the case of the movement of the sun about the earth).[30]

Let us be frank: if we fail to distinguish between the essence of capital and its appearance in competition, we are either rejecting Marx's methodology or demonstrating that we do not understand it.

---

the light of what occurs in and flows from the exchange between wage-labour and capital'.

[30] Marx 1994, p. 86.

Chapter Twelve
Too Many Blindspots About the Media

In a recent discussion in *Studies in Political Economy*, Robert A. Hackett began with the question, 'What is a socialist position on the control and functioning of the mass media in Canada?'[1] The answer, we soon learned, was not to be found in 'radical instrumentalist' approaches (such as that of Wallace Clement, *Canadian Dimension*, etc.) which focus on (quaint) matters like capitalist ownership of the media. Nor should one have 'romantic' illusions about such things as workers' control of existing media, So, where did Hackett seek the answer? In a Marxist-sounding communications theory known to friends and foes alike as the 'blindspot' paradigm.[2]

'A socialist analysis and strategy for the news media', Hackett proposed, 'must surely recognize that, like most branches of production in capitalism, most Canadian media industries must produce commodities and sell them in a market.'[3] With this innocent-sounding opening, Hackett proceeded to advance Dallas Smythe's proposition that the precise commodity sold by the media to advertisers is audiences! And so we entered a twilight zone of Marxist terminology and 'vulgar' analysis – one

---

[1] Hackett 1986, p. 141.
[2] The discussion takes its name from Dallas Smythe's original article (1977). See also Smythe 1981.
[3] Hackett 1986, p. 148.

where anything can happen if the right (or, rather, left) discourse is employed.

Consider Smythe's original argument, the explicit theoretical basis for Hackett's subsequent inferences. Rejecting what he described as an idealist view (held by, among others, Lenin, Baran and Sweezy, and Marcuse), Smythe argued that mass communications within monopoly capitalism have a commodity-form and that a materialist (i.e., Marxist) analysis required us to recognise that the audience itself was the commodity in mass-produced, advertiser-supported communications. The audience, produced by the media-capitalists and sold as a commodity to the advertisers, worked for the advertising capitalist (by learning to buy particular brands) – and, as such, produced surplus-value for the advertising capitalist.[4] Thus, the worker was exploited not only in the direct production process but also at home during 'free time', while watching – a *double* exploitation.

With this argument, designed to remove the blindspot of Western Marxists, Smythe introduced a paradigm sufficiently bold and unique to attract (to the process of 'normal science' within the confines of the paradigm) others like Hackett seeking a radical approach to communications. Among them Sut Jhally and Bill Livant, while rejecting many of the particulars of Smythe's argument, proceeded to take the position several steps forward (or backward).[5] For them, rather than the audience as commodity, the commodity was identified as time – watching time, sold by the media-capitalists to the advertisers. The audience, compelled to work by watching advertising for a period of time in excess of the cost of producing programmes, provides surplus labour-time ('surplus watching time') to the media-capitalist, which is the basis of the latter's surplus-value. This surplus-value, however, is only *realised* in the course of the sale of advertising time by the media-capitalists to the advertisers.

Now, obviously, the focus shifts here from the original 'blindspot' story – from surplus-value for the advertiser to surplus-value for the media. But, the audience still works. It still works for someone else. It is still exploited. It is

---

[4] As a possible measure of 'surplus-value created by people working in audiences', Smythe suggested that we compare the sum of advertising expenditures with 'value added' by retailing of consumer goods. Smythe 1977, pp. 19–20.

[5] Jhally and Livant 1984. Several points included in this note were contained in my original comments on the Jhally and Livant paper.

still the source of surplus-value. And, there is still the sale of audience-time as a commodity.

Nor would the new argument challenge the original story. It would be entirely consistent with this framework to propose that the audience, after working for the media-capitalists, *also* proceeds to secure consumer information from the advertisers and thereby to perform marketing functions for the advertising capitalist – i.e., that it works for *both* (although in different ways). In place of the double exploitation in Dallas Smythe's original argument, we would now have *triple* exploitation.[6]

The whole business bears some looking into – especially when we see the blindspot paradigm, drawing upon Marxist terminology, deployed as the theoretical basis for a criticism of a focus on capitalist ownership of the media.

Although a blind Western Marxist (at last, my confession) is not in principle opposed to the theoretical demonstration of two, three, many forms of exploitation, it must be admitted that we do have a proprietary interest in ensuring that there is enough of the worker left over to be exploited in the direct process of production. That, after all, continues to be the blindspot of Marxism – the tenet that surplus-value in capitalism is generated in the direct process of production, the process where workers (having surrendered the property rights over the disposition of their labour-power) are *compelled* to work longer than is necessary to produce the equivalent of their wage. Perhaps it is for this reason that there is hesitation in accepting the conception that *audiences* work, are exploited, and produce surplus-value – in that it is a paradigm quite different to the Marxist paradigm. One might go so far as to characterise this alternative paradigm as *in essence* stressing surplus-value as the result of the ripping-off of consumers – although its form of presentation, presumably under the influence of the Marxist paradigm, emphasises that these consumers are workers.[7]

---

[6] The subtitle of the Jhally/Livant paper, 'Extensions of the Domain of Capital' here would have a very vivid meaning.

[7] Consider the following 'The logic of the production of surplus-value in watching is the same as it is in the factory....[W]atchers labour for capital to the same extent as do wage-labourers in a factory. There is no qualitative difference.' Jhally and Livant 1984, p. 37.

.

It was Marx's argument that one of the tasks of science is to reduce the visible and merely apparent movement to the actual, inner movement. He approached this task by considering capital in general – capital in the abstract as it moved through its necessary circuits – before exploring the real forms of existence of capital as subdivided, as existing in competition.

Let us consider, then, capital-in-general – before looking at how it must appear. We begin with capital which possesses commodities which contain surplus-value latently – surplus-value which is the result of the exploitation of workers within production but which can only be made real (realised) through the sale of those commodities. As we saw in Chapter 7, every moment those commodities remain unsold is a cost to capital: a lengthy time of circulation ties up capital in the sphere of circulation and requires the expenditure of additional capital if production is to be continuous; similarly, a lengthy period of circulation reduces cash flows, reduces the turnover of capital – and thus reduces the annual surplus-value.[8]

Accordingly, it is in the interest of this capital to undertake expenditures which will reduce the time of circulation, and thus the total costs of circulation. Any such expenditures are rational so long as their cost is less than what is saved through more rapid sales, through a reduced time of circulation. Certain expenditures will be undertaken on advertisements, programmes and media in order to reach markets and sell commodities more rapidly. What it buys with these expenditures is more rapid sales – and, thus, a lesser deduction from the surplus-value generated in the sphere of production. The costs of the media department of this capital are credited to selling expenses.

Now, let us propose that we have a functional subdivision of this one capital into two, in which we separate from capital as a whole (for accounting purposes) one media-capital. In this case, the media-capital will sell its various services to 'industrial' capital, which will purchase those so long as it still gains by the reduction of circulation time. The media-capitalist here will obtain its appropriate share of the surplus-value generated within the sphere of production; it will obtain this share by charging industrial capital a price in excess of the costs of programmes.

It will be noted that both in this version and the preceding one, consumers enter into the calculation only as buyers; if they respond to exhortations and

---

[8] See also Lebowitz 1972.

sales efforts, there will be reduced circulation time and costs, more rapid turnover of capital, increased annual surplus-value. Whether they shut their eyes during the ads or study them astutely, searching for consumer clues, is irrelevant; all that matters is that they buy.

Now, finally, let us approach the surface, the realm of competition. Here we have differing, competing media-capitalists competing for the expenditures of competing industrial capitalists. The media-capitalists compete by attempting to demonstrate that they will be able to increase the commodity sales of industrial capitalists most rapidly – i.e., will permit the greatest possible reduction in circulation time. The *basis* of such competition necessarily is the size and nature of audience which may be reached through a particular medium. Thus, part of the competition of media-capitalists is the attempt to obtain the largest possible audience – which is, of course, in the interests of industrial capitalists (and capital-in-general).

On this surface, marked by competition of capitals, nothing in essence is altered. We have industrial capital seeking a means of reducing its total costs of circulation to a minimum – in order to maximise the valorisation of capital; we have it choosing among various avenues for its selling expenditures in order to maximise its increase in sales relative to the expenditures undertaken. Profits of media-capitalists are a share of the surplus-value of industrial capital. And, we have consumers doing their part by buying.

However, consider the self-conception of the media-capitalist in competition. From the perspective of the media-capitalist, what it does is to produce audiences for the advertiser; what it does is sell audiences and audience-time to the advertiser. From the perspective of the individual media-capitalist, its profit is a direct function of its size of audience. *Rather than as part of the process of selling the commodities of industrial capital to consumers, it necessarily appears as if the media-capitalists in competition sell consumers to industrial capital.*

Now, as Marx noted on many occasions, in competition everything is inverted. The ideas and conceptions of the actual agents of capitalist production on the surface are 'necessarily quite upside down'. These are the illusions created by competition. Consider Marx's discussion of the illusions of the merchant capitalist:

> It will be completely self-evident that, in the heads of the agents of capitalist production and circulation, ideas must necessarily form about the laws of production that diverge completely from these laws and are merely the

expression in consciousness of the apparent movement. The ideas of a merchant, a stock-jobber or a banker are necessarily quite upside down.[9]

To which we must add – the ideas of the media-capitalist.

Precisely because of this necessary inversion of the underlying relations and movements, Marx insisted on the necessity to begin by considering capital-in-general abstractly rather than relying upon the way things appear to the real actors. That is what Marx meant by science – in contrast to the perspective of 'vulgar economy' which begins from appearances. That is why science was necessary. In the so-called blindspot paradigm, however, *the starting-point is the self-conception of the media-capitalists*. The starting-point – buttressed by evidence of these self-conceptions – is the inverted concept of the sale of audiences and audience-time to industrial capitalists.

In short, the starting-point reveals a complete rejection of Marx's methodological premise. And, however much Marxian verbiage may *subsequently* enter into the discussion (value, surplus-value, valorisation, surplus watching-time, etc.) it cannot alter the fact that what is produced is an entirely un-Marxian argument with un-Marxian conclusions which follow from the initial premise. Should we then be surprised that this premise leads to the conclusion that audiences work, are exploited in this work and are a source of surplus-value?

Let us return to Hackett, who accepts that audiences are sold and that 'audience-power is a form of work in which audience members both market goods to themselves, and reproduce their labour power?'[10] It should be recognised that the first problem begins with his commonsense observation that the media produces and sells a commodity. Accepting this, it is only logical to attempt to identify the commodity and to observe that the media sells something to advertisers. From a *Marxist perspective*, however, the media produces and sells a commodity as such only insofar as there is a transaction with a consumer (newspapers, magazines, etc.); insofar as it sells advertising space/time (and thus, apparently, audiences) it functions within the circuit of capital performing a service *which takes a commodity-form*. Within this view of the media as two-sided, providing two use-values – a product (to the consumer) and the 'right' to accompany that product (to the advertiser) – there

---

[9] Marx 1981b, p. 428.
[10] Hackett 1986, p. 148.

is considerable basis to explore the contradictions and the interpenetration between the media as commodity-producer, and the media as moment within the sphere of circulation of capital.

How much credibility, however, can be assigned to a paradigm which starts from the assumption that the media sells what it can never have property rights over: the audience? Ultimately, the blindspot paradigm collapses on the point that if media-capitalists sell an audience to industrial capitalists, it must first be theirs to sell. The begged question then becomes: how did this commodity become the property of the media-capitalists in the first place? What is the transaction in which the property rights over the disposition of 'watching-power' were transferred from the original owners, the audience, to the media-capitalists? How is the contract specified – and how is it enforced? Although the ultimate test of any theory is its ability to explain (and what it *fails* to explain), the blindspot paradigm would appear to lead from a false premise to a dead-end.

So, what about the 'important implications' and new socialist strategies which are said to follow from this blindspot paradigm? Some of Hackett's points do not in *any* sense require acceptance of the paradigm, and can be reached equally well by a two-sided Marxist perspective (as in the case of his emphasis on exploiting the inherent contradictions within the media).[11] Certainly his fine discussion of 'objectivity', ideology and the importance of the struggle for hegemony owes nothing to the blindspot paradigm. In this respect, one might suggest that Hackett apply Occam's Razor – cut his losses and avoid legitimising the blindspot paradigm any further.

However, the blindspot paradigm is not entirely incidental to Hackett's conclusions. Its starting-point in the self-conception of media-capitalists is reflected in his sensitivity to the powerlessness of the media in the face of competition and markets – in the *'market as censor'* ('quite independently of the intentions and manipulations of owners').[12] Similarly, that starting-point in the self-conception of media-capitalists is reflected in the view of audiences as 'complicit' – the 'sense in which commercial media '"give people what they want"' and thus the problem of 'established audience expectations as a

---

[11] Hackett 1986, p. 154.
[12] Hackett 1986, pp. 149–50.

constraint on media reform'.[13] Giving sufficient 'weight to the role of audiences in the media system, and to the structural imperatives of production for a market' is the basis upon which Hackett scorns the radical-instrumentalist 'overemphasis' on capitalist ownership of the media (and the prescription of social ownership).[14]

Hackett's own strategy involves the creation of 'democratized, decentralized and decommercialized communication networks' in which audiences are active rather than positioned as consumers.[15] Such a goal is desirable, of course, and its achievement would appropriately be seen as a victory (in the same way as Marx viewed the co-operatives of his time as a great victory); its realisation, however, faces the problems (as Hackett notes) of how to finance such alternative media and (as he does not note in this context) 'established audience expectations'. The prospect of 'dwarfish forms', resulting from restriction to the private efforts of individuals, which 'will never transform capitalistic society' is real indeed.[16]

In contrast, what Hackett calls the radical-instrumentalist position is part both of a general struggle against capital and also of a particular struggle to extract *existing* media from their position within the circuit of capital. (And those struggles, insofar as they occur, enable the participants to produce themselves in an altered manner – as other than audience.) Hackett's 'socialist position on the control and functioning of the mass media in Canada', however, sets aside the problem of (and the struggle against) capitalist ownership and control of existing mass media. No one (to my knowledge) has denied the critical importance of alternative media as part of a hegemonic struggle against capital, but his comments on the limitations of the radical instrumentalist position reveal the existence of yet another blindspot – a beam in this case.

---

[13] Hackett 1986, pp. 150, 154.
[14] Hackett 1986, p. 148.
[15] Hackett 1986, p. 151.
[16] Marx n.d., p. 346.

Chapter Thirteen

The Theoretical Status of Monopoly-Capital

Monopoly-capital?

In 1966, Paul Baran and Paul Sweezy published *Monopoly Capital*, a book which was extremely influential in introducing a Marxian perspective to a new generation of critics of aspects of capitalism. More than simply an attempt to popularise Marx, however, *Monopoly Capital* also boldly advanced the argument that Marxian social science had *stagnated*, stagnated because of its reliance on the assumption of a competitive economy: 'the Marxian analysis of capitalism still rests in the final analysis on the assumption of a competitive economy.'[1]

Modern capitalism, however, was characterised by monopoly; the typical economic unit, they noted, 'has the attributes which were once thought to be possessed only by monopolies'.[2] And, recognition of this and its significance had to be at the core of analysis. The emergence of monopoly-capital anticipated but not investigated by Marx, had to be seen not as 'effecting essentially quantitative modifications of the basic Marxian laws of capitalism', – but as a 'qualitatively new element in the capitalist economy'.[3] Thus, monopoly power, rising surpluses, expansion

---

[1] Baran and Sweezy 1966, pp. 3–4.
[2] Baran and Sweezy 1966, p. 6.
[3] Baran and Sweezy 1966, p. 5.

of unproductive expenditures and stagnation as the normal state of the economy – elements introduced earlier in Sweezy's *Theory of Capitalist Development* – constituted the qualitatively new character of modern capitalism.[4]

For some Marxists, however, all this has little to do with Marxism. The very concept of a monopoly stage of capitalism, it has been argued, is 'incompatible' with Marx's theory. For, rather than the reduction of competition, Marx believed that capitalism would 'tend to be *less* monopolistic' and competition more intense.[5] Rather than Marxism, according to these critics, the Baran-Sweezy theory of monopoly-capital is idealist, bourgeois and leads logically to reformism.[6] There is, it appears, what one critic has described as an 'ambiguous and unclarified relationship of American neo-Marxism to classical Marxism'.[7]

But, then, what is classical Marxism in this area? In Marx's *Capital*, there are two apparent themes which point in opposite directions.[8] In Volume I, there is the account of growing monopolisation, the 'expropriation of many capitalists by a few', the growing force of attraction and centralisation – and the explicit statement relating the intensity of competition to the number of capitals in a particular sphere: 'competition rages in direct proportion to the number, and in inverse proportion to the magnitude, of the rival capitals'.[9] In Volume III, on the other hand, equalisation of the profit rate and capital mobility are shown to depend upon the degree of development of capitalism. The less capital is 'adulterated and amalgamated with survivals of former economic conditions' and the more the credit system develops, the greater the extent to which capital succeeds in equalising profit rates among the various spheres of production.[10] For those who emphasise this latter theme, then, monopoly power, barriers to entry, differential profit rates are, at best, transitory phenomena; the very development of capitalism breaks down

---

[4] Sweezy 1956.
[5] Zeluck 1980, p. 44; For a reply to Zeluck, Foster 1981.
[6] Zeluck 1980, pp. 50–2; Weeks 1981, pp. 153, 157, 165–7; Weeks 1977, pp. 286, 301. See also Clifton 1977, p. 150.
[7] Mosley 1979, p. 53.
[8] Clifton 1977, p. 145; Williams 1982.
[9] Marx 1977a, pp. 929, 779, 777.
[10] Marx 1959, pp. 172, 177, 192, 426.

monopolies and intensifies the competition among capitals through the mechanism of capital mobility.

The basis of the division over the status of the concept of monopoly-capital, thus, appears to be present in Marx himself; and, the possibility that Marx was simply inconsistent must be acknowledged – an admission that would provide the degree of freedom allowing all to choose among competing quotations according to taste. Yet, the proper situation of the concept of monopoly-capital cannot rely simply upon the consideration of extrinsic quotations. Rather, it is necessary to attempt to reconstruct Marx's inner argument and to establish which, if any, of Marx's statements flow logically and necessarily from his theory.

Essence and appearance in Marx's method

To understand the place of monopoly-capital in Marx's framework, we must first be clear as to the relation which Marx posed between the concept of capital and capital as it really exists. Before one could understand the behaviour and the movements of capital on the surface, it was necessary to grasp the inner nature, the essential character, of capital – that which distinguished it; the understanding of 'capital in general', the concept of capital, 'an abstraction which grasps the specific characteristics which distinguish capital from all other forms of wealth – or modes in which (social) production develops' – this conscious abstraction from surface phenomena was required in order to comprehend the inner laws, immanent tendencies and intrinsic connections of capital.[11]

Only then could one proceed to consider capital as it really exists – as individual capitals, as many capitals, as capitals in competition. Only then could one understand the apparent movements on the surface:

> a scientific analysis of competition is possible only if we can grasp the inner
> nature of capital, just as the apparent motions of the heavenly bodies are

---

[11] Marx 1973, p. 449; 1968, p. 106. The discussion here draws heavily upon my original 1980 manuscript for 'Marx's Methodological Project' which was the basis for several essays here (see Introduction). See also Rosdolsky 1977.

intelligible only to someone who is acquainted with their real motions, which are not perceptible to the senses.[12]

Thus, with an understanding of the concept of capital, of capital as self-expanding value, value-for-itself, standing opposite wage-labour, the necessary impulse of capital to develop productive forces in order to secure relative surplus-value is readily grasped. On the surface, in competition, however, that process did not occur with the conscious goal of the reduction of necessary labour. Rather, individual capitals acted in order to reduce their individual cost-prices, in order to 'pocket the difference between their costs of production and the market-prices of the same commodities produced at higher costs of production'; they develop productivity in order to increase their individual profits.[13] In place of the essential opposition of capital and wage-labour, on the surface there is substituted the opposition of capitals.

Through their individual actions, then, many capitals in competition *execute* the inner laws of capital; it is the 'way in which the immanent laws of capitalist production manifest themselves in the external movement of the individual capitals, assert themselves as the coercive laws of competition'.[14] Competition, Marx noted, 'is nothing more than the way in which many capitals force the inherent determinants of capital upon one another and upon themselves'. It does not '*explain* these laws; rather, it lets them be *seen*, but does not produce them'.[15]

Thus, the action of capital upon capital, the real process of capital, invents no new laws or tendencies; it merely realises those inherent in the very nature of capital. To try to explain those laws by reference to surface phenomena, however, is to follow the course of vulgar political economy; 'to try to explain them simply as the results of competition therefore means to concede that one does not understand them'.[16] Indeed, remaining at the level of appearance, one can never establish *necessity*; it is only the inner insofar as it is manifested as outer, essence insofar as it appears, that has the character of necessity:

---

[12] Marx 1977a, p. 433.
[13] Marx 1959, p. 259.
[14] Marx 1977a, p. 433.
[15] Marx 1973, pp. 651, 552.
[16] Marx 1973, p. 752.

> Wherever it is competition as such which determines anything, the
> determination is accidental, purely empirical, and only pedantry or fantasy
> would seek to represent this accident as a necessity.[17]

It was not, of course, merely the understanding of the essential in the apparent
movements of capital which concerned Marx. Also critical was the necessity
to 'grasp the inner connection in contrast to the multiplicity of outward
forms', to locate and describe the concrete forms, to demonstrate the inner
connections within the forms of capital assumed 'on the surface of society'.[18]
That was, in part, the project of Volume III of *Capital* – to demonstrate why
essence, the inner nature of capital, necessarily appeared as it did.

   Thus, we see here in Volume III the consideration of the rate of profit (which
has the rate of surplus-value as its 'invisible and unknown essence') and
prices of production ('an utterly external and *prima facie* meaningless form of
the value of commodities, a form as it appears in competition').[19] Similarly,
various forms of capital and sources of revenue are shown to necessarily
emerge from the movements of capital as a whole; merchant-capital and
merchant-profits, interest-bearing capital and interest, landed property and
rent – all these apparently independent forms of wealth are reduced 'to their
inner unity by means of analysis'.[20] As he had earlier remarked about Ricardo,
Marx here explains

> in this way all phenomena, even those like ground rent, accumulation
> of capital and the relation of wages to profit, which at first sight seem to
> contradict it [his formula]; it is precisely that which makes his doctrine a
> scientific system.[21]

It was the same effort to demonstrate the consistency of the outer forms
with the inner nature of capital which underlies Marx's discussion of the
transformation of values into prices of production. Discussion of this process,
which occurs through the equalisation of the rate of profit, is intended to show
that logically there is a necessary redistribution of surplus-value and value
on the surface – but nothing which is inconsistent with the inner relations.

---

[17] Marx 1959, p. 356.
[18] Marx 1971, p. 500; 1959, p. 25.
[19] Marx 1971, pp. 43, 194.
[20] Marx 1971, p. 500.
[21] Marx 1963, pp. 49–50.

Thus, for what classical political economy offered up as its external 'law,' prices of production, Marx provides an inner explanation.

Yet, certainly, consideration of this particular process of transformation could not exhaust the relation of many capitals on the surface to the concept of capital. Logically, the consistency of the actions of many capitals, the action of capital upon capital, requires consideration of *all possible forms* of many capitals. Many capitals logically can include at one extreme an infinite number of capitals (the 'perfect competition' case) or, at the other extreme, two capitals within a society. In short, one possible or contingent form of capital is not sufficient to demonstrate the necessary consistency of the outer forms of capital with its inner nature. And, certainly, Marx was explicit as to the limits of his discussion of transformation of values through the equalisation of profit rates. Equalisation of profit rates, he noted, implies mobility of capital, its free movement between various spheres of production; 'the premise in this case is that no barrier, or just an accidental and temporary barrier, interferes with the competition of capitals'.[22]

Rather than fetishising the transformation process, Marx proceeded to argue that *where* such barriers existed, where prices received exceeded the price of production (and therefore yielded higher than the average profit rate), where, in short, capital took the form of monopoly, here too this contingency would not violate the inner relations established. Either the existence of a monopoly would produce a redistribution of surplus-value ('a local disturbance in the distribution of surplus-value') – as in the other case considered – or, it could produce a reduction in wages below the value of labour-power.[23] In either case, Marx considered the presence of monopoly a phenomenon which did not at all contradict his formula.

Thus, competitive capital (*if* we may so designate the capital considered in the transformation discussion) and monopoly-capital were simply two contingent forms of capital, two forms of capital as it exists, two forms by which the inner laws of capital were executed.[24] And, yet, we know that there is more than that to the question of monopoly-capital – that of the status

---

[22] Marx 1959, p. 743; cf. also, p. 192.
[23] Marx 1959, pp. 839–40.
[24] Sweezy explicitly presents this position in Sweezy 1981, p. 63.

of a contingent form of capital; there is also the question of *necessity*, of the necessary emergence of monopoly.

Monopoly: from contingency to necessity

The proposition that the competitive form of capital has a tendency to give way to a monopoly form had a long lineage for Marx. It appears in Engel's early 'Outlines of a Critique of Political Economy' as the 'law of the centralization of private property', where large capitals swallow small capitals; was repeated by Proudhon and then identified as a movement and process (rather than an abstract formula) by Marx in his *Poverty of Philosophy*; and, then, once again appears as the tendency toward concentration of land and capital in a few hands and the victory of large capitals over small capitals in their contest in the *Communist Manifesto* and *Wage Labour and Capital*.[25] So, it is not surprising to see the proposition re-appear in *Capital*.

In *Capital*, the argument is that of the centralisation of capital. Noting that he could not here develop the 'laws of centralization of capitals, or of the attraction of capital by capital', Marx proceeded to offer a few facts. And these facts were that the battle of competition was fought by the cheapening of commodities, that large capitals beat the smaller capitals and that small capitals were thereby ruined, leaving large-scale industry under the control of a few hands.[26] Centralisation of capital then re-appears in the discussion of the historical tendency of capitalist accumulation, where we find that 'one capitalist always strikes down many others' and there is 'a constant decrease in the number of capitalist magnates'.[27] All this plays a critical role in the account of the end of capital; the monopoly of capital becomes a fetter on the development of productive forces.

The argument, we note, is basically the same as that of *Wage Labour and Capital*: centralisation emerges out of competition of capitals, attraction out of repulsion; individual capitals reduce their cost-prices and compel other capitals to follow suit or fall by the wayside. And, it is, of course, an outer or external account, one which presupposes consideration of individual capitals

---

[25] Engels 1975, p. 441; Marx 1963, pp. 151–2; Marx and Engels 1962, pp. 57, 104.
[26] Marx 1977a, p. 777.
[27] Marx 1977a, p. 929.

and of the competition of capitals (which, in fact, requires the discussion of Volume III of *Capital*). Yet, consideration of competition itself was premature, was possible 'only if we can grasp the inner nature of capital'.

We have, in short, a process of centralisation of capital – which plays such a critical role in Volume I – presented as the result of an external movement of many capitals; it is presented as an outer movement determined by competition of capitals. *Is it, then, a process which is contingent, purely empirical which only pedantry would represent as necessary?* Is it an outer movement for which there is no inner law, no immanent tendency, which gives it the character of a *necessary* process?

Well, it is certain that Marx had in mind an inner law for which the process of centralisation was 'merely' a manifestation. It was a law which he noted could not be 'developed here', and thus he limited himself to a few facts, an outer account. Similarly, he identified centralisation of capital as the *means* by which 'the immanent laws of capitalist production itself' accomplished the expropriation of individual capitals.[28] But, what *was* that inner law for which the process of centralisation as described was an outer form?

The inner tendency of capital to become One

The inner tendency, we propose, is simply the tendency of capital to become One, a tendency to develop from the form of many capitals (a fragmentation of capital given in its beginnings) to one adequate to its concept, capital in general. It is a tendency seen to be inherent in the very concept of capital itself – for all capital to be integrated as One capital in one hand and for all others to be in the position of wage-labour in relation to that capital. There are two aspects here: (1) the separation of the conditions of labour from all who labour and (2) the integration of these in one hand.

In short, we are describing as the inner tendency of capital precisely what is present in its historical genesis and inherent in its concept – expropriation/ separation. Expropriation is

---

[28] Marx 1977a, pp. 777, 928–9.

the point of departure for the capitalist mode of production; *its accomplishment is the goal of this production. In the last instance, it aims at the expropriation of the means of production from all individuals.*[29]

Indeed, every moment in the development of capital is to be understood as the development of this separation, on the one hand, and integration, on the other. In the primitive or original accumulation of capital, that 'historical process of separation which transforms the conditions of labour into capital and labour into wage-labour', there is already contained the integration of the conditions of labour.[30] As soon as capitalist production stands on its own feet, however, 'it not only maintains this separation, but reproduces it on a constantly extending scale'.[31]

Thus, simple reproduction of capital, that heuristic device, 'reproduces in the course of its own process the separation between labour-power and the conditions of labour'.[32] And, the accumulation of capital 'reproduces the separation and the independent existence of material wealth as against labour on an ever increasing scale'.[33] Finally, we have the process described as centralisation:

This is only the last degree and the final form of the process which transforms the conditions of labour into capital, then reproduces capital and the separate capitals on a larger scale and finally separates from their owners the various capitals which have come into existence at many points of society and centralizes them into the hands of big capitalists.[34]

It is just a further instance of separating – 'raised to the second power' – the conditions of production from the producers, a process that 'forms the conception of capital' and which is finally expressed as 'centralization of existing capitals in a few hands and a deprivation of many of their capital'.[35] Thus, we are describing here simply the progressive development of what is

---

[29] Marx 1959, p. 430. Emphasis added.
[30] Marx 1971, pp. 314–15.
[31] Marx 1977a, p. 874.
[32] Marx 1977a, p. 723.
[33] Marx 1971, p. 315.
[34] Marx 1971, p. 315.
[35] Marx 1959, p. 241.

inherent in the concept of capital; discussing precapitalist formations in the *Grundrisse*, Marx commented:

> the relation of labour to capital, or to the objective conditions of labour as capital, presupposes a process of history which dissolves the various forms in which the worker is a proprietor, or in which the proprietor works.[36]

That process is clearly one which continues – i.e., is a product and result of capital itself.

But, what are the *limits*, the theoretical limits, to this process? In a number of cases, the limit is expressed as the centralisation in a *few* hands. Post-dating many of these comments, on the other hand, are the changes which Marx introduced in the 1872 French edition (incorporated by Engels into the fourth German edition):

> In any given branch of industry centralization would reach its extreme limit if all the individual capitals invested there were fused into a single capital. In a given society this limit would be reached only when the entire social capital was united in the hands of either a single capitalist or a single capitalist company.[37]

How do we choose among the various quotations? Does this process of separation proceed to the point of centralising capital into a few hands, those of the big capitalists, or does it proceed *further*? And how precisely do Marx's comments on the place and role of the credit system and the emergence of the corporation fit in? Are they manifestations of the inner law or are they merely coincidental, reinforcing contingent developments?

What must be acknowledged is that however often Marx repeated this inner law of which centralisation was a manifestation, it is one thing to present a proposition with the characteristic of Hegelian elegance – and quite another thing to demonstrate its *necessity*. In the absence of such a demonstration of necessity, we need not worry about whether the tendency of capital to become One stops before this point – because there *is* no such tendency at all.

---

[36] Marx 1973, p. 497.
[37] Marx 1977a, p. 779.

The three aspects of integration

To demonstrate the necessity of the tendency of capital to become One, we must show that the very separation and disintegration of capitals is contrary to the concept of capital, that there is a particular restriction to the growth of capital and the development of productive forces inherent in the separation of capital – and, that accordingly the adequate development of capital requires the cancellation of that separation and fragmentation. In general, it must be shown that the unity of producers with the conditions of production is a barrier to the growth of capital – and, thus, that expropriation is necessary.

We need, however, to be more specific. For capital to become One – i.e., for the entire social capital of a given society to be united in the hands of a single capitalist or a single capitalist company, three separate (though related) processes are required:

1. Horizontal integration – the integration of all capitals in a single sphere,
2. Vertical integration – the integration of capitals in spheres which are organically related in the production of use-values, and
3. Conglomerate integration – the integration of capitals in differing spheres independent of any organic relation.

For integration to be complete, all three tendencies must be present. Thus, it is necessary to demonstrate that the existence of separate capitals in *each* case is contrary to the concept of capital within Marx's argument.

1. *The case for horizontal integration*

Consider first the tendency for horizontal integration, the most readily apparent argument which Marx provides. Here, the task is to demonstrate that the existence of separate capitals in a given sphere of production is a barrier to capital – and, accordingly, that capital has a tendency to negate that barrier.

Capital in general, self-expanding value, has the tendency to grow; faced with wage-labour, which struggles for its own goals, capital must develop productive forces in order to secure relative surplus-value. Yet, the separation of capitals within a particular sphere of production means that each capital thwarts the growth of every other capital:

the part of the social capital domiciled in each particular sphere of production is divided among many capitalists who confront each other as mutually independent and competitive commodity-producers.[38]

A critical part of Marx's argument, though, is that the very development of the specifically capitalist mode of production entails the requirement for 'a definite and constantly *growing minimum amount of capital*'; 'the conditions of production now demand the application of capital on a mass scale'.[39] The separation and independence of capitals in a particular sphere, however, prevents at a certain point the development of capital:

the world would still be without railways if it had to wait until accumulation had got a few individual capitals far enough to be adequate for the construction of a railroad.[40]

The separation of capitals prevents the development of productive forces to the extent that integration of capital would permit; it is contrary to capital's tendency to reduce necessary labour and secure relative surplus-value.

And, thus, we have the tendency for attraction of capitals, which 'becomes more intense in proportion as the specifically capitalist mode of production develops along with accumulation.'[41] The process of integration destroys the 'individual independence' of existing capitals, transforms many small capitals into a few large ones; it allows for the development of processes of production 'socially combined and carried out on a large scale'; it 'intensifies and accelerates the effects of accumulation'; and, 'it simultaneously extends and speeds up those revolutions in the technical composition of capital'.[42]

This process of horizontal integration of capital, a redistribution of capitals within a particular sphere, is, of course, the familiar account of centralisation. It is executed by the actions of capitals upon capitals, by the competition of capitals whereby 'success and failure both lead here to a centralization of capital, and thus to expropriation on the most enormous scale'.[43] Since it is so familiar, it is also critical to emphasise that it is *only one form* of the process of

---

[38] Marx 1977a, p. 776.
[39] Marx 1977a, p. 1035; Marx 1971, p. 311.
[40] Marx 1977a, p. 780.
[41] Marx 1977a, p. 778n.
[42] Marx 1977a, pp. 777, 778n, 780.
[43] Marx 1959, p. 430.

integration and that it is inadequate in itself for a tendency for the entire social capital to be united in the hands of a single capitalist. Its limit (understood as a mathematical limit rather than a prediction) is a single capital in a given branch of industry; but, it leaves the possibility of a multitude of separate industries all producing different use-values and separated by commodity exchange.

2. *The case for vertical integration*

The tendency for vertical integration of capital is not nearly as well developed in *Capital*, and its relative de-emphasis must be regarded as an inadequacy of *Capital*. Nevertheless, it is certainly present. Here, the task is to demonstrate that the existence of capitals which are organically related in the production of use-values *but separated by commodity exchange* is a barrier to capital.

The matter here revolves around the difference between the purchase of a commodity by one capital from another and the purchase of the commodity labour-power. In the first case, the individual capitalist pays for all the labour he receives; in the second, he only pays for the *necessary* labour:

> when the capitalist enters the commodity market as a buyer,...he has to pay the full value of a commodity, the whole of labour-time embodied in it, irrespective of the proportions in which the fruits of the labour-time were divided or are divided between the capitalist and the worker. If, on the other hand, he enters the labour market as a buyer, he buys in actual fact more labour than he pays for.[44]

Consider, then, the implications for the introduction of machinery. For capital *in general*, machinery will be introduced as soon as it involves a net saving on labour – as soon as more labour is replaced in a particular process of production than is required to produce the given machine; in short, it is introduced as soon as it allows for the increase in productivity and thus the generation of relative surplus-value.

However, this is *not* the point at which the individual capitalist who must purchase machinery as a commodity will introduce the new technique. For the individual capitalist, it is not the difference between the labour contained in

---

[44] Marx 1971, p. 216.

the machine and the labour it displaces that matters; rather, it is the difference between the labour in the machine and the portion of the direct labour which that capitalist *pays* for:

> the limit to using a machine is therefore fixed by the difference between the value of the machine and the value of the labour-power replaced by it.[45]

It is only this difference which influences the action of the individual capitalist.

For the individual capitalist, it is not the increase in productivity – i.e., the reduction in the value of the commodity – which matters; it is the reduction in his individual cost-price. Thus, 'the law of increased productivity of labour is not, therefore, absolutely valid' for the individual capital, for capital as a whole when separated and fragmented by commodity exchange. Capital, here, goes against its historic mission:

> Its historic mission is unconstrained development in geometric progression of the productivity of human labour. It goes back on its mission whenever, as here, it checks the development of productivity.[46]

Thus, all other things equal, One capital will introduce machinery sooner and more extensively than individual capitals separated by commodity exchange. This point is the core of Marx's comment:

> The field of application for machinery would therefore be entirely different in a communist society from what it is in bourgeois society.[47]

But, it is not communist society nor (as Rosdolsky suggests) 'state-capitalist' society which is at issue here – it is simply the tendency in capital for vertical integration, the tendency to go beyond the barrier presented by the separation of capitals.[48]

Vertical integration of capital makes possible the further development of combined labour processes. It is present at the origin of the capitalist development of manufacture, where that which was previously separated by commodity exchange becomes part of a continuous process of production;

---

[45] Marx 1977a, p. 515.
[46] Marx 1959, pp. 256–7.
[47] Marx 1977a, p. 515n.
[48] Rodolosky 1977, pp. 524–9.

and, it grows ever more intense with the development of the specifically capitalist mode of production – where there is 'the progressive transformation of isolated processes of production, carried on by customary methods, into socially combined and scientifically arranged processes of production'.[49] Vertical integration of capital substitutes, for the anarchy, the 'chance and caprice' of commodity exchange, the *a priori* plan of combined labour processes.[50]

For capitals in competition, this tendency for vertical integration is realised as a result of the saving which will accrue to the individual capital which chooses to produce means of production rather than to purchase these as commodities – the savings which emerge by no longer paying for the surplus-value of another capital:

> If, therefore, he produces his raw materials and machinery himself instead of
> buying them, he himself appropriates the surplus labour he would otherwise
> have had to pay out to the seller of the raw materials and machinery.[51]

In the battle of competition, vertical integration (the tendency for means of production to be removed from commodity exchange) is executed by the competition of individual capitals to expand at the expense of competing capitals.

As a tendency, vertical integration of capital was inadequately stressed by Marx – and, as a result, this important aspect of the integration of capital tends to be overlooked; but its basis is clearly present in Marx's theory. Its limit is the complete removal of means of production from commodity exchange and the establishment of *fully* combined labour processes – from raw materials to final use-values for consumers. Combined with horizontal integration developed to its limit (with which it interacts), it yields one capital in every socially-combined sphere of production producing final use-values; but, it is still not adequate to the concept of all social capital in the hands of a single capitalist – because it retains the separation of the various spheres.

---

[49] Marx 1977a, pp. 454, 463–5, 780.
[50] Marx 1977a, p. 476.
[51] Marx 1971, p. 216.

3. *The case for conglomerate integration*

Finally, in what way is the separation of capital into independent, discrete spheres contrary to the concept of capital? Consider an *absolute* separation where the 'various spheres of production are related to one another, within certain limits, as foreign countries or communist countries'.[52] In this case, all surplus-value generated and realised within a particular sphere would have to be accumulated in that sphere or consumed. Capital could not expand to its utmost – because it would be denied access to the means for its maximum self-expansion. But, that is contrary to the concept of capital, where 'every limit appears as a barrier to be overcome'.[53] In seeking the highest possible rate of profit and in shifting, accordingly, capital from one sphere to another, the individual capitalist acts in accordance with the inner nature of capital:

> In acting thus the individual capitalist only obeys the immanent law, and
> hence the moral imperative, of capital to produce as much surplus-value
> as possible.[54]

Thus, the equalisation of the rate of profit is inherent in the concept of capital as self-expanding value; it occurs through the competition of capitals to expand, where 'the action of capitals on one another has the force to assert the inherent laws of capital'.[55] And capital's tendency is always to transcend any barriers to its growth:

> It is the perpetual tendency of capitals to bring about through competition
> this equalization in the distribution of surplus-value produced by the total
> capital, and to overcome all obstacles to this equalization.[56]

The process by which this occurs, of course, is the shift of capital from one sphere to another, the free movement of capital. But, this requires that capital exists in its universal form – *money-capital*. Only here does capital possess 'the form which enables it as a common element, irrespective of its particular employment, to be distributed amongst the different spheres, amongst the

---

[52] Marx 1959, p. 174.
[53] Marx 1973, p. 174.
[54] Marx 1977a, p. 1051.
[55] Marx 1968, p. 94.
[56] Marx 1959, pp. 742–3.

capitalist class, according to the production needs of each separate sphere.'[57] Only here, in money-capital, in the money-market, do all distinctions as to the quality of capital disappear:

> All the different forms assumed by capital according to the different spheres of production or circulation in which it is invested, are obliterated here. It exists here in the undifferentiated, always identical form, that of independent exchange-value, i.e., of money.[58]

Here, in the money market, 'capital appears as the general element as opposed to individual capitals'; here, there is a real presence of capital as a whole:

> In the money market, capital is posited in its totality; there it *determines prices, gives work, regulates production*, in a word, is the *source of production*.[59]

Capital is always latently One in the form of money-capital, the form by which the equalisation of profit rates is accomplished – a process which 'implies, furthermore, the development of the credit system, which concentrates the inorganic mass of the disposable social capital vis-à-vis the individual capitalist'.[60]

What, then, is this money-capital which is concentrated in the credit system and which stands opposite individual capitals? Simply, it is the capital which has been realised in the form of money-capital in the course of the circuit of capital but for which the individual capital has no use at the moment – latent money-capital for the individual capital; it is 'released capital', which is put at the disposal of other capitalists.[61] With the development of the credit and banking system, for which this latent money-capital provides one of the foundations, this money-capital is put at the disposal of a mediator, the banker:

> the banker, who receives the money as a loan from one group of the reproductive capitalists, lends it to another group of reproductive capitalists, so that the banker appears in the role of a supreme benefactor; and at the

---

[57] Marx 1971, p. 465.
[58] Marx 1971, p. 464.
[59] Marx to Engels, 2 April 1858, in Marx and Engels 1965, p. 104; Marx 1973, p. 275.
[60] Marx 1959, p. 192.
[61] Marx 1957, p. 182 and *passim*.

same time, the control over this capital falls completely into the hands of the banker in his capacity as middleman.[62]

Thus, money-capital

> assumes the nature of a concentrated, organized that capital mass, which, quite different from actual production, is subject to the control of bankers, i.e., the representatives of social capital.

Here,

> the bankers confront the industrial capitalists and the commercial capitalists as representatives of all money-lenders. They become the general managers of money-capital.[63]

Yet, this movement of capital from sphere to sphere in this manner is, by its very nature, a *short-term movement*. The money-capital is capital to which the particular lender, the capitalist for whom it is latent money-capital, is *not indifferent*; it is capital ultimately intended for return to his own particular circuit of capital. The very development of the specifically capitalist mode of production, however, generates a requirement for *long-term* capital, for large masses of capital to be 'welded together' on a long-term basis.[64] It is for this very reason that Marx could announce: 'the *ultimate positing* of capital in the form adequate to it – is joint-stock capital'. Or, as he informed Engels – '*Share capital* as the most perfect form' of capital.[65]

Thus, the development of the corporation is immanent in the concept of capital. And, as is well-known, here we see the further separation between labour and the conditions of labour, the further dissolution of 'the various forms in which the worker is a proprietor, or in which the proprietor works'. In the corporation, the function of capital 'is entirely divorced from capital ownership, hence also labour is entirely divorced from ownership of means of production and surplus-labour'.[66] The ownership of capital is separated here from those who are not indifferent to its particular employment – those

---

[62] Marx 1959, p. 494.
[63] Marx 1959, pp. 361, 394.
[64] Marx 1977a, p. 780.
[65] Marx 1973, pp. 657–8; Marx–Engels, 2 April 1858, Marx and Engels 1965, p. 104.
[66] Marx 1959, p. 428.

who combine both the ownership of capital and the function of capital within one person. Capital, here, 'is employed by people who do not own it and who consequently tackle things quite differently than the owner, who anxiously weighs the limitations of his private capital insofar as he handles it himself'.[67] We have 'the mere manager who has no title whatsoever to the capital', who performs 'all the real functions pertaining to the functioning capitalist', on the one hand, and the owner of capital, who disappears from the production process, a 'mere money-owner capitalist' on the other hand. Capital, here in its 'most perfect form', is:

> directly endowed with the form of social capital (capital of directly associated individuals) as distinct from private capital. . . . It is the abolition of capital as private property within the framework of capitalist production itself.[68]

With the development of corporations in different spheres of production, money-capital (that undifferentiated, homogeneous form of capital) can now be distributed in large masses among the different spheres according to the requirements of those various spheres; it can now be made available to those who actually put it to work, those who perform the function of capital. Are, then, 'many corporations', many separate and distinct congelations of money. capital, adequate to the concept of capital? One would have to answer – no. Separate ownership in the various spheres could still inhibit the free entry of capital (through the determination of the particular requirements for money-capital); separate and distinct ownership, here, is consistent with a barrier to the equalisation of profit rates which is immanent in the concept of capital.

The adequate form of capital, then, is One corporation (or, many corporations which are identical) – a unitary authority which can shift capital from sphere to sphere in such a way as to maximise the self-expansion of capital. In conglomerate integration, the tendency for the integration of capitals in different spheres independent of any organic relation, we have the third aspect of the tendency of capital to become One. And, as in the other aspects, its real emergence to its limit is latent within the nature of capital. Just as vertical integration is latent in the addition of constant capital to new living labour in the formation of value, and just as horizontal integration is latent

---

[67] Marx 1959, p. 431.
[68] Marx 1959, pp. 380, 427.

in the formation of market-value, so also is conglomerate integration latent in the equalisation of the profit rate, where every capitalist is to be regarded 'actually as a shareholder in the total social enterprise'. In the equalisation of the profit rate, the formation of the general rate of profit:

> the various capitalists are just so many stockholders in a stock company … so that profits differ in the case of the individual capitalists only in accordance with the amount invested by each in the aggregate enterprise, i.e., according to his investment in social production as a whole, according to the number of his shares.[69]

And, how does the process of conglomerate integration occur within competition? The formation of corporations, of course, occurs due to the requirement of individual capitals to amass the funds required to expand; and, the movement into different spheres occurs as capitals competing to expand *diversify* in order to maximise their individual rate of self-expansion. Diversification, thus, is the manifestation of conglomerate integration – another manifestation of the tendency of capital to become One.

The combination of the three aspects of integration (horizontal, vertical and conglomerate) thus has as its limit the case 'when the entire social capital [is] united in the hands of either a single capitalist or a single capitalist company'.

The 'perfecting' of capital

How do we stand, now, in relation to the concept of monopoly-capital? It must be recognised that one-sidedness in stressing one or another aspect of the tendency of capital to become One has marked the controversies over the theoretical status of monopoly-capital. The inconsistency between Marx's own statements is only an apparent inconsistency; their inner unity is revealed in the notion of the tendency of capital to become One.

And, this tendency is the very process of development of capital itself. Beginning on the basis of the fragmentation of capitals, capital develops by transforming its historical presuppositions into a form increasingly adequate to its inner nature. Always One in essence, capital increasingly becomes so in

---

[69] Marx 1959, pp. 205, 156.

phenomenal form by acting upon itself – through the process of competition of individual capitals. Thus, capital is increasingly 'posited, not only *in itself* in its substance, but is posited also in its *form*'.[70] It is potentiality, that which is always inherent in the concept of capital, increasingly realised, increasingly emerging into existence. Adapting an argument from Hegel, we might say that the development of capital is the advance from the germ of the perfect to the perfect.[71]

Monopoly-capital represents this 'perfecting' of capital, this qualitative alteration in the phenomenal form of capital. From a Marxist (in contrast to a bourgeois) perspective, monopoly-capital is a more perfect, purer form of capital than that found in its historical infancy. As Sweezy has recently proposed, 'the transformation of competitive into monopoly capital not only does not negate this relationship [capital/wage-labour relationship – M.L.], it refines and perfects it'.[72] The inner nature of capital thus comes increasingly to the surface. That which, for the very unfinished and undeveloped nature of capital, was the 'esoteric possession of a few individuals' becomes 'exoteric, comprehensible, and capable of being learned and possessed by everybody'.[73] The illusions created by competition, the fetishism of commodities, the appearance of freedom for wage-labour, the illusory form of exploitation – all these are increasingly dissipated in the very development of capital, its tendency to become One.

To deny, then, a qualitative alteration in the phenomenal character of capital is a misplaced loyalty to the concept of capital. The problem with the Baran-Sweezy notion of monopoly-capital has not been its focus on the need for a special theory of monopoly-capital but, rather, its one-sided focus on the aspect of horizontal integration (with its corollaries of barriers to entry and differential profit rates). Just as incorrect is a position which privileges capital flows between branches of production as the highest form of competition, treating competition within particular branches as 'primitive'; it is a position which, focussing on a form of capital's tendency, loses sight of its essence.[74] Both positions are one-sided. They fail to capture the whole of capital's

---

[70] Marx 1973, p. 530.
[71] *Cf.* Hegel 1956, pp. 22, 54, 57.
[72] Sweezy 1981, p. 65; Weeks 1981, p. 167.
[73] Hegel 1967, p. 76.
[74] Weeks 1981, pp. 167–8.

tendency to become One, a tendency which, in the real world, proceeds unevenly (and which, accordingly, generates partial and one-sided analyses). Only the whole – the recognition of the three sides of capital's tendency to become One – however, represents Marx's position.

At this late date, it should not be necessary to stress the importance of a special theory of monopoly-capital, a theory which reflects the qualitative alteration of capital as its phenomenal form increasingly corresponds to its inner nature, a theory which focuses on those essential features which become increasingly manifest as capital perfects itself. Perhaps it is important, however, to emphasise the necessity for developing such a theory immanently out of Marx's concept of capital rather than through the usual practices of induction and empiricism so characteristic of post-Marx studies.

The former approach, attempted here, allows us to situate a theory of monopoly-capital in relation to Marx and reveals the later developments as already latent in the concept of capital; the latter approach, however, necessarily always leaves unclarified the precise relation to Marx's work.[75]

---

[75] Marx 1973, pp. 414, 310.

Chapter Fourteen

Analytical Marxism and the Marxian Theory of Crisis

Introduction

Methodology, it is often claimed, is what above all distinguishes Marxism from 'bourgeois social science'. In his classic articulation of this position, Georg Lukács argued many years ago that Marxian method constitutes the 'decisive difference':

> Orthodox Marxism...does not imply the uncritical acceptance of the results of Marx's investigations. It is not the 'belief' in this or that thesis, nor the exegesis of a 'sacred' book. On the contrary, orthodoxy refers exclusively to *method*.[1]

For Lukács, the distinguishing characteristic of that Marxian method was obvious. It was 'the point of view of totality', 'the all-pervasive supremacy of the whole over the parts'; and, it was this, he proposed, which was 'the bearer of the principle of revolution in science'.[2]

More recently, a similar claim for methodological distinctiveness has been made forcefully by two Marxist biologists, Richard Levins and Richard Lewontin, in their book, *The Dialectical Biologist*.

---

[1] Lukács 1972, pp. 27, 1.
[2] Lukács 1972, p. 27.

In contrast to a Cartesian method which begins from individual parts, each with its own intrinsic properties, and proceeds to explain the system as a whole, Levins and Lewontin stress an alternative, dialectical view in which 'parts acquire properties by virtue of being parts of a particular whole, properties they do not have in isolation or as parts of another whole'. What, indeed, distinguishes the dialectical view is its emphasis upon wholes.[3]

Yet, if there is, as has been proposed, a 'near-consensus view' with respect to an 'unreconcilable methodological fissure' between Marxism and its rivals, it is nevertheless rather difficult to find the clear articulation of this 'point of view of totality' in the particular sphere of Marxian economics.[4] Although there are isolated examples of such a focus, as in the work of Stephen Resnick and Richard Wolff or Alain Lipietz, most apparent in Marxian economics is an eclecticism which proceeds as if 'the point of view of totality' is deserving of lip service (and occasional aphorisms or exhortations) but is not to be taken seriously when it comes to analysis.[5]

This rejection in practice of the focus upon the whole can be seen in many places; anywhere Marxists explain essential characteristics of capitalism (such as the drive for accumulation or the substitution of machinery for direct labour) by the competition among individual capitalists, it represents a departure from the approach that Marx took from the time of the writing of the *Grundrisse*.[6] 'It is easy,' Marx noted there, 'to develop the introduction of machinery out of competition and out of the law of the reduction of production costs which is triggered by competition'. However, the theoretical requirement was to develop the introduction of machinery 'out of the relation of capital to living labour, without reference to other capitals'.[7] And, there was a critical reason for this approach.

For Marx, it was necessary to understand the essential nature of 'capital in general' before exploring the manner in which its inherent tendencies are executed through the actions of individual capitalists in competition. Rather

---

[3] Levins and Lewontin 1985, pp. 2–3, 273.
[4] Levine, Sober and Wright 1987, p. 67.
[5] Resnick and Wolff 1987, 1989 or Lipietz 1985.
[6] One of many examples can be found in Ernest Mandel's 'Introduction' to Volume I of *Capital* (Marx 1977a, p. 60), where Mandel proposes that the drive to accumulate capital 'is essentially explained by competition, that is by the phenomenon of "various capitals"'.
[7] Marx 1973, pp. 776–7.

than the external phenomena of competition, only the inner connections within the whole, 'the obscure structure of the bourgeois economic system', can yield an understanding of the system.[8] Thus, competition, he noted,

> is nothing more than the way in which the immanent laws of capitalist production manifest themselves in the external movement of the individual capitals, assert themselves as the coercive laws of competition.

In short, competition as such does not '*explain* these laws; rather, it lets them be *seen*, but does not produce them'.[9]

Thus, Marx was quite explicit in rejecting analyses of the tendencies of capitalism based merely upon the observation of individual capitals in competition: 'to try to explain them simply as the results of competition therefore means to concede that one does not understand them'.[10] Indeed, he argued that a focus upon surface phenomena, the results of competition, could never establish *necessity*:

> Where, as here, it is competition as such that decides, the determination is inherently accidental, purely empirical, and only pedantry or fantasy can seek to present this accident as something necessary.[11]

In this respect, the prevalence of Marxist arguments based upon the competition among capitalists suggests an implicit rejection of (or, at least, a confusion over) Marx's own method. Yet, currently at issue is not this implicit rejection but, rather, a quite explicit one.

Analytical Marxism

In recent years, a new phenomenon has appeared on the scene – a self-designated school of 'analytical Marxism', centred in particular around the work of John Roemer (a US economist at the University of California at Davis), Jon Elster (a Norwegian political scientist at the University of Chicago) and G.A. Cohen (a Canadian philosopher at Oxford). In addition to editing the Cambridge University Press series on Studies in Marxism and Social Theory,

---

[8] Marx 1968, p. 165.
[9] Marx 1973, pp. 651, 552.
[10] Marx 1973, p. 752.
[11] Marx 1981b, p. 485.

these three also form the core of a group of scholars which has met annually to discuss each other's work.[12]

'Rigor and clarity' has been identified by Elster as the underlying principle behind the group; yet, what has thus far marked the analytical Marxists has been their particular methodological stance. Rather than for *Making Sense of Marx* (the title of one of Elster's books), the attention attracted by the 'analytical Marxists' has come largely from their success in making *fun* of Marx. Their technique is well-designed to achieve the desired result. First, one begins by asserting a methodological principle precisely contrary to that of the author of whom one presumably wants to make sense. Then, from this very standpoint, one investigates the propositions of said author and finds, *mirable dictu*, – *non*sense. In defence of this singular approach to the rational reconstruction of a given theory, it may be said that it rarely fails to satisfy its practitioner.

Analytical Marxism begins with the unsupported premise of methodological individualism. It is not supported because it need *not* be: the power of conventionalism in contemporary social science ensures that such a premise will be accepted as the common sense of scientific practice. Thus, confident that those who count will genuflect, analytical Marxism points out that all institutions and social processes must be explained in terms of individuals alone.

For Jon Elster, one of the three founding partners, any explanation which 'assumes that there are supra-individual entities that are prior to individuals in the explanatory order' must be rejected.[13] In short, without microfoundations, no explanation is acceptable. Nor, for that matter, need it even be considered – as when Elster peremptorily dismisses Lipietz's discussion of the 'so-called "transformation problem"' with the comment that Lipietz uses 'an approach that completely neglects the need for microfoundations'.[14]

Guided by their methodological given, the analytical Marxists find Marxian theory, on the whole, rather inadequate. After all, Elster comments, 'Marx believed that capital had a logic of its own, which was somehow prior in the

---

[12] The nature and composition of the group, which also has designated itself as the 'No Bullshit Marxism Group', is described in Lebowitz 1988a (see Chapter 4) and Wright 1989.

[13] Elster 1985, p. 6.

[14] Elster 1985, p. 135n.

explanatory order to market behavior and competition'.[15] Similarly, John Roemer proposes that Marxists engage in teleological reasoning by their focus on capital as a supra-individual entity; 'in a competitive economy,' he explains, 'there is no agent who looks after the needs of capital'.[16] Thus, Marxian analysis, Roemer also announces, requires microfoundations.

Of course, a pre-emptive methodological strike is not the sole element in the analytical-Marxist campaign. Using analytical tools based upon their methodology, the analytical Marxists have also attempted to demonstrate that much of Marx is internally incoherent. Thus, in his long march through Marxian economics in his *Analytical Foundations of Marxian Economic Theory*, Roemer left among the casualties the 'fundamental Marxian theorem', the falling rate of profit, the law of value and the transformation problem, and theories of crisis.[17] The labour theory of value as a measure of exploitation, left standing, was subsequently disposed of in his *A General Theory of Exploitation and Class*.[18] Small wonder, then, that Elster (who characteristically dismisses Marx's crisis theory as 'trivial', 'rambling and repetitive', 'obscure', 'nebulous and opaque', and 'virtually devoid of content') could declare that 'Today Marxian economics is, with a few exceptions, intellectually dead'.[19]

Yet, if they judge Marxian method (and conclusions deriving therefrom) as wrong-headed, the analytical Marxists are not prepared to break entirely with Marx. The 'substantive research agenda' of Marxian economics, they propose, remains valid. Thus, Roemer argues that, using neoclassical tools, rational-choice models and the like, Marxian economics has made great progress in Marx's agenda by providing the necessary microfoundations and thereby substituting science for teleology.[20]

As noted in an earlier examination of analytical Marxism (see Chapter 4), this particular self-evaluation, however, is rather debatable. As a study ('pathbreaking' in Elster's words) which generates 'class relations and the capital relationship from exchanges between differently endowed individuals in a competitive setting', Roemer's *General Theory* provides crucial support

---

[15] Elster 1986, p. 24.
[16] Roemer 1986a, pp. 191–2.
[17] Roemer 1981.
[18] Roemer 1982.
[19] Elster 1985, pp. 161–5; 1986, pp. 60, 192.
[20] Roemer 1986a, pp. 191–201.

for analytical Marxism's quest for microfoundations.[21] Yet, not only does this prototype, constructed according to analytical Marxism's specifications, provide a basis for a rather strange Marxian progress (as in the case of the concept of 'just' exploitation), but its central propositions are questionable. At the core of his privileging of unequal endowments (and, thus, the dismissal of the importance of capitalist relations of production) is Roemer's finding that 'truly it does not matter whether labor hires capital or capital hires labor: the poor are exploited and the rich exploit in either case'.[22] Nevertheless, as we have seen in Chapter 4, the equivalent results demonstrated in this 'isomorphism theorem' (despite the critical difference in residual claimants) follow only from the assumptions embedded in Roemer's model which obliterate Marx's critical distinction between labour and labour-power.

In the end, then, rather than demonstrating the robustness of the analytical-Marxist project, Roemer succeeds merely in proving what is already present in his assumption set. Nevertheless, this particular failure is not sufficient in itself to dismiss *a priori* any analytical-Marxist argument which rejects a focus on supra-individual entities. Such a dismissal requires a closer examination of the central issues.

The limits to individuals

To say that only individual human beings act is neither a matter of dispute nor a *prima facie* guide to the selection of an appropriate methodology. Rather than attributing impulse to abstractions, Marx never denied that real human beings are the only actors. Indeed, he asserted this over and over again. What he always stressed, however, is that they act within constraints. (They make history but not under conditions of their own choosing.) From this perspective, what was essential was to understand those constraints – constraints not necessarily apparent to the individual actors.

Surprisingly, the concept of such constraints is a spectre that preoccupies at least one of the analytical Marxists. Having delivered his funeral oration for much of Marx's work, Elster does find one important and living contribution (indeed, Marx's 'most important methodological achievement') – the study of

---

[21] Elster 1985, p. 7.
[22] Roemer 1982, p. 93.

'social contradictions'. In particular, he has in mind Marx's exploration of the fallacy of composition, the unintended consequences of individual actions, 'counterfinality', the 'local-global' fallacy and the like.[23] Here is the basis, Elster announces, of a 'powerful methodology'.[24]

By the fallacy of composition, Elster understands the inference which takes the following form: 'what is possible for any single individual must be possible for them all simultaneously'. As he points out in his *Logic and Society*, such an inference is false if the relevant property is 'non-universalizable'.[25] In short, generalising from what is true for any single agent or group of agents to what is true of *all* agents may involve a fallacy of composition.[26]

Yet, for the actors themselves, nothing may be more natural. Elster indicates that

> Marx's most original contribution to the theory of belief formation was...his idea that the economic agents tend to generalize locally valid views into invalid global statements, because of a failure to perceive that causal relations that obtain *ceteris paribus* may not hold unrestrictedly.[27]

More is involved, too, than simply a theory of endogenous belief formation. Where individuals then proceed to *act* on the basis of such mutually invalidating beliefs, the result will be counterfinality – unintended consequences which have as their basis a fallacy of composition. We have, then, what Elster describes as

> perhaps the most powerful part of the Marxist methodology: the demonstration that in a decentralized economy there spontaneously arises a *fallacy of composition* with consequences for theory as well as for practice.[28]

There appears to be somewhat of a paradox here. It is obvious from the many examples that Elster offers – ranging from the cobweb phenomenon to the effect of wage reductions on effective demand, that he considers such 'social contradictions' to be central to social science in general and economics in

---

[23] Elster 1986, pp. 38–9, 194.
[24] Elster 1985, p. 43.
[25] Elster 1978, p. 99.
[26] Elster 1985, pp. 44–5.
[27] Elster 1985, p. 19.
[28] Ibid.

particular.[29] Indeed, Elster describes this 'extremely powerful' idea as 'Marx's central contribution to the methodology of social science'.[30] *Yet, implicit in the concepts of the fallacy of composition and counterfinality is the existence of constraints and limits upon individuals.*

How can there be a fallacy of composition and counterfinality ('the embodiment of the fallacy of composition') unless the group as a whole faces a constraint that no individual member of the group faces? Insofar as the fallacy of composition revolves around the non-universality of a given property, a specific limit to universality is obviously a *presupposition*. However, the refusal of analytical Marxism to entertain supra-individual entities means that such limits are revealed only *ex post facto* as counterfinality.

Consider in this respect a case set out by G.A. Cohen, the third of the founding partners, in his 'The Structure of Proletarian Unfreedom'. Ten people are placed in a locked room. There is a single heavy key on the floor which anyone can pick up. Whoever picks up that key can unlock the door and leave. But, *only* that person will be able to leave. In this case, to generalise from what is true of each (the ability to leave the room) to what is true of all is, of course, an example of the fallacy of composition. In fact, as Cohen points out, each person is free to leave the room – but '*only on condition that the others do not exercise their similarly conditional freedom*'. What makes their freedom contingent (a state which Cohen calls 'collective unfreedom') is that there are limits and constraints which are placed on the whole group: 'whatever happens, at least nine people will remain in the room'.[31]

Significantly, in this example, we have *prior knowledge* that the relevant property (freedom to leave the room) is 'non-universalizable'. Knowledge of the specific whole in this case is prior in the explanatory order to understanding the conditional and contingent state of the individuals within this whole. More is involved, too, than simply a question of epistemology; it is also an ontological question: the true properties of the individuals are only given by the characteristics of the whole.

Clearly, the importance one assigns to knowledge of global constraints depends upon the extent to which interaction effects are deemed significant. If

---

[29] Elster 1978, Chapter 5.
[30] Elster 1985, p. 48.
[31] Cohen 1986, pp. 244, 242.

one assumes the latter to be of a small order of importance, then the whole can be treated simply as the sum of its parts taken individually; in this case, one proceeds from the individual blithely (as in the case of much of neoclassical economics) without concern for fallacies of composition that emerge from interdependence.[32] By assumption, no investigation of constraints upon the whole is required; the macro can be safely left behind in the search for microfoundations.

If, on the other hand, interaction effects such as those captured by the concept of the fallacy of composition are considered important, a focus upon the macro-level and of constraints of the whole upon the individual parts would seem to follow (as it did for Keynes).[33] So, here is the paradox: while stressing the significance of interaction effects, analytical Marxism nevertheless remains committed to the Cartesian priority of the part over the whole characteristic of methodological individualism.

In Marx's methodological holism, by contrast, investigation of structural limits to individual actions is precisely the result of considering the whole first. Discussing the division of value, Marx noted that the length of a line

> is not determined by the lengths of the segments into which it is divided. It is rather the relative lengths of the latter that are limited in advance by the limits of the line of which they are parts.[34]

Value, in short, pre-exists its subdivision. The magnitude of value is measured by the amount of labour expended, and 'the commodity value cannot be resolved into anything further, and consists of nothing more'. Thus, total social labour exists as a limit on the distribution of income, which 'presupposes this substance as already present, i.e. the total value of the annual product, which is nothing more than objectified social labour'.[35]

Not only were there inherent limits on the total, but Marx also argued in the *Grundrisse* that the reproduction of capitalism as an organic system required specific proportions and internal relations. Thus, he spoke of an 'inner

---

[32] See, in this context, the discussion of the analysis of variance in Levins and Lewontin.

[33] The adage that an acceptance of Keynes is a precondition for acceptance of Marx is strengthened by Elster's complaint (Elster 1986, p. 63) about the lack of microfoundations for Keynesian macroeconomics.

[34] Marx 1981a, p. 462.

[35] Marx 1981b, p. 961.

division' of necessary and surplus labour and of direct labour and means of production.

> This inner division, inherent in the concept of capital, appears in exchange in such a way that the exchange of capitals among one another takes place in *specific and restricted proportions* – even if these are constantly changing in the course of production.

The inner relation, he proposed, 'determines both the sum total of the exchange which can take place and the proportions in which each of these capitals must both exchange and produce'.[36]

On the other hand, Marx certainly did not argue that capitalism as such operates as if the agents of production are *conscious* of those limits. Exchange and production were not absolutely bound to these 'specific and restricted proportions'; rather, it was the very nature of a commodity-producing society that there was no *a priori* plan. Thus, he continued,

> *Exchange* in and for itself gives these conceptually opposite moments an indifferent being; they exist independently of one another; their inner necessity becomes *manifest* in the crisis, which puts a forcible end to their seeming indifference towards each other.[37]

We have here what has been called a 'possibility theory' of crisis in Marx.[38] On the one hand, there are the necessary inner limits 'inherent in the concept of capital'; on the other hand, since capitalism is a commodity-money exchange economy, the very nature of real activity by capitalists occurs as if those limits are not present.[39]

> Exchange does not change the inner characteristics of realization; but it projects them to the outside; gives them a reciprocally independent form, and thereby lets their unity exist merely as an inner necessity, which must therefore come forcibly to the surface in crises.[40]

---

[36] Marx 1973, p. 443. Emphasis added.
[37] Marx 1973, pp. 443–4.
[38] Kenway 1980.
[39] Note that Kenway (1980) and Lavoie (1983) focus upon the separation of selling and buying inherent in a commodity-money economy as the basis of the 'possibility theory' they identify in Marx.
[40] Marx 1973, p. 447. Marx made the same point in *Theories of Surplus Value* (Marx 1971, p. 518): 'It is *crises* that put an end to this apparent *independence* of the various

Thus, crises result from growing divergences between the results of the action of autonomous economic agents and what Alain Lipietz describes as 'the internal connections and immanent laws', which 'express only the unity of the capitalist structure, that is, its reproduction'.[41] Counterfinality occurs when economic agents act in such a way as to violate the 'specific and restricted proportions' determined by the inner requirements for reproduction.

From this perspective, if we are to understand what places limits upon the individual actors, making their autonomy a conditional autonomy, neither individuals nor market behaviour nor competition can come first in the explanatory order. Rather, the requirement is the identification of the 'intrinsic connection existing between economic categories or the obscure structure of the bourgeois economic system'.[42] For, as Marx noted, 'there would be no crisis without this inner unity of factors that are apparently indifferent to each other'.[43] In the absence of such a consideration of those limits, it will not be surprising if Marx's theory of crisis appears (as it does for Elster) incomprehensible.

Yet, if we have here in this combination of inherent limits and individual capitalists indifferent to those limits the basis for a possibility theory of crisis, it must be acknowledged that, for Marx, demonstration of the *possibility* of capitalist crisis was a relatively trivial and self-evident matter. Far more critical was the demonstration of an inner tendency to *violate* those inner limits, an inherent tendency for capitalist crisis – i.e., what Kenway calls an 'actuality' theory of crisis.[44]

Realisation and crisis

Let us consider Marx's 'nebulous and opaque' discussion of crises which are the result of the inability to realise surplus-value.[45] As Marx stressed,

---

elements of which the production process continually consists and which it continually reproduces'.

[41] Lipietz 1985, p. 69.
[42] Marx 1968, p. 165.
[43] Marx 1968, p. 500.
[44] Kenway 1980, p. 25.
[45] The tendency of the falling rate of profit (FROP) is not our subject. We will simply note with respect to FROP that its ultimate basis is lagging productivity increases in Department I (the sector producing means of production). This was a point well understood by Marx (if not by analytical Marxists and others) as indicated by his

the conditions for the realisation of surplus-value differ significantly from the conditions for the production of surplus-value; they are restricted by 'the proportionality between the different branches of production and by society's power of consumption'. Since the latter exists within the framework of 'antagonistic conditions of distribution' which restrict the consumption of the vast majority of the population, there is a specific reason for the emergence of crises within capitalism.[46]

For Marx, overproduction, 'the fundamental contradiction of developed capital', was specific to the very nature of capitalism:

> The bourgeois mode of production contains within itself a barrier to the free development of the productive forces, a barrier which comes to the surface in crises and, in particular, in *overproduction* – the basic phenomenon in crises.[47]

Rather than occurring in the proper proportions, capitalist production takes place 'without any consideration for the actual limits of the market or the needs backed by the ability to pay'.[48] Thus, Marx observed that there is a 'constant tension between the restricted dimensions of consumption on the capitalist basis, and a production that is constantly striving to overcome these immanent barriers'.[49]

In particular, he argued that the limit was the result of bounds upon the consumption of workers, which capital attempts to keep to a minimum. As he commented in Volume II of *Capital*, in a well-known note for future elaboration:

> Contradiction in the capitalist mode of production. The workers are important for the market as buyers of commodities. But as sellers of their commodity – labour-power – capitalist society has the tendency to restrict them to their minimum price.[50]

---

comment in Volume III of *Capital* (1981b, p. 333) that FROP would not hold 'when the productivity of labour cheapens all the elements of both constant and the variable capital to the same extent'. See Lebowitz 1976; 1982a (Chapters 7 and 8 above) and Perelman 1987.

[46] Marx 1981b, p. 352.
[47] Marx 1973, p. 415; Marx 1968, p. 528.
[48] Marx 1968, p. 535.
[49] Marx 1981b, p. 365.
[50] Marx 1981a, p. 391n.

What Marx was describing was an inherent tendency of capitalism to produce more surplus-value than it could realise through the sale of commodities. And, since the problem was manifested in inadequate consumer demand, it followed that overproduction has a logical sequence: it appears in Department II (the sector producing articles of consumption) and spreads to Department I. For general overproduction, Marx argued, it suffices that there be overproduction of the principal commercial goods.[51] Thus, the demand for means of production may appear 'adequate and sufficient', but 'its inadequacy shows itself as soon as the final product encounters its limit in direct and final consumption'.[52]

It is essential to recognise, of course, that limits upon workers' consumption are *always* present. Accordingly, they cannot be the proximate (as opposed to ultimate) cause of periodic crises of overproduction. Precipitating the emergence of overproduction was an increase in the rate of surplus-value in the sphere of production. The very efforts of capital 'to reduce the relation of this necessary labour to surplus labour to the minimum' posit 'a new barrier to the sphere of exchange'.[53]

Overproduction, Marx commented, arises precisely because the consumption of workers 'does not grow correspondingly with the productivity of labour.'[54] Yet, it was not simply a matter of inadequate workers' consumption. Capitalists were also restricted in their consumption since they were preoccupied with 'the drive for accumulation'. Thus, the limit to the realisation of surplus-value was that workers could not consume enough whereas capitalists, attempting to maximise profits and to accumulate, *would not*.[55]

The result, then, is the tendency for crises, those 'momentary, violent solutions for the existing contradictions, violent eruptions that re-establish

---

[51] Marx 1968, p. 505. Given the interdependence of industries, overproduction in Department I was an 'effect' (Marx 1968, p. 524); 'the *overproduction* of coal is implied in the *overproduction* of iron, yarn etc. (even if coal was produced only in proportion to the production of iron and yarn etc.)' (Marx 1968, p. 531).

[52] Marx 1973, p. 421n.

[53] Marx 1973, p. 422.

[54] Marx 1968, p. 468.

[55] Given these antagonistic conditions of distribution, there was too much accumulation, too much capital – and accordingly, also, overproduction of commodities: 'the statement that there is *too much capital*, after all means merely that too little is consumed as *revenue*, and that more cannot be consumed in the given conditions' (Marx 1968, p. 534).

the disturbed balance for the time being'.[56] The emerging crisis acts 'to restore the correct relation between necessary and surplus labour, on which, in the last analysis, everything rests'.[57]

Thus, the following points appear to follow from this brief consideration of the texts:

(1) There is a 'specific' rate of surplus-value (e*) required for balance (i.e., successful reproduction) in the economy.
(2) Productivity increases which exceed real wage increases have the effect of increasing the rate of surplus-value above e*.
(3) The effect of the increase in the rate of surplus-value above e* is sooner or later to create a crisis of overproduction, manifested initially in Department II, the sector producing articles of consumption.
(4) The result of the crisis is to restore the appropriate rate of surplus-value, e*.[58]

As can be seen, we have here a simple set of propositions which implies a pattern of periodic crises of overproduction and a long-run constant wage-share of national income. But, in this unqualified form, it is far *too* simple. In particular, there is no apparent link between this 'actuality' theory, based upon capital's tendency to increase the rate of surplus-value beyond the 'specific and restrictive proportions' inherent in the concept of capital, and the 'possibility' theory, which focuses on the tension between the inherent limits and the existence of autonomous individual capitalists. To resolve this requires us to take seriously 'the point of view of totality'.

A holistic thought-experiment

Since our purpose here is to demonstrate the importance of considering the whole explicitly, let us conduct a holistic thought-experiment which represents capitalism as a relationship between one capitalist and his wage-labourers.

---

[56] Marx 1981b, p. 357.
[57] Marx 1973, p. 446.
[58] This concept of an 'equilibrium share of wages' appears to be the interpretation of David Harvey in a recent book (Harvey 1982, pp. 55, 77, 174). See Lebowitz 1986a.

The justification for this procedure is straightforward: Marx did the same thing repeatedly.[59] Indeed, many of the central relations developed in *Capital* implicitly assume capital as a whole or One Capital. This is certainly the basis for Marx's determination that, within capitalism, surplus-value does not originate in the exchange of non-equivalents in the sphere of circulation. His 'proof' ('The capitalist class of a given country, taken as a whole, cannot defraud itself') is simply an announcement that the true subject of study is capital as a whole rather than any single capitalist.[60]

Similarly, Marx often drew upon the image of capitalism as composed of two unified blocs – the capitalist class as a whole and the working class as a whole – in order to distinguish essential relations from apparent surface phenomena. By representing capitalism as an organic whole characterised by one capitalist and his wage-labourers, we capture what Marx described as the 'essential relation':

> the relation of *every* capitalist to his *own* workers is the *relation as such* of *capital and labour*, the essential relation.[61]

Indeed, he explicitly argued that one could not understand the nature of capital as the result of exploitation unless we consider the capitalist and the worker 'in their totality, as the capitalist class and the working class confronting each other'.[62] All this, of course, is precisely the focus upon 'supra-individual entities' that analytical Marxism abhors.

By abstracting from any consideration of competition and the separation of capital into many capitals, our thought-experiment effectively assumes the planning of production and distribution of means of production by the One Capitalist. It is, of course, an abstraction. It does not suggest that capital really acts as a whole (or as One); nor does it depart from Marx's insistence that 'capital exists and can only exist as many capitals'.[63] Nevertheless, it is our contention that such a thought-experiment yields some interesting insights

---

[59] As Duncan Foley observes (1986, p. 6), 'Marx often fails to be explicit about the level of aggregation at which he is working. He frequently explains the aggregate behavior of a system by discussing a typical or average element of it'.
[60] Marx 1977a, p. 266.
[61] Marx 1973, p. 420.
[62] Marx 1977a, p. 732. See the discussion in Lebowitz 2003, Chapter 9.
[63] Marx 1973, p. 414.

into Marx's argument (and, what is immediately relevant, the question of those inherent limits and restricted proportions).

Assume the optimising single capitalist wants to maximise the production and realisation of surplus-value. We treat workers here as objects rather than subjects; that is, aside from permitting them to push sufficiently in the opposite direction to capital to permit us to assume that both the real wage and the workday are constant, we are looking explicitly here only at capital's side of the totality which is capitalism as a whole. Thus, the thought-experiment explored here is inherently one-sided.[64]

Since we also will assume that our optimising capitalist is faced with a given number of workers, it follows that he can only increase the level of surplus-value by reducing the necessary portion of the workday. This is achieved by an increase in the level of productivity; and the condition is the substitution of means of production for living labour (i.e., an increase in the technical composition of capital). What emerge, then, as inherent tendencies of capital in general from our thought-experiment are a rising technical composition of capital, rising productivity and a rising rate of surplus-value.

Will increases in the rate of surplus-value in the sphere of production, however, generate problems of realisation? Let us suggest that our One Capitalist, as an optimiser, will only increase the technical composition of capital and will only strive for more surplus-value if he intends to *use* this surplus-value. To secure the additional articles of consumption and means of production that he desires, he will choose the appropriate increase in the technical composition of capital; i.e., we assume that he acts purposively and is not subject to myopia.

Thus, as long as our One Capitalist respects the 'specific and restricted proportions' necessary for reproduction (and there is no reason to assume that he will not), there is no basis for overproduction. Through our thought-experiment, we posit a specific relation between the rate of surplus-value and the level of capitalist expenditures (both consumption and investment) which constitutes the required proportions for inner balance. The rate of surplus-value (or, alternatively stated, the profit-share of national income) can be

---

[64] Among other things, this excludes consideration of the manner in which workers' struggles impose upon capital the necessity to revolutionise the means of production. See the discussion of this one-sidedness in Lebowitz 1982b, 2003 and Part V below.

increased without violating the necessary proportions – so long as capitalist expenditures themselves increase accordingly.

The point can be considered by reference to Michal Kalecki's argument, which itself drew upon Marx:

$$Y= P+W \text{ (1)}$$
$$Y= Ck + Cw + I \text{ (2)},$$

where Y, P, W, Ck, Cw and I are national income, profits, wages, capitalists' consumption, workers' consumption and investment, respectively. Since we assume that W= Cw (i.e., that workers spend what they get), then the equilibrium condition is:

$$P= Ck +I \text{ or,}$$
$$Y(P/Y)= Ck +I. \text{ (3)}$$

Kalecki's central point can be illustrated simply in Figure 14-1 (The Kaleckian Cross). With the profit-share of $(P/Y)^*$ (which is equivalent to $e^*/e^* +1$), the equilibrium output is OA; all surplus-value generated within the sphere of production (BA) is realised. If capitalists succeed, however, in increasing the rate of surplus-value (i.e., raising the profit-share) to $(P/Y)'$, then at the existing output of OA, profits (or surplus-value) generated within production (CA) will exceed that realisable at the given level of capitalist expenditures, BA; i.e., CB is unrealisable surplus-value. Thus, assuming no commensurate increase in capitalist expenditures (or, for Kalecki, a budget deficit or export surplus), the equilibrium income level will fall to OD: 'The level of income or product will decline to the point at which the higher relative share of profits yields the same absolute level of profits'.[65]

What the argument indicates, of course, is that any increase in the rate of surplus-value is sustainable (i.e., does *not* violate the necessary conditions for balance) so long as it is accompanied by the appropriate increase in capitalist expenditures. That is precisely the point that Marx himself stressed in his reproduction models in Volume II of *Capital*: 'the capitalist class as a whole...must itself cast into circulation the money needed to realize its

---

[65] Kalecki 1968, p. 61.

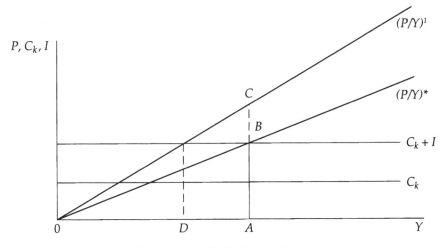

Figure 14–1. The Kaleckian Cross

surplus-value'. Not only was this point not paradoxical, 'it is in fact a necessary condition of the entire mechanism'.[66]

Thus, our thought-experiment yields an inference quite *different* to that of our earlier consideration of Marx's texts on crises of overproduction; it suggests that an increase in the rate of surplus-value is *not* sufficient to generate a crisis. Rather, there appears to be no inherent check to the growth of the profit-share. For One Capital, there are no apparent barriers in the sphere of circulation to the growth of capital.

Of course, what should be immediately apparent is the relationship of this thought-experiment to Ricardo's treatment of accumulation without any regard for potential crises of overproduction. This similarity, however, is not accidental, since our thought-experiment has a familial relationship to Ricardo's corn model.

The world of many capitals

If these are the tendencies inherent in our One Capital experiment, what about those of a real world characterised by many capitals in competition? In this régime, the operative motive of each capitalist will not be to reduce the

---

[66] Marx 1981a, p. 497.

necessary portion of the workday in order to increase the surplus portion. Such a perspective is clearly beyond the ken of any individual capitalist. Rather, each capitalist attempts to increase his profits by reducing his cost of production vis-à-vis his competitors; he does this by substituting machinery for labour and by finding more efficient methods of production. Thus, 'there is a motive for each individual capitalist to cheapen his commodities by increasing the productivity of labour'.[67] In the real régime of competition, the tendencies are rising technical composition of capital, rising productivity and a rising rate of surplus-value – tendencies already seen in the régime of One Capital.

We have reproduced here Marx's distinction between 'the general and necessary tendencies of capital', on the one hand, and 'their forms of appearance', the way in which those inner laws 'manifest themselves in the external movement of the individual capitals' and 'assert themselves as the coercive laws of competition'.[68] In the one case, we have capital as a purposeful actor; in the other, many individual capitalists (also purposeful actors) driven by competition. We can see, then, what Marx meant in the *Grundrisse* when he asserted that 'competition executes the inner laws of capital; makes them into compulsory laws towards the individual capital, but it does not invent them'.[69]

Yet, what about the specific and restricted proportions that Marx discussed? In the régime of competing capitalists, there is *ex post* validation of private activities (in contrast to the planning of One Capital). Yet, as Marx asked,

> since, on the basis of capitalist production, everyone works for himself and a particular labour must at the same time appear as its opposite, as abstract general labour and in this form as social labour – how is it possible to achieve the necessary balance and interdependence of the various spheres of production and the proportions between them, except through the constant neutralisation of a constant disharmony?[70]

---

[67] Marx 1977a, p. 435.
[68] Marx 1977a, p. 433.
[69] Marx 1973, p. 752.
[70] Marx 1968, p. 529.

In short, as noted earlier, precisely because there is not planned production in the régime of many capitals, there exists the *possibility* of crisis – crisis because the inner requirements for balance are not achieved. Nevertheless, we must recall that Marx wanted to do more than establish the possibility of crisis inherent in a capitalist commodity-money economy. More importantly, he wanted to establish its *necessity*.

This was precisely Marx's point with respect to the régime of many capitals. From Marx's perspective, the problem of Ricardo and his followers was one of reductionism: they treated the real world of many capitals as if it were the régime of One Capital and, thus, as a régime in which capital was distributed among the various spheres as if according to a plan. This, however, excluded by assumption what is specific to the real world of capital:

> All the objections which Ricardo and others raise against overproduction etc. rest on the fact that they regard bourgeois production either as a mode of production in which no distinction exists between purchase or sale – direct barter – or as *social* production, implying that society, as if according to a plan, distributes its means of production and productive forces in the degree and measure which is required for the fulfilment of the various social needs, so that each sphere of production receives the *quota* of social capital required to satisfy the corresponding need. This fiction arises entirely from the inability to grasp the specific form of bourgeois production....[71]

Let us consider, then, what is specific to the régime of many capitals. As we have already seen by examination of the régime of One Capital, an increase in the rate of surplus-value is not in itself sufficient to generate a realisation crisis. The question before us, accordingly, is why do 'many capitals' *necessarily* drive beyond the proper proportions?

In the régime of One Capital, we assumed that, in order to secure a given increase in surplus-value (to satisfy desired increments in means of production and articles of consumption), our rational capitalist initiates a given increase in the technical composition of capital. Since he is aware of the interdependencies between various sectors, it is assumed that he makes the correct decisions to achieve his goals (i.e., that the proper proportions are respected).

---

[71] Marx 1968, pp. 528–9.

Let us assume that each individual capitalist in the régime of many capitals similarly chooses the appropriate increase in the technical composition of capital to achieve his desired growth in surplus-value *on the basis of the information available to him.* What the individual capitalist does *not* know, however, is that he will be the beneficiary not only of productivity increases in his *own* production process but also of productivity increases elsewhere in the economy; 'capitalist X benefits not only from the productivity of labour in his firm, but also from that of other firms as well'.[72]

Thus, productivity increases in a Department I sector not only reduce the value of the constant capital of all industries using its commodities as inputs (thereby increasing the rate of profit directly) but also cheapen these commodities and thus lower the value of labour-power insofar as these commodities enter into workers' consumption.[73] Similarly, the actions of each capitalist in Department II will contribute to the reduction in necessary labour and thus to an increase in the general rate of surplus-value.[74]

Consider the implications of the absence of foresight into developments in interdependent industries. Under these conditions, in order to achieve his given target (to meet requirements for planned expenditures), the individual capitalist reduces his cost of production more than he would if he had foresight. Thus, compared to the régime of One Capital, the tendency will be for greater increases in the technical composition of capital. Characteristic of the world of real capital will be a period that Marx described as one of 'feverish production'.[75]

Conversely, the period in which production occurs on its new basis (the increased technical composition of capital) will be one in which total social productivity will increase more than the sum of the separate acts of individual capitalists. The benefit that accrues to the capitalist – indeed, to all capitalists – is the advantage produced by social labour. Elster describes this very case as a Marxian example of 'invisible hand' effects – unintended consequences characterised by positive externalities.[76]

---

[72] Marx 1981b, p. 177.
[73] Marx 1981b, p. 174; 1977, p. 442.
[74] Marx 1977a, p. 433.
[75] Marx 1977a, p. 580.
[76] Elster 1985, pp. 24–5, 144.

What Elster does not recognise, however, is that *violated* under these circumstances are precisely the proper proportions that Marx stressed. Social productivity and the rate of surplus-value in the sphere of production increase more than the individual capitalists expect. Surplus-value grows more than their anticipatory expenditures on means of production and capitalist consumption.[77]

Stated in the context of Figure 14.1, the inherent tendency of capitalist production is to generate a profit-share of income which cannot be sustained without a fall in the level of income. Although capitalist expenditures may increase sufficiently to validate the increased profit-share $(P/Y)'$, the effect of the interaction among individual capitalists is unintentionally to drive the profit-share higher than $(P/Y)'$. The period here is that of the 'consequent glut on the market' which follows that of feverish production.[78] As Marx's Volume II footnote on the contradiction of capital continued:

> Further contradiction: the periods in which capitalist production exerts all its forces regularly show themselves to be periods of over-production; because the limit to the application of the productive powers is not simply the production of value, but also its realization.[79]

Thus, 'invisible-hand' effects in the sphere of production will tend to have as their counterpart counterfinality in the sphere of circulation. It is as if, in the régime of One Capital, the capitalist were to find to his surprise that he had produced more surplus-value than he wanted – i.e., the myopic capitalist. Myopia in the régime of many capitals necessarily exists, however, because of the separation of capitals.

Our specific concern here has been to identify the nature of the necessary inner limits that Marx stressed. As we have seen, Marx proposed that the result of going beyond the proper proportions was a crisis which restores the 'correct relation' between necessary and surplus-labour. But, what *is* that correct relation? It will not be the *original* rate of surplus-value (e*) but, rather, the increased rate of surplus-value that would be found in the régime of One Capital (represented in Figure I by $(P/Y)'$). There are 'specific and restricted

---

[77] The immediate effect is the unanticipated increase in money-capital (i.e., capitalists who sell but do not buy), which meets the conditions of the 'possibility theory' as stated by Kenway 1980 and Lavoie 1983. See note 5.

[78] Marx 1977a, p. 580.

[79] Marx 1981a, p. 391n.

proportions', but as Marx noted, 'these are constantly changing in the course of production'.[80]

The specific fallacy of composition

The precise nature of the limit is clear if, taking a leaf from Elster's book, we restate the problem in the context of the fallacy of composition which underlies counterfinality in this case. *Any individual capitalist, it may be argued, can lower his cost of production and realise the additional surplus-value thereby generated.* A fallacy of composition, however, may be committed if we attempt to generalise from this locally valid statement to all capitalists simultaneously. The familiar case, of course, is the Keynesian discussion of the effect of wage reductions.

That particular illustration of the fallacy was certainly understood by Marx. 'Every capitalist,' Marx noted in the *Grundrisse*, 'knows this about his worker, that he does not relate to him as producer to consumer, and [he therefore] wishes to restrict his consumption, i.e. his ability to exchange, his wage, as much as possible.'[81] Yet, at the same time, each capitalist looks upon the workers of *other* capitalists simply as consumers (i.e. as if they are not workers similarly restricted to a minimum). The result was an inherent tendency to violate the restricted proportions:

> Here again it is the competition among capitals, their indifference to and independence of one another, which brings it about that the individual capital relates to the workers of the entire remaining capital *not as to workers*: hence is driven beyond the right proportion.[82]

As our discussion has indicated, however, the fallacy of composition in question is not limited in its application to the case of a wage decrease. Where the reduction in the cost of production occurs through an increase in productivity, it may *also* hold. The mechanism, of course, is different. In this case, counterfinality emerges because, given the ('invisible-hand') interaction effects, increases in productivity will generate a rate of surplus-value in excess

---

[80] Marx 1973, p. 443.
[81] Marx 1973, p. 420.
[82] Ibid.

of that 'warranted'. More surplus-value is produced than can be realised, and the 'inner necessity' therefore comes forcibly to the surface in a crisis.

The limit which, when violated, produces counterfinality is the same in both cases: *the limit as to how high the rate of surplus-value in the sphere of production can rise without generating a realisation crisis is given by the level of expenditures on means of production and capitalist consumption.* So long as this condition is satisfied, neither in the case of reduced wages nor increased productivity will there be a fallacy of composition and counterfinality resulting from a local-global generalisation. Central to Marx's 'actuality' theory of crisis, however, was the view *contra* Ricardo that, precisely because of the independence of individual capitalists but the necessary interdependence of their actions, the tendency was for that inner necessity to be violated and therefore manifested in crises.[83]

What this exercise accordingly has provided is a reconciliation between Marx's focus on the effects of increases in the rate of surplus-value and the analysis based on 'the point of view of totality'. All this yields an interesting inference. Insofar as the 'correct relation' of necessary and surplus-labour which crisis acts to restore is that of the régime of One Capital, the trajectory (the inner tendency) of capital remains that of our thought-experiment: rising technical composition of capital, rising productivity and rising rate of surplus-value – *despite the periodic fluctuations about this trajectory which necessarily result from the competition of capitals.*[84] The 'necessary balance and interdependence of the various spheres of production and the proportions between them' is achieved 'through the constant neutralisation of a constant disharmony', but *in themselves* crises imply nothing about a 'breakdown' of capitalism.[85]

Conclusion

As the above discussion illustrates, our argument is not at all with Elster's focus on the fallacy of composition, counterfinality, unintended consequences,

---

[83] This argument corresponds to that of Lipietz 1985 and Harvey 1982. I incorrectly criticised the latter on this question in Lebowitz 1986.

[84] Recall, however, that we are considering here only the tendencies of capital (and not those of wage-labour). See note 13 above.

[85] Marx 1968, p. 529. Rather, as Gramsci (1971, p. 184) argued, crises 'can simply create a terrain more favourable to the dissemination of certain modes of thought, and certain ways of posing and resolving questions involving the entire subsequent development of national life'. Cf. Lebowitz 2003.

etc. Elster, indeed, is correct to emphasise the importance of such concepts in Marx. In the absence of a prior consideration of the structure as a whole, however, what is lost is an understanding of the structural limits which generate counterfinality as a phenomenon. This may explain why Elster's discussion of Marx's theory of crisis is 'virtually devoid of content' – despite his own recognition of 'invisible hand' effects in the sphere of production.[86]

In Marx's methodological holism, consideration of supra-individual entities as prior in the explanatory order is a central part of his examination of the structure within which individuals act and which conditions their autonomy. In this respect, Roemer's truism that 'in a competitive economy there is no agent who looks after the needs of capital' entirely misses Marx's point about the logical priority of the whole.[87] Not only do the analytical Marxists fail to advance Marx's substantive research agenda, but they also fail to understand the method they are challenging.

Analytical Marxism, on the other hand, has performed an important service. For, in their insistence in performing an 'erase and replace' operation with respect to Marxist methodology, its champions do explicitly what many others who consider themselves Marxists without any modifying adjective have long done implicitly and eclectically.[88] What distinguishes analytical Marxism in this respect, then, is not its uniqueness in its methodological principles but, rather, its self-conscious articulation of those principles and rigorous consistency in applying them.

Accordingly, the greatest contribution of analytical Marxism may be its success in revealing the current confused state of Marxist methodology. Through its searching (and occasionally sneering) criticism, it has created the context for a better specification of an integral Marxist methodology. For this reason, recalling Oskar Lange's retort to von Mises, the future developers of an adequate Marxist economic theory may wish to erect a statue to the analytical Marxists. And, as Lange noted in his discussion, such a statue may serve well as a basis for a lecture on dialectics.[89]

---

[86] Elster 1985, pp. 161–5.
[87] Roemer 1986a, p. 191.
[88] It would be wrong, of course, to equate the 'many-capital' theorists with the methodological individualism of analytical Marxism; however, an emphasis upon microfoundations is common to both.
[89] Lange 1964, pp. 57–8.

Chapter Fifteen
In Brenner, Everything Is Reversed

The excitement about Brenner[1]

As has been noted before, economic crisis tends to
bring with it a boom in the crisis-theory sector. Yet,
perhaps fitting at this particular time, the current
theoretical boom seems to be localised in one work –
Robert Brenner's *The Economics of Global Turbulence*,
published as a special issue of *New Left Review* last
summer.[2] The symposium organised by *Historical
Materialism* is only one reflection of the view that
the publication of Brenner's monograph marks an
important event.

The *New Left Review*, of course, has done its best to
generate this excitement both by choosing to devote
an entire issue to the single work and also by the
nature of its introduction. Noting his earlier work
on the importance of agrarian developments for
emerging capitalism which set off the well-known
'Brenner Debate', *NLR* promises that Brenner's
new study is 'set to provoke a still wider debate'.
In employing an 'original Marxism' which disposes
with 'what has often passed for orthodox deductions

[1] I am very grateful for the comments of Howie Chodos, Sam Gindin, Leo Panitch
and, particularly, Greg Albo on an earlier version, presented at 'The Asian Crisis and
Beyond: Prospects for the 21st Century', a conference sponsored by *Studies in Political
Economy* in Ottawa, January 1999.
[2] Brenner 1998a.

from *Capital'* and combining his 'clear-cut analytical model' with 'detailed historical narrative', Brenner's 'remarkable work', they assert, is 'a momentous achievement' – one which, it is even implied, deserves a Nobel Prize for 'the first thinker able to explain the laws of motion of the global economy in which we now live'. 'Marx's enterprise, '*NLR* declares, 'has certainly found its successor'.[3]

So, what precisely is the excitement about? Timeliness, for one. Brenner's monograph (clearly a long time in preparation) is particularly timely because he rejects an explanation of the Asian crisis as a local aberration but sees it clearly as part of a global economic crisis – one which can only be understood in the context of the postwar boom and the factors which brought it to an end. Beginning by recounting the success of German and Japanese manufacturers during the so-called Golden Age in capturing from US firms significantly increased shares of world trade based upon their lower-cost production, Brenner's study focuses, in particular, upon the continuing competitive struggle between US, German and Japanese capital. Between 1965 and 1973, he notes, US manufacturing profits dropped 40.9% because of

> the increased downward pressure on prices that resulted from the unanticipated entry into the market of lower cost producers, especially from abroad.[4]

Over the next two decades, decades marked by significantly reduced rates of growth, investment and productivity gains and also by rising unemployment levels, an intense struggle over market shares would continue. Although he credits US success in repressing workers for its part, Brenner particularly stresses the currency valuation shifts arising from the Plaza Accord of 1985 for improving the state of US manufacturing and deteriorating those of Japan and Germany: the yen and mark appreciated 10.5 and 12.7% respectively *annually* against the dollar between 1985 and 1990 and then at annual rates of 9.1 and 2.5 between 1990 and 1995.[5] The ultimate effect, he proposes, was to stagnate the German economy and to bring the Japanese economy to the point of collapse.

---

[3] Brenner 1998a, pp. i–v.
[4] Brenner 1998a, pp. 95, 102.
[5] Brenner 1998a, pp. 196, 202.

Where does the Asian crisis fit into this picture? Simply because the over-valued yen encouraged an 'impetuous' increase in productive capacity throughout East and Southeast Asia during the 1990s, 'invading markets previously held by Japanese producers, particularly in North America'.[6] It was an expansion, he argues, undermined once the yen collapsed and the US dollar (to which local currencies were pegged) rose:

> It was thus the reduction in the value of the yen beginning in spring 1995, so vital for keeping the Japanese economy afloat, which propelled the Asian economies into their current profound crisis and ended up threatening not only Japanese recovery but that of the entire system.

All of this is consistent with what Brenner describes as 'a central theme of this text' – that 'competitive advantages secured by one major economy have tended to imply losses for others'.[7] In addition to his focus upon uneven development and the ensuing struggle for re-division of world markets, however, there is another essential part of his argument; at every step of the way, he tells the same story: a spectre has been haunting capitalism – the spectre of overcapacity. As he indicates in a subsequent essay:

> My argument is that the roots of long-term stagnation and the current crisis lie in the squeeze on manufacturing profits that resulted from the rise of manufacturing overcapacity and overproduction, which was itself the expression of intensified international competition.[8]

Overcapacity and overproduction, thus, emerged in the latter part of the 1960s, continued over the long slump and now, he argues, has become increasingly serious:

> It is the worsening of manufacturing overcapacity that has prepared the ground for the chain of events through which today's crisis has come into being.[9]

However, while the existence of overcapacity as such may help to explain movements in profits, investment, productivity and other important

---

[6] Brenner 1998a, p. 258.
[7] Brenner 1998a, pp. 257–8.
[8] Brenner 1998b, p. 24.
[9] Brenner 1998b, p. 25.

phenomena, Brenner is well aware that it is itself an effect which requires explanation. The core of his work, accordingly, is an attempt to demonstrate precisely *why* overcapacity has emerged as a problem in the modern capitalist world economy.

Situating his theory

Brenner, of course, is not the first person working within the framework of Marx's theory to write about the postwar crisis. Since explanations focusing upon such favoured factors as profit squeeze, rising value composition of capital and overproduction have long vied for support, Brenner's first chore is to attempt to settle accounts with some existing left accounts. Beginning with a critique of supply-side theories of the long downturn, he particularly targets those on the Left (such as Bowles, Gordon and Weisskopf as well as the French regulation-school theorists) who stressed the weakness of capital – a weakness resulting presumably from both the salutary effect of the long postwar boom upon the strength of workers and also the 'Keynesian' state arrangements put in place to prevent another Great Depression.

Brenner's critique is, firstly, an 'orthodox deduction from *Capital*'. Challenging the supply-side argument that extended full employment led to a profit squeeze through the effect of a tight labour market on wages and productivity growth, Brenner proposes that such a situation will 'call forth counteracting tendencies that make for the increase in profitability and thereby tend to prevent an actual profit squeeze from taking place'.[10] For example, the substitution of machinery for labour stressed by Marx leads both to 'relatively reduced labour demand and to increased productivity growth'.[11] Thus, it follows, emerging profit squeezes will be short-term and cannot explain a system-wide long downturn. Further, Brenner declares that supply-side arguments focusing upon national institutions (capital-labour 'accords', welfare states, etc.) in particular countries fail an important empirical test: they cannot explain why 'the downturn has been *universal, simultaneous* and *long-term*'. With respect to this last point, he concludes that:

---

[10] Brenner 1998a, p. 18.
[11] Brenner 1998a, p. 17.

It is almost impossible to believe that the assertion of workers' power has been so effective and so unyielding as to have caused the downturn to continue over a period of close to a quarter century.[12]

Faring even worse in Brenner's eyes as an adequate theoretical explanation of the long downturn is the traditional falling rate of profit argument, which he labels 'the Fundamentalist Marxist theory'.[13] Brenner describes the FROP thesis as the proposition that increasing mechanisation must lead to declines in the output-capital ratio which cannot be counteracted by rising productivity (i.e., the output-labour ratio) and, thus, to a falling rate of profit. Malthusian, he sneers, noting that the FROP thesis amounts to 'the impeccably Malthusian proposition' that the rate of profit falls because the effect of capital accumulation is to lower *total* factor productivity.[14] Were this incantation not sufficient in itself to exorcise the falling rate of profit explanation of crisis, Brenner also draws upon the critiques of Okishio and Roemer which conclude that individual capitalists will raise, rather than lower, the profit rate by introducing technical changes. The entire logic of the theory, thus, is suspect for him:

> For the Fundamentalist Marxist theory to hold, therefore requires the assumption – again paradoxical in terms of Marx's own premises – that capitalists adopt new techniques that *decrease their own rate of profit* – and, again, end up reducing overall productivity.[15]

If both the profit-squeeze and FROP theories of crisis are dismissed so summarily as explanations of the long downturn, attention then logically turns to the theory often identified as the third in the triumvirate of Marxian crisis arguments – the classic overproduction theory. We refer here to Marx's argument that overproduction is the 'fundamental contradiction of developed capital', that it emerges because of the 'constant tension between the restricted dimensions of consumption on the capitalist basis, and a production that is constantly striving to overcome these immanent barriers' and that its proximate cause is that the consumption of workers 'does not

---

[12] Brenner 1998a, p. 22.
[13] Brenner 1998a, p. 11.
[14] Brenner 1998a, p. 11.
[15] Brenner 1998a, p. 12n.

grow correspondingly with the productivity of labour' – i.e., is the result of the increase in the rate of exploitation.[16]

By introducing his own account of the long-term downturn as one which 'finds the source of the profitability decline, schematically speaking, in the tendency of the producers to develop the productive forces... without regard for existing investments and their requirements for realization', Brenner would seem, at first glance, to accept the classic overproduction thesis as his own.[17] Yet, while he neither directly introduces nor challenges this crisis theory as an explanation of the long downturn and the current crisis, Brenner's explicit rejection of the theoretical focus on a rising rate of exploitation is clear from his citation of his 1991 collaboration with Mark Glick for a criticism of 'the under-consumptionist interpretation of the interwar crisis'.[18]

In that earlier critique of the regulation school, Brenner and Glick took direct aim at theoretical explanations of the 1920s and 1930s based upon the tendency of productivity to increase more rapidly than real wages. Why, they asked, is the 'supposedly insufficient demand for consumer goods' not offset by rising 'demand for capital goods by firms seeking to remain competitive through investment and technical change?'[19] Indeed, they proposed there that 'none of the many different theorists of the inevitability of realization/underconsumption crises has yet put forward a systematic and general argument to show that realization will not take place by way of the increased aggregate demand' under a number of circumstances.[20] Would not, for example, the 'expansion of capital investment (demand for capital goods) under the pressure of competition' and ensuing increases in consumption prevent the emergence of realisation problems?

Given this Brenner-Glick 'Say's Law' formulation which essentially queries why an excess demand for Department I output does not compensate for any excess supply of Department II output, it is not surprising that Brenner does not build his overcapacity argument here on the effects of an increasing rate

[16] These quotations and an argument developing this crisis theory can be found in Lebowitz 1994 (see Chapter 14 above). See also Lebowitz 1982 and Lebowitz 1976 (see Chapters 7 and 8 above) for a discussion of Marx's crisis theory and a critique of the FROP argument.

[17] Brenner 1998a, pp. 23–4.

[18] Brenner 1998a, p. 14n.

[19] Brenner and Glick 1991, p. 80.

[20] Ibid.

of exploitation.[21] True, he acknowledges, realisation of surplus-value may pose problems. However, for Brenner, the problems originate not in any tendency of capital to overexploit but, rather, are due to 'capitalism's unplanned competitive nature'.[22] Indeed, at the core of his argument is the position that overcapacity is the result of the competition of capitals; it is, as noted above, the 'expression of intensified international competition'.

Two cheers for Brenner

Those who acknowledge the unique character of Marx's methodological approach will sense immediately a serious problem in Brenner's argument. Before undertaking a methodological critique (which, alas, by its nature, can not escape a focus upon 'orthodox deductions from *Capital*'), however, it is essential to acknowledge his salient achievement in this work.[23] Not only does Brenner skewer well those supply-side arguments which implicitly treat the nation and national capital as the One, but he also points to the inherent problems in the oblivious empiricism characteristic of many technically sophisticated studies.

By stressing, for example, the manner in which the increasing intensity of international competition was reflected in reduced mark-ups in US manufacturing in the 1965–73 period (and focusing upon the contrasting experience of manufactures and non-manufactures), Brenner demonstrates that the fall in the US profit share ('the profit squeeze') in manufacturing was due not at all to the weakness of capital (i.e., the strength of workers) but, rather, to the effect of growing international competition upon selling prices. Empirical studies, then, which emphasise the profit squeeze but lack a variable to capture the effects of international competition at a time when

---

[21] Note that their argument did not explore the extent to which, under conditions of declining profits in Department II, capitalists may choose not to convert their money-capital into new means of production but just to place them in banks.

[22] Brenner 1998a, p. 24.

[23] The focus of this particular critique will be on methodological rather than empirical issues. In addition, I will leave the defence of profit-squeeze and FROP theories to those who feel particularly criticised. My own comments on FROP can be found in Lebowitz 1982, 1976 (Chapters 7 and 8 above).

it was clearly increasing are revealed thereby to have misdirected readers despite their sophisticated techniques.[24]

Similarly, Brenner directly takes on those who have stressed declining output-capital ratios in their explanation of falling profit rates in the US. Yes, he acknowledges, 'output-capital ratios did fall significantly during this period' (1965–73); however, it is wrong to infer support from this for a FROP argument stressing growing inefficiency of investment.[25] And, the reason is that the 23% decline in *nominal* output-capital ratios includes the effects of changes in relative prices: expressed in constant output and capital stock prices, 'the (real) output-capital ratio in manufacturing fell barely at all between 1965 and 1973'. Here again, then, inferences from individual country studies which assign high weight to falling output-capital ratios (or rising value-compositions of capital) should be questioned – regardless of how good their regressions – if they have excluded at the outset Brenner's alternative that:

> the fall in profitability originated in the inability of US manufacturers to fully realize their investments because of the increased downward pressure on prices that resulted from the unanticipated entry into the market of lower cost producers, especially from abroad.[26]

In short, all other things equal, the very introduction of new, low-cost producers into an industry can mean that existing capitals no longer realise all their individual value of output and the surplus-value generated within production. Considering only these particular individual capitals, we would find the value of their output down relative to advanced capital, their profit share down and a lower rate of profit; yet, we could not reason from these individual capitals to understand the industry as a whole. The same caveat holds for studies focusing on national capitals.[27]

---

[24] Note that Bowles, Gordon and Weisskopf introduced the international dimension into their study of US profits through the terms of trade – thereby stressing foreign sellers of *inputs* rather than sellers of competing manufactures. Bowles, Gordon and Weisskopf 1986.

[25] Brenner 1998a, p. 101.

[26] Brenner 1998a, p. 102.

[27] Brenner's account provides support for an earlier proposition:
  The discovery of declining rates of productivity increase and falling rates of exploitation in particular national centres of capital...is quite consistent with precisely the *opposite* characteristics for world capital as a whole. To

The treatment, thus, of individual capitalist countries as the appropriate unit of analysis has built into it the inability to deal adequately with the problem of overcapacity, a matter which can be explored only at the level of capital as a whole, world capitalism. With his focus upon overcapacity and his critique of supply-side theories which offer country-specific explanations of patterns which are universal, simultaneous and long-term, Brenner's work here is an important corrective to many earlier analyses of the postwar period. However, although he promises to make the international economy his 'theoretical vantage point', Brenner does not substitute for the focus on national capital as One the alternative emphasis of world capital as One.[28] Rather, he makes his centrepoint *many* ones – i.e., many competing national capitals; consequently, he falls into predictable traps.

A methodological distinction

To understand the central problem in Brenner's explanation of developments in this period, it is essential to recall his membership in the analytical-Marxist fraternity. At the core of this group was the concept of methodological individualism, which Jon Elster (a founding father) described as the principle that all social phenomena are 'explicable in ways that only involve individuals – their properties, their goals, their beliefs and their actions'. It is a position, Elster argued, that rejects any explanation that 'assumes that there are supra-individual entities that are prior to individuals in the explanatory order'. 'Good science' for the analytical Marxists, indeed, had to meet the standard set by modern scientific practice, which meant (according to John Roemer) that 'Marxian analysis requires microfoundations' and (according to Phillipe Van Parijs) that 'no explanatory theory is acceptable unless it is provided with *microfoundations*'. In this respect, analytical Marxism distinguished itself by its explicit criticism of Marx where he appeared to deny methodological individualism.[29]

---

reason from the situation of particular capitals to the whole involves a logical fallacy of composition. For, with a growing intensity of international capitalist competition, individual national capitals may appear as weak (because of their inability to maintain mark-ups) at the very time when capital is strengthening on a world scale. (Lebowitz 1988b, pp. 138–9.)

[28] Brenner 1998a, p. 23.

[29] Lebowitz 1988a. See also Lebowitz 1994 (Chapter 14 above).

While Brenner always seemed an unlikely member of the group and was not himself inclined to criticise Marx, his own commitment to methodological individualism is the context in which to understand his statement as to the requirements of a good crisis theory:

> A sufficient theory of crisis must explain not only why what individuals and collectivities do in pursuit of their interests leads to an aggregate pattern of production and distribution in which profitability is undermined, thereby reducing the capacity and incentive to invest. It must also explain why that same pattern leads producers to take remedial action that fails to bring about an adjustment and ends up exacerbating the difficulties of the initial situation.[30]

Not only the 'sufficient theory of crisis' but also the explanation of growth must meet the methodological-individualist test. Brenner begins his theoretical account by attributing the 'relentless and systematic development of the productive forces' within capitalism to the actions of 'individual units' which act to maximise their profits. As these individual firms seek the lowest cost techniques and move to produce what the market desires *and* as 'competition on the market...weeds out those units that fail to produce at a sufficient rate of profit', the result is 'the inherent dynamism of the capitalist economy'.[31] This is the same dynamism arising from 'inter-capitalist competition' that Brenner and Glick had earlier described as imposing

> an inexorable pressure on firms to maximize cost-cutting so as to realize temporary surplus profits or technological rents, thereby maintaining themselves against competitors, and to accrue sufficient surpluses for adequate further investment.[32]

From the actions of individual capitals to the beneficial effects of an invisible hand – Adam Smith's familiar mixture of atomism and a harmonious universe.

Indeed, Brenner's focus on the centrality of the competition of capitals for capitalist development is a theme which can also be found in his essay on the emergence of capitalism in Roemer's *Analytical Marxism* collection. There,

---

[30] Brenner 1998a, p. 23.
[31] Brenner 1998a, p. 10.
[32] Brenner and Glick 1991, p. 55.

Brenner explicitly set out Adam Smith's invisible hand account of capitalist economic development resulting from competition among producers who, following their individual rational self-interest, cut costs, accumulate and innovate. Brenner's central point, though, was that the unacknowledged premise for these beneficial unintended consequences is the prior existence of capitalist property relations. Smith, he noted,

> begged the fundamental question: *under what conditions* will or will not the patterns of economic action pursued by individuals correspond to the requirements of economic growth of the economy as a whole?[33]

Thus, under precapitalist property relations, Brenner argued, the actions of individuals, 'although individually rational, are nonetheless systematically subversive, in the long run, of economic development'.[34] Only where capitalist relations prevail 'will the individual economic actors necessarily have the motivation (survival) to adopt new techniques; only under capitalism will there obtain a process of natural selection to weed out those who do not'. Indeed, 'only under capitalist property relations can we expect a pattern of modern economic growth'.[35]

Of course, Brenner's acceptance of the Smithian argument *once capitalist relations are in place* does not help us to understand the emergence of capitalist crisis. That is, indeed, one of the central themes of Brenner's current work, where he proposes that, if we are to grasp 'the historical regularity of secular capitalist downturn, we therefore need a theory of a malign invisible hand to go along with Adam Smith's benign one'.[36] We need, in short, a theory that can explain how rational individual actors, under capitalist relations, act in such a way as to produce *negative* unintended consequences, thereby undermining profitability and the economic growth of the economy as a whole.

The competition of individual capitals, thus, is always in the foreground in Brenner's explanation of capitalism's dynamics – both its periods of growth and slump. Indeed, he chides supply-side theorists for focusing too much on the 'vertical' relations of capitalists and workers:

---

[33] Brenner 1986, p. 25.
[34] Brenner 1986, p. 26.
[35] Brenner 1986, pp. 34, 45.
[36] Brenner 1998a, p. 23.

As a result, they have tended to underplay not only the productive benefits, but also the economic contradictions, that arise from the 'horizontal' competition among firms *that constitutes the capitalist system's economic mainspring.*[37]

Yet, emphasis upon the competition of capitals to explain the dynamics of the system is precisely what Marx rejected. Rather, he stressed that competition was simply the 'way in which the immanent laws of capitalist production manifest themselves in the external movement of the individual capitals'.[38] Competition, Marx argued, does not '*explain* these laws; rather, it lets them be *seen*, but does not produce them'.[39] Thus, Marx was quite explicit in rejecting analyses of the dynamics of capitalism based merely on the observation of individual capitals in competition. Challenging Smith's explanation of a falling rate of profit by reference to the competition of capitals, he declared 'to try to explain them [capital's laws] simply as the results of competition therefore means to concede that one does not understand them'.[40]

Marx, of course, was not denying that developments occurred *through* the actions of the competing capitals. He was not asserting that there was a single actor (capital in general or capital as a whole) that functioned within society. Rather, while competing capitals execute the inherent tendencies of capital, Marx concluded that the nature of capital and of those 'general and necessary tendencies' could be grasped only by beginning from consideration of capital as a whole.[41]

Precisely for this reason, in *Capital* (and before it, the *Grundrisse*), Marx's deduction of capital's tendency to increase productivity in order to generate relative surplus-value is conducted at the level of capital as a whole – in contrast to the analyses of his youth, which had focused on competition. 'It is easy,' Marx now commented in the *Grundrisse*, 'to develop the introduction of machinery out of competition and out of the law of the reduction of production costs which is triggered by competition.' (Nothing, indeed, could be easier.)

---

[37] Ibid. Emphasis added.
[38] Marx 1977a, p. 433.
[39] Marx 1973, pp. 651, 552.
[40] Marx 1973, p. 752. In their comments on Brenner, Ben Fine and his co-authors also have stressed some of the problems in Brenner's focus on competition and the relation to the influence of 'analytical Marxism'. Fine, Lapavitsas and Milonakis 1999.
[41] Marx 1977a, p. 433.

However, the theoretical requirement was to develop the introduction of machinery 'out of the relation of capital to living labour, without reference to other capitals'.[42] In short, it is precisely Marx's insistence upon exploring 'supra-individual entities...prior to individuals in the explanatory order' which is the distinctive characteristic of his method.

Nevertheless, once one grasps what Marx was attempting to demonstrate in *Capital* – i.e., that capital is the result of exploitation, what does the difference in methodology matter? Granted that Brenner's approach differs fundamentally from Marx's esoteric methodology in the analysis of the dynamics of capitalism, can that be in itself sufficient to reject Brenner's analysis or even to describe it as non-Marxist? Since what matters is the effect, if any, of rejecting Marx's holism in favour of methodological individualism in the particular case, let me suggest three areas of concern which arise out of Brenner's focus upon the competition of capitals: the explanation of causation, the determination of limits and the treatment of essential relations.

'In competition, everything is reversed'

One of the important differences Marx identified between an inner analysis and outer observation relates to the direction of causality. 'That in their appearance things are often presented in an inverted way,' he commented, 'is something fairly familiar in every science, apart from political economy.'[43] In order, therefore, to stress the necessity to go beyond appearances, Marx repeatedly used the analogy of the manner in which appearances falsify the real movement of the planets: 'having once made sure of the real movement of the celestial bodies, we shall be able to explain their apparent or merely phenomenal movements'. Although 'everyday observation' would suggest that the sun moves around the earth, he noted, 'scientific truth is always paradox, if judged by everyday experience, which catches only the delusive appearance of things'.[44]

It was the work of 'science', then, to go beyond appearances, 'to resolve the visible, merely external movement into the true intrinsic movement'. To

---

[42] Marx 1973, pp. 776–7.
[43] Marx 1977a, p. 677.
[44] Marx 1985b, pp. 127–8.

follow Marx along this path, of course, requires that we acknowledge that there is a difference between the extrinsic and the intrinsic: 'all science would be superfluous if the outward appearance and the essence of things directly coincided'.[45] Further, it is necessary to recognise that in political economy as elsewhere the understanding of essence must come first:

> A scientific analysis of competition is possible only if we can grasp the inner nature of capital, just as the apparent motions of the heavenly bodies are intelligible only to someone who is acquainted with their real motions, which are not perceptible to the senses.[46]

Clearly, for Marx, understanding the concept of value must precede an analysis of its components. Just as the segments of a line 'are limited in advance by the limits of the line of which they are parts', so, too, the sum of value logically precedes its subdivisions.[47] Yet, the focus on individual capitals in competition (characteristic of vulgar economics) yields a quite different picture. It appears that wages, profit and rent are the original constituents of price – an order precisely the opposite to the inner analysis; 'in short, here all determinants appear in a position which is the *inverse* of their position in capital in general'.[48]

Especially frustrating in this respect for Marx was Adam Smith because he traced both 'the intrinsic connection existing between economic categories or the obscure structure of the bourgeois economic system' and also 'the connection as it appears in the phenomena of competition and thus as it presents itself to the unscientific observer...'. Having initially grasped that inner connection, Smith then became 'obsessed...with the *connection, as it appears in* competition, and in competition everything always appears in inverted form, always standing on its head'.[49]

For Marx, Smith thereby was abandoning the perspective of the scientific analyst and accepting the way things appear to the actual participants in economic activity. Whereas the former considers the system as a whole and employs abstract thought (deduction) in order to grasp the system's necessary

---

[45] Marx 1966, pp. 313, 817.
[46] Marx 1977a, p. 433.
[47] Marx 1981a, p. 462.
[48] Marx 1973, p. 657.
[49] Marx 1968, pp. 165, 217.

conditions for reproduction, individual capitals are concerned only with their own conditions of existence – their costs and the possibilities for profit:

> In the competition of individual capitalists among themselves as well as in the competition on the world-market, it is the given and assumed magnitudes of wages, interest and rent which enter into the calculation as constant and regulating magnitudes.... Here, then, experience shows theoretically, and the self-interested calculation of the capitalist shows practically, that the prices of commodities are determined by wages, interest and rent, by the price of labour, capital and land, and that these elements of price are indeed the regulating constituent factors of price.[50]

Why exactly does this reversal occur? What individual capitals see as the premise of their activity Marx, in contrast, grasped as result. The problem here is not unique. Permeating, indeed, the political economy which begins from individual capitals in competition is that 'the pattern of the process of reproduction is not understood – how it appears not from the standpoint of individual capital, but rather from that of total capital...'.[51] Since individual actors do not concern themselves with the necessary conditions for the whole, the real premise is to be determined logically rather than accepting the order of causation as it appears to competing capitals. On few matters was Marx more consistent than in his understanding that reasoning from the forms of daily existence is an abandonment of science and a falsification of the inner relations:

> *Thus, everything appears reversed in competition*. The final pattern of economic relations as seen on the surface, in their real existence and consequently in the conceptions by which the bearers and agents of these relations seek to understand them, is very much different from, and indeed quite the reverse of, the inner but concealed essential pattern and the conception corresponding to it.[52]

This brings us, then, to Brenner's reversal. As might be predicted from his focus on the competition of individual capitals to explain the dynamics of capitalism, Brenner reverses the order of Marx's explanation: *whereas, for*

---

[50] Marx 1966, pp. 874–5.
[51] Marx 1966, p. 844.
[52] Marx 1966, pp. 209, 225.

Brenner, it is the intensified competition of capitals that leads to overcapacity, for Marx, the inherent tendency for overcapacity leads to the intensified competition of capitals. For Marx, rather than a cause, intense competition is itself a result:

> The rate of profit would not fall under the effect of competition due to over-production of capital. It would rather be the reverse; it would be the competitive struggle which would begin because the fallen rate of profit and over-production of capital originate from the same conditions.[53]

We thus have two alternative orders of explanation – (1) from the increase in the rate of exploitation to overcapacity to intensified competitive struggle or (2) from intensified competitive struggle to overcapacity. While neither denies the importance of the increasing intensity of competition in the real world, differing methodologies assign it differing locations. If we begin from consideration of capital as a whole, that increasing intensity of competition is not an external matter; its basis is the relative overproduction of capital, the expansion of capital beyond the ability to valorise that capital. In contrast, from the perspective of the capital of an individual country, that increased competition necessarily appears as an external force. We see here a classic example of how 'the immanent laws of [world] capital manifest themselves in the external movement of the individual capitals... [and] assert themselves as the coercive laws of [international] competition'.[54]

How, then, can we choose between these two orders of explanation? Brenner himself, after all, is an excellent source for the position that underlying the problem of overcapacity is an increase in the rate of exploitation. At every step of his detailed historical narrative, he points out that the capitals that expanded were those able to combine low-cost labour with high productivity and that capital's expansion in centres characterised by high rates of exploitation generated an overwhelming export orientation as a necessity for realisation, thereby producing this intensification of competition.

Rather than attempting to distinguish empirically between what Marx called 'the general and necessary tendencies of capital' and 'their forms of appearance', it is essential to recognise that we are talking about two quite distinct logical planes. In the former, capital generates relative surplus-value

---

[53] Marx 1966, p. 252.
[54] Marx 1977a, p. 433. *Cf.* Lebowitz 1988b.

by driving down necessary labour; in the latter, individual capitals do so by competing to lower their production costs (wage bills among them). That the latter is an accurate description of the actual process is not sufficient to make it the basis upon which to understand the nature of capital and its tendencies. Given the form in which capital necessarily exists, what is the likelihood of an increase in the rate of exploitation *except* through the competition of capitals – or the growth of capital except as uneven development?

If an explanation based upon the competition of capitals is to be demonstrated as inadequate, then the demonstration must be logical rather than empirical. In the case of Brenner's theoretical explanation, there is such a logical test: given Brenner's description of inter-capitalist competition as the source of the inherent dynamism of capitalism, what turns it into the source of capitalism's problems? Why, in short, does the invisible hand turn bad?

Why the invisible hand turns bad

As discussed in 'Analytical Marxism and the Marxian Theory of Crisis', Marx's investigation of the 'obscure structure of the bourgeois economic system' reveals the existence of structural limits to individual actions. By identifying the necessary conditions for reproduction of capital as a whole, Marx's theory points to the tension between those structural limits and individual capitals that proceed *as if no limits exist*. Crises, for Marx, thus occur not simply because of capitalism's unplanned nature but because (1) there are 'specific and restrictive proportions' required for realisation and (2) there is an inherent tendency of individual capitals to violate those proportions.[55] As Marx noted, 'there would be no crisis without this inner unity of factors that are apparently indifferent to each other'.[56] Precisely because individual capitalists functioning in the market are indifferent to the requirements for capitalist reproduction, they tend to violate them in the course of their drive to increase surplus-value:

> Exchange does not change the inner characteristics of realization; but it projects them to the outside; gives them a reciprocally independent form,

---

[55] Lebowitz 1994 (Chapter 14 above). Marx 1973, pp. 443–4.
[56] Marx 1966, p. 500.

and thereby lets their unity exist merely as an inner necessity, which must therefore come forcibly to the surface in crises.[57]

Thus, capital's tendency to increase the rate of surplus-value beyond the level warranted by the conditions for realisation – i.e., its tendency to produce more surplus-value than can be realised – generates the crisis according to Marx's overproduction theory. Given that the purpose of capitalist production is surplus-value and that purpose can be realised only through the sale of commodities, there is a limit to how high the rate of exploitation can be driven; sooner or later, capital's thrust 'to reduce the relation of necessary labour to surplus labour to a minimum' produces barriers to realisation of surplus-value and thus a barrier to the growth of capital.[58] Overcapacity results from violation of the limits to the market under existing conditions – workers cannot spend more and capitalists will not.

In the absence of a prior determination of the requirements of the system as a whole, however, it is not possible to identify the structural conditions which, when violated, turn a benign invisible hand into a malign one. Because of his adherence to methodological individualism, Brenner's theory of the malign invisible hand fails to explain the turning points.

Consider his explanation as to how 'intensified international competition' generated overcapacity. Brenner describes the process as one in which individual firms, when adding to capacity, do not know what their competitors will do. They function under conditions of uncertainty. So, in attempting to maximise individual profits, they cut their costs and lower their prices, thereby pressuring old firms, which are no longer able to maintain old profit levels.[59] 'There is over-capacity and over-production, *with respect to the hitherto-existing profit rate.*'[60] The problem is, however, that the high-cost firms do not simply disappear from the market: their investments in fixed capital as well as their established relations with suppliers and purchasers in existing product lines are 'sunk capital', and the firms remain in the industry in question even with reduced profits.[61] Accordingly, the exit necessary to restore the old levels

---

[57] Marx 1973, p. 447.
[58] Marx 1973, p. 422; Lebowitz 1976, p. 236; Lebowitz 1982, pp. 16–20.
[59] Brenner 1998a, pp. 24–5.
[60] Brenner 1998a, p. 26.
[61] Brenner 1998a, p. 33.

of profitability does not take place; and, to the extent that firms respond to the competitive pressure with new investments of their own, the problem of overcapacity increases.

Within this framework of the competition of capitals and uneven development, things go from bad to worse. Still lower-cost producers appear as the drive intensifies to find 'even lower production costs through the combination of even cheaper labour with even higher levels of techniques in still later-developing regions...'.[62] Thus, rather than correcting itself, an initial pattern of overinvestment in the postwar period led to the long downturn and the underlying basis of the current financial crisis.

What Brenner describes here is a market failure – a particular capitalist's dilemma in which no individual capitalist firm finds it rational to scrap its fixed assets, with the result is that capitalism is locked into a path which is increasingly self-destructive.[63] What he *fails* to explain, however, is why the maximising activities of individual capitals cease to generate benign results. After all, that very 'inter-capitalist competition' which he describes as the source of capitalism's dynamism now reappears as the source of its misery. But, what has changed? That there is fixed capital? That firms have sunk costs not only in fixed capital but also in established routines and relationships? That firms function under conditions of uncertainty?

Having rejected the prior necessity to understand the structure within which that competition of capitals occurs – i.e., the logical priority of the whole, Brenner is unable to explain exactly why market failure has emerged. The question of limits to the market receives no attention in his account how competition generates overcapacity. Yet, a limit to the market is precisely the necessary condition for the emergence of overcapacity since, as Marx noted, 'if the expansion of the market had kept pace with the expansion of production there would be no glut of the market, no over-production'.[64] Indeed, this is the *premise* of Brenner's own argument. Before raising the question of the failure

---

[62] Brenner 1998a, p. 34.

[63] It is difficult not to see this as a particular version of the FROP supply-side argument that Brenner so summarily dismisses. Is not the focus here upon the manner in which the result of rational individual investment decisions is the declining efficiency of investment – falling output-capital ratios, rising value compositions of capital and the like?

[64] Marx 1968, p. 524.

of firms to scrap fixed capital and/or to exit, the context in which overcapacity emerges has already been set; as the result of the entry of the new, lower-cost firms:

> The line can be said to be characterized by over-capacity or over-production because – or in the sense that – *there is insufficient demand* to allow the higher cost firms to maintain their former rates of profit....[65]

Brenner, however, offers no explanation as to *why* 'there is insufficient demand'.

To illustrate the problem in Brenner's argument, let us conduct a thought-experiment. Consider a particular counter-factual proposition: assume that there is a global régime in which not only have wages been removed from competition (i.e., there is no possibility of firms securing rents by access to cheap labour) but, also, where real wages are a direct and constant function of productivity – not only over time but also cross-sectionally. Under these extreme golden-age conditions, we may suggest, firstly, that overcapacity would not have emerged as a problem – both because of less capital accumulation but also because the demand for Department II output would be stronger. Further, under these counterfactual conditions (which, all other things equal, imply a constant rate of exploitation), we propose that the degree of competition of capitals would be significantly lower – which suggests that the intensity of competition is properly grasped as an effect rather than a cause.

Of course, as Brenner well knows, sooner or later, any such assumed conditions would disappear to the extent that capital's drive for surplus-value and its victories in class struggle allow it to find ways to increase the degree of exploitation; and, as Marx knew, those successes in the sphere of production, sooner or later, would recreate the problems resulting from capital's tendency to expand production without regard for the limits in the sphere of circulation given by capitalist relations of production. That all this looks like the result of the increasing intensity of competition of capitals should not obscure its roots in the violation of the structural limits that are hidden from methodological individualists.

---

[65] Brenner 1998a, p. 25. Emphasis added.

Obscuring the essential relation

Finally, let us consider the nature and implications of the story Brenner has told. Given his acceptance of methodological individualism, it is not surprising that the competition of capitals displaces class relations in his account. Only when analysis begins from capital as a whole and workers as a whole – i.e., from consideration of capitalism as a whole – is there not a distortion of the essential relation of capital and wage-labour.[66] Whereas a focus upon individual capitals directs attention to the conditions under which individual capitals ensure their survival by producing more cheaply than their competitors, starting from capital as a whole puts the condition for the survival of capital itself – the maintenance of the dependence (and the *feeling* of dependence) of workers upon capital – at the centre of analysis.[67]

Thus, in one account, 'relentless and systematic development of the productive forces' as the result of inter-capitalist competition; in the other, the reproduction of capitalist relations of production as workers are weakened by their displacement by machinery, the geographical redistribution of capital and state repression. Whereas the former focuses upon the increased degree of competition among capitals in order to tell its story of capitalist growth and slump in the second half of the century, for the latter it is the increased degree of separation among workers – the resultant of capital's greater success in the two-sided class struggle – which is the real story of this period. The expansion of capital in localities characterised by low labour costs relative to productivity, in short, can be considered from the perspective of its effect upon older, high-cost competitors or it can be seen as a way in which capital divides and separates workers. Focus upon the competition of capitals invariably introduces a one-sidedness in which the only relevant actors are capitalists; it is a form of the one-sided Marxism that ignores the role of workers' struggles in shaping capitalism's dynamics.[68]

---

[66] Lebowitz 1992a, pp. 135–9.
[67] Marx 1977a, pp. 899, 936.
[68] 'The silence as to the opposition from wage-labour has produced the theoretical substitution of the opposition of individual capitals as the explanation for the development of productive forces within capitalism.... Thus, a phenomenal, outer explanation similar to that which Marx rejected in the course of (and after) the *Grundrisse* displaces an inner account based upon the opposition of capital and wage-labour; lost is the extent to which workers' struggles impose upon capital the

Given his own critique (which set off the 'Brenner Debate') of writers who failed to place class at the centre of their analyses, Brenner should know better than this.[69] And, indeed, the story he tells (his 'detailed historical narrative') is sensitive to the offensives launched by capital against workers and to the importance of the state of class struggle; he acknowledges, for example, that while direct action and general militancy by US workers was successful in pressuring capital until the latter part of the 50s, the latter launched an assault in the early 60s and 'achieved what turned out to be a fundamental shift in the balance of class power' which 'persists right up to the present'.[70]

Nevertheless, as we have seen, when it comes to his 'clear-cut analytical model', Brenner criticises arguments which focus too much on the 'vertical' relations between capitalists and workers and understate both the positive and negative effects of the 'horizontal' competition among firms. His methodology drives him in a direction contrary to his earlier focus on class struggle, back to a Smithian emphasis upon the manner in which inter-capitalist competition generates both the development of productive forces and also its contradictions.

And, where does this argument lead? Brenner's explanation of the slump leads him to criticise Keynesian demand stimulus because of its effect in keeping redundant manufacturing capacity from being scrapped. Keynesian policies in the US until the early 90s, he argues, 'actually contributed to the perpetuation of overcapacity and overproduction and thus helped to keep down rates of profit in aggregate'.[71] On the other hand, the alternative of allowing the crisis to deepen to the point where it is severe enough to compel weak capitals to exit – i.e., to ensure that 'sufficient high-cost, low profit means of production can be forced from lines affected by over-capacity/over-production and reduced profitability...' has its own drawbacks for capitalism.[72] Even though the 'rollback of that redundant manufacturing capacity and output' could be seen as 'the precondition for restoring the system to health', restrictive macroeconomic policies and the embrace of neoliberalism worsen

---

continuing necessity to revolutionise the instruments of production.' Lebowitz 2003, p. 121.

[69] Brenner 1985.
[70] Brenner 1998a, p. 58.
[71] Brenner 1998a, p. 152; Brenner 1998b, p. 25.
[72] Brenner 1998a, p. 24.

the situation by their effect upon aggregate demand.[73] Competitive austerity and the competitive struggle over the incidence of scrapped capital intensify the struggle for exports and 'exacerbate the secular problem of manufacturing overcapacity'. The break from Keynesianism, Brenner accordingly concludes, was a 'crucial enabling condition for today's economic turmoil, opening the way for the international economy's turn from long-term stagnation to intense crisis'.[74]

Thus, a crisis which brings to the fore the problem of Brenner's 'malign invisible hand' – the paradox that individual profit-maximising and competitive market mechanisms, the very source of capitalism's dynamism, generate long-term stagnation and crisis. The result, Brenner proposes, is an important ideological opening for the Left:

> once it ceases to be possible to simply take it for granted as a first principle
> that free market allocation per se will always yield the best possible outcome,
> the way is opened to question the appropriateness of market allocation in all
> areas of economic life – market allocation of long-term investments, market
> allocation of commodities and, most centrally of course, market allocation
> of labour power.[75]

It is an opportunity, he argues, to make the claim for 'the indispensability of socialism – i.e., of democratic, social control over the economy from the bottom up by the working class'. And, yet, insofar as Brenner's analysis of the slump is essentially that of a market failure, another direction is already implicit in that description – to substitute for the anarchy of capital a way to co-ordinate the actions of capital to reduce capacity and to monitor new additions on a world-scale. In short, the implicit solution is a depression-cartel. Brenner, in fact, reveals the cartel solution inherent in his argument about sunk fixed capital and the failure to exit by calling attention to the parallel between his analysis and 'late nineteenth-century literature on "ruinous competition", which often sought to justify cartels and trusts'.[76]

Here, again, regardless of his own political perspective, the methodology permeating his analytical model drives him in the direction of a political

---

[73] Brenner 1998a, pp. 152–3, 156.
[74] Brenner 1998b, p. 25.
[75] Brenner 1998b, p. 23.
[76] Brenner 1998a, p. 26n.

strategy in which the logic is not one of class struggle but, rather, of a search for transnational agencies to stabilise the competition of capitals. However, what else could be expected of an analysis that stresses 'capitalism's unplanned competitive nature'? Nothing in the implied solution, in short, would focus upon workers as such – because the analysis does not.

In contrast, an analysis which sees the rise of overcapacity as rooted in the increase in the rate of exploitation places at the centre struggles for higher real wages and for increased satisfaction of needs for producers around the world and looks to reduce the ability of capital to divide workers – the struggle, in short, to reduce the rate of exploitation. This is a position which, having identified the central problem as class exploitation, focuses upon class struggle. Not, of course, because a reduced degree of separation among workers and a lower rate of exploitation will solve capitalism's problems. But, rather, insofar as the central thrust of capital as a whole to expand surplus-value is grasped as itself the source of misery, struggles on the part of workers to satisfy their own need for development provide both the direction and basis for that claim for the 'indispensability of socialism'.[77]

It is striking how far Brenner's current analysis moves him away both from a focus on class struggle and from the class-centred analysis of his earlier work on the emergence of capitalism. Given, indeed, the thrust of that early work which criticised Smithian Marxism, it is ironic that, whereas one of Marx's achievements was to go beyond Smithian atomism, Brenner has returned to it. As Marx commented about Smith:

> Having revealed the intrinsic connection, he is suddenly obsessed again with the aspect of the phenomenon, with the *connection, as it appears in competition*, and in competition everything always appears in inverted form, always standing on its head.[78]

In this respect, given the *New Left Review*'s praise of Brenner's 'momentous achievement', we should think about the message that has been communicated. For, an important part of *NLR*'s praise for Brenner is because of 'his open-mindedness as a historian'. Whereas his earlier work focused upon class

---

[77] See, in particular, Chapters 10 and 11 in Lebowitz 2003.
[78] Marx 1968, p. 217.

relations between peasant producers and feudal lords – i.e., placed the class relation at its heart, *NLR* notes that in his analysis of recent changes:

> Brenner reaches the opposite conclusion. Here it is not the vertical relationship between capital and labour that in the last resort decides the fate of modern economies, but the horizontal relationship between capital and capital. It is the logic of competition, not class struggle, that rules the deeper rhythms of growth or recession.[79]

One may suggest that this accurate description of Brenner's text brings a rather different meaning to *NLR*'s closing declaration that, in this work, 'Marx's enterprise has certainly found its successor'. In Brenner, everything is reversed.

---

[79] Brenner 1998a, p. iii. While the most vexing statements in this volume have been made by the *New Left Review* editors rather than Brenner, it is difficult to imagine that they were made without his knowledge.

PART FIVE

CONSIDERING THE OTHER SIDE OF *CAPITAL*

Part Five

Considering the Other Side of *Capital*

The essays in this part all explore questions raised in my *Beyond 'Capital'*. Chapter 16 presents my argument that there was no organic system presented in *Capital* and that the silences that have been identified in that work (including a silence related to the revolutionary subject) have their roots in the missing side of capitalism, the side of workers. In responding to a critique of the book by a prominent supporter of the Uno school, Chapter 17 stresses the importance of the variable, the degree of separation of workers, and argues that this school displaces class struggle from the core of capitalism by a general-equilibrium model. Chapter 18 asks what happens to our concept of the capitalist state when we look at capitalism as two-sided and sets out the logic of social democracy, identifying the condition that makes the capitalist state the basis for preserving capitalist relations rather than destroying them. Finally, the book concludes by demonstrating that Marx's assumption in *Capital* that the standard of necessity is given for a given time and place was by no means neutral. In 'The Politics of Assumption, the Assumption of Politics', a slightly revised version of my Deutscher Memorial Prize Lecture for 2005, we can see that once this assumption is relaxed, the familiar argument for relative surplus-value collapses.[1] In the absence of recognising the implications of Marx's assumption (and incorporating something like the concept of the degree of separation of workers), I propose that Marxist economists will continue to have difficulty in incorporating class struggle into their work – thus making it relevant to the real class struggle.

---

[1] The slight revision demonstrates my inability to restrain myself from making a little observation about the implicit assumptions in all those learned discourses on 'the transformation problem'.

Chapter Sixteen
The Silences of *Capital*

Not too long ago, Michael Burawoy commented that 'two anomalies confront Marxism as its refutation: the durability of capitalism and the passivity of its working class'.[1] So, has it come time, more than 125 years after the publication of *Capital*, to admit that the 'facts' (which meant something to Marx) simply do not support Marx's theory?[2]

It depends. It depends on what aspect of Marx's theory we have in mind. What reason would we have on the basis of historical experience to reject Marx's analysis of the nature of capital? Should we scuttle the idea that capital rests upon the exploitation of workers, that it has an insatiable appetite for surplus-labour, that it accordingly searches constantly for ways to extend and intensify the workday, to drive down real wages, to increase productivity? What in the developments of world capitalism in the last two centuries would lead us to think that capital is any different?

Do we think that, for example, Marx's statement that capital 'takes no account of the health and the length of life of the worker, unless society forces it

---

[1] That these 'anomalies' are identified as separate is itself interesting. Burawoy 1989, p. 51.
[2] 'I was delighted to find my theoretical conclusions fully confirmed by the FACTS.' Marx to Engels, 24 August 1867, in Marx and Engels 1987, pp. 407–8.

to do so' no longer holds – and, indeed, that it does not apply as well to capital's treatment of the natural environment?[3] Was Marx wrong in proposing that 'the entire spirit of capitalist production, which is oriented towards the most immediate monetary profit' is contrary to 'the whole gamut of permanent conditions of life required by the chain of human generations' or that all progress in capitalist agriculture in 'increasing the fertility of the soil for a given time is a progress towards ruining the more long-lasting sources of that fertility'? Does our modern experience with chemical pesticides and fertilisers refute Marx's perspective on capitalism and nature, on what capitalist production does to 'the original sources of all wealth – the soil and the worker'?[4]

Much has, of course, changed in the last two centuries – indeed, in the last quarter of this century. But, is the nature of capital among them? The apparent victory of capitalism over its putative alternative is not a challenge to the theory of *Capital*. Modern celebrants of capital would find in Marx an unsurpassed understanding of capital's dynamic, rooted in the self-valorisation that serves as motive and purpose of capitalist production. That capital drives beyond 'all traditional, confined, complacent, encrusted satisfactions of present needs, and reproductions of old ways of life', that it constantly revolutionises the process of production as well as the old ways of life, 'tearing down all the barriers which hem in the development of the forces of production, the expansion of needs, the all-sided development of production, and the exploitation and exchange of natural and mental forces' – all this was central to Marx's conception of production founded upon capital.[5] Thus, if capital today compels nations to adopt capitalist forms of production, creates a world after its own image and indeed shows once again that all that is solid (including that made by men of steel) melts into air, this in itself cannot be seen as a refutation of Marx.[6]

Nor, finally, in these days of shutdowns, growing unemployment and devaluation of capital, can we forget the contradictory character of capitalist reproduction that Marx stressed – his injunction that capital's tendency

---

[3] Marx 1977a, p. 381.
[4] Marx 1981b, p. 754n; 1977a, p. 638.
[5] Marx 1973, p. 410; 1977a, p. 617.
[6] Marx and Engels, *Manifesto of the Communist Party* in Marx and Engels 1976, pp. 487–8.

towards the absolute development of productive forces occurs only in 'the first act' and that the realisation of surplus-value produced requires a 'second act' in which commodities must be sold 'within the framework of antagonistic conditions of distribution' marked by capitalist relations of production.[7] In the signs of capitalist crisis about us, we have yet another demonstration that the understanding of the nature and logic of capital contained in Marx's *Capital* is as valid as ever.

And, yet, there is that so-obvious failure, that apparent anomaly. And, that is that capital is still with us and shows no signs of taking its early departure. For some on the Right (as well as adherents to the thesis of the primacy of productive forces), this is simply proof that capitalist relations of production are not a fetter on the development of productive forces and, indeed, that capitalism is 'optimal for the further development of productive power'.[8]

All this, of course, is despite Marx's assurance that capitalism was doomed, that it would come to an end with 'the revolt of the working class, a class constantly increasing in numbers, and trained, united and organized by the very mechanism of the capitalist process of production'. But, the 'knell' has not sounded for capitalism, and the expropriators have not been expropriated.[9]

We need to know why. What in Marx's *Capital* can explain it, what should have prepared us for understanding this historic failure? The answer, I suggest, is not what is in *Capital* but, rather, what is not.

The 'real silences'

What is missing in *Capital* was stated quite well by E.P. Thompson in his *Poverty of Theory*. *Capital*, he argued, is 'a study of the logic of capital, not of capitalism, and the social and political dimensions of the history, the wrath and the understanding of the class struggle arise from a region independent of the closed system of economic logic'.[10] For Thompson, the problems in Marx originated when he proceeded from Political Economy 'to *capitalism...*, that is, the whole society, conceived as an "organic system"'. The flaw was that 'the whole society comprises many activities and relations...which are

---

[7] Marx 1981b, p. 352.
[8] Cohen 1978, p. 175.
[9] Marx 1977a, p. 929.
[10] Thompson 1978, p. 65.

not the concern of Political Economy, which have been *defined out of* Political Economy, and for which it has no terms'.[11] And, the critical 'missing term' for Thompson is that of 'human experience'. When we raise this point, he proposed, 'at once we enter into the real silences of Marx'.[12]

Who could deny that there is indeed this silence in *Capital*? There is no place in *Capital* for living, changing, striving, enjoying, struggling and developing human beings. People who produce themselves through their own activities, who change their nature as they produce, beings of praxis, are not the subjects of *Capital*. The idea of the *'rich* human being' – 'the man in whom his own realisation exists as an inner necessity, as *need*' is entirely foreign to *Capital*.[13] In its place, we have structures which dominate human beings, a logic of capital that means that the individual consumption of the worker 'remains an aspect of the production and reproduction of capital, just as the cleaning of machinery does'; we have a working class that 'is just as much an appendage of capital as the lifeless instruments of labour are'.[14]

Why, however, is there this silence? Thompson argues that it is the result of the mature Marx's preoccupation with the critique of political economy. That, in contrast to his early attack on the latter for not considering the worker 'when he is not working, as a human being', Marx fell into a *trap*: 'the trap baited by "Political Economy". Or, more accurately, he had been sucked into a theoretical whirlpool' – one in which 'the postulates ceased to be the self-interest of man and became the logic and forms of capital, to which men were subordinated'. For Thompson, the problems of Marxism are the result of the 'system of *closure*' in which all is subsumed within the circuits of capital, where capital posits itself as an 'organic system'.[15]

And, yet, if we accept Marx's concept of an organic system as one in which 'everything posited is thus also a presupposition' (i.e., in which all premises are the results of the system itself), that claim cannot be conceded. There *is* no organic system established in *Capital*.[16] At the very point of the discussion of simple reproduction, intended to consider capitalism as an organic system,

[11] Thompson 1978, p. 62.
[12] Thompson 1978, pp. 164–5.
[13] Marx 1975d, p. 304.
[14] Marx 1977a, pp. 718–19.
[15] Marx 1975d, pp. 241–2; Thompson 1977, pp. 59, 60, 65, 163–4, 167.
[16] Marx 1973, p. 278.

we see there is an element which is not part of capital, which is not produced and reproduced by capital – a point of departure but not one of return in the circuit of capital, a premise which is not a result of capital itself. And, it is one necessary for the reproduction of capital, required for the very existence of capital itself:

> The maintenance and reproduction of the working class remains a necessary condition for the reproduction of capital. But the capitalist may safely leave this to the worker's drives for self-preservation and propagation.[17]

Thirty-two words – and, then, theoretical silence. What is missing from the circuit of capital is the second moment of production ('Moment IV'), the consideration of the production of the wage-labourer. And, this question, the subject matter for the projected book on wage-labour which was to complete 'the inner totality', involves far more than concern with physical reproduction or the household; it encompasses as well the social reproduction of wage-labour.[18] Rather than a 'system of closure', *Capital* is only a moment in the development of an organic system.[19]

Situating the silence

Let us attempt to identify a few of the problems associated with the absence of the book on wage-labour. A full discussion of these and other issues can not be pursued here but is the subject of my book, *Beyond 'Capital': Marx's Political Economy of the Working Class*.

1. *The struggle for higher wages*

While *Capital* presents well the manner in which workers, indeed all human beings, are means for capital in its drive for self-valorisation, it does not do the same for the side of the worker. Little is said about what Marx identified as the goal of the worker, about 'the worker's own need for development', or how she strives to achieve that goal.[20] We understand quite well why,

---

[17] Marx 1977a, p. 718.
[18] Marx 1973, pp. 520–1, 264.
[19] Lebowitz, 2003, Chapter 4; Lebowitz 1982b.
[20] Marx 1977a, p. 772.

for example, capital struggles to 'reduce wages to their physical minimum and to extend the working day to its physical maximum', but we do not know precisely why 'the working man constantly presses in the opposite direction'.[21] Further, there is no discussion at all in *Capital* about the struggle for higher wages.

One aspect of *Capital*'s silence is that it does not explore the manner in which new needs are constantly created for workers. Marx consistently stressed that the creation of 'new needs arising from society itself' is 'a condition of production founded on capital' and that the capitalist searches for means to spur workers on to consumption, 'to give his wares new charms, to inspire them with new needs by constant chatter, etc'. Yet, although Marx emphasised that the growth of capitalist production meant that the worker's 'subjective poverty, his need and dependence grow larger in proportion', none of that plays a role in *Capital*.[22] Even though each new need becomes a new link in the golden chain which secures workers to capital, even though Marx in the *Grundrisse* announced that it is upon this creation of new needs for workers that 'the contemporary power of capital rests', *Capital* is silent here.[23]

Thus, the underlying basis for the struggles of workers to secure higher wages is not present. But, then, what would be the point anyway? *Capital*, after all, assumes the standard of necessity for workers to be a 'constant magnitude' for a given country at a given period; and, Marx did this in order to avoid 'confounding everything'.[24] As he noted in the *Grundrisse*, no matter how much the standard of necessity may change, 'to consider those changes themselves belongs altogether to the chapter treating of wage labour'.[25] Marx was very clear and consistent on this point: changes in the needs of workers were not properly part of the subject matter of *Capital*. As he indicated in his 1861–3 draft notebooks for *Capital* (known as *Zur Kritik* and newly translated into English):

---

[21] Marx 1985b, p. 146.
[22] Marx 1973, pp. 287, 409–10; Marx 1977a, p. 1062.
[23] Marx 1973, p. 287.
[24] Marx 1977a, pp. 275, 655; Lebowitz, 2003, pp. 44–50.
[25] Marx's reference to this section as a 'chapter' may be placed in context by noting that it occurs in his 'chapter' on capital, which comprises pages 239 to 882 in this edition. Marx 1973, p. 817.

The problem of these movements in the level of the workers' needs, as also that of the rise and fall of the market price of labour capacity above or below this level, do not belong here, where the general capital-relation is to be developed, but in the doctrine of the wages of labour.... All questions relating to it [the level of workers' needs] as not a given but a variable magnitude belong to the investigation of wage labour in particular....[26]

The point was exactly the same in the material Marx drafted for Volume I of *Capital* in 1864–5:

The level of the necessaries of life whose total value constitutes the value of labour-power can itself rise or fall. The analysis of these variations, however, belongs not here but in the theory of wages.[27]

Not only does this assumption of a constant standard of necessity (the assumption in *Capital* which was to be removed in the book on wage-labour) mean that there can be no examination of the implications of changes in real wages, but it is not at all surprising that Marx had little to say in *Capital* about trade unions ('whose importance for the English working class can scarcely be overestimated').[28] There is no discussion of how the organised worker 'measures his demands against the capitalist's profit and demands a certain share of the surplus value created by him'; there is no consideration of how, despite capital's own tendency, workers would not permit wages 'to be reduced to the absolute minimum; on the contrary, they achieve a certain quantitative participation in the general growth of wealth'.[29] As Engels commented, the great merit of the trade unions is that 'they tend to keep up and to raise the standard of life.[30] But all this is missing from *Capital*.

The point is that *Capital* does not have as its object the examination of the movement when 'the workingman presses in the opposite direction' to capital. Even in the case of the struggle over the workday (which Marx did introduce

---

[26] Marx and Engels 1988, pp. 44–5.

[27] Marx 1977a, pp. 1068–9.

[28] Marx 1977a, p. 1069. See Lebowitz 2003, p. Chapter 6 for a consideration of problems in the discussion of relative surplus-value when the assumption of a fixed standard of necessity is relaxed. A further discussion occurs in Chapter 19 below.

[29] Marx 1973, pp. 597; 1971, p. 312.

[30] Engels 1967, p. 102. Engels's comment in his critique of the Erfurt Programme was: 'The organisation of the workers, their constantly increasing resistance, will most probably act as a certain barrier against the increase of poverty.' Engels 1970.

into *Capital*), rather than a theoretical exploration of the inherent tendency of workers to struggle for a reduction of the workday because of their need for more time and energy for their own process of production, he focuses upon the effort of workers to retain the 'normal' workday (i.e., a defensive action). In general, while we see capital's tendency to increase the rate of surplus-value, there is no treatment of wage-labour's tendency to *reduce* the rate of surplus-value. The very tendencies of wage-labour which emerge from 'the worker's own need for development' and which are the basis of the struggles of workers *for themselves* are absent.[31] There is no theoretical framework for dealing with increases in the standard of necessity because *Capital* is meant to explain the logic of capital but not the logic of wage-labour.

2. *The inherent functionalism*

Precisely because the worker as subject is absent from *Capital*, precisely because the only subject is capital – and the only needs and goals those of capital, there is an inherent functionalist cast to the argument which flows from *Capital*. Characteristic of a one-sided Marxism that fails to recognise that *Capital* presents only one side of capitalism is the presumption that what happens occurs because it corresponds to capital's needs (which are the only ones acknowledged).

Thus, for one-sided Marxism, if the workday declines, it is because capital needs workers to rest. If the real wage rises, it is because capital needs to resolve the problem of realisation. If a public healthcare system is introduced, it is because capital needs healthy workers and needs to reduce its own costs; if a public-school system, capital requires better educated workers. If sectors of an economy are nationalised, it is because capital needs weak sectors to be operated by the state. Such arguments are inherently one-sided. When the needs of workers are excluded at the outset and only capital's needs are recognised, it cannot be considered surprising that a one-sided Marxism will find in the results of all real struggles a correspondence to capital's needs.

Yet, this problem is not unique to those who have followed Marx. The same functionalist argument can be found in *Capital* itself. Regardless of his

---

[31] Among these is the tendency to combine and reduce the separation among them. *Cf.* Lebowitz 2003, p. Chapter 7.

account of the struggle by workers to limit the workday and of the resistance by capital, Marx nevertheless could comment that, due to the deterioration of its human inputs, 'the limiting of factory labour was dictated by the same necessity as forced the manuring of English fields with guano'. The limiting of the workday, in short, occurred (was 'dictated') because it corresponded to capital's requirements (just as farmers had to replenish the fertility of the soil). That clear functionalist statement appears even though Marx later commented that capital concerns itself with the degradation of the human race as little as with 'the probable fall of the earth into the sun' and must be 'forced by society' to do so.[32]

A similar problem is apparent in Marx's description of the value of labour-power as determined by the '*value of the necessaries* required to produce, develop, maintain, and perpetuate the labouring power'.[33] The premise is that, since the worker unfortunately depreciates and has a limited life, the maintenance of the use-value of this instrument with a voice includes expenditures not only to redress its daily wear and tear but also for those 'means necessary for the worker's replacements, i.e., his children'.[34] Since 'the man, like the machine,' Marx proposes, 'will wear out, and must be replaced by another man', there must be sufficient necessaries 'to bring up a certain quota of children that are to replace him on the labour market and to perpetuate the race of labourers.'[35]

Frankly, to propose that the value of labour-power contains provisions for the maintenance of children *because capital wants future recruits* twenty years hence – rather than because workers have struggled to secure such requirements – is a teleological absurdity! However, it is a logical result of the disappearance of wage-labour-for-itself from *Capital*. Marx himself must bear responsibility for some of the functionalist absurdities of his disciples.

For those who have followed Marx in this regard and who have furthermore treated *Capital* as a completed epistemological project, the results have been disastrous. Failing to grasp what is missing from *Capital*, failing to investigate the worker as subject, they are left with the Abstract Proletarian, the mere negation of capital. That productive worker for capital within the sphere of production (i.e., the wealth producer) and epitomised as the factory worker,

---

[32] Marx 1977a, pp. 348, 381.
[33] Marx 1985, p. 130.
[34] Marx 1977a, p. 275.
[35] Marx 1985b, p. 129.

that productive instrument with a voice which can gain no victories which allow it to take satisfaction in capitalist society (any apparent victories being in fact those of capital), that not-capital who is united and disciplined as the result of capitalist development – the Abstract Proletarian has no alternative but to overthrow capital.

3. *The dependence of the wage-labourer*

The expropriators, however, have not been expropriated. And, it is not at all difficult to grasp why when we focus upon the worker rather than upon capital as the subject. For, it is the dependence of the wage-labourer upon capital, that need and dependence which grows larger in proportion to capitalist production, which becomes critical to understand. Consider the position of the wage-labourer. In order to satisfy her needs, she must secure use-values from outside her own process of production. Under the prevailing circumstances, she must take the only potential commodity she has, living labour capacity, and find the buyer for whom it is a use-value – capital. To be for herself, the wage-labourer must be a being for another. We have here the worker as wage-labourer-for-herself – as one who approaches capital as a means, a means whose end is the worker for herself.

Capitalism, in short, encompasses not only a relation in which the worker is the mediator for capital in securing its goals (K-WL-K) but also a relation in which capital is the mediator for the worker in securing hers (WL-K-WL). Once we articulate this second side, there is no mystery behind the dependence of the worker upon capital. Within this relation, workers need capital; it must appear as the *necessary* mediator for the worker. The maintenance and reproduction of capital remains a necessary condition for the reproduction of the worker as wage-labourer. As Marx noted in the *Grundrisse*, if capital cannot realise surplus-value by employing a worker, then:

> labour capacity itself appears outside the conditions of the reproduction of its existence; it exists without the conditions of its existence, and is therefore a mere encumbrance; needs without the means to satisfy them;...[36]

---

[36] Marx 1973, p. 609.

The worker, accordingly, is produced as one conscious of her dependence upon capital. And, everything about capitalist production contributes not merely to the relation of dependence but also to the 'feeling of dependence'.[37] The very nature of capital is mystified – 'all the productive forces of˙social labour appear attributable to it, and not to labour as such, as a power springing forth from its own womb'. Having surrendered the right to his '*creative power*, like Esau his birthright for a mess of pottage', capital, thus, becomes 'a very mystical being' for the worker because it appears as the source of all productivity.[38]

Fixed capital, machinery, technology, science – all necessarily appear only as capital, are known only in their capitalist form:

> The accumulation of knowledge and of skill, of the general productive forces
> of the social brain, is thus absorbed into capital, as opposed to labour, and
> hence appears as an attribute of capital....[39]

Thus, as Marx commented, this transposition of

> the social productivity of labour into the material attributes of capital is so
> firmly entrenched in people's minds that the advantages of machinery, the
> use of science, invention, etc. are *necessarily* conceived in this *alienated* form,
> so that all these things are deemed to be the *attributes of capital*.[40]

In short, wage-labour assigns its own attributes to capital in its mind because the very nature of the capital/wage-labour relation is one in which it has already done so in reality.

Insofar as this sense of dependence upon capital is regularly reproduced, capital can safely leave its own condition of existence, the maintenance and reproduction of the working class, to the worker's own drives. The very process of capitalist production produces and reproduces workers who consider the necessity for capital to be self-evident:

> The advance of capitalist production develops a working class which by
> education, tradition and habit looks upon the requirements of that mode

---

[37] Marx 1977a, p. 936.
[38] Marx 1981b, p. 966; 1973, p. 307.
[39] Marx 1973, p. 694.
[40] Marx 1977a, p. 1058.

as self-evident natural laws. The organization of the capitalist process of production, once it is fully developed, breaks down all resistance.[41]

Breaks down all resistance! In the light of Marx's comment, how can we possibly talk about the durability of capitalism and the passivity of the working class as *anomalies*? Indeed, given Marx's statement that 'the great beauty of capitalist production' consists in its ability to constantly replenish the reserve army of labour and thereby to secure 'the social dependence of the worker on the capitalist, which is indispensable', how can we talk about the revolt of the working class (however well it may be 'trained, united and organized')?[42] On the contrary, as Marx noted about developed capitalism:

> In the ordinary run of things, the worker can be left to the 'natural laws of production', i.e. it is possible to rely on his dependence on capital, which springs from the conditions of production themselves, and is guaranteed in perpetuity by them.[43]

By education, tradition and habit, the worker in developed capitalism necessarily looks upon the requirements of capital as common sense; and, that feeling of dependence is indispensable in ensuring capitalism's necessary premise and making it an organic system – in perpetuity.

Understanding the silence of *Capital*

So, if the book on wage-labour was so important to an understanding of capitalism (rather than of just the logic of capital), why did Marx not write it? To answer this requires us first to be absolutely clear as to why Marx wrote *Capital* (and, indeed, Volume I over and over again). The answer is precisely his understanding of the dependence of the worker upon capital. Given the inherent mystification of capital, *demystification* is a necessary condition for workers to go beyond capital.

For this very reason, Marx considered it essential to reveal the nature of capital, to reveal what cannot be apparent on the surface – that capital itself is the result of exploitation. To counter the inherent mystification of capital

---

[41] Marx 1977a, p. 899.
[42] Marx 1977a, p. 935.
[43] Marx 1977a, p. 899.

required the theory of *Capital*. Significantly, however, for this particular purpose only *Capital* – and not the originally projected six books (or even the first three) – is required; indeed, only Volume I of *Capital* is required!

Capital was Marx's attempt to make the proletariat 'conscious of the condition of its emancipation', conscious of the need to abolish capital's ownership of the products of labour – i.e., 'to inscribe on their banner the *revolutionary* watchword, "*Abolition of the wages system!*"'.[44] That was a limited object but, nevertheless, a crucial one given Marx's understanding of capital's inherent tendency to develop a working class which looks upon capital's requirements as 'self-evident natural laws'.

If we fail to recognise that limited object, however, we may misunderstand entirely *Capital's* place and importance. In the absence of the demystification of capital, there is no going-beyond capital. Immiseration, crises, stagnation, destruction of the natural environment do not lead beyond capital because so long as capital appears as the source of all wealth and as the only means to satisfy their own needs, workers are necessarily dependent upon it. Thus, *Capital* is not merely a moment in the understanding of capitalism as an organic system; it is also a moment in the revolutionary struggle of workers to go beyond capital. Marx did not write his projected volume on wage-labour because, ultimately, he was less interested in the completion of his epistemological project than in his revolutionary project. What E.P. Thompson forgets is that, as Engels indicated in speech at Marx's graveside, 'Marx was before all else a revolutionist'.[45]

The most serious silence

And, yet, the failure to focus upon the worker as subject and upon the process by which the worker produces herself has had a serious effect both upon Marxism and upon the revolutionary project itself. If one proceeds simply from the contradictions inherent within capital, the central issue may become (as it has for adherents of the regulation school) an explanation of how capital *nevertheless* is reproduced; investigation accordingly focuses upon the particular modes of regulation which manage to sustain capitalist relations.

---

[44] Marx 1985b, p. 149.
[45] Engels 1978, p. 682.

If, on the other hand, we begin from a consideration of the worker as subject, the central question becomes – how, under the necessary circumstances, can capital *not* succeed? We are led necessarily to the central place of the process of class struggle in Marx's theory.

The silence of Marx in *Capital* has meant a de-emphasis upon the process of struggle itself as a process of production. Just as every activity of the worker alters her as the subject who enters into all activities, similarly the process in which workers struggle for themselves is also a process in which they produce themselves in an altered way. They develop new needs in struggle, an altered hierarchy of needs. Even though the needs which they attempt to satisfy do not in themselves go beyond capital, the very process of struggle is one of producing new people, of transforming them into people with a new conception of themselves – as subjects capable of altering their world.

Nothing is more essential to Marx than this conception. The failure to understand the centrality of 'the coincidence of the changing of circumstances' and of self-change – that coincidence that can only be understood as *'revolutionary practice'* – is the failure to understand the dynamic element without which there can be no end to the feeling of dependence and thus no transcendence of capital![46] Understanding struggle as a process of production is the most serious gap as the result of Marx's failure to go beyond *Capital*. Limited to *Capital*, we have only the mechanical laws of capital, a structure without subjects, a one-sided Marxism – or, to be more exact, the *absence* of Marxism!

If, then, we accept the importance of 'revolutionary practice', it is clear what *cannot* be a basis for going beyond capital – the absence of people in motion.[47] And, this is what we need to think about as we approach the beginning of a new millenium. We need to think about 1967, one hundred years after *Capital* was first published. *Capital* meant something more then (as it did at its 50th anniversary). Why? Not because its account of capitalism was any truer then but because people were in motion (and were changing themselves). That is what made the theory of *Capital* a use-value. As Marx well-knew, the struggle of workers is indispensable for 'preventing them from becoming apathetic,

---

[46] Marx 1976a, p. 4.
[47] Note that this concept also points to the nature of the state necessary to go beyond capital. See Chapter 18 below.

thoughtless, more or less well-fed instruments of production'.[48] Although Marx wrote *Capital* to explain to workers why they were struggling, 'it is not enough for thought to strive for realisation, reality must itself strive towards thought'.[49]

When we teach *Capital*, we need to teach what it left out, its silences – i.e., not only what is in *Capital* but what is not. And, we have to help to bring an end to that silence. This is at the core of a revitalised Marxism, a Marxism that will continue the revolutionary project that we observe in *Capital*.

---

[48] Marx and Engels 1979, p. 169.
[49] Marx 1975c, p. 183.

Chapter Seventeen

Beyond the *Capital* of Uno-ism

In his curiously titled 'Returning to Marx's *Capital*', Robert Albritton's review of my *Beyond 'Capital'* begins with a summary of some themes from my book, segues into an extended celebration of his own particular brand of Japanese Marxism and ends with a string of invectives, among them – 'unquestioning embrace of humanist essentialism', 'old simplistic humanism', 'class struggle functionalism' and 'a theory prepared to sacrifice the law of value in order to advance a humanist self-realization of the working class'.[1] So it occasionally goes, unfortunately, when paradigms clash.

It should be stressed, though, that at no time in my book did I criticise the Uno school of Japanese Marxism of which Albritton is a prominent advocate; indeed, I must confess that at no point did I even think about this school of thought. Yet, Albritton's charges (which I barely understand) suggest that the particular arguments that I advanced hit a sensitive nerve and, indeed, that they represent a challenge to his interpretation of Marxism. Upon reflection, I agree – *Beyond 'Capital'* undermines the credibility of the Uno school as a reading of Marx.

---

[1] Lebowitz 2003. Albritton 2003.

Consider the central thesis of my book – Marx's *Capital* is one-sided. One-sided because critical themes for his intended book on wage-labour (which was to complete 'the inner totality' of capitalism) were not taken up; one-sided because, according to Marx's own methodological standard, capitalism cannot be seen as an organic system unless all its premises (in particular, the 'necessary condition for the reproduction of capital') can be demonstrated to be produced by the system itself; and, one-sided because the tendencies of workers are critical in producing the dynamic properties of capitalism. What *Capital* offers, then, is one side of capitalism – the side of capital.

Without consideration of the second side of capitalism, however, my chapter on 'one-sided Marxism' argues that not only are capital's tendencies 'taken as objective, even technical, laws inherent in its own essence' but even our understanding of capital is necessarily flawed:

> Only with the completion of the totality are new sides of capital revealed. Only then do we have capital that faces workers who are struggling for their goals, workers who are more than mere technical inputs to be stretched to emit more labour or to be produced more cheaply.[2]

This argument does not drop from the sky – it follows chapters detailing the evidence on the missing book on wage-labour, exploring the dialectical structure of *Capital*, setting out Marx's political economy of the working class (the alternative logic within capitalism), and finally the pivotal chapter on 'Wages' which removes the critical assumption of *Capital* which Marx designated for removal in the book on wage-labour – the assumption that the standard of necessity is given for a 'given country in a given period', i.e., that the subsistence requirements of workers can be 'treated as a constant magnitude'.

None of this is addressed directly in Albritton's review of *Beyond 'Capital'*. He does not challenge any evidence or reasoning. What he challenges is the project itself – the idea of continuing Marx's project to explore the implications of the missing five books that Marx himself identified. Missing books, Albritton scoffs – and suggests twenty-nine books (including ones on heterosexism, religion, war and disability)! All these things must be theorised, he argues, '*but not at the level of the theory of capital's inner logic*'. And, there

---

[2] Lebowitz 2003, p. 121.

we have the apparent core of Albritton's argument (and, indeed, of his Uno school) – *Capital* must be accepted as writ, as the fount of knowledge of the inner logic of capital. Everything besides that inner logic belongs at a different level of analysis which explores more concrete subject matter; it is *there* that we can 'begin to formulate really interesting theories'.

Except it is not Marx's *Capital* that sets those bounds between that inner logic of capital and a 'stage theory' which examines particular phases of capitalism (Albritton's own interest). Rather, the rock upon which Albritton has built is the Uno-Sekine '*Capital*', a unique construction of 'the theory of a purely capitalist society' (TPCS); this 'overhauling and complete restatement of *Capital* as a theory of pure capitalism' is the standard for every judgement of Albritton and the basis for all the incantations – e.g., law of value (twenty-five times) and inner logic of capital (twenty times) – with which he would drive away the enemy.[3]

The enemy, as it happens, is anyone who does not accept that the inner logic of capital is a general-equilibrium model in which market mechanisms (the law of value) ensure the reproduction of capitalism. Not only does TPCS surgically remove history from Marx's *Capital* (severing Marx's links between the logical tendencies of capital and the historical trajectory of capitalism) but it also redefines Marx's concept of 'the inner nature of capital' to include 'the external movement of the individual capitals' in the market (thereby making a muddle of Marx's own clear distinction).[4] In TPCS, there is no assumption of a given standard of necessity and, thus, no need to remove anything. Rather, as with similar neoclassical interpretations of Ricardo and the classical school, the real wage is determined here endogenously (simultaneously with rates of surplus-value, profit and accumulation).

So, of course, there is no place for class struggle in this Stepford edition of *Capital* which Sekine calls 'the dialectic of capital'.[5] Everything has already been determined by supply and demand in a perfectly competitive model. Simply assume a natural rate of population growth and a desired rate of accumulation out of the surplus, and the atomised workers who compete against each other (but do not combine) receive as wages what is necessary

---

[3] Uno 1980, p. xxvi.
[4] Marx 1977a, p. 433.
[5] Sekine 1984.

to keep everyone more or less happy and the system running. Nothing in 'this liberal utopia, in which the existing resources are optimally allocated for the production of all use-values' and where workers 'enjoy a historically feasible standard of living in a state close to full employment' would make a neoclassical economist uneasy – as long as the term 'positive non-wage income' were to be substituted for 'exploitation'.[6] In place of Marx's workers, who struggle collectively over the workday and over their wages (except where constrained by *Capital*'s critical assumption) and achieve results depending upon the 'respective powers of the combatants', meet the Stepford worker – the worker who must conform to capital's requirements if she is to survive.

But, leave this pure capitalist utopia and return to Marx's *Capital*. And, now, remove Marx's assumption that workers receive 'a definite quantity of the means of subsistence'.[7] What happens when productivity rises in the production of those means of subsistence? Without that assumption fixing the standard of necessity, increased productivity does not in itself generate relative surplus value (Marx's Chapter 12 story); rather, all other things equal, the result is increased real wages without any change in surplus value – something Marx sets out clearly as an option in his *1861–3 Economic Manuscripts*.[8] In short, the result of productivity increases as such is that workers rather than capitalists are the beneficiaries. Relative surplus-value (its existence and growth) requires a variable not explicitly identified by Marx.

In *Beyond 'Capital'*, I defined this variable as 'the degree of separation among workers' and set out the necessary conditions for relative surplus value to emerge with rising productivity. To articulate this variable immediately focuses theoretical attention both on the tendency for workers to combine and also on the tendency of capital to divide and separate workers – a tendency which may be satisfied not only through the effects upon the labour market of the substitution of machinery for workers. Racism and sexism and the choice of technique and location of investment can also be important for capital – even where the immediate effect may be lower productivity and efficiency – because of their effects upon the transaction costs of workers in their attempt to combine. In short, recognition of the importance of the degree of separation

---

6 Sekine 1984, p. 98.
7 Marx 1977a, p. 276.
8 Lebowitz 2003, pp. 114–17.

among workers as a variable means that rather than a stress solely upon capital's tendency for an increasing scale of productive plant ('which has its unintended consequence the centralizing, uniting and organizing of the working class'), another side of capital comes to the fore: 'Much of capitalist globalization, indeed, may be driven by the desire to weaken workers – by an attempt to *de*centralize, *dis*unite and *dis*organize workers'.[9]

Providing the theoretical logic for decentralisation of capital is just one example of how developing the side of wage-labour undermines reliance upon the Uno-Sekine construction of the theory of pure capitalism which Albritton substitutes for Marx's *Capital*. To the extent that the continuation of Marx's project can yield theoretical insights that are precluded by the premature closure enacted by the peculiar combination of a general-equilibrium model and Hegelian mysticism most marked in Sekine's work, it demonstrates that what appears in Albritton's 'stages' level as contingent, in fact, belongs to an inner level of analysis – i.e., as 'general and necessary tendencies of capital'.[10]

That recognition is precisely what Albritton resists. It is why he complains over and over again about efforts to 'put too much of history into capital's inner logic' (by which he means only the Uno-Sekine pure theory of capitalism); and, it is why he argues that

---

[9] Lebowitz 2003, p. 123.

[10] Marx 1977a, p. 433. In Lebowitz 1998, I commented on Sekine's version of Uno as follows (citations from Sekine in the original):

> As developed within the perspective of Sekine and the Uno School, the dialectic of capital treats capitalism as an eternal, self-contained and reproducing totality which is the counterpart of Hegel's dialectic of the Absolute. The dialectic of capital, indeed, is the dialectic of the Absolute [God], tracing out the same logical structure. 'The exact correspondence between the dialectic of capital and Hegel's *Logic* can scarcely be doubted'. Just as Hegel's discussion in the Book of the Notion in his *Logic* 'copies the self-revealing wisdom of the Absolute,' so also does the dialectic of capital reveal the subject-object identity in capital as it 'follows the self-synthesising logic of capital'. 'There is clearly no escape,' Sekine announced (57), 'from the conclusion that what Hegel believed was the Absolute was in fact capital in disguise.'

With respect to this general perspective (as reflected in the argument of another Sekine disciple), I continued:

> We know capital, thus, through its works – a general equilibrium system in which the goal of capital is realised through the subjective self-seeking of individual capitals. With the revelation of an Invisible Hand, the logic of capital comes to an end.

the weakness of Marxian political economy stems from those like Lebowitz, who, instead of developing these more concrete levels tend to remain at the level of capital's logic precisely because they think it explains so much that more concrete levels are unnecessary.

The issue, though, is not whether concrete study is or not necessary. There is no dispute between Albritton and me as to what needs to be explained. Rather, we differ on whether Marx's attempt to explain historical movement logically and theoretically should be scuttled in favour of the Uno-Sekine-Albritton combination of a general-equilibrium model and eclecticism under the rubric of stages theory. Whereas I retain Marx's focus on revealing 'the economic law of motion of modern society' and his dialectical understanding of 'every historically developed form as being in a fluid state', Sekine's 'dialectic of capital' stresses that 'capitalism possesses a consistent system of logic' and that it only 'ceases to exist when external conditions become sufficiently unfavourable to the operation of its logic, as they did after the War of 1914'.[11] Here, as elsewhere, Albritton's position is quite clear: he accepts Sekine's 'dialectic of capital' as superior to Marx's *Capital* and, indeed, perfect; accordingly, he proposes that 'Marxian Political Economy can revive itself by creatively developing levels of analysis and by integrating aspects of poststructuralist theories of subjectivity'.

The enormous gap between the two perspectives on the link between theory and history in Marx becomes manifestly clear in Albritton's response to my proposal that latent within Marx's political economy of the working class, the alternative logic within capitalism, one can see the elements of the society of free and associated producers, communist society. Characteristically, rather than examining my evidence and reasoning, Albritton declares this to be 'theory as wish-fulfillment and not a theory as rigorous analysis of capitalism' and proceeds to erupt in Althusserian outrage over 'humanism' and 'essentialism'. There is no surprise here – the Uno-Sekine conception of pure capitalism at its very core rejects any suggestion that capitalism contains the seeds of its own destruction; its purpose is to present capitalism 'as if it were a self-perpetuating entity'.[12]

---

[11] Marx 1977a, pp. 92, 103; Sekine 1984, p. 96.
[12] Uno 1980, p. 125.

In the Uno-Sekine view, pure capitalism *is* a solid crystal, an organism that is *not* constantly engaged in a process of change.[13] Rather than continuing to build upon this crippled, indeed dead, conception of capitalism (and declaiming against all who would introduce elements contrary to its 'law of value'), Albritton should return to Marx's *Capital*. He should attempt to see how much of his work on concrete stages of capitalism can be placed within a different paradigm – that of Marx's *Capital*, in short, how much can be demonstrated to reflect inner tendencies within capitalism.

---

[13] Marx 1977a, p. 93.

Chapter Eighteen
Situating the Capitalist State

When, theoretically, can Marxists talk about the capitalist state? In the original conception of his 'Economics', Marx placed the 'State' as the fourth of his six intended books.[1] 'The concentration of bourgeois society in the form of the state', 'the concentration of the whole', was to follow the book on wage-labour which itself would complete 'the inner totality'.[2] Thus, as revealed by its placement, the concept of the capitalist state would be developed out of the consideration (in a dialectical manner) of capital, landed property and wage-labour – the subjects of the first three books. Only when that 'inner totality' is completed can we examine the state as 'the concentration of the whole'.[3]

The problem, of course, is that Marx never went beyond *Capital* in his original plan. Some of the implications of this (and, in particular, of the missing book on wage-labour) have been explored in *Beyond*

---

[1] Lebowitz 2003, Chapter 3.

[2] Marx 1973, pp. 264, 108, 227.

[3] By the same logic, the concept of the state itself as initially developed in Book IV must be incomplete. The full and adequate development of the concept of the capitalist state occurs only when the state is considered in the context of the world-market (the subject matter of the concluding book) 'in which production is posited as a totality together with all its moments' (Marx 1973, pp. 264, 273). I.e., the aspect that the state takes on in the context of competing national capitals and nation-states is essential to understanding the capitalist state. See the strong argument to this effect in von Braunmühl 1978. This side of the capitalist state, however, is not explored here.

'Capital'.[4] Not only was *Capital* one-sided with respect to its examination of capitalism (presenting the side of capital but *not* 'the completed bourgeois system') but, in particular, the treatment of workers as subjects – as they struggle for their own goals and as they produce themselves through their own activities – is revealed to be both essential to the understanding of capitalism and missing from *Capital*.

None of this, however, has stopped Marxists from theorising about the capitalist state based upon *Capital* alone. Central to the extensive state-debates of the 1970s was the contribution of the 'state-derivationist' or 'capital-logic' school, which attempted to avoid the eclecticism characteristic of so many Marxian treatments by logically deriving the category of the state directly from the concept of capital.[5] Yet, as Simon Clarke has indicated in his fine survey, these efforts were simply a variant of a structural-functionalist orthodoxy which considers the state in terms of its functional necessity for capital; the determining role of class struggle was necessarily displaced.[6] And, this judgement cannot come as a surprise – when we understand that *Capital* has only capital as its subject and considers only capital's needs and tendencies but not those of workers.[7]

It does not mean, however, that the project of state-derivation is inherently flawed. By explicitly considering the 'intermediate link' omitted by the capital-logic school (i.e., the side of wage-labour), it is possible to reconstruct Marx's concept of the capitalist state as the object and result of class struggle. Further, the resulting understanding of the capitalist state as the 'concentration of bourgeois society in the form of the state' is the link to Marx's view of the form of state necessary to go *beyond* capital.

Wage-labour's latent state

There is a concept of the state implicit in the concept of capital. Since this is, however, ground well-covered in the earlier state-derivation discussions (cf. Holloway and Picciotto), it is sufficient here to note that inherent in capital's need for valorisation are state activities to ensure the availability of appropriate

---

[4] Lebowitz 2003.
[5] Cf. Holloway and Picciotto 1978.
[6] Clarke 1991.
[7] Lebowitz 2003.

labour-power at wages consistent with capital's requirements (drawing upon the power of the state wherever 'the sheer force of economic relations' is not adequate), to ensure the existence of material conditions of production (where these are deemed 'necessary but not productive in the capitalist sense', i.e., profitable) and to protect the fruits of capitalist exploitation through the existence of a legal system enforcing private property rights.[8]

In short, as the capital-logic school demonstrated, it is possible within Marx's framework to develop aspects of a state latent in the concept of capital. Yet, precisely the same can be done by starting from the concept of wage-labour (both within *Capital* and as developed in *Beyond 'Capital'*).[9]

Just as consideration of the concept of the capitalist state implicit in capital begins with the understanding of capital's drive for surplus-value, examination of wage-labour's latent state begins with a focus upon the impulse of workers to satisfy their needs – their needs for use-values, for time and energy for their own production process and, ultimately, 'the worker's own need for development'. Yet, insofar as we speak of wage-labour, we are not considering abstract producers; rather, we mean workers who exist within the capital/wage-labour relation and are thus dependent upon capital to realise those needs.

In this respect, like other commodity-sellers, wage-labourers have the need for contract enforcement, a standard measure of prices and the determination of a circulating medium (as well the provision of stable conditions of exchange) which are attributes 'proper to the state' in a commodity-exchanging society.[10]

Yet, there are specific aspects of a state if it is to serve as an agency for wage-labourers as sellers of labour-power. Since capital is able to capture the fruits of co-operation because of the separation among wage-labourers – a disunion 'created and perpetuated by their *unavoidable competition amongst themselves'*, the condition for being able to achieve a quantitative participation in the general growth of wealth is the ability of wage-labourers to combine in

---

[8] We cannot concern ourselves here with the capital-logic discussions of the inherent necessity for the 'autonomy' of the state or of the state as 'ideal' total capitalist acting against individual capitals. On the former, see Clarke 1991, p. 186; on the latter, my position is implicit in Lebowitz 1992b.

[9] Except where otherwise noted, supporting arguments and textual evidence may be found in Lebowitz 2003.

[10] Marx 1977a, pp. 221–2.

trade unions.[11] In this respect, the state is central; for, the state has the power either to prevent (or restrict) such combinations of workers or to permit (and facilitate) them. There is, thus, an inherent logic to the struggle of workers to make the state serve their interests by legalising and supporting the existence of trade unions.

To keep up and raise their wages, however, more is required than the ability to form trade unions. Inherent in the wage-labour relation is the dependence of the worker upon the willingness of capital to purchase labour-power (which itself depends upon capital's ability to realise the surplus-value produced by workers); if that requirement is not met, then labour-power 'exists without the conditions of its existence, and is therefore a mere encumbrance; needs without the means to satisfy them'.[12] Further, since the existence of unemployment clearly weakens workers, the state latent in the needs of wage-labourers is one which will foster conditions of full employment.

While wage increases will permit workers to purchase more means of subsistence, the use-values which correspond to their social needs are not limited to those which take a commodity-form. A state acting as an agency of wage-labourers would expand the provision of *'that which is needed for common satisfaction of needs,* such as schools, health services, etc' for workers.[13] Similarly, insofar as qualities of nature (such as clean air and sunlight) are part of the worker's set of needs and correspond to the 'worker's own need for development', latent in the state are activities to protect and repair natural conditions impaired by capitalist production.[14]

Further, the moment of production which *Capital* does not consider, the worker's own process of production, requires labour-power as well as the use-values which are inputs into that labour process. Implied, accordingly, is the struggle of wage-labourers over the length and intensity of the capitalist workday in order to have time and energy for themselves. It is a victory for 'the political economy of the working class' when the state legislates restrictions on the workday.[15]

[11] Marx n.d., p. 347.
[12] Marx 1973, p. 609.
[13] Marx 1962, p. 22.
[14] For discussions of capital's tendency to impair the conditions of production, see Jim O'Connor's work in *Capitalism, Nature, Socialism* (and, in particular, the recent symposium on 'the second contradiction of capitalism').
[15] Marx 1985a, pp. 10–11.

Thus, considered from the side of wage-labour, we see that, acting as an agency of wage-labour, the state will restrict the workday, support increases in real wages, assist in the realisation of other social needs and, in general, foster the expanded reproduction of wage-labourers. In this respect, the state latent in the concept of wage-labour functions much like trade unions. However, whereas trade unions act in opposition to specific and particular capitals, in themselves they cannot confront the power of capital as a whole.

For that reason, Marx stressed not merely the *possibility* of moving beyond purely economic struggles in order to use the power of the state on behalf of workers but, rather, the *necessity*. The real victory of the political economy of the working class in the case of the Ten Hours' Bill was the demonstration that wage-labour required political struggle and the use of the state. The Ten Hours' Bill, after all, was a legislative act – which it *had* to be. As Marx argued, the limitation of the working day 'was not to be attained by private settlement between the working men and the capitalists. This very necessity of *general political action* affords the proof that in its merely economic action capital is the stronger side'.[16] Only by going beyond 'a purely economic movement' to act as a class *politically* could the working class enforce 'its interests in a general form, in a form possessing general, socially coercive force'.[17]

And, here, we see immediately a stark contrast between the requirements of capital and wage-labour that Marx identified with respect to the state. Whereas capital may be able (through the regular reproduction of a reserve army) to dispense with the power of the state and rely upon 'the sheer force of economic relations' to secure its goals, workers *require* the social force of the state.[18]

This is especially true because of the particular contradiction between wage-labour as a whole and individual wage-labourers. Whereas the competition of individual capitals manifests the inner laws of capital, when individual wage-labourers compete, they do not manifest and execute the inner tendencies of wage-labour in general. Rather, by competing with each other, workers press not in the opposite direction to capital but in the *same* direction. For this reason, the socially coercive force of the state is necessary

---

16 Marx 1985b, p. 146.
17 Marx and Engels 1965, pp. 270–1.
18 Marx 1977a, pp. 899, 935, 382.

to bind not only capital but *also wage-labourers as individual self-seekers*. As Marx noted in the case of the workday,

> the workers have to put their heads together and, as a class, compel the passing of a law, an all-powerful social barrier by which they can be prevented from selling themselves and their families into slavery and death by voluntary contract with capital.[19]

In such cases, he commented, 'the working class do not fortify governmental power. On the contrary, they transform that power, now used against them, into their own agency'.[20]

The logical necessity of the state from the side of wage-labour is clear (and, indeed, is stronger than that from the side of capital – given capital's relative strength in 'merely economic action'). In this respect, it cannot be considered surprising that, in practice, workers have looked upon the state as a means of enforcing their interests within capitalism. Nevertheless, like trade unions, the state latent in the concept of wage-labour does not go beyond the capital/wage-labour relation. Nor can it avoid (any more than trade unions) any limits given by capital's need for valorisation. In short, to consider the capitalist state, we need to situate it within the totality which is capitalism as a whole, as 'the concentration of bourgeois society'.[21]

The capitalist state as concentration of the whole

Between two conceptions of right, force decides. Inherent in capital and wage-labour are two concepts of the capitalist state in struggle – whether the state will be a mediator for capital or whether it will be a mediator for wage-labour. On matters such as restrictions on the length of the workday, the legalisation and fostering of trade unions, the orientation to full employment and the provision of use-values to permit the common satisfaction of needs, capital and wage-labour push the state in opposite directions. The fixation of the actual practices of the state 'resolves itself into a question of the respective powers of the combatants'.

---

[19] Marx 1977a, p. 416.
[20] Marx n.d., pp. 344–5.
[21] It should be obvious that, in developing the logic of the state from the side of wage-labour, we are identifying the logic – and limits – of social democracy.

But, is this an indeterminacy between specific limits? Are there any 'laws' which determine those limits? Consider the case of a state under the complete domination of capital, where capital is able to use the power of the state without check. In this case, capital will be successful in reducing wages to a minimum and extending the workday to a maximum; so long, indeed, as capital is able to find substitutes for specific labour or material conditions of production, the tendency will be one of non-reproduction of particular workers and natural conditions.

In this respect, there is no immediate limit to capital's ability to use the state on its behalf. Yet, at the same time, to the extent that capital has been successful in using the power of the state to break down the resistance of workers, the expanded reproduction of capital does not require a state.[22]

Consider the other extreme – a capitalist state completely dominated by wage-labour. Here, we would expect to find workers using the state to foster increases in wages and the reduction of the work-day – thus, a tendency toward the reduction of the rate of surplus-value, toward the inability of capital to engage in expanded reproduction. Is there a limit here? Clearly, capital may respond by ceasing accumulation, which (within the framework of capitalist relations) will produce a crisis – a reduced demand for labour-power and the weakening of the position of wage-labour. Or, there may be an accelerated increase in the technical composition of capital (and accompanying displacement of workers). Between these two cases, the differences are significant; yet, they have in common the implication of limits to the ability to use the state on behalf of wage-labour within capitalism. The prospect is one of the balance of forces shifting to favour capital both in the economic sphere and with respect to control of the state.

Recall, however, the scenario of the *Communist Manifesto* where wage-labour uses the power of the state to make 'despotic inroads' on capitalist property – i.e., to introduce measures 'which appear economically insufficient and untenable, but which, in the course of the movement, outstrip themselves, necessitate further inroads upon the old social order'.[23] In this case, the

---

[22] As Clarke notes, in the strictest sense for Marx, the state is not necessary for the reproduction of capital. Indeed, 'if there were no class struggle, if the working class were willing to submit passively to their subordination to capitalist social relations, there would be no state', Clarke 1991, p. 190.

[23] Marx and Engels 1976b, p. 504.

combination of restrictions upon capital (which limit the possibility of its reproduction) and the development of state sectors would be part of a process of displacing capital as the mediator for wage-labour and substituting the state. To the extent that *this* outcome is possible, there would appear to be no limit to the state as an agency of workers.

And, yet, there is a critical premise for this last potential case. It presupposes workers who do not look upon capital as a *necessary* mediator. However, everything about capitalist production fosters not merely the relation of dependence but also that 'feeling of dependence'upon capital.[24] Having surrendered the right to his '*creative power*, like Esau his birthright for a mess of pottage', capital becomes 'a very mystical being' for the worker because it appears as the source of all productivity.[25] Considering as well the effect of the regular reproduction of the reserve army, Marx concluded that the very process of capitalist production produces and reproduces workers who consider the necessity for capital to be self-evident:

> The advance of capitalist production develops a working class which by education, tradition and habit looks upon the requirements of that mode as self-evident natural laws. The organization of the capitalist process of production, once it is fully developed, breaks down all resistance.[26]

Even, accordingly, if wage-labourers succeed in turning the state into their own agency, *so long as they remain conscious of their dependence upon capital* that state must act to facilitate conditions for the expanded reproduction of capital. That is the necessary result of functioning within the bounds of a relation in which the reproduction of wage-labour as such requires the reproduction of capital.

Thus, even though there may be considerable variation based upon the 'respective powers of the combatants', the capitalist state remains within the bounds of the capitalist relation and supports its continued existence. Not because a state within capitalist society *must* support the reproduction of capital. Nor because the gains workers can make through the state create illusions and sap their otherwise revolutionary spirit. Rather, capital *itself* spontaneously produces illusions – illusions which tend to dissuade a

---

[24] Marx 1977a, p. 936.
[25] Marx 1981b, p. 966; 1973, pp. 307, 694; 1977a, p. 1058.
[26] Marx 1977a, p. 899.

challenge to capitalism as such. Ultimately, it is precisely insofar as workers look upon the requirements of capitalism 'as self-evident natural laws' that makes the capitalist state the guarantor of the reproduction of capital.[27]

Beyond the capitalist state

There is, of course, more to the story. Marx, after all, believed that workers would succeed in going *beyond* capital. And that would be the result not of some automatic crisis of capitalism but, rather, as the result of that process (not considered in *Capital*) by which workers produce themselves through their own activities.

Nothing is more central to Marx's entire conception than the coincidence of the changing of circumstances and self-change – i.e., the concept of 'revolutionary practice' set out in his Third Thesis on Feuerbach.[28] When workers struggle for higher wages, struggle against capital in the work-place and for the satisfaction of their social needs in general, that very process is one of transforming them into people with a new conception of themselves – as subjects capable of altering their world.

And, the same is true of the struggle to make the state the workers' agency. Not only is this struggle necessary (because 'in its merely economic action capital is the stronger side'), it is also an essential part of the process by which workers transcend their local interests and take shape as a class against capital as a whole. Thus, for example, the struggle to make the state expand its provision of use-values *'needed for common satisfaction of needs* such as schools, health services, etc.' not only is an effort to substitute the state for capital as a mediator for workers but also unifies workers (skilled and unskilled, waged and unwaged). In this respect, the struggle for the state is an essential moment

---

[27] In *Build it Now: Socialism for the 21st Century* (Lebowitz 2006), under the heading, 'The Failure of Social Democracy', I argue: 'When capital goes on strike, there are two choices, *give* in or *move* in. Unfortunately, social democracy in practice has demonstrated that it is limited by the same things that limit Keynesianism in theory – the givens of the structure and distribution of ownership and the priority of self-interest by the owners. As a result, when capital has gone on strike, the social-democratic response has been to give in.... Rather than maintaining its focus on human needs and challenging the logic of capital, social democracy has proceeded to enforce that logic.'

[28] Marx 1976a, p. 4.

in the process of producing the working class as a class-for-itself, an essential moment in the process of going beyond capital.

And, yet, all of this refers only to the very *process* of struggle. *Past* victories are *incorporated* – just as are the results (e.g. increased wages) of past trade-union victories. Fixated in existing state practices, the transformative effects of their achievement are constantly undermined by that spontaneous process by which the dependence of wage-labourers upon capital is reproduced as common sense. Accordingly, the struggle to make the state an agency of workers must be *continuous*; only the constant effort to compel the state to satisfy (directly or indirectly) the social needs of workers can change both circumstances and people. This emphasis upon the centrality of revolutionary practice, however, points as well to specific characteristics of a state which will be *other* than the 'concentration of bourgeois society'.

In short, as Marx concluded, we cannot be indifferent to the *form* of the state as an agency of workers. Only insofar as state functions are 'wrested from an authority usurping pre-eminence over society itself, and restored to the responsible agents of society' are the activities of the state those by which workers produce themselves as capable of governing. Only where the state as mediator for (and power over) workers gives way to the 'self-government of the producers' is there a continuous process whereby workers can change both circumstances and themselves.[29]

Implicit in the concept of revolutionary practice is, then, a form of state in which workers themselves determine their needs and the means of satisfying them, in which capital's position as mediator between producers and their needs is transcended – i.e., a state of the Paris-Commune type. 'The working class,' Marx commented, 'can not simply lay hold of the ready-made state machinery, and wield it for its own purposes.' And, that was because the very nature of the existing state was inherent in 'the historical genesis of capitalist production' where 'the rising bourgeoisie needs the power of the state' – a state infected because its very institutions involve a 'systematic and hierarchic division of labour', because it assumes the character of 'a public force organized for social enslavement, of an engine of class despotism'.[30]

---

[29] Marx 1971b, pp. 72–3.
[30] Marx 1971b, pp. 68–9.

For the state to be 'the political form...under which to work out the economical emancipation of Labour', Marx argued that this required 'the reabsorption of the state power by society as its own living forces instead of as forces controlling and subduing it, by the popular masses themselves, forming their own force instead of the organized force of their suppression'.[31] For the struggle to make the state the agency of workers to produce more than the representation of workers' interests in the capitalist state, it requires the conversion of 'the state from an organ standing above society into one completely subordinate to it'.[32]

One thing, then, is certain. When we proceed from the vantage point of the self-production of workers, it underlines the inadequacy of attempts to use the capitalist state ('the concentration of bourgeois society in the form of the state') to go beyond capital. For Marx, it was clear that what was called for was a struggle to transform 'the ready-made state machinery' into a political form which ensures a continuous process of revolutionary practice.

---

[31] Marx 1971b, p. 75; 1971a, p. 153.
[32] Marx 1962, p. 30.

Chapter Nineteen
The Politics of Assumption, the Assumption of Politics

I am very much honoured by this prize[1] – because of the commitment of its namesakes (especially Isaac Deutscher from I learned much in my early reading and whose appreciation of *Capital* on the BBC formed part of my first lecture every time I gave my Marx course). And also honoured because it links me to such a stellar group of previous recipients including István Meszárós who, thirty-five years after delivering the first Deutscher Prize Lecture, continues to remind us what the point is. I hope that my own thoughts here can help.

Assume a perfectly competitive capitalist economy with costless freedom of entry and exit, and the attempt to raise taxes on capital in one jurisdiction will lead capital to exit for other jurisdictions. Accordingly, we conclude, there is no point in trying to tax capital.

Assume that a set of productive relations exists so long as it does not fetter the development of productive forces; therefore, we conclude that the reason capitalism persists is because it is 'optimal for the further development of productive power'.[2]

---

[1] The Isaac and Tamara Deutscher Memorial Prize Lecture for 2005 on the occasion of receiving the Deutscher Prize for 2004 for *Beyond 'Capital': Marx's Political Economy of the Working Class* (Lebowitz 2003) in London on 4 November 2005.
[2] Cohen 1978, p. 206.

Assume identical production functions in a credit-market island and a labour-market island, where the delivery of labour for the wage is 'as simple and enforceable a transaction as the delivery of an apple for a dime'.[3] We conclude from identical mathematical results in the two islands that capitalist exploitation does not require domination at the point of production but flows, simply, from unequal property endowments.

In each case, the conclusions are present in the premise. What is proven is what is already embedded in the assumptions. And, these examples point to the necessity always to interrogate conclusions to see whether they flow from our assumptions.

So, if we accept this simple point, a *very* simple point, what conclusions are latent in the assumption that 'in a given country at a given period' the quantity of the means of subsistence required by workers is given and 'can therefore be treated as a constant magnitude'?[4] Does this assumption imply that productivity increases as such will not benefit workers?

The assumption introduced

I began to worry about Marx's assumption that the standard of necessity is given once I started the process of trying to understand the *Grundrisse*. For one, there was Marx's stress in the *Grundrisse* about capital's tendency to create new needs for workers, on which, he noted, 'the contemporary power of capital rests'.[5] There is no mention of this in *Capital*. How could such an important source of capital's power be reconciled with the assumption that the worker's necessary needs were constant? Clearly, this was a critical assumption to be removed, I concluded many years ago, in that book on wage-labour that Marx had promised.[6]

But, there was another aspect of the *Grundrisse* that troubled me. That volume revealed the relation between Marx's discussion of capital in general, his inner analysis, and the necessary form of existence of capital as many capitals in competition. Over and over again, we see Marx stress that competition does not create the inner laws of capital, that competition merely

---

[3] Roemer 1986a, p. 269; Lebowitz 1988a.
[4] Marx 1977a, pp. 275, 655.
[5] Marx 1973, p. 287.
[6] Lebowitz 1977–8.

lets them be seen.[7] He said this often enough that it could not be dismissed as a casual comment. And, once you grasp that relation between the essence and appearance of capital, it is there to be seen clearly in *Capital*, where Marx explicitly indicates that 'the general and necessary tendencies of capital must be distinguished from their forms of appearance'.[8]

If the competition of capitals executes and manifests the inner laws of capital, however, we should be able to demonstrate the same results on both logical levels. And, sometimes this is very simple. For example, in his examination of capital in general Marx explains that capital's drive to expand leads it to attempt to lengthen and intensify the workday and to increase productivity. Look, then, at the struggle of individual capitals against each other – we see that their attempt to expand leads them to do everything possible to reduce production costs and that they are driven by competition to precisely the same results. In short, here we can demonstrate that 'the immanent laws of capitalist production manifest themselves in the external movement of the individual capitals, assert themselves as the coercive laws of competition...'.[9]

So, what happens at each level when there are productivity increases? At the level of many capitals competing in the real world, growing productivity means, all other things equal, rising output, falling prices and thus increased real wages. At the level of capital in general, however, rising productivity yields, not rising real wages but relative surplus-value – this is, of course, the story presented by Marx in Volume I, Chapter 12. But, if competition reveals the inner laws of capital, how is that, in one case, workers benefit from rising productivity and, in the other case, capital benefits? *There* was the immediate puzzle.

Well, of course, the explanation is the assumption that Marx introduced at the level of capital-in-general – the premise that the quantity of means of subsistence for workers can be treated as given for a given period in a given country. He *initially* defended this assumption by stressing the need for simplification – for holding some things constant at the outset and removing these assumptions subsequently. 'Only by this procedure,' Marx explained to Engels, 'is it possible to discuss one relation without discussing all the rest.'

---

[7] Marx 1973, pp. 651, 751–2. See Chapters 1, 10 and 11 in this volume in particular.
[8] Marx 1977a, p. 433.
[9] Ibid.

Similarly, at the same time in his *Grundrisse* manuscript, he indicated that making such fixed assumptions was necessary in order to avoid 'confounding everything'.[10] But, was holding the standard of necessity constant the *only* option if you wanted to avoid confounding everything?

Within a few years, in his 1861–3 *Economic Manuscripts*, Marx offered an additional reason for the assumption. The physiocrats, he noted, had begun with this assumption of subsistence as a fixed magnitude and thereby had correctly identified the sphere of production as the source of surplus-value. This concept of a subsistence wage, Marx argued, was the foundation of modern political economy, and Adam Smith had followed their lead 'like all economists worth speaking of'.[11]

Of course, the assumption had nothing to do with a natural or physiological subsistence (a mistake the physiocrats were inclined to make). That subsistence wage could be high or low:

> The only thing of importance is that it should be viewed as given, determinate. All questions relating to it as not a given but a variable magnitude belong to the investigation of wage labour in particular and do not touch its general relationship to capital.[12]

Thus, what was critical was the particular insight that this assumption of a given standard of necessity provides about the nature of capital. It permits us to grasp the concepts of necessary labour and the value of labour-power (and, thus, the concepts of surplus-labour and surplus-value). And, being able to determine the basis of the value of labour-power, Marx insisted, was of 'the highest importance for grasping the capital-relation'. So, even though he was clear that the standard of necessity is a variable magnitude, Marx put that question aside until his study of wage-labour in particular:

> In our investigation, however, we shall everywhere assume the amount and quantity of the means of subsistence, and therefore also the extent of needs, at a given level of civilisation, is never pushed down, because this investigation of the rise and fall of the level itself (particularly its artificial lowering) does not alter anything in the consideration of the general relationship.[13]

---

[10] Lebowitz 2003, p. 46.
[11] Lebowitz 2003, p. 45.
[12] Marx 1988, pp. 44–5.
[13] Marx 1988, pp. 45–7.

It is not hard, then, to understand why Marx assumed the standard of necessity given – (a) a simplifying assumption was desirable, (b) it was an assumption already familiar in classical political economy (distinguishing that school from vulgar economy), and (c) this particular assumption illuminated the nature of capital as the product of the exploitation of workers. While Marx was clear, too, that 'the level of the necessaries of life whose total value constitutes the value of labour-power can itself rise or fall,' this was a matter that would be addressed later – 'the analysis of these variations, however, belongs not here but in the theory of wages'.[14]

But, was the assumption neutral? Did it illuminate some aspects of the nature of capital but leave others in the darkness? And, since we know that Marx never did get around to removing it, were there conclusions latent in that assumption?

The non-neutrality of Marx's assumption

Think about the implications of assuming a constant standard of necessity. In such a case, the only way that necessary labour (and its value-form, the value of labour-power) can fall is through a fall in the value of a given set of the necessaries of life. 'In our investigation,' Marx indicated, 'wages are only reduced by the DEPRECIATION of that labour capacity, or what is the same thing, by the cheapening of the means of subsistence entering into the workers' consumption.'[15]

To understand the nature of capital, in short, the only change in the wage to be considered is that which results from changes in the conditions of production of the commodities consumed by workers. Explicitly excluded from purview is any change related to the market for labour-power. Marx was quite clear in stating this:

> In so far as machinery brings about a direct reduction of wages for the workers employed by it, by e.g. using the demand of those rendered unemployed to force down the wages of those in employment, it is not part of our task to deal with this CASE. It belongs to the theory of wages.[16]

---

[14] Marx 1977a, pp. 1068–9.
[15] Marx 1994, p. 23.
[16] Ibid.

So, return to the concept of relative surplus-value. Given Marx's assumption, 'a change in the magnitude of surplus value presupposes a movement in the value of labour-power, brought about by a change in the productivity of labour'. We have here the basic relationship first accurately formulated, according to Marx by Ricardo.[17] Accordingly, the story of the growth of surplus-value becomes simply a story of the development of productive forces. It is the point that Marx makes over and over again in his elaboration of 'the concept of relative surplus-value': capital has an 'immanent drive', a constant tendency 'towards increasing the productivity of labour, *in order to cheapen commodities and, by cheapening commodities, to cheapen the worker himself*'.[18]

So, what is important about co-operation of workers? Social productivity of combined labour exceeds the sum of individual productivities. Productivity rises but capital, rather than workers, is the beneficiary. What occurs in manufacturing? Increase in productivity, capital benefits. What occurs in machinofacture? Increase in productivity, capital benefits. The important story told is that the development of productive forces benefits capital because it yields relative surplus-value by lowering necessary labour through the increase in productivity. 'It is only the shortening of the labour-time necessary for the production of a definite quantity of commodities that is aimed at.'[19] True, individual capitalists may want to destroy unions, may want to use machinery to defeat strikes, but capital as a whole, capital in general, has its eye on the prize – 'cheapening the means of subsistence entering into the workers' consumption'.

So, what drives the development of capitalism? Capital's desire for growth, its desire for surplus-value – and only that. Capital is the actor. Capital makes history (though not under conditions of its own choosing). The picture, in short, is one of capital propelling itself to develop the productive forces, one of a system that accordingly delivers better and better productive forces. And, when capital can *no longer* develop those productive forces, revolution is on the agenda. 'The function of the revolutionary social change,' Cohen inferred, 'is to unlock the productive forces.'[20] Accordingly, since capital has created

---

[17] Marx 1977a, pp. 658, 660.
[18] Marx 1977a, pp. 436–7. Emphasis added.
[19] Marx 1977a, p. 438.
[20] Cohen 1978, p. 150.

better, more efficient (and, of course, neutral) productive forces, the task now is both to take these achievements and give *workers* the benefits of them – the highest achievements of capitalism and soviet power – and also to build upon these.

How much of this particular story flows from that assumption of a constant standard of necessity? If we made a *different* assumption – a constant rate of surplus-value (the Volume III, Chapter 13 assumption underlying a tendency of the rate of profit to fall), the effect of productivity increases which reduce the value of the means of subsistence would be real wages which increase at the same rate as productivity. 'In this case, because the productivity of labour as risen,' Marx explained in his 1861–3 manuscripts, 'the quantity of use values he receives, his real wage, had risen, but its *value* has remained constant, since it continues to represent the same quantity of realized labour time as before.'[21]

Under this alternative assumption of a constant rate of surplus-value, in short, *workers* are the beneficiaries of productivity increases. The value of the worker's money wage would be unchanged but, with a doubling of productivity, it would 'represent twice as many use-values as before, and...each use-value would be twice as cheap as it was before'.[22] Of course, by assumption there would also be no generation of relative surplus-value. Thus, the direct link between productivity increase and relative surplus-value would be severed.

Yet, it is essential to understand that we do not *need* to make an explicit assumption of a constant rate of surplus-value to achieve this result in which real wages rise with productivity. All that is necessary is to drop the imposed assumption of the constant standard of necessity. Then, with a falling value of means of subsistence as the result of productivity increases, all other things equal, the real value of the worker's money wage would rise. The doubling of productivity would lead to a halving of commodity values and, thus, a doubling of real wages. Once we no longer impose the requirement of 'a definite quantity of commodities' consumed by workers, the constant rate of surplus-value, all other things equal, emerges as a *result* with productivity increases. This inference at the level of capital in general corresponds in this

---

[21] Marx 1994, pp. 65–6; Marx 1977a, p. 659; Lebowitz 2003, pp. 114–15.
[22] Marx 1977a, p. 659.

case to what occurs at the level of capitals in competition, all other things equal – i.e., when productivity changes drop from the sky.

The basis, in short, for relative surplus-value is *not* the growth of productivity (as presented in Chapter 12 of Volume I). We need to understand that Marx's assumption is not neutral. That assumption leads us to make this specific connection between productivity increases and relative surplus-value. However, if an increase in social productivity were to drop from the sky, all other things equal, it would be workers who benefit and there would be no relative surplus-value. Something *additional* is required for relative surplus-value. Something is missing from the story Marx told in Chapter 12. And, if it is missing here, the question is whether it is missing everywhere.

Another variable, another assumption

To capture what is missing, *Beyond 'Capital'* introduces at the inner level of capitalism a specific concept and new variable – the degree of separation among workers.

This concept reflects the fact that capitalism is not driven simply by the goals of capital. There are also the goals of workers. Capital has the explicit goal of the growth of surplus-value. Workers, though, have their explicit goals, too – they struggle for time for themselves (not only to rest and recuperate but also, Marx noted, 'the worker needs time in which to satisfy his intellectual and social requirements'); they struggle to reduce the intensity of their workday in order to have energy for themselves; and, they struggle to secure the use-values which correspond at that point to their 'social needs, the needs of socially developed human beings'. Underlying all these needs of workers is what Marx described in *Capital* as 'the worker's own need for development'.[23]

There are, thus, two 'oughts' in capitalism: 'the capitalist constantly tending to reduce wages to their physical minimum, and to extend the working day to its physical maximum, while the working man constantly presses in the opposite direction'.[24] What, then, determines 'the respective powers of the combatants'?

---

[23] Lebowitz 2003, pp. 66–76.
[24] Marx 1985b, p. 146; Lebowitz 2003, pp. 73–4.

I propose that we conceive of a variable (X), which represents the degree of separation among workers. 'The workers' power of resistance,' Marx pointed out, 'declines with their dispersal'; and, we can suggest that this X-factor will determine the strength of the ability of workers to struggle over wages, to struggle over the length and intensity of the work-day and to struggle against capital as a whole.[25]

Come back to the case for the generation of relative surplus-value. The necessary condition for relative surplus-value is the decline in necessary labour, a condition which is satisfied if productivity (q) rises more than real wages (U). What, then, determines the course of real wages? We can represent the course of real wages as a function of the relation of productivity to the degree of separation (q/X). Then, we can set out the following cases:

(a) if productivity rises and the degree of separation among workers is constant, then real wages rise at the same rate as productivity. In this case, necessary labour and the rate of surplus-value are constant; the worker is beneficiary of productivity gains;

(b) if productivity rises and the degree of separation increases at the same rate, then the real wage is constant. In this case, capital captures all the benefits of productivity increase as relative surplus-value; and,

(c) if productivity rises and the degree of separation of workers increases, but at a lesser rate, then there is both relative surplus-value and a rising rate of surplus-value as well as increased real wages.

From this perspective, then, the necessary condition for relative surplus-value is a rise in the degree of separation of workers (or, inversely, a fall in the degree of unity of workers). Productivity increases by themselves cannot explain the growth of relative surplus-value. But how can we say this when we understand that capital, as the owner of the products of labour, is the immediate beneficiary of *any* increase in productivity (whatever its source)? The answer, simply, is that a rise in the X-factor is essential for the growth of relative surplus-value because, if capital benefits immediately from productivity gains, the question would remain as to why the worker is not successful in capturing these benefits when he 'measures his demands against

---

[25] Marx 1977a, pp. 591, 638.

the capitalist's profit and demands a certain share of the surplus value created by him'.[26]

Why is there confusion in the understanding of the necessary conditions for relative surplus-value? Precisely because productivity gains are generally associated with the changes in the labour process initiated by capital, the effects of productivity changes and increases in the degree of separation among workers tend not to be disentangled. Take, for example, the substitution of machinery for workers, a case where use of the product of the social brain definitely fosters the development of social productivity. The begged question is why *workers* are not the beneficiaries, why they are not able to capture the gains in the form of real wages which rise at the same rate as the productivity gains. Chapter 12 of Volume I offers no answer to this.

Recall, though, that Marx excluded from his discussion of relative surplus-value the case where 'machinery brings about a direct reduction of wages for the workers employed by it, by e.g. using the demand of those rendered unemployed to force down the wages of those in employment'. Here is precisely the missing explanation. All other things equal, the displacement of workers increases the degree of separation of workers. As a result, productivity rises more rapidly than real wages, and the resulting fall in necessary labour yields the increase in surplus-value. We, further, can see this inner tendency manifested in competition, in that real world of many capitals and many wage-labourers. There, all other things equal, the weakened position of workers in the labour-market produces the downward pressure on money wages that is the condition for real wages to rise less than productivity.

Of course, all other things are not necessarily equal. While capital attempts to raise the degree of separation to its maximum, the worker 'constantly presses in the opposite direction'. In short, we cannot exclude the possibility that workers, by organising and by uniting, can *counteract* capital's tendency. The removal of the assumption of a given standard of necessity and the articulation of the variable X, the degree of separation among workers, in short, clearly bring class struggle to centre stage in the discussion of the development of capitalism.

---

[26] Lebowitz 2003, p. 91; Marx 1973, p. 597.

The assumption of class struggle

Class struggle, of course, is not absent from *Capital*. When Marx put aside the question of changes in the 'definite quantity' of means of subsistence until the book on wage-labour, he did not put aside the question of class struggle. However, he froze the *worker's* side of class struggle. What other basis could there be for assuming real wages constant in the face of rising productivity? In *Capital*, workers do *not* press in the opposite direction to increase their wages; rather, the degree of separation of workers increases to prevent them from sharing the benefits of the advance of social productivity.[27]

Once we recognise, however, that workers have their own goals and that they combine in order to struggle successfully, we can no longer assume that the link between productivity increase and surplus-value is automatic; nor can we assume that capital proceeds *as if* productivity increases automatically translate into relative surplus-value. Capital must negate its negation in order to posit itself – it must divide and separate workers as its necessary condition of existence.

The X-factor immediately allows us to see that part of the essence of capital, indeed an *essential* aspect of the logic of capital, is the tendency to divide workers by turning their differences into antagonism and hostility. It is a point Marx recognised well in his comment about the antagonism between Irish and English workers – this antagonism, he noted, is 'the *secret of the impotence of the English working class*, despite its organization. It is the secret by which the capitalist class maintains its power. And that class is fully aware of it.'[28] The use of racism and sexism, however, does not appear as part of the essence of capital in Marx's *Capital*; and, that is not an accident.

Similarly, once we recognise the importance to capital of dividing workers, then we can no longer look upon capital's tendency simply as one that inexorably yields an increasing scale of productive plant (and which has as its unintended consequence the centralising, uniting and organising of the working class). Capital's drive for surplus-value can lead to specific alterations in the mode of production that *lower* productivity as such – as long as they divide workers. For capital, what matters, after all, is not productivity but the relationship between productivity and the degree of separation (q/X).

---

[27] Lebowitz 2003, pp. 89–91, 117–19.
[28] Lebowitz 2003, pp. 159–60.

Much of capitalist globalisation, indeed, may be driven by the desire to weaken workers – by an attempt to *de*centralise, *dis*unite and *dis*organise workers. Does the assumption of a given standard of necessity help us to understand the phenomenon of modern capitalist globalisation or capital's drive for contracting-out?

But, that raises the *whole* question of the nature of the changes in productive forces sponsored by capital. We know that capital has the tendency to stimulate co-operation in production among workers. In choosing the forms of co-operation, though, how likely is it for capital to introduce changes in the labour process that strengthen the unity and self-consciousness of workers? Capital encourages the development of the collective worker in itself but has no interest in the emergence of the collective worker *for itself*.

Given that capital's goal is valorisation rather than the development of productive forces as such, the relation of productivity to the degree of separation of workers is what capital must consider when initiating changes in the labour process. The logic of capital accordingly demands that the changes in the productive forces introduced by capital *cannot* be neutral. Those productive forces, at any given point, reflect capital's goal within capitalist productive relations; and, insofar as that goal is relative surplus-value, in themselves, their nature must be such as to weaken workers.

And, this point about the non-neutrality of capital's achievements, which one would not grasp from a reading of Marx's Chapter 12, means that the society that would go beyond capitalism *cannot* simply take the achievements of capital and channel the benefits to workers instead of capital. As I proposed in *Beyond 'Capital'*:

> Precisely because capital's goal is not the development of productive forces for itself but is valorization, the character of instruments of production and of the organization of the capitalist production process at any given point expresses capital's goals in the context of two-sided class struggle. In short, unless the behaviour of capital is considered in the context of wage-labour for itself rather than just wage-labour in itself, the clear tendency is to think in terms of the autonomous development of productive forces and the neutrality of technology. Both conceptions are characteristic of economism.[29]

---

[29] Lebowitz 2003, p. 123.

There is no better way to grasp the class character of the productive forces than to recall what Marx learned about the nature of the workers' state as the result of the actions of workers in struggle in the Paris Commune. The parallels are striking. Just as the working class cannot use the 'ready-made' state machinery for its own purposes, so also it cannot use the ready-made *productive* machinery for its own purposes. Just as in the case of the capitalist state, the existing productive forces introduced by capital are *infected* – their very nature involves a 'systematic and hierarchic division of labour', and capitalist production assumes the character of 'a public force organized for social enslavement, of an engine of class despotism'.[30] No one could deny that Marx recognised this despotism of the capitalist workplace – with its 'barrack-like discipline'.[31] But, who would argue that this abomination flows *simply* from the drive to increase productive forces?

Understanding the importance of the X-factor, which is to say the pervasive character of class struggle, means that we recognise that building the society of associated producers necessarily requires us to go *beyond* seizing the capitalist state and *beyond* seizing capitalist productive enterprises. The associated producers inherit these but they must transform them to correspond to the essence of associated producers – the self-government of the producers, that form which allows the producers to transform both circumstances and themselves and which stimulates, rather than truncates, the development of their capacities.

When we begin *without* Marx's assumption, without freezing class struggle from the side of workers, we not only understand capitalism better; we also gain insights into process of going beyond it.

The politics of assumptions and variables

Can acceptance of assorted evils like economism, determinism and statism then all be traced to a simple assumption about the standard of necessity? We need to think about the importance of identifying variables and about the assumptions we make. As we should know from Marx, our variables, our

---

[30] Lebowitz 2003, p. 194.
[31] Marx 1977a, pp. 450, 549.

assumptions, the way in which we express formulae, direct our attention to what is important to understand.

Consider the variable labour-power, the capacity to perform labour. By articulating this variable, Marx enabled us to distinguish explicitly between the labour necessary to reproduce the worker and the labour the worker performs. It shines a light on the importance of the reproduction of the working class, the necessary condition of existence for the reproduction of capital, a central concept that finds no place in vulgar (or neoclassical) economics. Similarly, there are the concepts that he saw as so important to articulate – surplus-value (independent of its various subdivisions) and abstract labour, which is the key to unlocking the riddle of money. What would Marx's *Capital* be without these new concepts and variables he introduces?

We can also see the importance Marx attached to *assumptions* about variables. Recall his point about treating the standard of necessity as given. The physiocrats had made a great leap forward by making the subsistence wage, 'the equivalent of the necessary means of subsistence', the pivotal point in their theory. Even though they were mistaken in treating this 'unchangeable magnitude' as determined entirely by nature, 'the Physiocrats transferred the inquiry into the origin of surplus value from the sphere of circulation into the sphere of direct production'. In this way, they 'thereby laid the foundation for the analysis of capitalist production' and deserved to be recognised as 'the true fathers of modern political economy'.[32] And, we see that Marx retained this assumption in order to advance this 'inquiry into the origin of surplus value'. To understand the nature of capital, he stressed, 'the only thing that is important' about the standard of necessity is that 'it should be viewed as given, determinate'.

Finally, we know that Marx grasped that the way in which a formula presents a relation, in fact, can conceal the specific nature of the relation. Classical political economy, he noted, had worked out the formulae for the rate of exploitation and the rate of surplus-value 'in substance, but not in a conscious form'. Yet, Marx was very critical of the way these formulae presented the relation. He argued that, by expressing surplus-labour in relation to the entire workday and expressing surplus-value as a fraction of the total value-product, classical political economy mystified the nature of

---

[32] Lebowitz 2003, pp. 32, 44–5.

the capital-relation as a relation of exploitation, presenting instead 'the false semblance of a relation of association'.[33]

What was the problem? Clearly not that there was anything *false* about classical political economy's formulae. After all, their formulae were essentially the same – they were simply 'derivative' formulae. However, the problem is that the permissiveness of their derivative formulae allowed erroneous conceptions to be smuggled in. Not simply by permitting the idea that 'worker and capitalist divide the product in proportion to the different elements which they respectively contribute towards its formation'.[34] There were also assumptions that could be introduced without conscious formulation. By relating surplus-labour to the entire workday, Marx pointed out that:

> The political economists' favourite method of treating the working day as constant in magnitude became a fixed usage, because in those formulae surplus labour is always compared with a working day of a given length.[35]

As we know, the treatment of the workday as a given (and, thus, its disappearance as variable) meant that, for classical political economy (and, unfortunately, for some late interpreters of Marx), the coercive nature of the capitalist workday disappeared. With the obscuring of the compulsion to perform surplus-labour so apparent in absolute surplus-value, the source of the surplus was mystified – leaving the exploitation of workers no more compelling an explanation of the surplus than the exploitation of corn, steel or peanuts.

Assumptions and forms of expressing relations that open the door to mystification need to be challenged. And, this is not a purely academic or scientific question. There was a reason that Marx was very sensitive to the political implications of assumptions and formulae. Although definitely a man of science, he was (as Engels pointed out at his graveside) before all else a revolutionary, one whose 'real mission in life was to contribute, in one way or another, to the overthrow of capitalist society'.[36]

---

[33] Marx 1977a, pp. 668–70.
[34] Marx 1977a, p. 671.
[35] Marx 1977a, p. 670.
[36] Engels 1978, p. 682.

So, what would this revolutionary (and, indeed, what should *all* revolutionaries) think about the retention of an assumption which treats the lowering of the value of commodities consumed by workers as an immanent tendency but obscures capital's tendency to divide workers? What should we think about an assumption that prevents us from seeing that the story of the growth of surplus-value is not simply one of the growth of productive forces but, indeed, one of capital's continuing ability to divide workers in the face of the development of social productivity? What should we think of an assumption that portrays as neutral the productive forces introduced by capital? The economism that flows from the assumption that Marx intended to remove should be clear.

Theory and history

But, *when* should that assumption be removed? In *Beyond 'Capital'*, I followed Marx in proposing that the removal of the assumption belonged in the 'Book on Wage-Labour'. Yet, should not the assumption of the given standard of necessity be removed *before* the historical illustration of the development of productive forces which occurs under capitalist relations of production? After all, that account of manufacturing and modern industry in *Capital* is meant to be a test of the theory of relative surplus-value as set out in Chapter 12.

'Testing by facts or by practice respectively,' Lenin commented about *Capital*, 'is to be found here in *each* step of the analysis.'[37] We know, too, that the demonstration of the correctness of abstract thought was *critical* for Marx. As he wrote to Engels in 1867:

> As regards CHAPTER IV, it was a hard job finding *things themselves*, i.e., their *interconnection*. But with that once behind me, along came one BLUE BOOK after another just as I was composing the final *version*, and I was delighted to find my theoretical conclusions fully confirmed by the FACTS.[38]

Indeed, Marx insisted that only after the inner connections have been discovered (through the 'power of abstraction') 'can the real movement

---

[37] Lenin 1963, p. 320.
[38] Marx and Engels 1987, pp. 407–8.

be appropriately presented'.[39] Yet, the argument that I have made is that Marx did *not* elaborate all the inner connections. In focusing only upon capital's 'immanent drive' to cheapen commodities in order to cheapen the worker herself and in ignoring capital's immanent drive to divide workers, Marx presented 'the general and necessary tendencies of capital' only in part, only one-sidedly. Should not the theory that is 'tested' be one which focuses explicitly upon *both* productivity and the X-factor? Upon the relation of productivity to the degree of separation among workers?

The answer, I suggest, is obvious. What kind of historical account of the development of capitalism can be based upon an assumption that effectively freezes the workers' side of class struggle? The theory which should be tested by historical illustration is one which begins from two-sided class struggle, one which explicitly recognises the struggle over the degree of separation.

And, yet, think about that historical account. There is more in that account than just a description of productivity gains for the purpose of producing a definite quantity of commodities more cheaply. We also see, for example, how the competition of women and children in the factories breaks the resistance of male workers, how workers are forced to compete against machines, and we see the use of machines as weapons for 'suppressing strikes', as 'weapons against working class revolt'.[40] Those historical observations, however, are sparse and scattered; and, most significantly, they are *not theorised* – their premise has not been developed as part of the inner connections.

In this respect, the history presented is *not* simply a confirmation of the theory of relative surplus-value by 'the FACTS', by the real movement. When it comes to testing the theory that Marx presented in Chapter 12, there are clearly 'unexplained variations' in the historical account of manufacturing and modern industry. These observations would not, however, be unexplained by a theory which includes capital's goal of weakening workers and increasing the degree of separation of workers.

To demonstrate that capital is the product of surplus-labour, Marx explicitly put aside critical questions until his 'investigation of wage-labour in

---

[39] Marx 1977a, pp. 90, 102. Marx underlined this point when he commented about the concept of value that 'Even if there were no chapter on "value" in my book, the analysis of the real relations which I give would contain the proof and demonstration of the real value relation.' Marx and Engels 1965, pp. 209–10.

[40] Marx 1977a, pp. 526, 557, 562–3.

particular'. However, by choosing not to develop the side of wage-labour and the ensuing struggle over the degree of separation of workers theoretically *before* presenting the historical development of capitalism, Marx weakened both his own theory and how it was viewed by those who followed.

Did he recognise this? We know from Engels's Preface to the Third Edition of Volume I of *Capital* that 'it was Marx's original intention to re-write a great part of the text of the first volume, to formulate many theoretical points more exactly, to insert new ones, and to bring historical and statistical materials up to date'.[41] Would theoretical points raised here about the degree of separation of workers have been among those formulated more exactly or inserted in Volume I? Although we will never know Marx's intention, how can we *ourselves* proceed without formulating and inserting them?

Theory and politics

Do we need, however, specifically to articulate this X-factor? Could it not be said that all that is required is to be more explicit about the importance of class struggle and the balance of class forces? I suggest not. However salutary it is in the face of economism to repeat the phrase 'class struggle' over and over again, it is not enough.

We need to remember that identification of a variable can cast a particular light, that it can illuminate what has been in the shadows – and this, I propose, is precisely true about the X-factor, the degree of separation among workers. This variable shouts that what matters is the unity of the working class; it insists that it is the division and separation of workers by capital that defeats them and that prevents workers from being the beneficiaries of the growth of the productivity of social labour. And, it demands that we ask at all times two questions – (1) what divides us and (2) how can we break down those divisions?

Once you think about this variable, I suggest that there is no going back to the comfort of determinism or the scientism of the Marxist economists whose contribution to the overthrow of capitalist society would be the discovery of the correct solution to the 'transformation problem' (a puzzle whose

---

[41] Marx 1977a, p. 106.

assumptions, incidentally go unrecognised by these alchemists).[42] When you focus upon the struggle over the degree of separation among workers and when you recognise how seemingly-well-grounded and objective economic variables (like the rate of profit) are affected by the results of this struggle, then (however threatening this may be to economists – either by training or

---

[42] The *real* 'transformation problem' has been the transformation of scarce intellectual resources into endless forgettable articles. Not only have so many tended to mistake a special case demonstrating the logical consistency of essence and appearance for a real process occurring in real time (see Chapter 10), but the simple premise of the balance of class forces and class struggle underlying that demonstration has been submerged in formalism.

Prices of production (i.e., equilibrium prices based upon equal profit rates), it is argued, logically must differ from values based upon quantities of labour because the value-compositions of capital differ. A high ratio of constant to variable capital, all other things equal, means that sectors with a high value-composition of capital would have lower profit rates than average. Since this violates the condition that (in the absence of barriers to the movement of capitals) profit rates are equal, the logical resolution is that prices must deviate from values systematically to ensure compliance with that condition.

The familiar assumption of 'all other things equal', however, masks in this case the critical premise that the rate of surplus-value is equal in all sectors. Of course, if the rate of surplus-value does not tend to be equal but, rather, varies with the value-composition of capital, then there would be no logical basis for price deviating from value. So, what is the basis for this premise of equal rates of surplus-value?

Presumably, this is generated by the actions of many workers in competition: just as the efforts of individual capitals to maximise their growth will tend to produce the intersectoral movements which equalise profit rates, so also will the efforts of workers to maximise their goals as wage-labourers (insofar as they function as individuals) lead them to migrate from capital to capital and thus to produce a tendency for the rate of surplus-value to equalise. Thus, Marx comments in Volume I of *Capital* (Marx 1977a, pp. 791–2) that higher wages draw workers into the 'more favoured sphere' and then (in Chapter 10 of Volume III) that the assumption of equal rates of surplus value 'assumes competition among the workers, and an equalization that takes place by their constant migration between one sphere of production and another' (Marx 1981b, p. 275).

However, given that the wage necessarily appears as a payment for the entire workday rather than for the necessary portion, what workers observe are differing wages and differing lengths and intensities of the workday. Thus, the movements of wage-labourers as such would be based upon their search for a 'fair day's wages for a fair day's work'. What the competition of wage-labourers tends to produce is equal returns of wages per effort – i.e., equalisation as commodity-sellers; this is not the same, however, as equalisation of rates of exploitation because the latter is determined by the relation of real wages and productivity.

With differing degrees of separation among workers, rates of surplus-value can vary despite equalisation of wages per a workday of given intensity. All the transformation discussions presuppose equal ratios of q/X per sector, which is a condition for equal rates of surplus-value. Once, however, we acknowledge the role of class struggle, we understand that the relation of inner to outer is not a mathematical problem.

by inclination) what becomes obvious is *indeterminacy*. The indeterminacy inherent in struggle.

Articulating this variable for the degree of separation puts a searchlight on the need to go beyond the economism of the economists in another way. Obviously, the X-factor is not determined solely by the struggle over purely economic matters. There is the struggle against capital's deployment of racism, sexism and its fostering of divisions and competition among workers in different countries. These are struggles to create vehicles that can bring workers together, struggles over the state and struggles in the sphere of ideology. Indeed, at the core of these struggles is the battle of ideas – a struggle to demonstrate not only that capital is the result of exploitation but also that this exploitation is based upon the separation of workers.

In this respect, assertion of the need, firstly, to understand the inherent bias flowing from Marx's assumption, secondly, to remove that assumption and, thirdly, to introduce the variable I have called the X-factor should be seen as part of the battle of ideas, as an attempt to redirect the activity of Marxist thinkers to the focus of the revolutionary Marx. By introducing this variable explicitly into our theoretical work, our theory assumes politics and political struggle. Indeed, we put politics in command.

I concluded Chapter 9 of *Beyond 'Capital'* by stressing that the purpose of Marx's *Capital* was to give workers a weapon with which to go beyond capitalism. And, I asked, why did Marx not get around to writing the book on wage-labour? I answered that 'the completion of his epistemological project interested him less than his revolutionary project'.[43] In these days when Hugo Chavez (inspired by István Meszáros) has very clearly reminded us of the obvious point – that the choice before us is socialism or barbarism, it is time to remember that revolutionary project. What else should we expect from anyone whose mission in life is to contribute, in one way or another, to the overthrow of capitalist society?

---

[43] Lebowitz 2003, p. 177.

Bibliography

Albritton, Robert 2003, 'Returning to Marx's *Capital*: A Critique of Lebowitz's *Beyond "Capital"*', *History of Economic Ideas*, 11, 3: 95–107.
Antonio Callari et al. (eds.) 1995, *Marxism in the Modern World: Confronting the New World Order*, London: The Guilford Press.
Arthur, Chris 1998, 'Systematic Dialectic', *Science & Society*, 62, 3: 447–59.
Baran, Paul A. 1952, 'The Political Economy of Backwardness', *Manchester School* (January) reprinted in *The Economics of Underdevelopment*, edited by A.N. Agarwala and S.P. Singh, Oxford: Oxford University Press, 1958.
—— 1957, *The Political Economy of Growth*, New York: Monthly Review Press.
Baran, Paul A. and Paul M. Sweezy 1966, *Monopoly Capital: An Essay on the American Economic and Social Order*, New York: Monthly Review Press.
Blackburn, Robin (ed.) 1973, *Ideology in Social Science*, New York: Vintage Books.
Bowles, Samuel, David M. Gordon, and Thomas E. Weisskopf 1986, 'Power and Profits: The Social Structure of Accumulation and the Profitability of the Postwar U.S. Economy', *Review of Radical Political Economics*, 18, 1 & 2: 132–67.
Bradley, Ian and Ronald L. Meek 1986, *Matrices and Society*, Middlesex: Penguin Books.
Braverman, Harry 1974, *Labor and Monopoly Capital: The Degradation of Work in the Twentieth Century*, New York: Monthly Review Press.
Brenner, Robert 1985 [1976], 'Agrarian Class Structure and Economic Development in Pre-Industrial Europe', in *The Brenner Debate: Agrarian Class Structure and Economic Development in Pre-Industrial Europe*, edited by T.H. Aston and C.H.E. Philpin, Cambridge: Cambridge University Press.
—— 1986, 'The Social Basis of Economic Development', in *Analytical Marxism*, edited by John Roemer, Cambridge: Cambridge University Press.
—— 1998a, *The Economics of Global Turbulence: A Special Report on the World Economy, 1950–98*, *New Left Review*, I, 229.
—— 1998b, 'The Looming Crisis of World Capitalism: From Neoliberalism to Depression?', *Against the Current*, November/December: 22–6.
Brenner, Robert and Mark Glick 1991, 'The Regulation Approach: Theory and History', *New Left Review*, I, 188: 45–119.
Bukharin, Nikolai 1972, *Economic Theory of the Leisure Class*, New York: Monthly Review Press.
Burawoy, Michael 1989, 'Marxism Without Micro-Foundations', *Socialist Review*, 19, 2: 53–86.
Carling, Alan 1986, 'Rational Choice Marxism', *New Left Review*, I, 160: 24–62.
Chandler, Alfred D. 1969, *Strategy and Structure*, Cambridge, MA.: MIT Press.
Clarke, Simon (ed.) 1991, *The State Debate*, New York: St. Martin's Press.
Clawson, Patrick 1983, 'A Comment on Van Parijs's Obituary', *Review of Radical Political Economics*, 15, 2: 107–10.
Clifton, James A. 1977, 'Competition and the Evolution of the Capitalist Mode of Production', *Cambridge Journal of Economics*, 1, 2: 137–51.
Cogoy, Mario 1973, 'The Fall of the Rate of Profit and the Theory of Accumulation', *Bulletin of the Conference of Socialist Economists*, 8: 52–67.

Cohen, Gerald A. 1978, *Karl Marx's Theory of History: A Defense*, Princeton: Princeton University Press.

—— 1986, 'The Structure of Proletarian Unfreedom', in Roemer (ed.) 1986a.

De Vroey, Michel 1981, 'Value, Production and Exchange', in *The Value Controversy*, edited by Ian Steedman, London: Verso.

Desai, Meghnad 1979, *Marxian Economics*, Oxford: Basil Blackwell.

Elson, Diane 1979, 'The Value Theory of Labour', in *Value: The Representation of Labour in Capitalism*, edited by Diane Elson, London: CSE Books.

Elster, Jon 1978, *Logic and Society*, Chichester: Wiley.

—— 1985, *Making Sense of Marx*, Cambridge: Cambridge University Press.

—— 1986, *An Introduction to Karl Marx*, Cambridge: Cambridge University Press.

Engels, Frederick 1967 [1881], 'The Wages System', *The Labour Standard*, 21 May 1881, in Henderson (ed.) 1967.

—— 1970 [1891], 'Critique of the Draft Social-Democratic Programme (1891)', in *Marxism Today* (February).

—— 1975, 'Outlines of a Critique of Political Economy', in Marx and Engels, *Collected Works*, Volume 3, New York: International Publishers.

—— 1978 [1883], 'Speech at the Graveside of Karl Marx', in *The Marx-Engels Reader*, edited by Robert C. Tucker, Second Edition, New York: W.W. Norton.

Fine, Ben, Costas Lapavitsas, and Dimitris Milonakis 1999, 'Addressing the World Economy: Two Steps Back', *Capital & Class*, 67: 47–90.

Foley, Duncan K. 1986, *Understanding 'Capital': Marx's Economic Theory*, Cambridge, MA.: Harvard University Press.

Foster, John Bellamy and Henryk Szlajfer (eds.) 1984, *The Faltering Economy: The Problem of Accumulation under Monopoly Capitalism*, New York: Monthly Review Press.

—— 1981, 'Is Monopoly Capital an Illusion?', *Monthly Review*, 33, 4: 36–47.

—— 1986, *The Theory of Monopoly Capitalism: An Elaboration of Marxian Political Economy*, New York: Monthly Review Press.

Gerdes, Paulus 1985, *Marx Demystifies Calculus*, Minneapolis: Marxist Educational Press.

Gilbert, Richard et al. 1938, *An Economic Program for American Democracy*, New York: Vanguard.

Gramsci, Antonio 1971, *Selections from the Prison Notebooks*, edited and translated by Quintin Hoare and Geoffrey Nowell Smith, New York: International Publishers.

Gray, John 1983, 'The System of Ruins', *Times Literary Supplement*, December 30: 1461.

Hackett, Robert A 1986, 'For a Socialist Perspective on the News Media', *Studies in Political Economy*, 19: 141–56.

Hansen, Alvin 1939, 'Economic Progress and Declining Population Growth', *American Economic Review* (March), reprinted in American Economics Association, *Readings in Business Cycle Theory*, Homewood: Richard D. Irwin, 1951.

Hardach, Gerd, Dieter Karras, and Ben Fine 1978, *A Short History of Socialist Economic Thought*, London: Edward Arnold.

Harvey, David 1982, *The Limits to Capital*, Chicago: University of Chicago Press.

Hegel, G.W.F. 1956, *The Philosophy of History*, New York: Dover.

—— 1929, *Hegel's Science of Logic*, Translated by W.F. Johnston and L.G. Struthers, London: Unwin.

—— 1967, *The Phenomenology of Mind*, New York: Harper and Row.

Henderson, W.O. (ed.) 1967, *Engels: Selected Writings*, London: Penguin.

Himmelweit, Susan and Simon Mohun 1978, 'The Anomalies of Capital', *Capital and Class*, 6: 67–105.

Hodgson, Geoff 1974, 'The Theory of the Falling Rate of Profit', *New Left Review*, I, 84: 55–82.

Holloway, John and Sol Picciotto (eds.) 1978, *State and Capital: A Marxist Debate*, London: Edward Arnold.

Huberman, Leo and Paul M. Sweezy 1960, 'The Steel Strike in Perspective', *Monthly Review*, 11, 10: 357–61.

Hunt, Emery K. and Jesse G. Schwartz (eds.) 1972, *A Critique of Economic Theory: Selected Readings*, Middlesex: Penguin.
Hunt, Emery K. and Howard Sherman 1972, 'Value, Alienation, and Distribution', *Science & Society*, 36, 1: 29–48.
Itoh, Makoto 1978, 'The Formation of Marx's Theory of Crisis', *Science and Society*, 42: 129–55.
Jhally, Sut and Bill Livant 1984, 'The Valorisation of Consciousness: Extensions of the Domain of Capital', Paper presented to the Canadian Communications Association (June).
Kalecki, Michal 1968, *Theory of Economic Dynamics*, New York: Monthly Review Press.
Kenway, Peter 1980, 'Marx, Keynes and the Possibility of Crisis', *Cambridge Journal of Economics*, 4, 1: 23–36.
Lange, Oskar 1964 [1938], *On the Economic Theory of Socialism*, New York: McGraw-Hill.
Lavoie, Don 1983, 'Some Strengths in Marx's Disequilibrium Theory of Money', *Cambridge Journal of Economics*, 7, 1: 55–68.
Lebowitz, Michael A. 1966, 'Monopoly Capital', *Studies on the Left*, 6: 61–71.
—— 1972, 'The Increasing Cost of Circulation and the Marxian Competitive Model', *Science & Society*, 36: 331–8.
—— 1975, 'Human Needs, Immiseration and Alienation', Paper presented at the annual meeting of the Canadian Economics Association, June 1975.
—— 1976, 'Marx's Falling Rate of Profit: A Dialectical View', *Canadian Journal of Economics*, 9, 2: 232–54.
—— 1977–8, 'Capital and the Production of Needs', *Science & Society*, 41, 4: 430–47.
—— 1982a, 'The General and the Specific in Marx's Theory of Crisis', *Studies in Political Economy*, 7: 5–25.
—— 1982b, 'The One-Sidedness of *Capital*', *Review of Radical Political Economics*, 14, 4: 40–51.
—— 1984, 'Review of John Roemer's *A General Theory of Exploitation and Class*', *Canadian Journal of Economics*, 27, 2: 407–11.
—— 1985, 'Kornai and Socialist Laws of Motion', *Studies in Political Economy*, 18.
—— 1986a, '*Capital* Reinterpreted', *Monthly Review*, 38, 2: 33–41.
—— 1986b, 'Transcending the Crisis of Socialism', *Socialism in the World*, 54.
—— 1988a, 'Is "Analytical Marxism" Marxism?', *Science & Society*, 52, 2: 191–214.
—— 1988b, 'Trade and Class: Labor Strategies in a World of Strong Capital', *Studies in Political Economy*, 27, 3: 137–48.
—— 1992a, *Beyond 'Capital': Marx's Political Economy of the Working Class*, London: Macmillan.
—— 1992b, 'Capitalism: How Many Contradictions?', *Capitalism, Nature, Socialism*, 3, 3: 85–96.
—— 1994, 'Analytical Marxism and the Marxian Theory of Crisis', *Cambridge Journal of Economics*, 18, 2: 163–79.
—— 1998, 'Review of Felton Shortall's *The Incomplete Marx*', *Historical Materialism*, 3: 173–88.
—— 2000, 'Kornai and the Vanguard Mode of Production', *Cambridge Journal of Economics*, 24, 3: 377–92.
—— 2003, *Beyond 'Capital': Marx's Political Economy of the Working Class*, Revised Edition, London: Palgrave Macmillan.
—— 2004, 'Ideology and Economic Development', *Monthly Review*, 56, 1: 14–24.
—— 2006, *Build it Now: Socialism for the 21st Century*, New York: Monthly Review Press.
Lefebvre, Henri 1968, *Dialectical Materialism*, London: Jonathan Cape.
Lekachman, Robert 1966, *The Age of Keynes*, New York: Random House.
Lenin, Vladimir I. 1963, *Philosophical Notebooks*, in *Collected Works*, Volume 38, Moscow: Foreign Languages.
Levine, Andrew, Elliott Sober, and Erik Olin Wright 1987, 'Marxism and Methodological Individualism', *New Left Review*, I, 162: 67–84.

Levins, Richard and Richard Lewontin 1985, *The Dialectical Biologist*, Cambridge, MA.: Harvard University Press.

Lifshultz, Lawrence S. 1974, 'Could Karl Marx Teach Economics in America?', *Ramparts*, 12, 9: 27–30, 52–9.

Lipietz, Alain 1985, *The Enchanted World: Inflation, Credit and the World Crisis*, London: Verso.

Lukács, Georg 1972, *History and Class Consciousness: Studies in Marxist Dialectics*, translated by Rodney Livingston, Cambridge, MA.: MIT Press.

—— 1978, *Marx's Basic Ontological Principles*, London: Merlin.

Maarek, Gerard 1979, *An Introduction to Karl Marx's 'Das Kapital'*, Oxford: Martin Robinson.

Magdoff, Harry and Paul M. Sweezy 1977, *The End of Prosperity: The American Economy in the 1970s*, New York: Monthly Review Press.

—— 1987a, *Stagnation and the Financial Explosion*. New York: Monthly Review Press.

—— 1987b, 'Capitalism and the Distribution of Income and Wealth', *Monthly Review*, 39, 5: 1–16.

Marx, Karl n.d. [1866], 'Instructions for the Delegates of the Provisional General Council. The Different Questions', in *Minutes of the General Council of the First International, 1864–66*, Moscow: Progress Publishers.

—— 1906, *Capital*, Volume I, New York: Modern Library.

—— 1957, *Capital*, Volume II, Moscow: Foreign Languages Publishing House.

—— 1959, *Capital*, Volume III, Moscow: Foreign Languages Publishing House.

—— 1962 [1875], *Critique of the Gotha Programme*, in Marx and Engels, *Selected Works*, Volume 2, Moscow: Foreign Languages Publishing House.

—— 1963, *Poverty of Philosophy*, New York: International Publishers.

—— 1966, *Capital*, Volume III, Moscow: Progress Publishers.

—— 1968, *Theories of Surplus Value*, Volume II, Moscow: Progress Publishers.

—— 1971, *Theories of Surplus Value*, Volume III, Moscow: Progress Publishers.

—— 1971a [1871], 'First Outline of *The Civil War in France*', in Marx and Engels 1971.

—— 1971b [1871], *The Civil War in France*, in Marx and Engels 1971.

—— 1973, *Grundrisse*, New York: Vintage Books.

—— 1975a [1843], *Contribution to the Critique of Hegel's Philosophy of Law*, in Marx and Engels, *Collected Works*, Volume 3, New York: International Publishers.

—— 1975b [1843], 'On the Jewish Question', in Marx and Engels, *Collected Works*. Volume 3, New York: International Publishers.

—— 1975c [1844], 'Contribution to the Critique of Hegel's Philosophy of Law. Introduction', in Marx and Engels, *Collected Works*, Volume 3, New York: International Publishers.

—— 1975d [1844], *Economic and Philosophic Manuscripts of 1844*, in Marx and Engels, *Collected Works*, Volume 3, New York: International Publishers.

—— 1976a [1845], 'Theses on Feuerbach', in Marx and Engels, *Collected Works*, Volume 5, New York: International Publishers.

—— 1976b [1847], *The Poverty of Philosophy*, in Marx and Engels, *Collected Works*, Volume 6, New York: International Publishers.

—— 1977a, *Capital*, Volume I, New York: Vintage Books.

—— 1977b [1849], *Wage Labour and Capital*, in Marx and Engels, *Collected Works*, Volume 9, New York: International Publishers.

—— 1981a, *Capital*, Volume II, New York: Vintage Books.

—— 1981b, *Capital*, Volume III, New York: Vintage Books.

—— 1985, *Value, Price and Profit*, in Marx and Engels, *Collected Works*, Volume 20, New York: International Publishers.

—— 1985a [1864], 'Inaugural Address of the Working Men's Association', in Marx, and Engels, *Collected Works*, Volume 20, New York: International Publishers.

—— 1985b [1865], *Value, Price and Profit*, in Marx and Engels, *Collected Works*, Volume 20, New York: International Publishers.

—— 1988, *Economic Manuscripts of 1861–63*, in Marx and Engels, *Collected Works*, Volume 30, New York: International Publishers.

—— 1994, *Economic Manuscript of 1861–63*, in Marx and Engels, *Collected Works*, Volume 34, New York: International Publishers.

—— n.d., *Theories of Surplus Value*, Volume 1, Moscow: Foreign Languages Publishing House.

Marx, Karl and Frederick Engels 1962, *Selected Works*, Volume I, Moscow: Foreign Languages Publishing House.

—— 1965, *Selected Correspondence*, Moscow: Progress Publishers.

—— 1971, *On the Paris Commune*, Moscow: Progress Publishers.

—— 1976a [1846], *The German Ideology*, in Marx and Engels, *Collected Works*, Volume 5, New York: International Publishers.

—— 1976b [1848], *Communist Manifesto*, in Marx and Engels, *Collected Works*, Volume 6, New York: International Publishers.

—— 1979, *Collected Works*, Volume 12, New York: International Publishers.

—— 1983, *Collected Works*, Volume 40, New York: International Publishers.

—— 1987, *Collected Works*, Volume 42, New York: International Publishers.

—— 1988, *Collected Works*, Volume 30, New York: International Publishers.

McFarlane, Bruce 1982, *Radical Economics*, New York: Saint Martin's Press.

McLellan, David (ed.) 1972, *Karl Marx: The Grundrisse*, London: Macmillan.

Medio, Alfredo 1972, 'Profits and Surplus-Value: Appearance and Reality in Capitalist Production', in Hunt and Schwartz (eds.) 1972.

Meek, Ronald 1961, 'Sraffa's Rehabilitation of Classical Economics', *Science & Society*, 25, 2: 39–156.

Mosley, Hugh 1979, 'Monopoly Capital and the State: Some Critical Reflections on O'Connor's *Fiscal Crisis of the State*', *Review of Radical Political Economy*, 11, 1: 52–61.

Nell, Edward 1973, 'Economics: the Revival of Political Economy', in Blackburn (ed.) 1973.

Olson, Mancur 1965, *The Logic of Collective Action*, Cambridge, MA.: Harvard University Press.

Perelman, Michael 1987, *Marx's Crises Theory: Scarcity, Labor, and Finance*, New York: Praeger.

Resnick, Stephen and Richard Wolff 1987, *Knowledge and Class: A Marxian Critique of Political Economy*, Chicago: University of Chicago Press.

—— 1989, 'The New Marxian Economics: Building on Althusser's Legacy', *Economies et Sociétés*, Série Oeconomia, 11: 185–200.

—— (eds.) 1985, *Rethinking Marxism: Essays for Harry Magdoff & Paul Sweezy*, New York: Autonomedia.

Robinson, Joan 1967, *Economics: An Awkward Corner*, New York: Pantheon.

—— 1972, 'The Second Crisis of Economic Theory', *American Economic Review*, 62, 2: 1–10.

—— 1955, *Marx, Marshall and Keynes*, Delhi: Delhi School of Economics.

Roemer, John E. 1981, *Analytical Foundations of Marxian Economic Theory*, Cambridge: Cambridge University Press.

—— 1982, *A General Theory of Exploitation and Class*, Cambridge, MA.: Harvard University Press.

—— (ed.) 1986a, *Analytical Marxism*, Cambridge: Cambridge University Press.

—— 1986b, 'Reply to Nadvi on Marxian Matters', *Economic and Political Weekly*.

—— 1994, *A Future for Socialism*, Cambridge, MA.: Harvard University Press.

Rosdolsky, Roman 1977, *The Making of Marx's 'Capital'*, London: Pluto Press.

Samuelson, Paul 1971, 'Understanding the Marxian Notion of Exploitation: A Summary of the So-Called Transformation Problem Between Marxian Values and Competitive Prices', *Journal of Economic Literature*, 9, 2: 399–431.

—— 1973, 'Samuelson's Reply on Marxian Matters', *Journal of Economic Literature*, 11, 1: 64–8.

Sekine, Thomas T. 1984, *The Dialectic of Capital: A Study of the Inner Logic of Capitalism*, Volume I, York: Yushindo Press.

Smythe, Dallas 1977, 'Communications: Blindspot of Western Marxism', *Canadian Journal of Political and Social Theory*, 1, 3: 1–27.

—— 1981, *Dependency Road: Communications, Capitalism, Consciousness and Canada*, Norwood, NJ.: Ablex.

Sraffa, Piero 1960, *Production of Commodities by Means of Commodities: Prelude to a Critique of Economic Theory*, Cambridge: Cambridge University Press.

Steindl, Josef 1976, *Maturity and Stagnation in American Capitalism*, New York: Monthly Review Press.

Struik, Dirk 1948, 'Marx and Mathematics', *Science & Society*, 12, 1: 118–96.

Sweezy, Paul M. 1938, *Monopoly and Competition in the English Coal Trade, 1550–1850*, Cambridge, MA.: Harvard University Press.

—— 1939, 'Demand Under Conditions of Oligopoly', *Journal of Political Economy*, reprinted in American Economics Association, *Readings in Price Theory*, Chicago: Richard D. Irwin, 1952.

—— 1951, 'Introduction' to Joseph A. Schumpeter, *Imperialism and Social Classes*, New York: Augustus M. Kelley, Inc.

—— 1953, *The Present as History: Essays and Reviews on Capitalism and Socialism*, New York: Monthly Review Press.

—— 1954, 'Review of Steindl', *Econometrica* (October).

—— 1956, *The Theory of Capitalist Development: Principles of Marxian Political Economy*, New York: Monthly Review Press.

—— 1972, *Modern Capitalism and Other Essays*, New York: Monthly Review Press.

—— 1974, 'Some Problems in the Theory of Capital Accumulation', *Monthly Review*, 26, 1: 38–55.

—— 1974, 'Critique of Maurice Dobb, ', *Journal of Economic Literature*, June: 482–3.

—— 1979, 'Inflation Without End?' *Monthly Review*, 31, 6: 1–10.

—— 1980, 'The Crisis of American Capitalism', *Monthly Review*, 32, 5: 1–13.

—— 1981, 'Keynes as a Critic of Capitalism', *Monthly Review*, 32, 11: 33–6.

—— 1981a, *Four Lectures on Marxism*, New York: Monthly Review Press.

—— 1981b, 'The Economic Crisis in the United States', *Monthly Review*, 33, 7: 1–10.

—— 1987, 'Interview with Paul M. Sweezy', *Monthly Review*, 38, 11: 1–28.

Sweezy, Paul M. and Leo Huberman (eds.) 1965, *Paul A. Baran (1910–1964): A Collective Portrait*. New York: Monthly Review Press.

—— 1962, 'The Common Market', *Monthly Review*, 13, 9: 385–96.

—— 1967, 'End of the Boom?', *Monthly Review*, 18, 11: 1–9.

Sweezy, Paul M. and Harry Magdoff 1974, 'Twenty-Five Eventful Years', *Monthly Review*, 26, 2: 1–13.

—— 1977, 'Steel and Stagnation', *Monthly Review*, 29, 6: 1–9.

Thompson, Edward P. 1978, *The Poverty of Theory*, New York: Monthly Review Press.

Tsuru, Shigeto 1976, *Towards A New Political Economy (Collected Works of Shigeto Tsuru, Volume 13)*, Tokyo: Kodansha Ltd.

Uno, Kozo 1980, *Principles of Political Economy: Theory of a Purely Capitalist Society*, Brighton: Harvester Press.

Van Parijs, Philippe 1980, 'The Falling-Rate-of-Profit Theory of Crisis: A Rational Reconstruction by Way of Obituary', *Review of Radical Political Economy*, 12, 1: 1–16.

Van Parijs, Phillipe 1983, 'Why Marxist Economics Needs Microfoundations: Postscript to an Obituary', *Review of Radical Political Economics*, 15, 2: 111–24.

von Braunmühl, Claudia 1978, 'On the Analysis of the Bourgeois Nation State within the World Market Context. An Attempt to Develop a Methodological and Theoretical Approach', in Holloway and Picciotto (eds.) 1978.

Weeks, John 1977, 'The Sphere of Production and the Analysis of Crisis in Capitalism', *Science and Society*, 41, 3: 281–302.

—— 1981, *Capital and Exploitation*, Princeton: Princeton University Press.

Williams, Philip L. 1982, 'Monopoly and Centralization in Marx', *History of Political Economy*.

Wilson, Edmund 1953, *To the Finland Station*, Garden City: Doubleday.

Wolff, Robert Paul 1984, *Understanding Marx*, Princeton: Princeton University Press.

Wright, Erik Olin 1989, 'What Is Analytical Marxism?', *Socialist Review*, 19, 4: 35–56.

—— 1982, 'The Status of the Political in the Concept of Class Structure', *Politics & Society*, 11, 3: 321–41.

—— 1985, *Classes*, London: Verso.

Zeluck, Steve 1980, 'On the Theory of the Monopoly Stage of Capitalism', *Against the Current*, 1, 1.

Index

Index of Names

Albritton, Robert   319–25

Baran, Paul   158, 174–83, 188, 218,
   225–6, 245
Brenner, Robert   40, 49, 193, 273–97
Bukharin, Nicolai   30–1, 33
Burawoy, Michael   303

Chandler, Alfred   111
Clarke, Simon   328–9, 333
Clawson, Patrick   42, 58
Cohen, G.A.   39–40, 60–1, 249, 254, 344

Dobb, Maurice   18, 21, 158, 163–6,
   189

Elster, Jon   4–5, 39–41, 44, 47–51, 58–61,
   249–57, 267–71, 281
Engels, Friedrich   115, 121–2, 234, 242,
   309, 315, 341, 353–4

Glick, Mark   278, 282
Gramsci, Antonio   3, 270
Gray, John   40–1

Hackett, Robert   217–8, 222–4
Hansen, Alvin   169–72
Harvey, David   260, 270
Hayek, Friedrich   41, 63
Hegel, G.W.F.   xiv–xvi, 12, 25, 67, 69,
   71–75, 79–87, 101, 103–4, 110–1, 196,
   201–2, 234, 245, 323

Kalecki, Michal   168, 173–80, 184, 186,
   263
Keynes, John Maynard   6, 28, 31–2, 101,
   160, 171–2, 255

Lange, Oskar   62–3, 162, 271
Lenin, Vladimir   xiii, xvi, 62, 75, 81,
   83–4, 162, 182, 195, 201–2, 218, 354

Levins, Richard   42, 247–8, 255
Lewontin, Richard   42, 247–8, 255
Lipietz, Alain   248, 250, 257, 270
Lukacs, Georg   xiii, 83, 86, 247
Luxemburg, Rosa   166

Magdoff, Harry   143, 159, 179, 182,
   184–6, 188
Mandel, Ernest   214, 248

O'Connor, James   155, 330

Ricardo, David   20, 22–3, 36–7, 69–70,
   80, 84–5, 109, 112–4, 134, 137, 140–1,
   147, 163–5, 229, 264, 266, 270, 321,
   344
Robinson, Joan   17–8, 28–9, 32
Roemer, John   4, 39–44, 48, 50–64, 249,
   251–2, 271, 277, 281–2

Samuelson, Paul   18, 25
Schumpeter, Joseph   160, 169, 173
Schwartz, Jesse   19
Sekine, Tom   321, 323–5
Smith, Adam   36, 80, 163, 211, 213–4,
   282–4, 286, 294, 296, 342
Smythe, Dallas   217–9
Sraffa, Piero   18–28, 32, 163–5
Steindl, Joseph   173–80, 184, 186
Sweezy, Paul   101, 143, 157–90, 225–6,
   230, 245

Thompson, E.P.   305–6, 315
Tsuru, Shigeto   160, 164–5

Uno, Kozo   301, 319–25

Van Parijs, Phillippe   42, 48–9, 281

Wolff, Robert Paul   35–7
Wright, Erik Olin   40, 58

Subject Index

Abstract labour 89–98, 164, 198, 352
Abstract proletarian 311–2
Abstraction 40, 52, 73–84, 134, 143, 195–8, 202, 205, 227, 261, 354
Accumulation of capital 70, 116, 140, 207, 233
Alienated economics 27
Althusserian outrage 324
Analytical Marxism 3–4, 7, 39–64, 193, 247–71, 281–2, 284
Apologetics 3, 11
Appearance 4, 7, 11–5, 67, 69–73, 75, 85, 103, 126, 195–203, 207–15, 222, 227–9, 265, 285–8, 341, 357
  Everyday notions 4–15, 67, 71, 197, 205
  Law and appearance 72–3, 76, 79, 85, 109, 113, 133–4, 172, 198, 207
  Multiplicity of outer forms 69–72, 195–6, 200, 229
  Paradox of appearance 70–2, 211, 285
  Price of production as form 197–8
  Profit as form of existence 197–9
Aristocracy of labour 182
Associated producers 324, 351
  Socialism 28, 41, 61–64, 144, 153–4, 158, 161, 295–6, 335, 358
Assumptions 4, 12, 52, 57–8, 101, 113, 119, 130, 134–8, 166, 186, 223, 225, 252, 301, 309, 320–2, 340–58
  Assumption of constant standard of necessity 301, 308–10, 320–2, 340–5, 348–55
  Assumption of equal rates of surplus value 373
  Assumption of equal returns of wages per effort 357
  Assumption of uneven productivity increase 101, 119, 134–8, 141–2, 257–8
  Assumption of workday as given 36, 57, 353
  Neutral 119, 301, 343, 346
Atomistic individual 42–7, 51–2, 56

Barrier and Limit 101, 107–15, 118–9, 122–8
Being and Nothing 71, 79

Capital
  Capital as a whole 5–7, 15, 43, 83, 85, 88, 105, 132, 135, 193, 196–7, 200, 205–8, 220, 229, 238, 241, 260–4, 280–1, 284, 288–9, 293, 296, 331, 335, 344, 347

Capital as mediator 312, 334–6
Capital as unity of production and circulation 88, 104, 196
Capital attempts to divide workers 46, 48, 293, 296, 322, 346–50, 354–6
Capital perfects itself 126, 245–6
Centralization of capital 115, 124, 193, 226, 231–4, 236
Expropriation/separation 232
Integration of capital 231–46
Necessary tendencies of capital 10, 43, 73, 115, 134–5, 140, 200, 206–11, 227–8, 232, 265, 284, 288, 323, 341, 355
Ownership of capital 28–9, 32, 53–4, 242–4
Reproduction of capital 14, 143, 147, 200, 233, 255, 257, 289, 293, 306–7, 312–3, 320–1, 333–5, 352
Capitalist expenditures 262–3, 268
Capitalist relations of production 51–8, 143, 145–56, 252, 283, 292–3, 305, 354
Formal subsumption of labour 54
Labour power as commodity 4, 12–5, 20–1, 23, 50, 53–6, 60, 81, 109, 214, 329–32
Precapitalist relations 54–8, 283
The essential relation 15, 45, 149, 151, 261, 285, 293–4
Vertical relationship between capital and labour 294, 297
Capitalist state 317, 327–37, 351
Capitalist's dilemma 291
Cartesian reductionism 49, 248, 255, 428
Circulation time 107, 121–4, 206, 220–2
Class struggle 13, 19, 79, 153–5, 181, 189, 193, 209, 215, 292–7, 301, 305, 316, 319, 321, 328–37, 348–51, 355–7
  Antagonism between Irish and English workers 349
  Class struggle functionalism 319
  Coercive nature of capitalist workplace 12, 36, 353
  Demystification of capital 19, 314–5
  Despotic inroads on capital 333
  Self-evident natural laws 313–5, 334–5
  Trade unions 125, 309, 330–2
  Two-sided class struggle 222–3, 293, 350, 355
  Unity of working-class 347–50, 356

Competition 7–10, 43–51, 132, 193, 197–200, 205–15, 220–3, 226–32, 236, 239–49, 251, 257, 261, 264–71, 275, 278–97, 331, 340–1, 346, 348
  Competition among workers 46, 331, 355–8
  Competition executes inner laws of capital 43–4, 49, 51, 208–9, 211, 225–46, 265, 341
  Competition reverses everything 43, 70–1, 193, 211–2, 214, 221–2, 273, 285–7, 296
Contingency and Necessity 15, 73, 112, 132, 152–3, 155, 193, 200, 207–11, 228–35, 249, 256, 266, 323
Contradiction 79, 81, 86, 88, 106, 108, 110–1, 117, 126, 132, 202, 206, 253, 331
  Contradiction in the capitalist mode of production 79, 109–11, 123, 125, 132, 148–50, 166, 184, 258, 268, 315
  Contradiction of capital 124, 127, 165, 184, 206, 253, 284
  Fundamental contradiction of capitalism 148–9, 166, 258, 277
  Principal contradiction 182
  Specific barrier of capital 143, 147–56
Crisis 17, 123, 131–2, 153, 155–6, 166–8, 256–60, 266, 268, 270, 273–97
  Crisis of intelligence 172, 282
  Crisis of theory 31–2
  Marx's crisis theory as "trivial" 251
  Overaccumulation 167–70, 179, 184, 277, 290
  Overcapacity 275–81, 288, 290–6
  Postwar crisis 193, 274–6, 291, 294–5
  Underconsumption 109, 149, 152, 166–74, 179, 266, 270, 278

Degree of separation of workers 293, 296, 301, 322, 346–50, 355–8
  X-Factor 347, 349, 351, 355–6, 358
Determinism 351, 356
Dialectic of capital 321, 323–4
Dialectical and dialectics 42–3, 61, 75, 80, 103–5, 120–1, 126, 151, 195, 201, 232, 248, 324
  Concept of the real 200–1
  Concrete to abstract 75, 195, 197
  Concrete totality 81–5, 195, 202
  Dialectical derivation 67, 81, 83, 85
  Dialectical moment 81–2
  Dialectical reasoning 67, 83–5, 195
  Distinction 81–5, 88, 90, 93
  Enrichment of concepts 76, 82–5, 120–1, 123
  Negation of negation 82

Point of view of the totality 85, 200, 248
Rich totality 74, 80–3, 185
Scientifically correct method 25, 74–5, 80, 195
Testing by facts 83, 87, 201–3, 354–5
Theory of knowledge 72, 202
Unity of opposites 78, 106
Disciples 134–5, 153, 311, 321

Empiricism 72–3, 134, 246, 279
Essence
  Immanent laws 43–4, 49, 51, 132, 200, 206–11, 227–46, 249, 257, 265, 270, 284, 288, 325, 331, 340–1, 344, 348, 354–5
  Inner and outer 69–72, 196–8, 209–13, 228–232, 285, 293, 357
  Inner connection 9–11, 25, 43, 69, 71–4, 76, 80–1, 85, 196, 198, 200, 210, 212–4, 227, 229, 249, 257, 286–7, 296, 354–5
  Inner structure 43–4, 193, 197
  Invisible essence 13–5, 197–9, 206, 212, 229
  Obscure structure 43, 71, 85, 186, 189, 195, 200, 213, 249, 257
Exploitation 7, 13, 26, 30, 53, 55–60, 63, 168, 176–8, 180–1, 198, 206, 209, 214–5, 220, 261, 278, 285
  Exploitation of audience 218–9, 222
  Exploitation of corn, steel, peanuts 37, 353
  'Just' exploitation 58, 252

Fallacy of composition 21, 22, 28, 31, 76, 269, 270, 271, 285–6, 297
Falling rate of profit 41–2, 67, 101, 103–31, 133–43, 165, 171, 188, 251, 257, 277, 280, 284
  Falling rate of profit classical argument 104, 113, 119, 123
  FROP 101, 133–5, 137, 140, 143, 145, 152–3, 156, 165–6, 188–9, 257–8, 277–280, 291
Functionalist 49, 310–1, 328

General barrier 143–7, 152–6
General Theory of stagnation 184, 186–7
Golden Age 158, 174, 180, 187, 274, 292

Hegelian mysticism 323

Invisible hand 267–71, 282–3, 289–90, 295, 323

Keynesian 6, 31–2, 101, 171–4, 184–5, 269, 280, 294–5, 335
  Keynesian policies 294
  Keynesian social democracy 32

Law of value 319, 321, 325

Market failure 291, 295
Methological individualism 3, 47–50, 56, 193, 250–5, 271–2, 285, 290, 293
  Microfoundations 47–9, 250–2, 255, 271, 281
  Supra-individual entities 46–7, 49, 250–2, 255, 271, 281, 285
Monopoly capital 162, 167, 175–87, 210, 218, 225–46
Movement of the planets 70, 211, 285

Nature and organic processes 23, 132, 139–48
Neoclassical 3–4, 11–2, 15, 18–9, 22, 28, 30–2, 42–3, 46–53, 57, 60–2, 158–9, 171, 186, 251, 255, 321–2, 352
  General equilibrium 27, 59, 67, 78, 317, 337, 339, 340
  Neoclassical Marxism 42, 48
Neo-Ricardian 3, 17–37, 153, 165, 189
Nobel Prize 274

One-sided Marxism 293, 310, 316, 320
Organic system 43, 60, 84, 199, 255, 301, 305–7, 314–5, 320

Political economy
  Classical political economy 20, 36–7, 69, 84, 104, 106, 120, 163, 165, 230, 343, 350–1
  Political economy of the working class 3–4, 320, 324, 330–1
  Vulgar political economy 3–4, 6, 10–5, 18, 20, 22, 69, 198, 210, 222, 228, 286, 343, 352

Productive forces, non-neutral 345–6, 350–1, 354
Profit squeeze 275–9

Qualitative value problem 163–4

Revolutionary practice 316, 335–7
  Struggle as a process of production 316

Sales effort 124–5, 178–9, 221
  Creation of new needs 111, 125–6, 207, 308, 316, 340
Say's law 172, 278
Science and method 12, 15, 69–73, 84–86, 202, 207, 211–2, 215, 220, 222, 247, 254, 285–7
Scientism 356
Stagnation 181–7, 226, 275, 295, 315
State derivation 328
Stepford edition of *Capital* 321–2
Surplus value
  Annual rate of surplus value 121–3
  Link between productivity and relative surplus value 117, 235, 322, 341, 344–9
  Relative surplus value 26, 117–8, 209, 228, 235–7, 284, 288, 301, 309, 322, 341, 344–8, 350, 354–5

Theory of a purely capitalist society 321
Transformation problem 20, 25, 37, 250–1, 301, 356–7

Unintended consequence 253, 267, 270, 283, 323, 349

Worker's own need for development 307, 310, 329–30, 346